IDIOT'S GUIDES.
AS EASY AS IT GETS!

W9-BCK-701

The
Bible

by Benjamin Phillips, PhD

ALPHA

A member of Penguin Group (USA) Inc.

Shippensburg Public Library
73 West King Street
Shippensburg PA 17257

For Joelyn, Robby, and Caroline—(Prov 31:10; Ps 127:3)

ALPHA BOOKS

Published by Penguin Group (USA) Inc.

Penguin Group (USA) Inc., 375 Hudson Street, New York, New York 10014, USA · Penguin Group (Canada), 90 Eglinton Avenue East, Suite 700, Toronto, Ontario M4P 2Y3, Canada (a division of Pearson Penguin Canada Inc.) · Penguin Books Ltd., 80 Strand, London WC2R 0RL, England · Penguin Ireland, 25 St. Stephen's Green, Dublin 2, Ireland (a division of Penguin Books Ltd.) · Penguin Group (Australia), 250 Camberwell Road, Camberwell, Victoria 3124, Australia (a division of Pearson Australia Group Pty. Ltd.) · Penguin Books India Pvt. Ltd., 11 Community Centre, Panchsheel Park, New Delhi—110 017, India · Penguin Group (NZ), 67 Apollo Drive, Rosedale, North Shore, Auckland 1311, New Zealand (a division of Pearson New Zealand Ltd.) · Penguin Books (South Africa) (Pty.) Ltd., 24 Sturdee Avenue, Rosebank, Johannesburg 2196, South Africa · Penguin Books Ltd., Registered Offices: 80 Strand, London WC2R 0RL, England

Copyright © 2014 by Penguin Group (USA) Inc.

All rights reserved. No part of this book may be reproduced, scanned, or distributed in any printed or electronic form without permission. Please do not participate in or encourage piracy of copyrighted materials in violation of the author's rights. Purchase only authorized editions. No patent liability is assumed with respect to the use of the information contained herein. Although every precaution has been taken in the preparation of this book, the publisher and author assume no responsibility for errors or omissions. Neither is any liability assumed for damages resulting from the use of information contained herein. For information, address Alpha Books, 800 East 96th Street, Indianapolis, IN 46240.

IDIOT'S GUIDES and Design are trademarks of Penguin Group (USA) Inc.

International Standard Book Number: 978-1-61564-627-2
Library of Congress Catalog Card Number: 2014935265

16   15   14   8   7   6   5   4   3   2   1

Interpretation of the printing code: The rightmost number of the first series of numbers is the year of the book's printing; the rightmost number of the second series of numbers is the number of the book's printing. For example, a printing code of 14-1 shows that the first printing occurred in 2014.

Note: This publication contains the opinions and ideas of its author. It is intended to provide helpful and informative material on the subject matter covered. It is sold with the understanding that the author and publisher are not engaged in rendering professional services in the book. If the reader requires personal assistance or advice, a competent professional should be consulted. The author and publisher specifically disclaim any responsibility for any liability, loss, or risk, personal or otherwise, which is incurred as a consequence, directly or indirectly, of the use and application of any of the contents of this book.

Most Alpha books are available at special quantity discounts for bulk purchases for sales promotions, premiums, fund-raising, or educational use. Special books, or book excerpts, can also be created to fit specific needs. For details, write: Special Markets, Alpha Books, 375 Hudson Street, New York, NY 10014.

Trademarks: All terms mentioned in this book that are known to be or are suspected of being trademarks or service marks have been appropriately capitalized. Alpha Books and Penguin Group (USA) Inc. cannot attest to the accuracy of this information. Use of a term in this book should not be regarded as affecting the validity of any trademark or service mark.

Publisher: Mike Sanders

Executive Managing Editor: Billy Fields

Executive Acquisitions Editor: Lori Cates Hand

Development Editor: Ann Barton

Senior Production Editor: Janette Lynn

Cover and Book Designer: Rebecca Batchelor

Illustration: Michael and Renee Wren, Wrensong Studio

Indexer: Heather McNeil

Layout: Ayanna Lacey

Proofreader: Jaime Julian Wagner

CONTENTS

INTRODUCTION

"Take up and read! Take up and read!" sang a young voice from across the garden wall. It was only a child singing in a children's game, but the words struck a Roman public speaking teacher sitting in the garden. Turning to the scroll beside him, he opened the book of Romans and started to read. So began a lifetime of reading the Bible for a man who would become one of the greatest thinkers of the ancient world, Augustine.

People pick up the Bible for many different reasons, and many wish they had a friend who would read along with them and help them better understand what the Bible says. One such person was an Ethiopian official returning home from Jerusalem. As he puzzled over the book of Isaiah, a Jewish man named Philip approached and asked if the official understood what he was reading. The Ethiopian's response has been echoed by many through the years, "Well, how could I, unless someone guides me?" (Acts 8:31)

This book is for anyone who, like Augustine, chooses to "Take up and read!," and like the Ethiopian official, wishes for friendly guide to go with them.

Reading with *Idiot's Guides: The Bible*

This book introduces the history of the Bible and helps those unfamiliar with it get started in reading and understanding it. Each book of the Bible is introduced with a short summary and explanation of its setting and origin. Important figures in each book are named and described. Key sections are noted in book outlines, which will help show how the books are structured. Many of these important passages receive more detailed explanation later in the book. Artwork on nearly every page will help readers visualize the Biblical scenes, and maps will help place the events in the world. Short explanations of historical and cultural background, important concepts and patterns, as well as interpretive issues and debates will allow readers to see more clearly what is going on as they read the Bible. Biblical links will help readers see the way in which the Bible fits together as a literary whole.

Idiot's Guides: The Bible is intended simply to describe the Bible on its own terms. Readers will be introduced to a few of the more important scholarly debates, but this book focuses on introducing the Bible itself more than the debates surrounding it. Most of all, however, this book is not intended to replace reading the Bible itself. It will best serve those who want to read the Bible and will use the Guide to help them read better. Some readers may wish that different emphases were highlighted or passages discussed. Thinking about what might have been done differently and why makes readers part the great conversation about the Bible; all are welcome.

Bringing a *Guide* to Bible Readers

Philip didn't just happen to be available to guide the Ethiopian official; an angel helped him to be in the right place at the right time (Acts 8:26). So also, this book is far more than the product of one person's work. *Idiot's Guides: The Bible* was edited by Lori Hand and Ann Barton, whose gracious comments and perceptive questions made them effective advocates for the readers. This book is a much more useful tool for new Bible readers because of their generous efforts. The original artwork throughout this book is the result of the amazing creativity of Michael and Renee Wren. Readers can see more of their work at Wrensong Studio (www.wrensongstudio.com).

Students at Southwestern Baptist Theological Seminary's Houston Campus (www.swbts.edu/houston) contributed background research for numerous Bible books. Thanks go to Sidney Broome, Hayley Dossey, Caleb Fleming, Emily Nesbitt, and Matt Wooster. Future Southwestern Seminary student Franky Dowdy contributed research on several books. I am also grateful for the assistance of colleagues who read and commented on various parts of this manuscript including David Hutchison, Stefana Laing, Miles Mullin, and Stephen Presley. My pastor, David Belk, is an incredible model of gracious Bible teaching. I have tried to follow the spirit of his example here. This book would not have happened without the initiative of John Wilsey, who introduced me to the project and provided wise counsel throughout.

Most of all, I am grateful for the support of my wife Joelyn and children Robby and Caroline. They cheerfully endured three months of writing and editing, spanning the Thanksgiving, Christmas, and New Year's holidays, and bore a heavy burden to make this book a reality. It is to them that this book is due and dedicated.

May the Author of the Book bless all who "Take up and read!" (Rev 1:3).

Benjamin Phillips
Houston, Texas
2014

Mural illustrations by Michael and Renee Wren, Wrensong Studio, © Dorling Kindersley

Maps by Ed Merritt © Dorling Kindersley

Greek gospel photo (page 5) by Alistair Duncan © Dorling Kindersley

HSCB Study Bible image (page 9) used with permission from Lifeway Christian Resources/B&H Publishing Group

Solomon's Temple illustration (page 104) by Russell Barnett © Dorling Kindersley

Understanding the Bible

The Bible comes to readers as a complete package—a book sitting on a shelf. But this book journeyed far to reach that shelf. It was written by approximately 40 authors, living on 3 continents, over a 1,400-year period that ended almost 2,000 years ago. A canyon of language and time stands between those authors and today's readers. Reading the Bible requires bridging that gap.

The book we call the Bible today is comprised of two main parts: the Old Testament, which was written to the nation of Israel between 1400 and 400 B.C.E, and the New Testament, which was written to Jewish and Gentile Christians in the Roman Empire between 50 and 100 C.E.

Languages of the Bible

The Old Testament was written primarily in Hebrew, the language of ancient Israel. The New Testament was written in Greek. Although these languages are unfamiliar to most English speakers today, using them actually maximized the number of people who could read the Bible at the time.

Biblical Hebrew was easier to learn and read than some other ancient languages of the day. It has only 22 characters and was one of the earliest languages to be written with symbols that represent individual sounds. These 22 sounds could be combined to form any Hebrew word. Hebrew was still challenging to learn because the symbols were all consonants, but context would usually make the appropriate vowels apparent for a Hebrew speaker. As a result, reading the Hebrew Bible (the Old Testament) was possible for many more people than if it had been written in Egyptian hieroglyphics.

The writings of the New Testament were also accessible to a wide audience because they were written in Greek. Koine Greek was the language of government and culture in the Roman Empire at the time of Christ. Documents written in this language could be read almost anywhere in the Empire.

Biblical Texts

The ability to read is important, but it would be useless without a way of getting the text from the author to the reader. For the biblical texts, relatively inexpensive, portable materials were typically used for writing, such as specially prepared animal skins (velum) and reeds (papyrus), which were rolled in scrolls. But these materials decayed quickly and had to be reproduced. Professional copyists, or scribes, developed in order to preserve the original writings and make them more widely available.

The most famous Hebrew scribes were the Masoretes (500 C.E. to 1000 C.E.). These copyists developed elaborate methods for ensuring the accuracy of their work. Their success can be seen by comparing the earliest Masoretic copy of Isaiah (c. 1000 C.E.) to the Dead Sea Scrolls copy of Isaiah (c. 150 B.C.E.). Despite over 1,000 years of copying by hand, the differences between the two are minimal, usually on the level of minor spelling variations.

Greek manuscripts of the New Testament are more widely available than any other ancient text and were transcribed much closer to the dates of their original writing. There are about 5,600 manuscripts of the Greek New Testament (with many more early translations). The earliest copies of complete books date to within 150 years of the original writings. Recently, fragments of Greek manuscripts from the late first to early second century C.E. have been found, which date to within 25 years of the original writings. That short timespan leaves little room for corruption to the text.

TEXTUAL TERMS

Biblical scholars distinguish among manuscripts, text, and autographs. The *autographs* are the original, handwritten physical documents. The Biblical autographs are no longer extant (available). The word *text* refers to the actual words, regardless of whether conveyed by the original or a copy. Finally, *manuscripts* are handwritten copies of the text.

The Modern Bible

Today, these ancient manuscripts are compiled through *textual criticism*, a discipline in which specialists compare differences in manuscripts to compile a unified text of the Bible. There are two major approaches to this task. The "Majority Text" takes the reading offered by the most manuscripts available. The "Critical Text" evaluates the reliability of the available manuscripts in order to determine the most likely reading.

Although there are some places where differences occur, the vast majority do not affect the meaning of the text. The Hebrew Bible is available as the *Biblia Hebraica Stuttgartensia* (1997). The most widely used critical Greek New Testaments are the *Nestle-Aland* (2012) and *United Bible Society* (2001). These critical texts form the basis for most modern translations of the Bible.

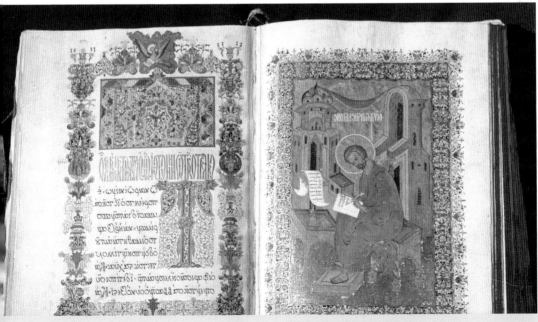

From the original Hebrew and Greek scrolls, parts of the Bible have been translated into over 2,500 languages and published in many different forms. This sixteenth-century Greek Gospel features ornate illustrations.

The Bible was written by many authors over a long period of time, but none of them provided a prophetic table of contents. In order to be printed as a single book, works recognized as scripture had to be complied and so distinguished from books that are not authoritative. This process began with Israel's acceptance of the Torah (which is made up of Genesis through Deuteronomy) as the foundation of the Hebrew Bible (the Old Testament). For Christianity, it closed with the recognition of the 27 books of the New Testament. Together, the 66 books of the Hebrew Bible and the New Testament form a unanimously accepted list for Christianity.

The Hebrew Bible divides its 22 books into 3 parts:

- Torah (Law)
- Nevi'im (Prophets)
- Ketuvim (Writings)

Taken together, they are called the *Tanakh*. Though the order of the books differs, the 39 books of the Christian Old Testament are the same as the 22 in the Hebrew Bible. The difference in number comes from the fact that in the Christian Old Testament, several books are divided into two parts and listed separately (for example, 1 & 2 Kings). The 12 minor prophets (in other words, the short books) in the Old Testament are the same as the single book called *The Twelve* in the Hebrew Bible.

The Old and New Testaments

The division of the Bible into Old and New Testaments reflects the promise of Jeremiah 31:31–34 of a "new covenant" or "testament" and the conviction that this promise was fulfilled in Jesus Christ. The distinction between Old and New Testaments does not imply a lesser status for the Hebrew Bible (see Matthew 5:17). The New Testament authors quote or allude to as many as 16 of the 22 books of the *Tanakh*, providing more than 10 percent of the content of the New Testament.

Many of the books of the Bible take place concurrently.

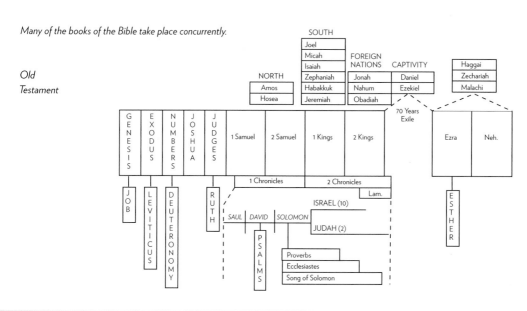

Old Testament

UNDERSTANDING THE BIBLE

The New Testament canon is composed of 27 books: 4 Gospels, Acts, 13 Pauline letters (letters written by Paul), 8 other letters, and the book of Revelation. The development of this list began in the wake of an early Christian controversy over the status of the Hebrew Bible. Marcion, a bishop in Alexandria (c. 68–140 C.E.), rejected the Old Testament and published a list of Christian writings he accepted as scripture (mainly Luke and Paul's letters). Other bishops soon affirmed the Old Testament as scripture and began producing lists of Christian writings they took to be scripture as well. The earliest such list available is the Muratorian Fragment (c. 170 C.E.), which names 20 of the 27 New Testament books. The final list emerged by c. 450 C.E. and stands without serious challenge today.

Reading the Bible

The major question for a new Bible reader, however, is not what to read. That issue is settled by picking up a Bible. The real question is where to begin reading the Bible. There are several good options:

Book by book   Begin with Genesis and keep going. With this approach you will hit everything, but you can lose narrative flow.

Chronological order   Refer to the charts shown here, or get a Bible that orders the books according to when they were written and what they discuss. This approach helps readers to see the flow of Biblical history, but the distinct nature of each book of the Bible may be lost.

Begin at the center   Start with the Gospels of Mark and John, which focus on Jesus' deeds and words, respectively. This way, you read the historical and literary climax of the Bible first. However, without familiarity with the Hebrew Bible, significant details can easily be missed.

Dive in the deep end   Start with Romans. This approach introduces the central theological themes of the Bible with lots of Hebrew Bible quotations, but presumes a basic knowledge of Biblical history.

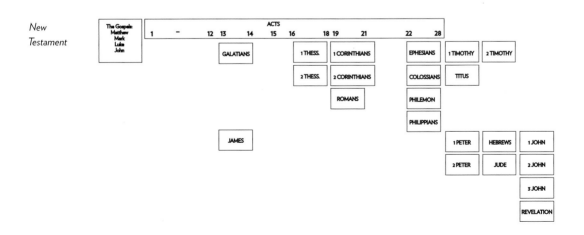

Modern English translations of the Bible are part of a history of Bible translations almost as old as the Bible itself. The first great project, the *Septuagint* (LXX), translated the Hebrew Bible into Greek between 200 and 100 B.C.E. In 382 C.E., Jerome revised the Old Latin translation of the Bible. His work became the foundation of the Vulgate, the official Latin Bible of the Roman Catholic Church. In 1534, Martin Luther completed translation of the *Lutherbibel*, a cornerstone of modern German.

Though there were earlier English Bibles, the most famous and influential English translation is the Authorized Version (AV), commonly called the King James Version (KJV), first published in 1611. The King James Version of the Bible is the most printed book in history, with over one billion copies printed.

BIBLE TRANSLATION HISTORY

200 B.C.E.: Septuagint (LXX)

382 C.E.: Jerome's Latin Vulgate

1384 C.E.: Wycliffe Bible

1454 C.E.: Gutenberg's Printing Press: Gutenberg Bible (Latin)

1522 C.E.: Martin Luther's Bible (German)

1526 C.E.: Tyndale's New Testament

1535 C.E.: Coverdale Bible

1539 C.E.: The "Great Bible"

1560 C.E.: The Geneva Bible

1609 C.E.: The Douay Bible

1611 C.E.: The Authorized Version (King James Bible)

1971 C.E.: The New American Standard Bible (NASB)

1973 C.E.: The New International Version (NIV)

2002 C.E.: The English Standard Version (ESV)

2004 C.E.: The Holman Christian Standard Bible (HCSB)

Approaches to Translating the Bible

Modern American-English translations typically opt for one of two approaches to translating the Bible. *Formal equivalence* attempts to minimize the influence of interpretation in translating the Bible. The most prominent of these "word-for-word" translations are the New American Standard Bible (NASB) and the English Standard Version (ESV). *Functional equivalence* utilizes greater interpretive liberty in hopes of reproducing meaning and impact. The most prominent of these "thought-for-thought" translations are the New International Version (NIV) and the New Living Translation (NLT).

This edition of *Idiot's Guide: The Bible* has adopted the Holman Christian Standard Bible (HCSB) for Biblical quotations. The HCSB attempts to combine the advantages of both formal and functional equivalence, aiming for an "optimal" (readable-formal) equivalence. Where functional equivalence is required in order to be readable, literal translations are provided in footnotes so readers can see the formal equivalent.

Modern English Bibles

Modern English Bibles come in a variety of forms. Some reproduce little more than the translation along with the later addition of standard chapters (1200s C.E.) and verses (1500s C.E.). Many now print the text to clearly show sentences and paragraphs or poetic structures, which don't always correspond neatly to the standard chapter and verse divisions. Beyond the actual translation, publishers often add other features to aid reading, comprehension, and study of the Bible. When detailed explanatory or devotional material is added in footnotes or insets, the edition is called a "Study Bible."

22 — Chapter number

40 — Verse number

Paul's Testimony

Section header (not part of original text)

Other features not shown:

Red letters to identify the words of Christ

Book titles

Use of font changes (**boldface** and SMALL CAPS) to indicate Old Testament quotations

Alternative readings/ translations

Explanatory notes

1907   Acts 22:22

40After he had given permission, Paul stood on the steps and motioned with his hand to the people. When there was a great hush, he addressed them in the ᵃHebrew languageᵃ:

22 **1**"Brothers and fathers, listen now to my defense before you." **2**When they heard that he was addressing them in the Hebrew language, they became even quieter.ᵇ Heᶜ continued, "I am a Jewish man, born in Tarsus of Cilicia but brought up in this cityᴬ at the feet of Gamalielᵈ and educated according to the strict view of our patriarchal law. Being zealous for God, just as all of you are today,ᵉ **4**I persecuted this Wayᶠ to the death, binding and putting both men and women in jail,ᵍ **5**as both the high priest and the whole council of elders can testify about me. After I received letters from them to the brothers, I traveled to Damascus to bring those who were prisoners there to be punished in Jerusalem.ʰ

Paul's Testimony

6"As' I was traveling and near Damascus, about noon an intense light from heaven suddenly flashed around me. **7**I fell to the ground and heard a voice saying to me, 'Saul, Saul, why are you persecuting me?'

8"I answered, 'Who are You, Lord?'

"He said to me, 'I am Jesus the ᵏNazarene, the One you are persecuting!' **9**Now those who were with me saw the light,ᴮ but they did not hear the voice of the One who was speaking to me.ˡ

10"Then I said, 'What should I do, Lord?'

"And the Lord told me, 'Get up and go into Damascus, and there you will be told about everything that is assigned for you to do.'

11"Since I couldn't see because of the brightness of that light, I was led by the hand by those who were with me, and came into Damascus.ᵏ **12**Someone named Ananias, a devout man according to the law, having a good reputation with all the Jews residing there,ˡ **13**came and stood by me and said, 'Brother Saul, regain your sight.' And in that very hour I looked up and saw him. **14**Then he said, 'The God of our fathers has appointedᵐ you to know His will, to seeⁿ the Righteous One,ᵒ and to hear the sound of His voice.ᶜ **15**For you will be a witness for Him to all people of what you have seen and heard.ᵖ **16**And now, why delay? Get up and be baptized, and wash away your sinsᑫ by calling on His name.'ʳ

17"After I came back to Jerusalem and was praying in the ᵗemple complex, I went into a visionary stateˢ **18**and saw Him telling me, 'Hurry and get out of Jerusalem quickly, because they will not accept your testimony about Me!'

19"But I said, 'Lord, they know that in ᵗsynagogue after synagogue I had those who believed in You imprisoned and beaten.ᵗ **20**And when the blood of Your witness Stephen was being shed, I was standing by and approving,ᴰ and I guarded the clothes of those who killed him.'ᵘ

21"The He said to me, 'Go, because I will send you far away to the Gentiles.'"ᵛ

Paul's Roman Protection

22"They listened to him up to his word. Then they raised their voices, shouting, "Wipe this person off the earth—it's a disgrace for him to live!"ʷ

Center column cross-references:

ᵃ**21:40** Jn 5:2; Ac 12:17
ᵇ**22:1–2** Ac 7:2; 21:40
ᶜ**22:3–16** Ac 9:1–22; 26:9–18
ᵈ**22:3** Dt 33:3; Ac 5:34; 9:11; 21:39; 2Co 11:22; Php 3:5
ᵉ**22:4** Ac 26:5; Rm 10:2; Php 3:6
ᶠ**22:4** Ac 9:2; 24:14, 22
ᵍ**22:4** Ac 8:3; 22:19–20; 26:10
ʰ**22:5** Lk 22:66; Ac 13:26; 1Tm 4:14
ⁱ**22:6–11** Ac 9:3–8; 26:12–18
ʲ**22:9** Dn 10:7; Ac 9:7; 26:13
ᵏ**22:10–11** Ac 9:8; 16:30
ˡ**22:12** Ac 9:10, 17; 10:22
ᵐ**22:14** Ac 3:13; 9:15; 26:16
ⁿ**22:14** 1Co 9:1; 15:8
ᵒ**22:14** Ac 3:14; 7:52
ᵖ**22:15** Ac 23:11; 26:16
ᑫ**22:16** Ac 2:38; 1Co 6:11; Heb 10:22
ʳ**22:16** Ac 9:14; Rm 10:13
ˢ**22:17** Ac 9:26; 10:10
ᵗ**22:19** Mt 10:17; Ac 8:3; 22:4
ᵘ**22:20** Ac 7:58; 8:1; Rm 1:32
ᵛ**22:21** Ac 9:15; 13:46
ʷ**22:22** Ac 21:36; 25:24

ᴬ**22:3** Probably Jerusalem, but others think Tarsus   ᴮ**22:9** Other mss add *and were afraid*   ᶜ**22:14** Lit to hear a voice from His Mouth   ᴰ**22:20** Other mss add *of his murder*

21:39 That **Paul** was a citizen of **Tarsus**, a city of importance in the Greco-Roman world, accounted for his knowledge of Greek

21:40 Though the text says **Hebrew**, Paul probably spoke Aramaic to the crowd in order to communicate clearly with them. Aramaic became the new hebrew, so to speak, among the Jewish people after the exile. In Paul's day Hebrew was used only by the religious elite.

22:1 Paul labeled his address a **defense** or an apology. This is his first apologetic speech in Acts.

22:3 Paul offered a number of important facts about himself. It appears that Paul spent his youth up to the age of 13 or so in Tarsus where he was probably educated in the first stage of Greek schooling. Then he went to Jerusalem (**this city**) and finished his education under Gamaliel. Elsewhere in Acts Paul indicated that much of his youth was spent in Jerusalem (26:4), and that he had relatives there (23:16).

22:4 Paul's admission that he **persecuted this Way to the death** indicates that he was more than a passive participant in events such as the stoning death of Stephen (7:58)

22:5–21 This is the second account of Paul's conversion in the book of Acts (9:7; 26:12–18)

22:9 According to 9:7, Paul's traveling companions heard the voice that spoke to him on the road to Damascus, but they did not see anyone. In this verse, Paul himself said that they **did not hear the voice** of the One who was speaking to him. The grammar here supports the idea that Paul's traveling companions may have heard the voice but they did not understand it, or at least they did not understand it as the voice of the Lord.

22:17–21 Only this account of Paul's conversion mentions the temple vision. In his answer to the Lord (**But I said**), newly converted Paul seemed to expect his dramatic reversal from persecutor to advocate for Christianity would make his testimony powerful among Christian Jews in Jerusalem, but the Lord knew at this point they would **not** accept him. On early skepticism about Paul's conversion, see note at 9:26. On the execution of Stephen, see notes at verse 4 and 7:58.

22:22 Paul's mention of his commission to the Gentiles struck at the heart of Jewish nationalism.

Sample page from the Holman Christian Standard Bible (HCSB)

As a subject of serious study for over 2,000 years, there is a wide range of scholarly opinion on the Bible. Some of it is shaped by faith, some by skepticism. This book introduces readers to a few of the debates among Bible scholars of different faiths. The primary goal, however, is to introduce the Bible on its own terms. One important aspect of the Bible's content is its view of itself.

The Word of the Lord

The Bible is composed of 66 books. That diverse collection of books is presented as a unified whole, in part because of the conviction of its authors and those who compiled it that it also has a single, divine Author. Old Testament prophets from Moses through Malachi called their pronouncements "the Word of the Lord" over 200 times. God was said to speak "through" the prophets (1 Kings 14:18). Prophets who did not speak from God were considered false prophets (Numbers 22:38; Deuteronomy 18:18–20). In the New Testament, Jesus often said "Truly, truly, I say to you" as an equivalent to prophet's phrase "Thus says the Lord." The Bible presents the words of its human authors as simultaneously the words of God (1 Timothy 3:16), which were written by men "moved by the Spirit" of God (1 Peter 1:21).

When written, the Old Testament manuscripts were called "scripture," as were the words of Jesus (1 Timothy 5:18) and Paul's letters (2 Peter 3:16). All were considered to be God's own speech, the "Word of God" through "inspiration." Inspiration encompassed more than divine quotes or dictation, although that was also included (for example, Isaiah 38:4-6; Revelation 2:1). Luke's Gospel and the Book of Acts were the result of research and interviews (Luke 1:1–3). Other material was produced in different ways (Hebrews 1:1). Each book, however, was considered to have God as its ultimate Author.

The Power of the Bible

As God's Word, the Bible claims the same power displayed when God created the world by speaking (Genesis 1:3). It was this powerful Word which God placed in the mouths of the prophets (Jeremiah 1:9–10). The result was the lifting up and casting down of nations. Most importantly, the Bible sees its power functioning to summon faith and new life in the hearts of its readers (Romans 10:13–17; 1 Peter 1:23).

Truthfulness of the Bible

The Bible also claims to be completely truthful in its affirmations and faithful in its reports. God is described as a truth-teller (2 Samuel 7:28, John 17:17), and the truthfulness of the Bible becomes proverbial: "Every word of God proves true" (Proverbs 30:5). Of course, truth can be expressed in the ordinary descriptive language of historical writing, the intense images and metaphors of poetry, loose or interpretive quotations, rounded numbers, and even uncommon grammar. All of these are found in the Bible.

The truthfulness of the Bible is tested by tensions within and challenges from outside the text. Differences between details in various narratives and apparent conflict between theological assertions form the majority of internal tensions. Close examination of narrative details usually suggests plausible accounts of the harmony between differing narratives. While context helps to resolve many of the theological issues, others have caused centuries of debate, with some interpretations becoming widely accepted and others continuing to spark spirited dissent.

Apparent Conflicts

From outside the text, the interpretation of historical evidence or scientific data may conflict or seem to conflict with the Biblical text. These differences sometimes prompt reconsideration of particular interpretations of the Bible. Sometimes they spur further historical or scientific research. Most significant, however, is the disparity between the events described in the Bible and the personal experience of most readers. People don't expect to see someone walk on water or die and return to life after three days in a grave. The plausibility of the Bible's story can be judged on the basis of personal experience or a worldview which allows only natural causes. But if there is a divine Being, the idea that He might speak and act in the world can be neither irrational nor inherently implausible.

IN THE MOVIES:
THE BOOK OF ELI (2010)

Eli (Denzel Washington) is crossing post-apocalyptic America when Carnegie, a local warlord, recognizes the book Eli carries as the Bible. Carnegie (Gary Oldman) insists, "I need that book; I want that book." Asked why, he responds, "I grew up with that book; I know its power." Carnegie sees a weapon to control people, but others see the key to rebuilding society.

"You have been born again—not of perishable seed but of imperishable—through the living and enduring word of God."

(1 Peter 1:23, HCSB)

From the first words penned on scrolls through transmission and translation, across more than 2,000 years, the journey of the Bible to the modern reader has been a long road. But learning about the Bible is only the beginning of the reader's journey. The Bible was written to be read, not to gather dust on a shelf.

Reading the Bible may seem like a challenge. The Bible is a complex book, which is why seminary students take whole courses on interpreting it, and doctoral candidates have been writing dissertations on it for almost as long as there have been universities. The Bible remains a book that inspires authors and artists, refines the most subtle theologians, and stimulates the lifelong reader. But the Bible also rewards the efforts of those who open it for the first time and requires no more than a willing mind.

Using Contextual Clues

At the most basic level, reading the Bible is no different than reading an *Idiot's Guide*. The main units of thought are sentences and paragraphs. Together these paragraphs make up larger episodes in a variety of literary genres. These are the natural elements in any text, and context will help make sense of them. Intentional sensitivity to details, such as "who, what, when, where, why, and how," and the meaning of words in context, will also help the reader see what is going on more clearly.

Reading Charitably and Humbly

The most important foundation for reading any text, however, is not skill. Reading well requires virtue, especially charity and humility. A charitable reader assumes that the author is writing rationally and looks for the best, strongest understanding of the text. A humble reader remembers that there is always more to learn. Even when a text doesn't immediately make sense to the reader, the author had some reason for what they wrote. The humble reader looks for the information that makes sense of what the author wrote and why.

One Book, Many Genres

Although the skills and virtues for reading the Bible are comparable to those needed to read any book, there are certain features of the Bible that require specific consideration.. The Bible includes a wide variety of literary genres: history, poetry, proverbs, genealogies, parables, epistles, and speeches. Many Biblical books include multiple genres. Each genre has unique characteristics, and many of them are introduced in sidebars throughout this book.

Biblical Themes

The Bible also has major themes that are often linked through common imagery, events, or patterns. Recognizing them when they occur will help a reader to see how the whole fits together. Among the significant themes of the Bible are the glory of God, human sinfulness, divine judgment and grace, the kingdom of God, and salvation. These and others are also pointed out in sidebars in this guide. Recurring patterns include falls from grace and failures of faithfulness, God's use of weak agents to accomplish great things, promise and fulfillment, redemption through suffering, and the preservation of at least a few people through times of divine judgment.

Finally, the Bible itself offers advice for its readers. The Bible was not merely written to inform people. It was written to form them (1 Timothy 3:16). The Biblical authors intended for their writings to be practically applied. Reflection on how the text suggests application to life will help readers grasp more fully what the authors were trying to communicate.

The Bible is a large, rich book. As a result, different people will have different insights into the text and understand some parts better than others. While wrong interpretation is certainly possible, readers can also benefit from the insights of other readers, especially those who have more experience reading the Bible (see Acts 9:31; Ephesians 4:11–12).

A great disadvantage in reading most books is the absence of the author. Readers can't ask the author to explain what he or she meant. In fact, the older the text, the more likely the author will be "unavailable for comment." But the Bible asserts that its ultimate Author is available to any reader. David prayed for insight into scripture (Psalm 119:18). So can any other reader.

THE BIG STORY

The apparent tension between God's love and holiness drives the Biblical narrative. Love offers mercy, but holiness requires judgment. Either move threatens God's goal of a sinless human society. The Bible presents a divine dilemma: How can God be just and yet justify fallen people, and rescue creation while remaining righteous?

The Old Testament

Scholars classify the Old Testament books in different ways, but one of the most common groups them in five different categories: Law (also called the Torah, Pentateuch, or Books of Moses), Historical Books, Poetry, Major Prophets (large prophetic books), and Minor Prophets (smaller prophetic books).

Law

Genesis

Exodus

Leviticus

Numbers

Deuteronomy

History

Joshua

Judges

Ruth

1 & 2 Samuel

1 & 2 Kings

1 & 2 Chronicles

Ezra

Nehemiah

Esther

Poetry

Job

Psalms

Proverbs

Ecclesiastes

Song of Solomon

Major Prophets

Isaiah

Jeremiah

Lamentations

Ezekiel

Daniel

Minor Prophets

Hosea

Joel

Amos

Obadiah

Jonah

Micah

Nahum

Habakkuk

Zephaniah

Haggai

Zechariah

Malachi

GENESIS

INTRODUCTION

Genesis begins the history of creation and God's rescue of sinful humanity. The Creator blesses Adam's family, despite their repeated failures, and offers hope for a new beginning with Abraham and his descendants.

LOCATION: Genesis unfolds in the Fertile Crescent (what is today Iraq, Syria, Israel, and Jordan) and Egypt.

ORIGIN: Modern scholars offer many opinions about who wrote Genesis. However, the rest of the Bible names Moses as the author of Genesis. He would have written it during the period described in Exodus and Numbers, probably between 1400 and 1200 B.C.E

KEY PASSAGES

The Beginning of History (1–11)

1:1–2:25	God Creates the World and Humanity
3:1–24	Man Falls, but God Gives Hope in Judgment

The Life of Abraham and Isaac (12–26)

12:1–9	God Calls and Blesses Abram
15:1–21	God Promises Abraham a Son and a Land
24:1–67	Rebekah Displays the Faith of Abraham

The Life of Jacob and Joseph (27–50)

27:1–46	Jacob Tries to Steal a Blessing
32:24–30	Jacob Loses a Wrestling Match with God
37:1–36	Joseph the Dreamer is Sold into Slavery
39:1–41:49	Joseph Rises to Serve Pharaoh
42:1–44:34	Joseph Tests His Brothers

PRINCIPAL FIGURES

God   The book of Genesis presents God as the Creator who judges and blesses humanity.

Adam   The first man who was made in the image of God and given dominion over creation, but who introduced sin into the world.

Eve   The first woman, also made in God's image, who was created to help Adam where he could not succeed alone. Her importance made her the focus of the serpent's temptation.

Cain   The first son of Adam and Eve. When his sacrifice was rejected, he murdered his brother, **Abel,** and was exiled by God.

Noah   The first "savior" of the human race. Noah built a ship to restore the human and animal population of the earth after the worldwide flood.

Abraham/Abram   He had the faith to follow God to a promised land, and trusted God to provide him an heir through whom all nations would be blessed.

Isaac   The son Abraham received by trusting God's promise. He became the heir of God's promise to bless the world through Abraham.

Rebekah   The greatest woman of faith in Genesis, comparable to Abraham. She left her home to go to a promised husband.

Jacob   The son of Isaac and Rebekah, he was a clever deceiver until he lost a wrestling match with God, and was given a new name, Israel.

Joseph   The son of Jacob. His brothers hated him for his dreams. But he survived slavery and prison to provide for his brothers and Egypt during a great famine.

IN THE BEGINNING
(Genesis 1:1–2:4)

The first chapters of Genesis begin the story of God's creation. History began when God spoke and creation exploded into existence. Over six days God spoke; it was so, and it was good. On the first three days there was separation: dark from light, sea from sky, and land from sea. On the next three days, that structure was refined. Light and dark became sun, moon, and stars. Sky and sea were filled with birds and marine life. The land was given animals of all kinds. God worked for six days, but then there was a seventh day. On that final day, God blessed creation with His presence at rest. But God didn't rest alone.

Of all the things He created, the crowning glory of His work was humanity. He formed a man out of the dust and blessed him with life. God made a garden in one corner of this new world and put Adam in it. Adam was to be fruitful and fill the earth with people. He was to be its steward, expanding and adapting the garden to the rest of the earth. But Adam couldn't do the job by himself. He needed someone who would work with him and do things he could not. So God took a rib from Adam's side and formed the first woman, Eve, to be his wife. Together, Adam and Eve were made in God's image, reflecting the divine character and enjoying divine fellowship with God and each other.

THE BIBLE AND SCIENCE

Genesis evokes ideas of conflict between faith and science. Significant differences exist between current scientific cosmology and Genesis, especially regarding time scale and macro-evolution. But the creation account also describes a structured world that can be understood and a vision of humanity's role that aided the development of Western science.

"So God created man in His own image; He created him in the image of God; He created them male and female. God blessed them, and God said to them, 'Be fruitful, multiply, fill the earth, and subdue it. Rule the fish of the sea, the birds of the sky, and every creature that crawls on the earth.'" (Genesis 1:27–28, HCSB)

GENESIS

Adam and Eve's Sin

God created the world and made Adam and Eve His stewards. He designed them to serve each other: Adam through responsibility for their mission, and Eve as his essential and indispensable helpmate. Together, they were to tend creation and rule over the animals for good as God ruled humanity for good. God placed Adam and Eve in the Garden of Eden and withheld only the Tree of the Knowledge of Good and Evil. Adam and Eve's need for knowledge to govern creation should have sent them to the Creator for answers, reminding them of His wisdom and power and building their relationship with Him.

Instead, humanity fell. Satan infiltrated the Garden as a serpent. Eve was essential to humanity's success, and she became the focus of the temptation. Satan mocked God's word, His honesty, and His goodness. Satan claimed to offer a way for humanity to fulfill its mission without God. As Adam looked on, Eve succumbed to the serpent's temptation and ate from the Tree of Knowledge, then handed the fruit to Adam, who also ate. Satan had succeeded in reversing the structure of creation. Rather than serving each other, the first couple had harmed each other. Humanity submitted to an animal and abandoned submission to God.

PARADISE LOST

In 1667, John Milton published his greatest work, *Paradise Lost*. Containing more than 10,000 lines of verse, this epic poem narrates Satan's rebellion and the relationship of Adam and Eve. It is one of the enduring classics of English literature. Though Milton stated his intent to "justify the ways of God to men," many critics from the eighteenth century on have argued that he was "of the Devil's party without knowing it."

God's Judgment

Only then did they realize how vulnerable they were. Since the responsibility for stewardship was his, God confronted Adam. Adam blamed Eve and implied that God was at fault. As judgment, God cursed the ground to rebel against humanity as humanity had rebelled against God. Instead of enjoying harmony through service, marriage would be marred by manipulation and tyranny. Having rejected the gift of divine fellowship, humanity lost direct access to God in the Garden.

But with judgment, God gave hope. Instead of executing Adam, God substituted animals, offering the first sacrifice. Then God spoke the first prophecy: the "seed of the woman" would crush the serpent—at great cost.

IT WAS JUST A BITE!

Adam and Eve's sin seems small, even understandable. But by eating the fruit, humanity rejected trust and dependence on God and attempted to seize the place of the Creator (motivated by the serpent's words, "you shall be like God"). That bite tasted of blasphemous unbelief and pride.

> *"I will put hostility between you and the woman, and between your seed and her seed. He will strike your head, and you will strike his heel."*
>
> (Genesis 3:15, HCSB)

BIBLICAL LINKS

"When the time came to completion, God sent His Son, born of a woman, born under the law," *(Galatians 4:4, HCSB)*

GENESIS

Sometime after leaving the Garden of Eden, Adam and Eve had a child. Eve rejoiced, not just crediting her husband with helping her to have a son, but affirming that God had granted her the one who would defeat sin and the curse. But Cain was not the one. She later gave birth to a second son, Abel.

Two Brothers, Two Offerings

When they became men, Cain and his brother Abel went to present an offering to God, each gave of their life's work. Abel's offering of a firstborn from his flock was presented in humility and faith. Cain's offering from his harvest was delivered with arrogant assurance of his righteous standing. God accepted Abel's offering, but rejected Cain's.

God confronted Cain and warned him of the danger he faced. Here was Cain's chance to accept a bruised heel in order to crush the head of the serpent. But instead of sacrificing himself for his brother, Cain killed Abel, committing the first murder. Instead of defeating sin, sin defeated Cain.

SIN IN WESTERN CULTURE

The theme of sin shows up frequently in Western culture as the idea that there is something fundamentally wrong with humanity as a whole. This concern is found in novels such as Nathaniel Hawthorne's *The Scarlet Letter* and Fyodor Dostoyevsky's *Crime and Punishment*, as well as in movies such as *Amadeus*, *Mystic River*, and *Inside Man*. Songs like "Ugly" (The Exies), "We're All to Blame" (Sum 41), and "Crawling in the Dark" (Hoobastank) also explore the idea that humanity is broken.

Cain's Exile

Again, God confronted Cain, who now denied that he had any responsibility to protect Abel. But God had made people to serve each other, and God's promise had directed Eve's hope to one who would defeat the serpent, at great cost to himself. Cain was the opposite of that vision; he served himself and was defeated, at great cost to his brother.

Cain was exiled, but he was not utterly destroyed. God preserved Cain's life as a wanderer and eventually as the founder of the first city. His descendants were credited with the development of arts and technology, but they also focused on exalting their own names.

A Third Son

Eventually, Adam and Eve would have one more son, Seth. Among all the contributions Seth's descendants made to human culture, the greatest was learning to trust and glorify God by calling on His name.

WHO WAS CAIN'S WIFE?

The Bible only notes that Eve gave birth to Cain, Abel, and Seth. The fact that Cain (and Seth) married and had children raises the question of where their wives came from. The most likely answer is that they married daughters of Adam and Eve whose births were not mentioned by the Bible. The prohibition in the Law of Moses against marrying blood-kin (consanguineous marriage) was not given until much later (Lev 18:6-18).

"If you do what is right, won't you be accepted? But if you do not do what is right, sin is crouching at the door. Its desire is for you, but you must rule over it."

(Genesis 4:7, HCSB)

BIBLICAL LINKS

"By faith Abel offered to God a better sacrifice than Cain did. By faith he was approved as a righteous man, because God approved his gifts, and even though he is dead, he still speaks through his faith." *(Hebrews 11:4, HCSB)*

Lamach, who descended from Adam and Eve's third son Seth, had a son and named him Noah, meaning "rest." He hoped that his son would be the one who would bring relief from the curse God had imposed in response to Adam's sin (Gen 5:29). Although Noah did not defeat sin, he did become the savior of the human race in another way.

God Speaks to Noah

As humanity became more sinful, God grieved and decided to wipe the slate clean. Only Noah found favor with God. God warned Noah of the destruction that would come in 120 years and instructed him to build an ark—a ship that could survive the flood. Despite ridicule, Noah warned others of God's judgment with his preaching and his actions. He built an ark that could carry enough people and animals to repopulate the earth.

The Flood Arrives

Eventually, the flood came. God closed Noah and his family into the ark along with one pair of every major kind of animal, and seven for those used in sacrifices. It rained for 40 days, and the floodwaters covered the land for another 110 days after that.

As the flood waters drained from the land, the ark came to rest on Mount Ararat, in what is today northeastern Turkey. It took another 40 days before the tops of the mountains became visible. At that point, Noah began sending out birds to see if the ground had dried enough to allow his passengers to disembark.

CUBITS AND KINDS

Noah's ark was a big ship, 300 cubits long (possibly over 500 feet) and 1.4 million cubic feet in volume. The ark was about two-thirds the size of the Titanic. It carried animals of every "kind," a broad category, probably a rough equivalent to the category of "family" in the modern biological classification system.

When a dove returned with an olive branch, Noah and his family emerged to see a rainbow in the sky. The rainbow represented God's promise not to destroy the whole world by flood again and reaffirmed humanity's place as His image in creation.

Sin Remains

The flood destroyed most of sinful humanity, but that alone would not solve the problem. Once again, humanity was defeated by sin. After planting a vineyard and celebrating to excess, Noah woke to find that his son, Ham, had sinned against him. Again, a curse was pronounced. Ham's son Canaan would be as great a failure to Ham as Ham had been to Noah. But blessing was conferred on Noah's sons Shem and Japheth, who had shown respect for their father.

THE "ARK"

The word *ark* has several uses in the Bible, each building on the idea of a wooden container designed to protect something valuable. In Genesis, it refers to the ship built by Noah to rescue humanity and the animals from the flood. Later, a wooden chest overlaid with gold carrying the Ten Commandments is called "The Ark of the Covenant" (Exod 25).

BIBLICAL LINKS

"As the days of Noah were, so the coming of the Son of Man will be. For in those days before the flood they were eating and drinking, marrying and giving in marriage, until the day Noah boarded the ark. They didn't know until the flood came and swept them all away. So this is the way the coming of the Son of Man will be:" *(Matthew 24:37–39, HCSB)*

"I confirm My covenant with you that never again will every creature be wiped out by the waters of a flood; there will never again be a flood to destroy the earth." (Genesis 9:11, HCSB)

GENESIS

THE TOWER OF BABEL
(Genesis 11)

After the great flood, the human race swelled in size. Not trusting God's promise to bless them, the people decided they needed to protect themselves from any future divine wrath. To achieve this goal, they decided to "help" God so that He would appreciate what they did for Him. So they began to build a tower.

A Tower for God

The Tower of Babel might have been something like a ziggurat, a solid pyramid of brick on the outside and dirt filling the center. When completed, steps would have risen along one side to a room at the top. A god could rest and eat there before using the stairs to aid his passage from the heavens to the earth.

At the bottom of the stairs would have been a Temple, where the god would receive worship from those who had served him by easing his travels. The people of Babel thought that if they built such a structure, God would be grateful and favor the people with His protection.

LANGUAGES AS JUDGMENT

Babel introduces the idea that the inability to understand others because they speak a different language is evidence of divine judgment (also see Deut 28:49, Isa 28:9–13; 1 Cor 14:20–22). On the other hand, the removal of language barriers was a sign of divine favor (see Isa 33:17–24; Acts 2:5–13).

TIRAS • GOMER • *Black Sea* • *Caspian Sea* • JAVAN • JAVAN • MESHECH • ▲ *Mt. Ararat* • LUD • TUBAL • ASSHUR • MADAI • ARAM • *River Tigris* • ARPHAXAD • *(Mediterranean Sea)* • *Great Sea* • CANAAN • *River Euphrates* • ELAM • PUT • MIZRAIM • *River Nile* • CUSH

After God made humanity speak many languages, the descendants of Noah settled in different lands.

The Consequence of Pride

But God knew what was going on. Mocking their foolish project, God descended to earth without using their tower. He had come to "see" what they were doing. It was as if the tower were so small that even God couldn't see it without stooping down low to the ground. Although the tower wasn't dangerous, the pride that prompted its construction was. As long as sinful humanity could work together easily, there would be no limit to the sin they could do. So God executed a judgment that was thorough and gracious: He caused them to speak different languages. As a result, humanity scattered across the earth, fracturing into different tribes and nations.

BIBLICAL LINKS

"There were Jews living in Jerusalem, devout men from every nation under heaven. When this sound occurred, a crowd came together and was confused because each one heard them speaking in his own language. And they were astounded and amazed, saying, 'Look, aren't all these who are speaking Galileans? ... we hear them speaking the magnificent acts of God in our own languages.'" *(Acts 2:5–7, 11, HCSB)*

THE VALUE OF GENESIS GENEALOGIES

The genealogies are long and difficult to read. Genesis 5 follows the descendants of Seth, suggesting that Enoch never died (5:24) and naming Methuselah as the oldest man who ever lived, dying at age 969 (5:27). Genesis 10 identifies nations that descended from Noah's sons. Genesis 11 traces the descendants of Noah's son Shem to Abraham. These lists provide the first serious barrier to a reader who might be hoping to read the Bible from the beginning. But together, these lists connect later figures (Abraham, David, and eventually Christ) to Adam and the problems he caused. They also demonstrate that God's gift of life, and so His plan to bless humanity, continued despite sin and death.

"The Lord said, 'If they have begun to do this as one people all having the same language, then nothing they plan to do will be impossible for them. Come, let Us go down there and confuse their language so that they will not understand one another's speech.'" (Genesis 11:6–7, HCSB)

GENESIS

From the people scattered after Babel, God called Abram. Abram abandoned the security of his home to follow a God he didn't know, to a land he had never seen, on the strength of God's promise to bless him and the world through him (Gen 12). As Abram wandered the land of Canaan, his faith waxed and waned like the moon.

Abram's Doubts

Eventually, Abram questioned God (Gen 15). God reaffirmed and refined His promise: Abram would have a son of his own. Again, Abram believed God. The deal was sealed with a covenant ceremony in which God alone signed the contract. Although Abram was warned that his descendants would become a slave nation for a time, God also promised to lead them out with the wealth of the nation they served.

The Birth of Ishmael

As time passed, it seemed God had forgotten His promise, so Abram and his wife Sarai took matters into their own hands. Sarai offered her slave Hagar, who gave birth to Abram's son, Ishmael. Abram loved Ishmael and asked God to accept him as heir of God's promise. Although God promised to bless Ishmael, He refused to make him heir of the covenant promise.

BIBLICAL LINKS

"Just as Abraham believed God, and it was credited to him for righteousness, then understand that those who have faith are Abraham's sons."
(Galatians 3:6–7, HCSB)

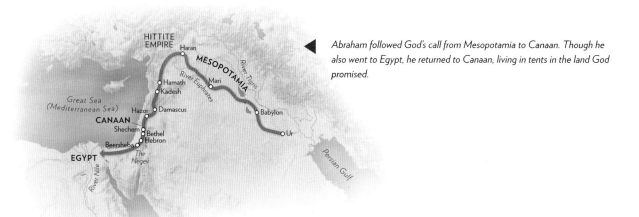

Abraham followed God's call from Mesopotamia to Canaan. Though he also went to Egypt, he returned to Canaan, living in tents in the land God promised.

God's Promise Fulfilled

Once again, God reaffirmed and refined His promise (Gen 17). This time, He changed Abram's name to Abraham and Sarai to Sarah. All the men of Abraham's household were required to be circumcised as a sign of their faithful participation in the contract. Then God promised that Sarah would bear Abraham a son. Since Sarah had passed menopause, it was laughable (Gen 17–18). But they trusted God enough to try one more time. When Sarah gave birth to Isaac as promised, God's promise was fulfilled (Gen 21).

POINTING TO THE PROMISED ONE

The Abrahamic Covenant begins to narrow the search for the one promised in Gen 3:15. Out of all nations, the promise would be fulfilled through Abraham. Of Abraham's sons, God chose Isaac instead of Ishmael. This covenant also introduces tension over the identity of the promised one: a faithful nation of Abraham's descendants, or an individual faithful son of Abraham. The answer to that question marks one of the primary differences between Jewish and Christian understandings of the Bible.

COVENANTS IN THE BIBLE

A covenant is a formal relationship between two parties, like a contract. In the Bible, God established several covenants to redeem humanity. Noah received the first explicit covenant (Gen 9), assuring that God would never again destroy humanity by flood. The Abrahamic Covenant (Gen 12, 15, 17) promised that God would bless humanity through Abraham's seed. The Mosaic Covenant (Exod 19-20) formalized the relationship between God and the nation of Israel. The Davidic Covenant (2 Sam 7) promised David an heir who would reign forever. Finally, Jeremiah promised a New Covenant (Jer 31) which would reconcile God's people to Him forever.

"Abram believed the Lord, and He credited it to him as righteousness." (Genesis 15:6, HCSB)

GENESIS

After Isaac's birth, conflict in the family led Abraham to send Hagar and Ishmael away (Gen 21). Then God called Abraham again (Gen 22). This time, it hurt. God's words reminded Abraham that his love for Isaac had resulted in the exile of another son whom he had hoped would be heir of God's promise. Worse, God commanded Abraham to take Isaac to the land of Moriah and sacrifice him.

The Journey to Moriah

As if in a daze, Abraham got up early, saddled the donkey, and gathered his son and servants before remembering to cut wood for the sacrificial fire. Apparently, they still hit the road before Sarah realized what was going on. The journey took three days.

Eventually, Abraham saw their destination. He and Isaac continued on alone. But Abraham promised his servants that both he and Isaac would return. When Isaac asked about the sacrifice, his father assured him that God would provide. Once again, Abraham trusted God.

BIBLICAL LINKS

"By faith Abraham, when he was tested, offered up Isaac. He received the promises and he was offering his unique son, the one it had been said about, Your seed will be traced through Isaac. He considered God to be able even to raise someone from the dead, and as an illustration, he received him back." *(Hebrews 11:17–19, HCSB)*

ANGEL OF THE LORD

The Angel of the Lord is a heavenly figure in the Old Testament that guided (Exod 14:19) and judged (2 Sam 24:16) the Israelites. Jewish interpreters have seen this figure as a divine messenger symbolizing God's distance (Exod 33:20) and presence, for example, when appearing to Elijah (1 Kgs 19:7). Christian interpreters have traditionally identified the Angel as appearances of Christ prior to the incarnation. This interpretation harmonizes Exodus 33:20 with the way in which the Angel is equated with God (Gen 31:11–13; Exod 3:2–10; Judg 13:21–22) and accepts worship as God (Josh 5:13–6:2; Judg 6:12–14).

Abraham's Faith is Tested

The action slowed to glacial speed as Abraham built an altar of stones, placed the wood upon it, and bound Isaac. After laying him on the altar, the knife rose and began to fall. Despite his previous failures, Abraham's faith had grown to the point where he trusted God's promises about Isaac enough even to sacrifice him at God's command. It was only then that the Angel of God called, "Stop!" Abraham looked up, and before him was a ram that had not been there before. At God's instruction, Abraham sacrificed the ram in Isaac's place.

Blessings From God

Abraham named the spot *Yahweh Yireh*, meaning God Will Provide. There God made His final promise to Abraham. Abraham's faith resulted in faithfulness, through which he experienced God's blessings. Abraham's descendants would outnumber the stars and the world would be blessed by his offspring.

BIBLICAL WORDPLAY

The original Hebrew text of Genesis 22 puns with the Hebrew word YRH (which means see, or see to). Abraham goes to the land of Provision (M'YRH), which he sees (YR) from a distance. He assures Isaac that God will provide (YRH) and looks up to see (YR) the sacrifice God provided. Here, Abraham's faith is finally seen in full.

"Abraham answered, 'God Himself will provide the lamb for the burnt offering, my son.'"
(Genesis 22:8, HCSB)

GENESIS

REBEKAH'S FAITH
(Genesis 24)

As Abraham neared the end of his life, he turned his attention to securing a good wife for Isaac. He called his senior servant and gave him a mission: return to Abraham's family in Mesopotamia and bring back a wife.

An Impossible Task

Abraham had two particular requirements. First, Isaac was not to develop a loyalty to the idols of the land by marrying a Canaanite woman. Second, Isaac was not to return to Mesopotamia, abandoning Abraham's faith in the promise God had made to give him the land of Canaan.

The servant was concerned. He was to find a woman who would leave the security of her family, travel to a land she had never seen, and marry a man neither she nor her family had ever met. It would have seemed an impossible task. Indeed, the conditions Abraham imposed could be met only by a woman whose faith was as strong as Abraham's.

A Sign from God

When the servant arrived, he asked for a clear sign of the woman God had chosen. The servant would ask a young woman for some water, a simple act of hospitality for a stranger. The chosen woman would be revealed by her offer to do the long labor of watering the camels also. Before he was even done praying, a beautiful girl approached the spring. When he asked her for a drink, she watered his camels also. Her name was Rebekah, and she was of Abraham's family.

FAMILIAL MARRIAGE

In the ancient world, marrying within the tribe was a common way of maintaining ethnic and cultural identity, often joining close relations. For example, Abraham's wife Sarah was his half-sister (Gen 20:12). The Law of Moses later outlawed this practice (Lev 18:6-18).

THE FAITH OF ABRAHAM

Abraham's faith is a significant image throughout the Bible. It refers to a trust in God resulting in obedience (Gen 12, 22). Rahab (Josh 2), Ruth, David (2 Sam 24), and Elijah (1 Kgs 18) are credited with this kind of faith. When Paul (Gal 3) and James (Jas 2) wrote about faith, Abraham was their main example. The author of Hebrews makes Abraham the centerpiece of his exposition of faith (Heb 11).

Rebekah Goes to Isaac

After giving Rebekah and her family gifts, he told them of Abraham's wealth and Isaac's position as sole heir. His story and gifts showed that Rebekah would be well cared for. The very next day, he prepared to leave. The family was reluctant, but when the question was put to Rebekah, she declared that she would go.

BIBLICAL LINKS

"Sons are indeed a heritage from the Lord, children, a reward. Like arrows in the hand of a warrior are the sons born in one's youth. Happy is the man who has filled his quiver with them. Such men will never be put to shame when they speak with their enemies at the city gate." *(Psalm 127:3–5, HCSB)*

"They blessed Rebekah, saying to her: Our sister, may you become thousands upon ten thousands. May your offspring possess the gates of their enemies."
(Genesis 24:60, HCSB)

GENESIS

JACOB STEALS ESAU'S BLESSING
(Genesis 27-28)

Isaac and Rebekah had twin boys, Esau and Jacob. Though God had promised that the Abrahamic Covenant would pass to Jacob, Isaac intended to pass its blessings to Esau, who was the first born of the twins and his favorite son. When Isaac's eyesight dimmed and he began to anticipate his death, he sent Esau out to hunt game and prepare his favorite meal. After eating the meal, he would bless Esau.

Jacob Deceives Isaac

Rebekah overheard her husband speaking to Esau, and, suspecting her husband's intentions, came up with a scheme of her own. She ordered Jacob to bring her two goats. Her plan was to cook the goats, dress Jacob in Esau's clothes, and have him feed the meal to Isaac. By pretending to be Esau, Jacob would secure the blessing instead of his brother. Jacob saw a flaw in the plan: Esau had hairy skin, while Jacob was smooth skinned. So when he went to Isaac, he wore the skins from the goats on his hands and neck.

Isaac was suspicious of the voice he heard and how quickly the meal was ready, but Jacob insisted he was Esau and claimed God had favored his hunt. Isaac grasped Jacob's hand and neck. Feeling the hairy skin, he gave the blessing: his son would receive abundant harvests, dominion over nations, and mastery over his brothers and he would become the agent of judgment and blessing in the world.

When Esau returned, he was enraged to find that his blessing had been stolen with nothing left for him. All Isaac could promise him was that he would live by the sword and eventually break free of his brother. Esau decided that as soon as Isaac died, Jacob would, too. Jacob fled for his life.

BIBLICAL LINKS

"You are the sons of the prophets and of the covenant that God made with your ancestors, saying to Abraham, 'And all the families of the earth will be blessed through your offspring. God raised up His Servant and sent Him first to you to bless you by turning each of you from your evil ways.'" *(Acts 3:25–26, HCSB)*

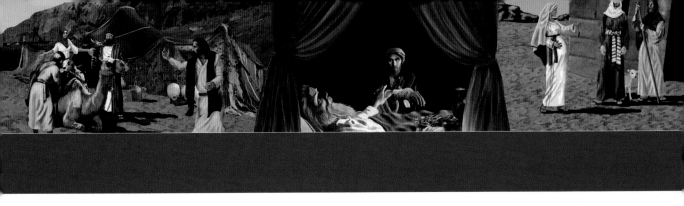

God Confers the Blessing

Although Isaac's family had schemed and fought over who would inherit Abraham's Covenant, it was not theirs to give. God alone could confer the blessing. While Jacob traveled, God confronted him in a vision and fulfilled His promise to give the Covenant to Jacob. Jacob lived for many years as an exile in Mesopotamia, working for his Uncle Laban.

A New Name for Jacob
(Genesis 32-33)

Eventually, Jacob returned to Canaan. On the return trip, he tried to make peace with Esau. But when he heard that Esau was coming to meet him with 400 warriors, he worried. After dividing his caravan into two groups, Jacob appealed to God for aid.

That night, Jacob *(yabbok)* found himself in a wrestling match *(yeabek)*. As dawn neared, his opponent ended the fight by dislocating Jacob's hip. Only then did Jacob recognize that he had been wrestling with God. He refused to let go unless the man blessed him. Acknowledging Jacob's refusal to let go even in defeat, God gave him the name Israel, meaning God Contended, and granted peace with his brother, Esau. Jacob had been humbled, allowing him to be reconciled to God and his brother and to return to the Promised Land.

FIRSTBORN AND YOUNGER SONS

Ancient near-Eastern cultures practiced primogeniture, the priority of the firstborn son in leadership and inheritance. Isaac's attempt to bless Esau reflects this practice. The Bible, however, shows a pattern of God raising younger sons to positions of prominence (for example Isaac, Jacob, Joseph, Judah, David, and Solomon).

"All the peoples on earth will be blessed through you and your offspring. Look, I am with you and will watch over you wherever you go. I will bring you back to this land, for I will not leave you until I have done what I have promised you."

(Genesis 28:14–15, HCSB)

GENESIS

THE LIFE OF JOSEPH
(Genesis 37–50)

Jacob had twelve sons, but Joseph was his favorite. Jacob showed his favor for Joseph by giving him a coat of many colors, which caused Joseph's brothers to envy and despise him. The dreams Joseph had indicating that his brothers would bow to him didn't help. So when Jacob sent Joseph to see to his brothers' welfare, they sold him into slavery and faked evidence of his death. But God was with Joseph.

Joseph Imprisoned

In Egypt, Joseph was sold to the captain of the guard, Potiphar. He became the senior manager of the household, and Potiphar prospered. But Potiphar's wife wanted Joseph and tried to seduce him. When Joseph spurned her, she accused him of attempting to rape her. Joseph was imprisoned, but God was with him.

An Interpreter of Dreams As a prisoner, Joseph became the warden's deputy. One day Pharaoh, the ruler of Egypt, imprisoned two of his important servants. They were responsible for protecting him from poison in his wine (cupbearer) and food (baker). Each had a strange dream, and both told Joseph their dreams. He gave God's interpretation: the cupbearer would be restored to his post, but the baker would be executed. The dreams proved to be accurate.

DREAMS AND INTERPRETATION

In the ancient world, dreams were considered divine messages. Egyptians, in particular, were fascinated by them. They kept detailed records of dreams and their meanings. These records were then used to train professional interpreters. Part of Joseph's reputation came from his success at interpreting dreams no one else could, without any professional training.

BIBLICAL LINKS

"We know that all things work together for the good of those who love God: those who are called according to His purpose." *(Romans 8:28, HCSB)*

Map legend:
- Joseph follows his brothers
- Joseph taken to Egypt

Map labels: Great Sea (Mediterranean Sea), Dothan, Shechem, River Jordan, Joppa, Jerusalem, Bethlehem, Gaza, Hebron, Beersheba, Salt Sea (Dead Sea), EGYPT

◀ *In the ancient city of Dothan, Joseph's brothers sold him into slavery.*

Joseph and Pharaoh

Two years later, Pharaoh had two nightmares. In one, seven healthy cows were consumed by seven sickly cows. In the other, seven plump heads of grain were swallowed up by seven thin heads of grain. When Pharaoh mentioned these dreams to his cupbearer, the cupbearer remembered Joseph and his skill for interpretation.

Pharaoh sent for Joseph who explained that God was promising seven years of record harvests, followed by seven years of famine. He advised Pharaoh to appoint someone to store the excess of the good years as a reserve for the famine. Pharaoh realized that God was with Joseph and gave him authority over the nation to carry out the plan he had proposed to Pharaoh.

During the famine, Jacob's sons came to buy grain. When they bowed before the Egyptian official in charge of the grain, they didn't realize it was Joseph. But he recognized them and tested them to see if they had changed. Eventually he revealed himself to his brothers and they were reconciled. Jacob moved to Egypt, where Pharaoh welcomed the family and provided them with rich land for their flocks. Joseph had accomplished his mission to see to the welfare of his brothers, but in a way no one had anticipated.

CULTURAL CONNECTIONS

The story of Joseph's coat of many colors provided the inspiration for Andrew Lloyd Weber's long-running musical, *Joseph and the Amazing Technicolor Dreamcoat*. In this interpretation, the role of Pharaoh is played in the style of Elvis Presley.

"You planned evil against me; God planned it for good to bring about the present result—the survival of many people."

(Genesis 50:20, HCSB)

JUDAH'S TRANSFORMATION
(Genesis 38)

The name of Jacob's son, Judah, means "praise God," yet his life did anything but. It was Judah who came up with the plan to sell his brother Joseph into slavery and fake his death. He cared nothing for his father's favorite son.

Judah and Tamar

Judah married his oldest son, Er, to a Canaanite woman, Tamar. But Er erred, and God executed him. This left Tamar without support, so the next brother, Onan, was to help her have a son. Onan took advantage of Tamar's vulnerability, preventing her from conceiving a son who would be Er's heir and not his own. As heir of the firstborn son, that child would have inherited most of Judah's wealth. Tamar had no recourse, but God stepped in and Onan also died.

Judah sent Tamar back to her family, saying that when his youngest son grew older, he would send for her. It was a promise he had no intention of keeping.

After Judah's wife died, he traveled to the shearing of the flocks. Along the way he saw what seemed to be a Temple prostitute and sought a "worship experience." Since he had no payment to offer, the woman demanded his staff and seal (the ancient equivalent of his driver's license and credit cards). Judah foolishly agreed. After reaching the flock, Judah sent a friend back with payment, but the woman was gone.

LEVIRATE MARRIAGE

The Levirate marriage was a custom designed to protect son-less widows from poverty and prostitution. The nearest kinsman was to marry the widow and care for her. The first son of their union would be the heir of the deceased husband, carrying his name and inheriting in his place. (See Deut 25:5–10.)

CULT PROSTITUTION

Many ancient female deities were associated with fertility and birth—this being the uniquely female mode of creating. Priestesses associated with these deities often served as substitutes for the goddess in ritual sex with male worshippers. Men gained the privilege of such worship by contributing gifts to the priestesses. Ritual sex acts were intended to aid the goddess in renewing the life of the world. This practice was forbidden by the Law of Moses (Deut 23:17).

Judah's Humiliation and Reformation

Shortly afterward, Tamar was found to be pregnant. Judah saw his chance to be rid of her and demanded that she be executed. However, she produced his staff and seal, revealing herself to be the woman from the Temple. Judah confessed, "She is more in the right than I." Tamar gave birth to twins, one of whom became an ancestor of King David.

Being humiliated by a Canaanite woman transformed Judah. When Joseph tested his brothers, Judah finally lived up to his name. He offered himself as a substitute, to go into slavery in Egypt in the place of his father's favorite son. As a result, Jacob made him the son who would succeed him as leader of the family.

BIBLICAL CONNECTIONS

"Ask of Me, and I will make the nations Your inheritance and the ends of the earth Your possession. You will break them with a rod of iron; You will shatter them like pottery." *(Psalm 2:8–9, HCSB)*

"The scepter will not depart from Judah or the staff from between his feet until He whose right it is comes and the obedience of the peoples belongs to Him."

(Genesis 49:10, HCSB)

EXODUS

Exodus describes God's liberation of Israel from slavery in Egypt. God calls Moses to confront Pharaoh and pronounce plagues on Egypt, culminating in the death of Egypt's firstborn sons at Passover. God leads Israel through the Red Sea to Mount Sinai, where Moses receives the Law of the Covenant.

KEY PASSAGES

The Life of Moses (1–4)

3:1–4:17   God Calls Moses from a Burning Bush

The Liberation of Israel (5–15:21)

7:14–11:10 God Brings Ten Plagues on Egypt

12:1–13:16 Israel Celebrates the First Passover

The Journey to Mount Sinai (15:21–18)

13:17–14:31 Israel Crosses the Red Sea

The Law of the Mosaic Covenant (19–24)

20:1–17   God Gives Moses the Ten Commandments

The Tabernacle of the Mosaic Covenant (25–40)

32:1–34:9   God Forgives Israel for Worshipping the Golden Calf

PRINCIPAL FIGURES

God   In Exodus, God is the Judge of Egypt, the Deliverer and Lawgiver who forgives Israel's unfaithfulness and provides during the nation's wilderness journey.

Moses   Drawn from the Nile River where his mother hid him, Moses was raised by an Egyptian princess, lived in the wilderness of Midian as a fugitive, and was commissioned by God to liberate Israel.

Miriam   Moses' older sister who protected him in the Nile River and became a prophetess during the Exodus.

Pharaoh   The title of the ruler of Egypt who ignored Joseph's legacy and refused to grant freedom voluntarily to Israel.

Aaron   Moses' older brother, who became his spokesman before Pharaoh and the first High Priest under the Mosaic Covenant.

Jethro   Moses' father-in-law, who counseled Moses to appoint elders to help him rule Israel during the Exodus.

Joshua   Moses' primary assistant during the Exodus journey, who acted as the commander of Israel's army.

LOCATION: The events in Exodus occur in Egypt and the Sinai Peninsula.

ORIGIN: Exodus indicates that Moses recorded God's instructions (Exod 24:4), and the rest of the Bible names Moses as the author of Exodus. He would have written it during the period described in Exodus and Numbers, probably between 1400 and 1200 B.C.E. Modern critical theories propose development of the text over time.

Although the Pharaoh whom Joseph served had honored Jacob's family, later Pharaohs came to fear Israel's numbers more than they valued Joseph's service (Exod 1). Israel was enslaved, and eventually Pharaoh ordered the murder of every Hebrew male child at birth. One Israelite woman had a son named Moses, whose name meant "draw out" or "deliverer." She hid him in a basket and left it floating in the reeds along the Nile River (Exod 2). An Egyptian princess found him and raised him as her son, though Moses knew of his Hebrew heritage.

As young man, Moses attacked and killed an Egyptian foreman who was beating a Hebrew slave. When his deed became known, Moses was forced to flee Egypt for his life. He found refuge in the wilderness of Midian, married a shepherdess, and tended her father's flocks.

After 40 years, God spoke to Moses through a bush that burned but was not consumed by flame (Exod 3–4). God recalled His promise to Abraham (Gen 15:13) and commissioned Moses to liberate the people of Israel. Moses was reluctant to go but God insisted.

God did not promise that the task would be easy, however. Though the Israelite leaders believed Moses, Pharaoh did not. God assured Moses that He would strike Egypt with plagues in order to force Pharaoh to release the people of Israel. Eventually, the Egyptians would be so glad to get rid of Israel that they would allow Israel to plunder the riches of Egypt as they left.

THE ORIGIN OF THE NAME "JEHOVAH"

The name "Jehovah" is derived from the four consonants in God's name YHWH (Exod 3:14). Latin transliterations rendered the name IHVH, and early German/English transliterations substituted "J" for "I" (JHVH). Because Jews avoided pronouncing this name, the vowel sounds from the word *Adonai* (Hebrew for "Lord") were added, yielding "JeHoVaH."

"Then the LORD said, 'I have observed the misery of My people in Egypt, and have heard them crying out because of their oppressors, and I know about their sufferings. I have come down to rescue them from the power of the Egyptians and to bring them from that land to a good and spacious land, a land flowing with milk and honey ....'" (Exodus 3:7–8, HCSB)

EXODUS

God sent Moses to demand that Pharaoh release the people of Israel from slavery, but Pharaoh's heart was hard. When he refused, Moses warned Pharaoh of the coming plagues. Initially, these plagues were only an irritation. But as Pharaoh continued to go back on promises to release the Israelites, they got worse. Later plagues destroyed crops and livestock. Both the magicians and the gods of Egypt were helpless before the God of the slaves.

Protection for Israel

Throughout the plagues, God protected the people of Israel from harm. The night of the tenth and final plague, the Israelites ate a special meal of lamb and unleavened bread. They smeared the blood of the lamb on their doorposts as a sign to the angel of death to pass over their home. That night, all the firstborn sons of Egypt died. Pharaoh then ordered the people of Israel to leave Egypt. The Passover celebrated God's rescue of the people of Israel; it was ancient Israel's "Independence Day."

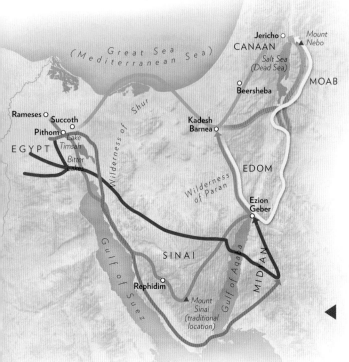

HARDENING PHARAOH'S HEART

God knew that Pharaoh would not allow his Israelite slaves to leave willingly (Exod 3:19). Yet God also warned Moses that He would harden Pharaoh's heart (Exod 4:21, 7:3). Indeed, Pharaoh refused (Exod 5:2) and hardened his own heart (Exod 8:15,32; 9:34). God responded by continuing to harden it (Exod 9:12; 10:1, 20, 27; 11:10; 14:8). This pattern led Augustine to conclude that sometimes God judges sin by condemning the person to more of the same.

◀ *There are several possible routes that the Israelites may have taken to reach Egypt.*

Moses Parts the Red Sea

When the Israelites left Egypt, they saw God's presence as a pillar of cloud during the day and a pillar of fire at night. This pillar led them on an erratic path toward Canaan. Pharaoh decided the people were lost and ordered his chariot army to wipe them out. When that army trapped the Israelites against the Red Sea, the people complained to Moses. The pillar of fire prevented the army from reaching the Israelites. So when Moses held up his staff and the Red Sea parted, there was time for the people of Israel to cross on dry ground. Once they crossed, the pillar of fire moved and the Egyptian chariots raced into the pass. When the sea rushed back in, the entire army drowned.

SLAVERY IN THE OLD TESTAMENT

Ancient slavery subjugated enemies and employed the poor (as in Genesis 47:13–26). After Egypt, Moses established slaves' rights: freedom after set periods or for harm, concubines could not be abandoned, and runaways could not be returned. Kidnapping into slavery incurred death. Although inconsistently applied, these laws made Israelite slavery more like indentured servitude than chattel-slavery.

> *"I will sing to the Lord, for He is highly exalted; He has thrown the horse and its rider into the sea. The Lord is my strength and my song; He has become my salvation. This is my God, and I will praise Him, my father's God, and I will exalt Him."*
>
> (Exodus 15:1–2, HCSB)

EXODUS

After crossing the Red Sea, the Israelites journeyed through the wilderness. Food and water quickly ran out, so God provided bread from heaven on a daily basis and caused a strong wind to blow quail into the camp. He also commanded Moses to strike a rock with his staff to cause water to flow for the people. God protected the people of Israel from an Amalekite attack, giving victory by extending the hours of sunlight as Moses held his arms up in a posture of supplication. But the complaints and problems of the people were so great that when Moses became exhausted, his father-in-law suggested a system of subordinate judges to help ease the load.

God Calls Moses

Eventually, the nation reached the base of Mount Sinai. The mountain was cordoned off as holy to God, and neither the people nor their flocks were to set foot on it. At an appointed time, the people gathered at the foot of the mountain. Sinai was enveloped in smoke and shook with fire and the sound of trumpets. From the turmoil, the voice of God called Moses up the mountain to receive God's law.

THE TEN COMMANDMENTS
(EXODUS 20:2–17, HCSB)

1. I am the Lord your God... Do not have other gods before me.
2. Do not make an idol for yourself.
3. Do not misuse the name of the Lord your God.
4. Remember the Sabbath day, to keep it holy.
5. Honor your father and your mother.
6. Do not murder.
7. Do not commit adultery.
8. Do not steal.
9. Do not give false testimony against your neighbor.
10. Do not covet... anything that belongs to your neighbor.

BIBLICAL LINKS

"I have been Yahweh your God ever since the land of Egypt; you know no God but Me, and no Savior exists besides Me." (Hosea 13:4, HCSB)

A Bond Between God and Israel

The Mosaic Covenant was the treaty that formally recognized the bond between God and the people of Israel. It took the form of an ancient suzerain-vassal treaty in which a vassal (usually a city or nation) submitted to an overlord (the suzerain). This kind of treaty described the basis for the agreement, usually past benefits rendered to the vassal by the overlord. It also listed the obligations of the vassal, and finally the blessings for covenant faithfulness and curses on unfaithfulness. The Law of Moses includes a wide variety of legal material, but the ethical heart of the covenant is the Decalogue, the Ten Commandments (Exod 20).

BIBLICAL ETHICS

The Ten Commandments were not arbitrary orders, they were practical expressions of love in light of the value of God and those made in His image. The first four commands describe love for God (Deut 6:5), based on the distinction between the Creator and creatures. Disobedience was a failure to respect God as the Creator. The remaining six commands describe love of neighbor (Lev 19:18), based on the human responsibility to help each other care for creation. Disobedience harmed the ability to steward creation as God intended (Gen 1:26).

"I am the Lord your God, who brought you out of the land of Egypt, out of the place of slavery. Do not have other gods besides Me."

(Exodus 20:2–3, HCSB)

EXODUS

When Moses went up on Mount Sinai to receive the Ten Commandments from God, he was gone for 40 days. While he was away, the people became impatient. They insisted that Aaron, Moses' brother, make a god for them. In fear, Aaron took golden jewelry and over-laid a wooden calf with gold. The people declared it to be the god that had delivered them from Egypt.

Moses Defends His People

On the mountain, God told Moses the people had be-trayed the Covenant. He challenged Moses, "Leave me alone, so... I can destroy them," and promised to make a great nation of Moses' descendants. Moses rose to the occasion and interceded for the people. He warned of how the Egyptians would mock God if the Israelites were destroyed and recalled God's promise to Abraham. God's anger abated.

The Price of Idolatry

When Moses descended, he saw the people worship-ping the calf. In rage, he shattered the stone tablets to the ground, symbolizing the breaking of the Covenant. When he confronted Aaron, his brother claimed the calf had simply emerged from the fire. Moses desecrat-ed the idol thoroughly by burning it, grinding it into powder, and scattering the ashes in the drinking water

so that it would eventually become human waste. He then executed the penalty for idolatry, "cutting off" over 3,000 of the idolatrous Israelites.

When Moses returned to seek God's forgiveness for the nation, he offered to be cut off in place of the people. God refused and told Moses to lead the people to Canaan without Him. He promised to send an angel to conquer the land for them. But Moses would not go without God; God was not a means to an end, He was the end. Again, God relented and He restored the Cov-enant by inscribing the Ten Commandments on a new set of stone tablets.

WARNINGS OF JUDGMENT

When God warned of impending judgment, it was usually an opportunity for the prophet to intercede or the people to repent. Notable examples include Abraham and Sodom (Gen 18:17–22), Amos and Israel (Amos 7:1–6), Joel and Judah (Joel 2), and though he tried to avoid it, Jonah and Nineveh (Jonah 3:4–5).

ARK OF THE COVENANT

During his 40 days on Mount Sinai, God instructed Moses to build a wooden chest to hold the stone tablets on which the Ten Commandments were inscribed. The chest was overlaid with gold and adorned with two angelic figures standing over the top of the box. The area between them was called the "mercy seat." This chest and its contents became known as the Ark of the Covenant.

"So Moses returned to the Lord and said, 'Oh, these people have committed a grave sin; they have made a god of gold for themselves. Now if You would only forgive their sin. But if not, please erase me from the book You have written.'" (Exodus 32:31–32, HCSB)

LEVITICUS

INTRODUCTION

Leviticus is the law code of the Mosaic Covenant. Although it is a separate scroll from Exodus, it records additional laws God gave to Moses at Mount Sinai (see Exod 19–25). The book highlights the demands of purity and holiness required of the priests and people belonging to the Holy One of Israel.

LOCATION: God gave the laws of Leviticus to Moses in the wilderness at Mount Sinai. The Tabernacle and the camp of Israel are the specific locations mentioned.

ORIGIN: Leviticus presents itself as laws God gave to Moses (Lev 1:1–2; 27:34). The rest of the Bible affirms Mosaic authorship. The laws would have been recorded at Mount Sinai, or while traveling to the Promised Land, between 1400 and 1200 B.C.E. Modern critical theories propose development of the text over time.

KEY PASSAGES

Sacrificial System and Priesthood (1–10)

8:1–10:7 Aaron and His Sons Become Priests

Laws of Purity and Festivals (11–25)

15:1–33 Bodily Discharges Symbolize the Taint of Sin

16:1–34 God Ordains Atonement for the Sins of the Nation

18:1–30 God Forbids Idolatry and Immorality

24:10–23 God Judges Blasphemy in the Camp

Covenant Blessings and Curses (26)

Laws for Supporting the Sanctuary (27)

PRINCIPAL FIGURES

God   In Leviticus, God is the Holy Lawgiver who will not be dishonored by sin among the priests or people of Israel.

Moses   Leviticus presents Moses as the human agent through whom God gave His laws to Israel and consecrated Israel's priests.

Aaron   Moses' older brother, who became the first High Priest under the Mosaic Covenant.

The Levites   The tribe of Moses and Aaron, chosen by God to be the priests for the nation of Israel under the Mosaic Covenant.

Nadab and Abihu   Two sons of Aaron, who were consecrated as priests but then consumed by fire from God when they elevated themselves over God's laws.

The Blasphemer   The son of an Israelite woman and an Egyptian man. Having blasphemed God's name, his name is never mentioned in Leviticus.

"For I am Yahweh your God, so you must consecrate yourselves and be holy because I am holy."

(Leviticus 11:44, HCSB)

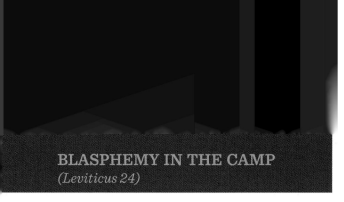

BLASPHEMY IN THE CAMP
(Leviticus 24)

God had demonstrated His power in the events of the Exodus, and His majestic holiness when He descended to Mount Sinai (Exod 19). Knowing the tendency of people to invoke powerful names for their own purposes, however, God had warned the people not to use His name wrongfully (Exod 20:7). Unfortunately, not everyone got the message.

A fight broke out between an Israelite and a man with an Egyptian father and Israelite mother. In his anger, the man invoked the name of God to curse the Israelite and was taken into custody. Because he dishonored God's name, the man's name is not mentioned and so was lost to history.

God told Moses to have the community execute the man by stoning. The people were to remember that blasphemy was a capital crime under the Covenant. But God also used the occasion to remind the people that killing someone made in God's image, any other human being, was equally evil. Punishment for any sin was to be proportionate to the crime; human life was to be valued alongside God's honor. Animal life was also valuable, but restitution could be made by replacing the animal killed. These laws were to apply equally to Israelites and to any foreigners living with the people of Israel.

Moses reported God's commands to the people. The blasphemer was taken outside the camp, symbolizing his expulsion from the people of God. The people then stoned him as God had commanded Moses.

CATEGORIES OF MOSAIC LAW

One common classification system for the Mosaic Law distinguishes ceremonial, civil, and moral law. Ceremonial law covers sacrifices, purity, and festivals. Civil law governs the daily function of the nation, including contracts, commerce, and lawsuits. Moral law includes the Ten Commandments. Some laws can be classified in multiple categories.

NUMBERS

Walking from Mount Sinai to the Promised Land takes less than two weeks. But the people of Israel took 40 years to enter the Promised Land. The book of Numbers tells the story of that journey. The people's disbelief that God could defeat the Canaanites led to judgment and a series of crises that left a whole generation dead in the wilderness.

KEY PASSAGES

Preparation to March from Mount Sinai (1–10)

Rebellion on the Edge of the Promised Land (11–15)

12:1–16	Miriam and Aaron Rebel Against Moses
13:1–14:45	Israel Refuses to Enter the Promised Land

Rebellion in the Wilderness (16–25)

16:1–50	Korah Rebels Against Moses and Aaron
20:1–12	Moses Rebels Against God's Instructions
22:1–24:25	Balaam Attempts to Curse Israel
25:1–18	Phinehas' Zeal Ends a Plague

A Faithful Generation Prepares to Enter the Promised Land (26–36)

PRINCIPAL FIGURES

God   In Numbers, God is portrayed as faithful through judgment on unfaithfulness.

Moses   Numbers presents Moses as the leader of the nation of Israel.

Aaron   Moses' older brother, the first High Priest of Israel, who dies on Mount Hor.

Miriam   Moses' older sister, who attempted to undercut his leadership of Israel and died during the wilderness wandering.

Joshua   Moses' primary assistant, who spied out the Promised Land with Caleb.

Caleb   Caleb was one of the 12 spies, and along with Joshua, the only one who recommended invasion and lived to enter the Promised Land.

Eleazar   Aaron's son, who succeeded him as the second High Priest of Israel.

Korah   A Levite who led a rebellion against Moses and was judged by being swallowed by the earth.

Balaam   The pagan prophet who attempted to curse Israel for King Balak of Moab.

Phinehas   Son of Eleazar, who was rewarded by God with a permanent priesthood because of his zeal for God's Law.

LOCATION: Numbers traces the Israelites journey from Mount Sinai to Kadesh-barnea and through the Negev Desert. The book ends on the plains of Moab across the Jordan River from Jericho.

ORIGIN: Numbers identifies Moses as its author (Num 1:1; 33:2). The book would have been written during the 40 years when the nation of Israel wandered in the wilderness, between 1,400 and 1,200 B.C.E. Modern critical theories suggest Numbers is the product of multiple unnamed editors.

When the people of Israel reached the southern border of Canaan (modern Israel), God ordered Moses to send spies into the Promised Land. At its fullest extent, the Promised Land was bounded by the Negev desert (south), the Euphrates River (north), the Mediterranean Sea (west), and the Arabian desert (east) (Exod 23:30–31). Of course, the land had long been controlled by other nations, known collectively as the Canaanites.

Moses sent one spy from each tribe, with orders to assess the richness and strength of the land and its inhabitants. The spies took 40 days and came back with ripe grapes and figs. They also brought discouraging news: the Canaanites were strong and lived in fortified cities.

Caleb and Joshua were confident that God would deliver the land to the Israelites, but the rest saw invasion as a suicide mission.

The people accused God of bringing them out of Egypt just to kill them in the wilderness. Amazingly, although their accusation named God as the Liberator who had defeated Egypt with miraculous plagues, they did not think He could defeat the Canaanites. They threatened to execute Moses and choose a new leader who would lead them back to slavery in Egypt.

God intervened and told Moses He would destroy the people with a plague. Moses implored God for pardon, and God granted it. However, He sentenced that generation of Israelites who had tested Him 10 times over to wander in the wilderness until everyone over the age of 20 had died. The younger generation would be shepherds for 40 years before entering the Land.

When the people heard this judgment, they admitted their rebellion and decided to invade the Land. Moses warned them that it was too late, but they did not listen. When they attacked, they were routed by the Canaanites.

REFINEMENT THROUGH SUFFERING

The Bible emphasizes that God refines people through suffering. Moses and David spent long periods in the wilderness before rising to prominence. God used the wilderness wandering and the Babylonian captivity to purify the nation. James (Jas 1:2–18) and Peter (1 Pet 1:3–9) both reflected on this theme.

The Promised Land: Canaan at the Time of the Exodus

Galilean Hills · Hazor
Sea of Chinnereth (Sea of Galilee)
▲ Mt. Carmel
Dor
Plain of Megiddo
GILEAD
Beth-Shan
River Jordan
Shechem
River Jabbok
Joppa
Bethel
Gezer · Jericho · Gilgal
Ashdod · Ekron · Jerusalem
Ashkelon
Bethlehem
Salt Sea (Dead Sea)
JUDAH
Gaza
Hebron
River Arnon
Beersheba
Central Highlands
(Mediterranean Sea)
Great Sea
The Negev

NUMBERS

BALAAM'S DONKEY
(Numbers 22)

The King Sends for Balaam

The King of Moab saw the Israelite exodus as a threat, so he sent for Balaam, a renowned prophet, to curse Israel. Moabite leaders came to Balaam with gifts and conveyed the King's request. Balaam asked God's permission to go to Moab but was refused. The people of Israel could not be cursed; they were blessed by God. The King sent for Balaam again, and this time God permitted him to go. However, God warned Balaam that he could only say what God told him to say.

Balaam reasoned that because God had given him permission to go to Moab, God could also be convinced to allow the prophet to curse the Israelites. Balaam set off for Moab, intending to do what the Moabite king had asked.

The Donkey Speaks

Knowing of his intentions, the Angel of the Lord ambushed Balaam on his way to Moab. Balaam didn't see the angel, but his donkey did. The donkey turned off the path, and Balaam beat her for disobedience. Then donkey pressed against a wall beside the path, and Balaam beat her again. Finally, the Angel of the Lord stood in a narrow spot between two vineyard walls.

This time, the donkey simply crouched down and refused to move. When Balaam beat her a third time, God enabled the donkey to speak. She asked Balaam what she had done to be beaten, and in a rage he answered her, "You made me look like a fool! If I had a sword in my hand, I'd kill you now!" The donkey pointed out that she had never acted this way before, and then God opened Balaam's eyes to see what the donkey had seen all along. The Angel of the Lord warned Balaam to say only what God told him, and Balaam finally got the message. The execution he threatened for his donkey after three acts of disobedience would fall on him should he try to disobey God a third time.

BLESSING AND CURSING

The words for blessing and cursing occur frequently in the Bible (544 and 282 times each, respectively). Blessings are gifts of life and things that enable life. Curses convey condemnation. Human blessing and cursing had no inherent power (as in Proverbs 26:2), but the Bible states that God's blessings and curses are always effective (Isaiah 55:10-11).

BIBLICAL LINKS

"I, Jesus, have sent My angel to attest these things to you for the churches. I am the Root and the Offspring of David, the Bright Morning Star."
(Revelation 22:16, HCSB)

Balaam Blesses Israel

When he arrived, the King of Moab took him up a mountain to see the Israelites and curse them. Instead, Balaam offered sacrifices and blessed Israel. The King was stunned. He took Balaam to three different spots, hoping a different perspective would bring different results. Each time, Balaam blessed the people Israel. Finally, the king gave up and dismissed the disappointing prophet.

TALKING ANIMALS IN THE BIBLE

Though there are angelic beings with animal-like features, Balaam's donkey and the serpent in the Garden of Eden (Gen 3) are the only two "normal" animals in the Bible that speak. The two events mirror each other: the Devil spoke through the serpent; God empowered the donkey. The serpent confused Eve and led humanity into sin; the donkey helped to set Balaam straight and prevented him from sinning.

"I see him, but not now; I perceive him, but not near. A star will come from Jacob, and a scepter will arise from Israel. He will smash the forehead of Moab and strike down all the Shethites."

(Numbers 24:17, HCSB)

NUMBERS

Although Balaam was not allowed to curse Israel, he did suggest an alternative strategy to the Moabite King. On his advice, the king sent young women of Moab and Midian to seduce Israelite leaders into worshipping Moab's god, Baal of Peor, through ritual prostitution. Their goal was to entice the Israelites into offering animal sacrifices to Baal and bowing down before their idols. The strategy was wildly successful and stirred God's wrath toward the people of Israel.

Moses Executes Judgment

Moses was instructed to execute judgment; the men who had pierced the pagan women in their dark tents were to be impaled in the sunlight. So Moses ordered the judges to kill all those who had betrayed the Covenant by worshipping Baal of Peor.

The first to act was Aaron's grandson, Phinehas. As the judgment was being pronounced and the people wept, Phinehas observed an Israelite bringing a foreign woman into his tent. But these were not just common folk. The man was the son of one of the leaders of the tribe of Simeon. The woman was a daughter of a tribal leader of Midian. Taking a short spear, he followed them into the tent and pinned them to the ground as they lay in each other's arms. God's wrath was averted. He acknowledged the righteousness of Phinehas' zeal and rewarded him and his zealous descendants with a covenant granting them permanent priestly status.

FLAGGING ZEAL

The zeal of Phinehas, grandson of Aaron the High Priest, contrasts with the unrighteousness of Phinehas, son of Eli the High Priest (1 Sam 2:22–36; 3:11–14; 4:4–11). The first Phinehas showed zeal for God's Law by initiating God's judgment on sexual sin in Israel. The later Phinehas was guilty defiling the Tabernacle by sleeping with the women who served there.

An Inspiration

Phinehas became an example of what it meant to have a total commitment to the Mosaic Covenant. He became the inspiration for the leaders of the Maccabean revolt in 167 B.C.E. and the anti-Roman rebels of the New Testament era, the Zealots. His example also energized a young rabbi named Saul to persecute the early Christians as a threat to the purity of Israel's covenant faithfulness.

ISRAEL AND PAGAN CULTURES

In the Old Testament, the influence of pagan cultures, particularly through intermarriage, is presented as a consistent problem for Israelite faithfulness to the Mosaic Covenant. Israel's unfaithfulness would eventually result in the nation's exile. Even after returning from Babylon, the problem of pagan influence persisted (as in Ezra 9–10).

BIBLICAL LINKS

"I [Paul] am a Jewish man, born in Tarsus of Cilicia but brought up in this city at the feet of Gamaliel and educated according to the strict view of our patriarchal law. Being zealous for God, just as all of you are today, I persecuted this Way to the death, binding and putting both men and women in jail, as both the high priest and the whole council of elders can testify about me. After I received letters from them to the brothers, I traveled to Damascus to bring those who were prisoners there to be punished in Jerusalem." *(Acts 22:3–5, HCSB)*

"I grant him My covenant of peace. It will be a covenant of perpetual priesthood for him and his future descendants, because he was zealous for his God and made atonement for the Israelites."

(Numbers 25:12–13, HCSB)

DEUTERONOMY

Deuteronomy is a second telling of the Law of Moses, given by Moses in his final addresses to the nation. Deutero and nomos are the Greek words for second and law. It retells the history of Israel in a way intended to humble the people and exhort them to faithfulness to the Covenant when they enter the Promised Land.

LOCATION: Moses addressed Israel on the Plains of Moab across the Jordan River from Jericho, then died on Mount Nebo, from which he saw the Promised Land.

ORIGIN: Deuteronomy identifies Moses as the author of its speeches (1:5; 5:1; 29:2) and the Law as a whole (33:9). Joshua may have written the account of Moses' death (Deut 34). Some critical theories suggest that Deuteronomy was written by priests in order to spur King Josiah's religious reforms (2 Kgs 22).

KEY PASSAGES

First Address: Israel's History (1–4)

4:1–40	Moses Exhorts Israel to Obey and Worship God

Second Address: The Law in the Promised Land (5–26)

6:1–25	Israel Teaches the Law to Future Generations
9:1–10:22	Moses Describes God's Reasons for Choosing Israel
17:14–22	God Identifies the Criteria for Future Leaders of Israel

Third Address: Appeal for Covenant Faithfulness (27–30)

28:1–14	God Promises Blessings for Covenant Faithfulness
28:15–68	God Promises Curses for Covenant Disobedience
30:11–20	Moses Appeals for Covenant Faithfulness

Transition to New Leadership (31–34)

31:1–21	God Commissions Joshua to Lead Israel
34:1–12	Moses Dies in Sight of the Promised Land

PRINCIPAL FIGURES

God Deuteronomy presents God as faithful to His Covenant with Israel.

Moses In Deuteronomy, Moses is the prophet-statesman who addressed the nation of Israel to appeal for Covenant faithfulness in the Promised Land.

Joshua Moses' primary assistant during the Exodus journey, who became leader of the nation after Moses' death.

As the nation of Israel approached the Promised Land, Moses prepared the people for new leadership. Moses knew that he would not be with them, because God had told him that he would not enter the Promised Land as punishment for his disobedience (Num 20:3–13). Moses also knew the tendency of the people to reject God's leadership in favor of the rule of men, so he warned the people of Israel about demanding to be ruled by a king, like the nations around them (17:14).

He told them that their king would have to be an Israelite who was not obsessed with building his military and his wealth, or with collecting wives. Most importantly, their king must write his own copy of the Mosaic Law in order to learn it and live by it. In this way, a king would remember that he was subordinate to God and no better than any other Israelite.

Moses also warned that the people must not imitate the idolatry of the Canaanites or follow prophets who encouraged worship of any idol (see Deut 13:1–5). Instead, Moses prophesied that God would send "a prophet like me" (Deut 18:15). That prophet would speak the words God had placed in his mouth, and God would hold everyone who did not listen accountable for their rejection. Any prophet that falsely claimed to speak a message from God, or who encouraged idolatry, was to be executed. Moses identified the fulfillment of a prophet's message as the test by which its source could be judged. Prophecies that were fulfilled came from God; those that were not fulfilled were false.

> *"The Lord your God will raise up for you a prophet like me from among your own brothers. You must listen to him."*
> (Deuteronomy 18:15, HCSB)

THE CENTER OF THE LAW

Deuteronomy articulates the heart of the Mosaic Covenant, "Listen, Israel: The LORD our God, the LORD is One. Love the LORD your God with all your heart, with all your soul, and with all your strength." (Deut 6:4–5) It asserted the absolute uniqueness of God and called for wholehearted love of God.

BLESSINGS AND CURSINGS
(Deuteronomy 28)

In his final sermon to the people of Israel, Moses exhorted them to be faithful to the Covenant with God and warned them of the consequences of unfaithfulness.

Reward for the Faithful

The divine blessings for faithfully obeying all the commands of God would place Israel far above all other nations. They would be blessed whether they lived in cities or in the country, and those blessings would extend to their descendants. Their enemies would be defeated and scattered. They would have many children and their flocks would grow. Nations would borrow of their wealth and their progress would grow unabated. The key was obedience to the Law, especially by refusing to worship idols.

The Price of Disobedience

But disobedience would have dire consequences. The nation would suffer in both the cities and the country, their descendants would suffer, and their flocks would shrink. Drought would turn the land to dust, and enemies would scatter them. Virgins engaged to be married would be defiled, those who built houses would not get to live in them, those who planted vineyards would not taste their fruit, and their cattle would be killed but they would eat none of the meat. They and their king would be exiled by a nation whose language they did not know.

THE SHEMA

Covenant faithfulness was encapsulated in the Shema, meaning hear, from Deuteronomy 6:4, "Listen, Israel: The Lord our God, the Lord is One." The uniqueness of Israel's God meant that obedience (listening) was not merely a matter of duty, but of relationship to the Creator of the world and Redeemer of the people. This point would be reinforced by James, who argued that mere intellectual assent to the Shema did not validate the claim to have Abrahamic faith (Jas 2:19).

The cities of Israel would be besieged and would starve. The hunger inside the walls would grow so great that parents would kill and eat their children but refuse to share the meal with even a brother. Even the most refined and delicate ladies would hoard their afterbirth to eat and consume their children. All the plagues of Egypt would come upon Israel. The people would be scattered across the nations but find no peace. Terror for their lives would be their constant companion. These harsh curses warned the people of Israel that their only hope for survival as a nation lay in faithfulness to the God of the Covenant.

BIBLICAL LINKS

"All Israel, foreigner and citizen alike, with their elders, officers, and judges, stood on either side of the ark of the Lord's covenant facing the Levitical priests who carried it. As Moses the Lord's servant had commanded earlier, half of them were in front of Mount Gerizim and half in front of Mount Ebal, to bless the people of Israel. Afterward, Joshua read aloud all the words of the law—the blessings as well as the curses—according to all that is written in the book of the law. There was not a word of all that Moses had commanded that Joshua did not read before the entire assembly of Israel, including the women, the little children, and the foreigners who were with them." *(Joshua 8:33–35, HCSB)*

"I call heaven and earth as witnesses against you today that I have set before you life and death, blessing and curse. Choose life so that you and your descendants may live, love the Lord your God, obey Him, and remain faithful to Him. For He is your life, and He will prolong your life in the land the Lord swore to give to your fathers Abraham, Isaac, and Jacob." (Deuteronomy 30:19–20, HCSB)

JOSHUA

The book of Joshua records Israel's initial conquest of the Promised Land. It traces the progress of the conquest, including the "conversion" of Rahab and the Gibeonites. The book ends with the partition of the land, plans for conquering the remaining territory, Joshua's farewell address, and the introduction of tension between the tribes.

LOCATION: Joshua begins with the Israelites crossing the Jordan River from the Plains of Moab to Jericho. The battles in Canaan ranged from Hebron (south) to Kadesh (north).

ORIGIN: The book identifies Joshua as its primary author (24:26) and was written prior to David's conquest of Jerusalem around 1000 B.C.E. (Josh 15:63). Modern critical theories argue that a later editor who shared Deuteronomy's theological perspective compiled the book.

KEY PASSAGES

Preparation for Invasion (1–5)
2:1–24   Rahab Protects the Spies in Jericho

3:1–4:24   Israel Crosses the Jordan River

Initial Conquest of Canaan (6–12)
6:1–27   The Walls of Jericho Fall

7:1–8:35   Achan's Sin Is Judged at the City of Ai

9:1–10:15 God Accepts the Gibeonites Despite Their Deception

Distribution of Canaan to the Israelite Tribes (13–22)
22:1–34   Construction of an Altar Divides the Tribes of Israel

Joshua's Farewell Addresses (23–24)
24:1–28   Joshua Challenges the People to Covenant Faithfulness

PRINCIPAL FIGURES

God   In Joshua, God blesses Israel's obedience and judges the Canaanites' sins by giving Israel the Promised Land.

Joshua   Moses' successor as leader of Israel and the military commander of Israel's army.

Rahab   A Canaanite prostitute in Jericho who was spared for helping Jewish spies escape capture.

Achan   After his sin led to Israel's defeat in battle, this Israelite was executed for stealing loot from Jericho in defiance of God's ban.

Phinehas   Son of Eleazar the High Priest, who arbitrated the first major dispute between the tribes of Israel after entering the Promised Land.

THE TRIBES OF ISRAEL

NORTH: ISRAEL	SOUTH: JUDAH
Asher	Judah
Dan	Benjamin
Ephraim*	Levi*
Gad	
Issachar	
Manasseh*	
Naphtali	
Reuben	
Simeon	
Zebulun	

THE GENTILE NATIONS

IN THE PROMISED LAND	NEIGHBORING NATIONS
Amalakites	Ammonites
Amorites	Arameans (Syria)
Canaanites	Edomites
Girgashites	Moabites
Hittites	Phoenicians
Hivites	
Jebusites	
Perezzites	
Philistines	

*Ephraim and Manasseh were sons of Joseph that Jacob adopted for the purpose of inheritance (Gen 48), replacing Joseph as tribes. They can be counted as "half-tribes" to keep the number of tribes at 12. Alternatively, the number 12 can be preserved by listing the tribes granted territory in the Promised Land and distinguishing them from the Tribe of Levi.

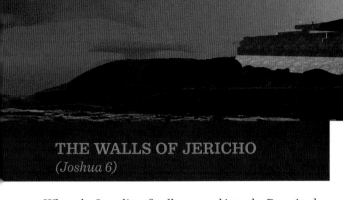

THE WALLS OF JERICHO
(Joshua 6)

When the Israelites finally crossed into the Promised Land, their first major obstacle was the walled city of Jericho in Canaan. It should have seemed unlikely that a nomadic people, without experience in siege-craft, could penetrate the massive walls. But when Jewish spies scouted the city, they were seen as a real threat (Josh 2).

The king of Jericho ordered their arrest, but the prostitute Rahab hid them and sent the searchers away. She told the spies that the people of Jericho were terrified of Israel's God and pleaded for protection. Though God had ordered the complete destruction of the Canaanites and all their possessions, Rahab's faith showed that she was no longer a Canaanite but was now one of God's people.

When Israel's army arrived at Jericho, they followed the battle plan God had given to Joshua (Josh 6). The army marched around the city once a day, for six days, carrying the Ark of the Covenant. On the seventh day, they marched around the walls seven times. The priests blew their horns, the people shouted, and the walls collapsed. The army killed every living thing in the city except Rahab and her family.

THE DESTRUCTION OF THE CANAANITES

God instructed Israel to kill every living thing in Canaanite cities (Deut 7:1–2). God's order demonstrated the gravity of sin and the totality of final judgment. However, it did not prevent individuals or nations from "switching sides" and becoming part of Israel (Rahab, Josh 2; Gibeon, Josh 9; Deut 20:10–18).

"[W]e have heard how the Lord dried up the waters of the Red Sea before you when you came out of Egypt .... When we heard this, we lost heart, and everyone's courage failed because of you, for the Lord your God is God in heaven above and on earth below."

(Joshua 2:10–11, HCSB)

JOSHUA

At the end of his life, Joshua assembled the tribes of Israel together. Large areas of Canaan had been conquered, and what remained had been divided between the tribes for future conquest. Joshua's goal was to remind the people of God's faithfulness and warn them that the conquest could be completed only if they remained faithful to the Mosaic Covenant.

The Threat of the Canaanites

The concern for Israel's faithfulness was well founded; much was at stake. If the people turned aside and began to worship the gods of the Canaanites, they would become just like the people God had sent them to destroy. Where they had once routed the militarily superior Canaanites because of God's aid, disobedience would cost them that aid and their conquest would fail. The great threat, Joshua warned, was blending into Canaanite culture. He appealed to the people to remember that while they had experienced God's blessings, abandoning God would result in experiencing God's wrath.

Joshua reviewed Israel's history, reminding them of how God had called Abraham, Isaac, and Jacob. He recalled the coming of Moses and Aaron to lead the Exodus and how God had triumphed at the Red Sea. The people had wandered the wilderness, but God protected them when Moab called Balaam to curse them. Finally, he celebrated God's conquest of Jericho and the wealth of the Promised Land.

BIBLICAL LINKS

"Then Elijah approached all the people and said, 'How long will you hesitate between two opinions? If Yahweh is God, follow Him. But if Baal, follow him.' But the people didn't answer him a word." *(1 Kings 18:21, HCSB)*

"The sorrows of those who take another god for themselves will multiply; I will not pour out their drink offerings of blood, and I will not speak their names with my lips. Lord, You are my portion and my cup of blessing; You hold my future. The boundary lines have fallen for me in pleasant places; indeed, I have a beautiful inheritance." *(Psalm 16:4–6, HCSB)*

A Promise to Remain Faithful

At the climax of his speech, Joshua demanded that the nation choose between serving the idols of their past and the God who had delivered them. The people promised to worship God just as Joshua did. But Joshua's response was brutally realistic, "You will not be able to worship Yahweh, because He is a holy God." (Joshua 24:19) The nation that had seen God's wonders and yet was quick to complain and turn to idols would never be able to live up to the standard of God's holiness. Still, the people of Israel insisted that they had it within them to remain faithful to the Covenant. So Joshua established a memorial stone to mark their promise.

THE MESSAGE OF THE LATER PROPHETS

Joshua's warning of Israel's faithlessness was tragically prescient. The historical books (Judges-Chronicles) would record the national cycle of disobedience, punishment, repentance, and restoration. One of the major themes of the prophet's preaching was to condemn the sins that fulfilled Joshua's fears (Joshua 24) and announce the curses that fulfilled Moses' warnings (Deuteronomy 28).

"But if it doesn't please you to worship Yahweh, choose for yourselves today the one you will worship: the gods your fathers worshiped beyond the Euphrates River or the gods of the Amorites in whose land you are living. As for me and my family, we will worship Yahweh."

(Joshua 24:15, HCSB)

JUDGES

INTRODUCTION

Judges describes Israel's declining cycle of Covenant unfaithfulness, oppression, and restoration. God's agents between Joshua's death and the beginning of the monarchy were called judges. The service of the 12 judges described may have overlapped instead of happening in sequence. The book also traces the increasing hostility of the Israelite tribes toward each other.

LOCATION: The events in Judges take place in the land of Israel and the Gentile areas: the Mediterranean coast (Philistines) and east of the Jordan River (Moabites, Amorites).

ORIGIN: The Bible does not identify the author of Judges, but tradition assigns it to Samuel. It was written before the conquest of Jerusalem around 1000 B.C.E. (Judg 1:21). Modern critical theories argue that Judges was compiled by a later editor who shared the theological perspective of Deuteronomy.

KEY PASSAGES

Israel's Failure to Conquer Canaan (1–2)

2:1–23	Israel Develops a Pattern of Unfaithfulness

The Judges and Israel's Cycle of Unfaithfulness (3–16)

3:12–30	Ehud Assassinates King Eglon of Moab
4:1–23	God Uses a Woman to Deliver Israel
6:1–8:35	Gideon Delivers and Deludes Israel
11:1–38	Jephthah Makes a Foolish Vow
13:1–16:31	Samson Displays Great Strength and Weakness

The Corruption of Israel (17–21)

19:1–21	Israel Nearly Destroys the Tribe of Benjamin

PRINCIPAL FIGURES

God   In Judges, God appears as the Judge of Israel's unfaithfulness, who grants mercy and peace when the nation cries out to Him.

Othniel   The nephew of the faithful spy Caleb, he became Israel's first judge after Joshua's death.

Ehud   A judge who rescued Jericho by assassinating the Moabite king.

Deborah   A prophetess and judge through whom God called Barak to attack the Canaanites.

Barak   The commander who refused to attack the Canaanites unless Deborah went with him.

Gideon, or Jerubbaal   The Israelite judge whose life most clearly reflected Israel's pattern of faithfulness followed by failure.

Jephthah   A judge who made a rash vow and ended up sacrificing his daughter.

Samson   A judge whose enormous strength resulted in great pride and a terrible end.

Delilah   The Philistine prostitute who seduced Samson into revealing the secret of his strength.

PHOENICIA

Great Sea (Mediterranean Sea)

SHAMGAR

Sea of Chinnereth (Sea of Galilee)

ELON

Ophrah   JAIR

GIDEON

GILEAD

MANASSEH

TOLA

River Jordan

Shamir

Pirathon   Shechem

ABDON   JEPHTHAH

EPHRAIM

EHUD/

DEBORAH   Jericho

DAN   Zorah

Bethlehem

SAMSON   IBZAN

JUDAH   Salt Sea (Dead Sea)

OTHNIEL

Origin of each judge

DEBORAH AND BARAK
(Judges 4)

During Israel's cycle of disobedience and punishment, God raised up a prophetess named Deborah as a judge among the northern tribes. People went to her to resolve difficult cases under the Law. One day, she summoned Barak and declared that God had commanded him to deploy 10,000 soldiers on Mount Tabor, overlooking the Jezreel Valley. She told him that God would lure the Canaanite general, Sisera, and his 900 chariots to the Wadi Kishon, a waterway at the foot of Mount Carmel that flooded in the rainy season, and hand them over to Barak to be destroyed. Uncertain about the plan, Barak agreed to go only if Deborah went with him. For his lack of courage and faith, Deborah told Barak that he would not be the one to defeat Sisera; instead, Sisera would be defeated by a woman.

When the battle began, God routed the Canaanite chariots with the Israeli infantry and Barak's army destroyed them all. Sisera, however, escaped the battle and fled on foot. He reached the tent of Heber, an Israelite whom Sisera believed to be a Canaanite sympathizer. There Heber's wife, Jael, welcomed the exhausted general. She invited him in and gave him milk to drink. When Sisera fell asleep, Jael took a tent peg and used a mallet to drive the peg through his Temple into the ground. When Barak arrived, she showed him the general's body, nailed to the floor.

THE OFFICE OF JUDGE

The word for "judge" means "deliverer." Judges delivered people from oppression caused by sin. Internally, that implied resolving cases under the Mosaic Law (a judicial role). But it also included restoring the Covenant by defeating foreign oppressors (a military role). Under the monarchy, the king became the highest judge in the land.

"Barak said to [Deborah], 'If you will go with me, I will go. But if you will not go with me, I will not go.' 'I will go with you,' she said, 'but you will receive no honor on the road you are about to take, because the Lord will sell Sisera into a woman's hand.'"

(Judges 4:8–9, HCSB)

JUDGES

THE LIFE OF GIDEON
(Judges 6–8)

When the Israelites ignored the Covenant, God allowed the people of Midian to oppress them by raiding their crops and flocks. The people cried out to God, and the Angel of the Lord appeared to Gideon as he was threshing wheat in a wine vat, hoping to hide the grain from the Midianites.

God Speaks to Gideon

The Angel commissioned Gideon to defeat the Midianites, but Gideon was nervous. He didn't understand why God seemed to have abandoned the Israelites to their enemies. Gideon couldn't imagine God using the youngest son of the weakest house in the tribe to liberate His people.

Gideon asked the Angel to accept a gift as a sign of God's favor. He brought food to the Angel, who called fire from a rock to consume it, so Gideon built an altar to the Lord there. That night, God sent Gideon to destroy the altar to Baal, one of the Canaanite gods. The townsmen demanded Gideon's life, but his father mocked their defense of Baal, nicknaming Gideon *Jerubbaal,* which meant "Let Baal prosecute him".

The Miracle of the Fleece

Next, God sent Gideon to attack the enemy in the Valley of Jezreel. Gideon called 4 tribes, and 32,000 men answered. But Gideon was still nervous. In order to show that God was really with him, he requested a miraculous sign. On two consecutive nights, he placed a fleece on the floor of the threshing room. The first night, he asked that the fleece appear wet with dew on dry ground in the morning, and it was so. The next night, he asked that the fleece remain dry and while the ground around it was wet with dew, and it was so. These signs symbolized God's intent and ability to do what seemed impossible.

DISUNITY OF THE TRIBES

One of the themes in Joshua and Judges is the disunity of the 12 Israelite Tribes. The tribes in Canaan distrusted those living east of the Jordan River. Victorious tribes were envied by less successful tribes. Eventually the tribe of Benjamin was almost wiped out by the others (Joshua 20–21).

Gideon's Victory

God tested Gideon, too. He informed Gideon that the army was too big. God wanted to ensure that there would be no way the Israelites could claim that they had gained the victory themselves. Fearful men were sent home. Then God told Gideon to keep just those who drank from the brook with cupped hands. Only 300 men remained. It should have been impossible for them to defeat the Midianites. But when Gideon spied on the Midianites, the huge army was terrified. He overheard one soldier relating a dream indicating that God had given the Midianites to Gideon. Gideon's men surrounded the camp in the night, sounded their ram's horns, shattered pots, and held up torches. The Midianites panicked, slaughtered each other, and fled for the Jordan River.

In the wake of the victory, the Israelites wanted to make Gideon their king. Gideon ostentatiously refused, but began to act like a king. He accepted a king's share of the spoils from which he made an *ephod* (breastplate) for an idol. This object became a snare for Gideon, his family, and the people of Israel. Eventually, one of his 70 sons made himself king and massacred his brothers before being betrayed himself.

BIBLICAL LINKS

"God, we have heard with our ears—our ancestors have told us—the work You accomplished in their days, in days long ago: to plant them, You drove out the nations with Your hand; to settle them, You crushed the peoples. For they did not take the land by their sword—their arm did not bring them victory—but by Your right hand, Your arm, and the light of Your face, for You were pleased with them." *(Psalm 44:1–3, HCSB)*

"The Lord said to Gideon, 'You have too many people for Me to hand the Midianites over to you, or else Israel might brag: 'I did it myself.'"

(Judges 7:2, HCSB)

THE LIFE OF SAMSON
(Judges 13–16)

Once again, the people of Israel had abandoned the Covenant, so the Philistines oppressed them. But because God remained faithful to His promises, He continued to raise up judges to rescue the Israelites when they called upon Him. One of the most famous judges was Samson.

Samson's Birth Is Foretold

The Angel of the Lord appeared to a barren woman and told her that she would have a son, Samson, and he would defeat the Philistines. The Angel said that Samson was not to cut his hair or drink wine. These odd requirements were unique to a Nazirite vow, which was normally made by an Israelite man for a limited duration. In Samson's case it would be for life.

Later, as the woman and her husband prepared a sacrifice at the altar, the Angel of the Lord appeared before them. The husband realized it was God and feared death, but his wife recognized that God, having accepted their sacrifice, would not kill them.

Samson's Strength

As the Angel said, the barren woman gave birth to a son named Samson. It became clear through the miraculous feats he performed, that God had endowed Samson with incredible strength. As long as he was faithful to his vow, God gave Samson victory over the Philistines. But violating his vow would make him vulnerable to his enemies.

The story of Samson's defeat began when he became enamored with a Philistine woman and married her. However, a riddle game at the wedding led Samson's new wife to put her loyalty to her people above Samson and he took revenge on the Philistines, just as God had intended. Her father gave her to another man, so Samson tied torches to foxes and released them in Philistine fields, burning their crops. Men from Judah arrested him and gave him to the Philistines, but with his great strength, Samson broke the bonds and killed 1,000 men using just a donkey's jawbone.

Samson and Delilah

Finally, Samson met Delilah, a beautiful Philistine woman. She wanted to know the secret of his strength in order to capture him and claim a reward from the Philistine leaders. Samson lied to her, and waking to find himself bound, burst the bonds. After several attempts, Delilah finally wheedled the secret of his strength from Samson: his long hair. Delilah cut it off as he slept, and when the soldiers arrived, Samson couldn't escape. His eyes were put out and he was put to work grinding grain like an ox. When the time came for the celebration of Samson's defeat, his hair had begun to grow back. When he was brought out to the feast, he appealed to God. With one last burst of strength, he toppled two columns, brought down the house, and killed more as he died than he had in his whole life.

THE PHILISTINE THREAT TO ISRAEL

The Philistines lived along the southwestern Mediterranean coast of Israel and were a constant threat. During Israel's Bronze Age, the Philistines had a major advantage because they could forge iron weapons. Though conquered by David, the Philistines do not disappear from the Biblical record until the New Testament era.

BIBLICAL LINKS

"I am not afraid of the thousands of people who have taken their stand against me on every side. Rise up, Lord! Save me, my God! You strike all my enemies on the cheek; You break the teeth of the wicked. Salvation belongs to the Lord; may Your blessing be on Your people." (Psalm 3:6–8, HCSB)

"For indeed, you will conceive and give birth to a son. You must never cut his hair, because the boy will be a Nazirite to God from birth, and he will begin to save Israel from the power of the Philistines."

(Judges 13:5, HCSB)

Ruth demonstrates that neither the faith of Abraham nor the compassion of God died out during the era of Judges. Though a Moabitess, rejected by the Mosaic Covenant, Ruth came to Bethlehem with Naomi. Boaz married Ruth as God's reward for her faith, and her son became King David's grandfather.

LOCATION: The events of Ruth take place in Moab and Bethlehem. Specific scenes take place on a road, in Boaz' field and threshing floor, and at the gate of Bethlehem.

ORIGIN: The book of Ruth does not identify its author. Rabbinic tradition attributes the book to Samuel. There is a wide range of modern theories about the authorship and date of the book. The story itself takes place during the period of the judges (before 1050 B.C.E.).

KEY PASSAGES

Scene 1: Ruth Displays Abrahamic Faith (1)

1:6–18   Ruth Insists on Going to Israel with Naomi

Scene 2: Ruth Gleans in Boaz' Field (2)

Scene 3: Boaz Commits to Protect Ruth (3)

3:8–13   Ruth Appeals to Boaz as Her Kinsman-Redeemer

Scene 4: Boaz Becomes Ruth's Kinsman-Redeemer (4)

4:9–17   God Blesses Boaz and Ruth

PRINCIPAL FIGURES

God   In Ruth, God shows compassion on the defenseless who depend on Him.

Elimelech   Naomi's husband, who abandoned the Promised Land during a famine.

Naomi, also called Mara   An Israelite woman whose life was made bitter by loss, yet was restored to pleasantness by Ruth's faith.

Mahlon   Naomi's son, who married Ruth, a Moabite woman.

Chilion   Naomi's son, who married Orpah, a Moabite woman.

Orpah   A Moabite woman who returned to Moab when Naomi sent her home.

Ruth   A Moabite woman whose faith led her to refuse Naomi's command to return to Moab when she had no prospect but poverty in Israel.

Boaz   A Judean of Bethlehem who married Ruth as her kinsman-redeemer.

At some point in the period of the judges, God judged the southern tribes with a famine. Elimelech abandoned his home in Bethlehem and took his wife, Naomi, and his sons to Moab, where he died. His two sons chose to marry Moabite women, but then they also died. The three widows now had no one to support them.

As an Israelite with no family in Moab, Naomi's best option was to return to Bethlehem and hope for the generosity to widows required by the Mosaic Law. As Moabites, however, Orpah and Ruth's best option seemed to be to go back to their families and hope for a new husband. This is exactly what Naomi ordered her daughters-in-law to do. Orpah reluctantly complied, but Ruth insisted on staying with Naomi. She identified herself with Naomi's people, the Israelites, and with Naomi's God. In that moment, Ruth ceased to be a Moabite and became an Israelite, one of God's people.

When Naomi and Ruth arrived in Bethlehem, the local women were amazed to see Naomi back after more than a decade's absence. Saddened by the loss of her husband and sons, Naomi rejected her given name, which meant "pleasantness" and identified herself as Mara, meaning "bitter." Though there had been a famine in the land, she had left Israel full (married with two sons). But returning now at the beginning of harvest, God was bringing her back empty (a widow with no sons).

FAMINE IN THE ANCIENT WORLD

The greatest disasters of the ancient world were famine, plague, and war (see Lam 4:9). Political stability and predictable, moderate rainfall were necessary for adequate harvests. Famine could force migrations, cannibalism, and widespread death. God warned the people of Israel that He would use famine as punishment for unfaithfulness to the Covenant (Lev 26:14–20; Deut 11:17).

"Do not persuade me to leave you or go back and not follow you. For wherever you go, I will go, and wherever you live, I will live; your people will be my people, and your God will be my God."

(Ruth 1:16, HCSB)

RUTH

Upon returning to Israel, Naomi and Ruth were destitute. In order to find food, Ruth took advantage of a Mosaic Law that allowed the poor to follow harvesters in the fields and gather any grain that fell (Lev 19:9–10).

Boaz Helps Ruth

As Ruth worked, the owner of the field, Boaz, saw her. He approved of her faithfulness to Naomi and called on God to reward her for taking refuge with Him. Boaz then went beyond the Law's requirement by offering her protection, food, and water as she worked, and extra grain. That night Ruth returned to Naomi with an astonishing amount of grain.

When Naomi realized who had helped Ruth, she informed her that Boaz was a "kinsman-redeemer" to their family, one tasked under the Mosaic Law with helping impoverished members of the family (Lev 25:25–26). In this case, Boaz could help and protect their family by marrying Ruth.

THE MOABITE CURSE

Because of their treachery, the Moabites were permanently cursed (Deuteronomy 23:3–6). But the blessing of Ruth suggests that when she declared her loyalty to Naomi and Israel's God, she ceased to be a Moabite under the curse. God showed mercy to the condemned when they repented and trusted Him.

Boaz Fulfills His Promise

Toward the end of the harvest, Naomi sent Ruth to offer herself to Boaz. She crept into the sleeping shelter that night and curled up at his feet. When he woke in the night, he asked her what she wanted. She asked for his protection as a kinsman-redeemer since he was related to Naomi's dead husband, Elimelech. Though there was another family member with the more immediate responsibility, Boaz promised to marry her if that man refused (Deut 25:5–10).

The next morning, Boaz found the other man and publicly informed him of a field Naomi wished to sell. The man was eager to "redeem" it for the family. But when Boaz informed him that he would also have to marry Ruth, and that their first son would inherit the field for Ruth's deceased husband, he refused. Boaz then married Ruth with the blessing of the elders, who prayed that Ruth would become like other pagan women who had joined Israel: Rachel, Leah, and Tamar.

BIBLICAL LINKS

"When brothers live on the same property and one of them dies without a son, the wife of the dead man may not marry a stranger outside the family. Her brother-in-law is to take her as his wife, have sexual relations with her, and perform the duty of a brother-in-law for her. The first son she bears will carry on the name of the dead brother, so his name will not be blotted out from Israel. But if the man doesn't want to marry his sister-in-law, she must go to the elders at the city gate... If he persists and says, 'I don't want to marry her,' then his sister-in-law will go up to him in the sight of the elders, remove his sandal from his foot, and spit in his face. Then she will declare, 'This is what is done to a man who will not build up his brother's house.'" *(Deuteronomy 25:5–9, HCSB)*

"May your house become like the house of Perez, the son Tamar bore to Judah, because of the offspring the Lord will give you by this young woman. ...and they named him Obed. He was the father of Jesse, the father of David."
(Ruth 4:12, 17, HCSB)

1 & 2
SAMUEL

The books of Samuel record Israel's transition from judges to kings. The books continue the theme of Israel's unfaithfulness to the Covenant, but they also describe fulfillment of the promised scepter for Judah (Gen 49:10), linking David to God's promises to Eve (Gen 3:15) and Abraham (Gen 12:1–3).

LOCATION: These books describe events in Israel. Notable locations are the Tabernacle, the Philistine cities, Mizpah, the Valley of Elah, the Judean wilderness, Hebron, and Jerusalem.

ORIGIN: Tradition assigns these books to Samuel and others. "The Book of Jashar" (2 Sam 1:18) was a source. Other available sources were David's court records (1 Chr 27:24) and the records of Samuel, Nathan, and Gad (1 Chr 29:29). The events described occurred between 1105 and 970 B.C.E.

KEY PASSAGES

1 Samuel

The Lives of Samuel and Saul (1–15)

1:1–4:1	Samuel Becomes a Judge
8:1–11:15	Israel Demands a King
15:1–34	God Rejects Saul

The Rise of David (16–31)

16:1–13	Samuel Anoints David as King
17:1–58	David Defeats Goliath
24:1–26:25	David Spares His Enemies

2 Samuel

David Becomes King (1–10)

5:1–25	David Is Crowned King Over All Israel
7:1–28	God Makes a Covenant with David

David's Sins and Their Consequences (11–24)

11:1–12:22	David Commits Adultery and Murder
13:1–14:33	David's Sons Mimic His Sins
15:1–19:43	Absalom Tries to Overthrow David
24:1–25	David Takes an Unlawful Census

PRINCIPAL FIGURES

God The books of Samuel present God as the rejected King of Israel, who nevertheless continues to govern the nation through His chosen rulers.

Eli The High Priest whom Samuel served and whose family was judged by God for their abuse of priestly power.

Hannah Samuel's mother, who dedicated her son to God's service in gratitude for becoming a mother.

Samuel The last of the judges, who anointed Saul as king and prophesied God's rejection before anointing David as Saul's replacement.

Saul An Israelite of the tribe of Benjamin who became Israel's first king but was rejected for foolish disobedience.

Jonathan Saul's son, who became David's closest friend and placed David's right to the throne above his own.

David An Israelite of the tribe of Judah, who became Israel's second, but greatest, king despite his flaws.

Bathsheba Wife of Uriah the Hittite, who committed adultery with David and eventually gave birth to Solomon.

Nathan The prophet who confronted David over his sin with Bathsheba and murder of Uriah.

Absalom David's favorite son, who attempted to overthrow David and was killed by Joab.

THE CAPTURE OF THE ARK
(1 Samuel 5)

The people of Israel remembered how the waters of the Jordan River (Josh 3) had parted and the walls of Jericho had fallen (Josh 6) when the priests had carried the Ark of the Covenant before the armies of Israel. They came to think of the Ark itself as being a powerful talisman by which God could be forced to fight for Israel. So when Samuel was a young man, Eli's evil sons carried the Ark into battle against the Philistines. But Israel was defeated and the Ark was captured.

But things didn't go well for the Philistines, either. The Ark was taken to the Temple of Dagon in Ashdod, where it was placed beside the idol, claiming that Dagon had conquered Yahweh. The next morning, however, the statue had fallen on its face before the Ark. The priests put the idol back, but in the morning it was found prostrate before the Ark again. This time, however, the head and hands of the statue had broken off. Yahweh had conquered Dagon.

After a plague broke out in Ashdod, the Philistines sent the Ark to Gath. Again, plague broke out, as it did in each of the Philistine cities where the Ark was sent. Finally, the people of Ekron demanded that the Ark be returned to the Israelites. The Philistines put the Ark on a cart, along with five golden rats and five golden tumors (one set for each of the five major Philistine cities) to acknowledge that God had sent the rats and the plague they carried. Then they hitched two cows that had just given birth to the cart and turned it lose to see where they would go. Instead of seeking their calves, the cows carried the Ark back to Israel.

IN THE MOVIES:
RAIDERS OF THE LOST ARK (1981)

The Ark of the Covenant disappeared from the Biblical narrative between 621–586 B.C.E. and has been sought ever since. In Steven Spielberg's classic movie, Nazis seek the Ark, believing that it "level[s] mountains and lay[s] waste to entire regions. An army that carries the Ark before it... is invincible." But the Ark proved to be no weapon men could wield.

THE RISE AND FALL OF SAUL
(1 Samuel 8–15)

The people of Israel came to Samuel and exercised their option to have a king (Deuteronomy 17:14–20). Samuel was hurt, but the people were rejecting God's leadership, not his. Samuel tried to dissuade the people by telling them of the harm kings would do, taking their sons as soldiers and fieldworkers and their earnings for his treasury. But the people insisted. They wanted a king like the nations, to rule them and defeat their enemies. Though Samuel ceased to be a judge, he continued to be a prophet until Saul's death (1 Sam 28).

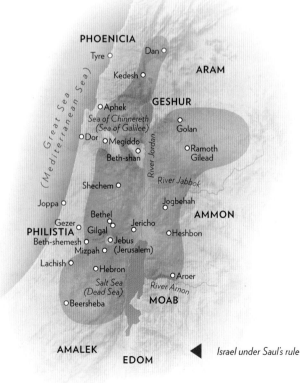

PHOENICIA
Tyre ○   Dan ○
Kedesh ○   **ARAM**
Great Sea
(Mediterranean Sea)
○Aphek   **GESHUR**
Sea of Chinnereth
(Sea of Galilee)
○Golan
○Dor ○Megiddo
○Ramoth
Gilead
Beth-shan
River Jordan
River Jabbok
Shechem ○
Jogbehah ○
Joppa ○
Bethel   **AMMON**
Gezer ○ ○ Jericho
PHILISTIA ○Gilgal
Beth-shemesh ○ ○Jebus ○Heshbon
Mizpah ○ (Jerusalem)
Lachish ○
○Hebron
○Aroer
Salt Sea
(Dead Sea)   *River Arnon*
○Beersheba   **MOAB**
AMALEK
EDOM   ◄   *Israel under Saul's rule*

God Choses Saul

God chose Saul, a young Benjamite, to be the king. But Saul didn't feel up to the job, so when Samuel announced him, Saul hid among the supplies and then returned to his home. Soon, however, the Ammonites attacked. God's Spirit empowered Saul and he called out the Israelite armies. Saul led the army to victory, and as the people celebrated Saul finally accepted his role as king. In his parting speech, Samuel warned the people that disobedience to God would destroy both them and their king.

Saul's Mistakes

Saul's reign was characterized by increasing sin, paranoia, and insanity. As he prepared for his first battle against the Philistines, Saul despaired of waiting for Samuel to arrive as promised to offer sacrifices to God. Instead, Saul decided to offer the sacrifices himself. Though he won the battle, he lost the chance to demonstrate complete trust in God and secure his throne permanently. More missteps followed until Saul again snatched defeat from the jaws of victory.

God ordered Saul to destroy Amalek, a Canaanite nation that had not yet been conquered, and all living creatures there. Saul did as God asked, up to a point. Though he destroyed most of the city, he spared the best livestock and the king. When Samuel confronted him, Saul claimed that he had obeyed God, and that the livestock was to be for sacrifices.

Saul Loses His Kingdom

But sacrifice is meant to atone for sin, not become its justification. Since Saul had rejected God's word, God rejected Saul as king. Finally, Saul confessed and grabbed Samuel's robe. A piece tore away, symbolizing God ripping the kingdom from Saul. Though Saul continued to rule, his mind was increasingly tormented by evil spirits and paranoia. Meanwhile, God sent Samuel in secret to anoint the next king, the Judean shepherd-boy David.

In the end, Saul spent more time trying to kill David, who had become his son-in-law and greatest supporter, than he did defending the people of Israel. He massacred a family of God's priests. Eventually, he became so desperate for a word from God that he consulted a medium and afterward committed suicide in battle.

THE OFFICE OF KING

God anointed Israel's kings as His representatives to make Israel faithful and defend them from enemies. They were to make their own copy of the Law of Moses, keeping it to guide their decisions. Unlike pagan kings, they were to be one of the people, not acquiring many wives or horses and chariots to secure their throne.

BIBLICAL LINKS

"Then the scribe said to Him, 'You are right, Teacher! You have correctly said that He is One, and there is no one else except Him. And to love Him with all your heart, with all your understanding, and with all your strength, and to love your neighbor as yourself, is far more important than all the burnt offerings and sacrifices.'" *(Mark 12:32–33, HCSB)*

"The people refused to listen to Samuel. 'No!' they said. 'We must have a king over us. Then we'll be like all the other nations: our king will judge us, go out before us, and fight our battles.'"

(1 Samuel 8:19–20, HCSB)

1 & 2
SAMUEL

DAVID AND GOLIATH
(1 Samuel 17)

The Philistines and the Israelites met for battle in the Valley of Elah. The Philistines sent out Goliath to call for single combat with an Israelite champion. He was a huge man, over 9 feet tall, wearing armor that weighed 125 pounds. He roared his defiance of Israel's army and of Israel's God for 40 days, and Saul's soldiers were terrified. None of them had the strength or skill to defeat Goliath. Saul offered rewards, exemption from taxes, and even his daughter in marriage, but it was not enough to entice any Israelite to volunteer for that suicide mission.

An Unlikely Hero

David, who had been a servant of Saul's in earlier years, came to the Israelite camp with supplies for three of his older brothers in Israel's army. When David heard Goliath's challenge, he wanted the chance to take down the giant. David began to ask around about the king's offer, irritating his brothers but gaining Saul's attention. Initially, the king dismissed David as too young and inexperienced, but David told him God had helped him kill lions and bears that had attacked his father's flocks. Reluctantly, Saul accepted David's offer. He wanted to dress David in the royal armor, but David took only his shepherd's sling and five smooth stones in a bag.

An Uneven Match

Goliath saw David coming and mocked him. But David sneered at the Philistine's need of weapons. He shouted that everyone would know that the people of Israel have a God who doesn't need swords to save His people. When Goliath lumbered forward, David swung his sling and hit Goliath between the eyes with a stone. Goliath collapsed, and David drew his enemy's own sword and lopped off his head. When the Philistines saw their champion fall, they panicked and fled.

BIBLICAL LINKS

"A king is not saved by a large army; a warrior will not be delivered by great strength. The horse is a false hope for safety; it provides no escape by its great power. Now the eye of the Lord is on those who fear Him—those who depend on His faithful love to deliver them from death and to keep them alive in famine." *(Psalm 33:16–19, HCSB)*

HEROIC WARRIORS

Ancient warfare occasionally featured battles decided by single combat. Everyone was to accept the result as deciding the battle. Other notable Biblical warriors were Nimrod (Gen 10:8–9), Ehud (Judg 3), Jephthah (Judg 11–12), the 24 champions (2 Sam 2:12–16), David's mighty men (2 Sam 23:8–39), and Jehu (2 Kgs 9–10).

David Secures the People's Favor

David's victory over Goliath caused the people to sing his praises. The women of Israel sang, "Saul has killed his thousands, but David his tens of thousands!" (1 Sam 18:7). This also marked the beginning of Saul's paranoia about David. The fact that David had been anointed as Israel's next king was a closely held secret. But Saul knew that he no longer had God's approval, and this miraculous victory suggested that His favor had landed on the young shepherd from Bethlehem.

"You come against me with a dagger, spear, and sword, but I come against you in the name of Yahweh of Hosts, the God of Israel's armies—you have defied Him. Today, the Lord will hand you over to me. .... Then all the world will know that Israel has a God, and this whole assembly will know that it is not by sword or by spear that the Lord saves, for the battle is the Lord's. He will hand you over to us."

(1 Samuel 17:45–47, HCSB)

THE DAVIDIC COVENANT
(2 Samuel 7)

The death of King Saul did not automatically give David the throne of Israel. After Saul committed suicide in battle, the nation was wracked by civil war. Judah made David king in the south, but for seven years the other tribes followed Saul's son Ish-bosheth. However, when Saul's general, Abner, defected to David, support for Ish-bosheth evaporated. Two of his soldiers assassinated him and delivered his head to David. They expected to be rewarded, but David ordered them executed for their crime. Only then were the tribes reunited as one kingdom.

A House for David

With his throne secure, David determined to build a house (a Temple) for God. The prophet Nathan encouraged him, but then returned with a message from God. God's sanctuary had been a tent since the Exodus and He had never asked the nation to build Him a Temple. By raising David from tending sheep to tending His people, God demonstrated that He was the One doing the blessing. Instead of David building a house for God, God promised to build a house (dynasty) for David.

God promised that a son of David would inherit the throne. This son would build a house (Temple) for God, and if he was faithful to the Mosaic Covenant (1 Kgs 2:4), his throne would endure forever. He would also have a Father-son relationship with God. God would discipline, not destroy, him. The kingdom would never be ripped from the house of David as it had been from Saul.

BIBLICAL LINKS

"Now listen: You will conceive and give birth to a son, and you will call His name Jesus. He will be great and will be called the Son of the Most High, and the Lord God will give Him the throne of His father David. He will reign over the house of Jacob forever, and His kingdom will have no end." *(Luke 1:31–33, HCSB)*

A Blessing Fulfilled

David's coronation fulfilled Jacob's blessing on Judah (Genesis 49:10). God's promise to Abraham would be mediated through the Davidic Covenant. Though the promise would be partially fulfilled in David's son, Solomon, it would also be tested by Solomon's sin. The nation would split into a northern kingdom (Israel) and a southern kingdom (Judah). These two kingdoms would be rivals for more than 200 years. David's capital, Jerusalem, would eventually fall to Babylon.

The Babylonian exile would not be the end of God's people, however. Some would return and rebuild the Jerusalem and its Temple. But the return from exile did not reestablish David's throne, leading some to hope that a Son of David would rise to restore the kingdom.

SON OF DAVID

Pre-Christian expectations for a "Son of David" varied widely, and included hopes for both priestly and royal leaders. Some looked for multiple leaders, and others for a single individual to combine multiple roles. Others saw no such promise. The Dead Sea scrolls mention "the Messiah(s) of Aaron and Israel" (The Rule of the Congregation, 100–75 B.C.E.), and "the Messiah of Justice, the branch of David" (100–0 B.C.E.). What held all these expectations together, however, was the conviction that their fulfillment would mean a full restoration of the nation to the blessings God had promised Abraham and Moses.

"The Lord Himself will make a house for you. When your time comes and you rest with your fathers, I will raise up after you your descendant, who will come from your body, and I will establish his kingdom. He will build a house for My name, and I will establish the throne of his kingdom forever."
(2 Samuel 7:11–13, HCSB)

DAVID AND BATHSHEBA
(2 Samuel 11–12)

If David had one weakness, it was for beautiful women. When he defeated Goliath, he earned the right to one of Saul's daughters, and he eventually married the younger one, Michal. However, Saul's paranoid anger eventually caused David to flee, and Saul gave Michal to another man. David then took two wives, Abigail and Ahinoam. When he became king, he acquired even more wives and concubines.

David Meets Bathsheba

After Saul's general, Abner, defected to David, David demanded that he bring Michal to him. Her second husband didn't want to give her up, but Abner threatened to kill him if he refused. Michal had been wrongfully taken, but even so, this seemed to violate the Law of Moses, which stated that a remarried woman could not return to her first husband. Then, David saw Bathsheba. David had married a princess, and then a widow, and even reacquired a former wife. But Bathsheba was different. She was rightfully married to Uriah the Hittite.

David met Bathsheba during the season for military campaigns. Instead of leading his army, he was home in Jerusalem. Walking on his roof one night, he saw Bathsheba bathing. He sent for her, and soon she reported that she was pregnant.

David attempted a cover-up by sending for her husband, Uriah. But Uriah refused to sleep in his own bed with his wife, thinking that it wasn't right for him to relax while the troops were in the field. David himself had traditionally forbidden his soldiers from having sex while campaigning (1 Sam 21:5).

Uriah's purity ruined David's desperate gambit. David even tried getting him drunk, but when that failed, David sent a message back to the front with Uriah. David's general, Joab, was to leave Uriah exposed in battle so that he died. It almost worked.

David's Judgment

Uriah died in battle, and David married Bathsheba as he had wanted. But then the prophet Nathan asked David to judge the case of a rich man who had stolen a poor man's pet lamb and killed it for a meal. David rose in self-righteous anger and sentenced the rich man to death. Nathan rounded on the king, "You are the man!"

Though David's repentance was immediate and genuine, he had trampled on God's Law. God forgave David, but even the king could not stand above the Law of Moses. David's sin with Bathsheba brought turmoil to his family. Just as he had ordered the fictional rich man to pay fourfold for his sin, David lost four of his sons.

The first was Bathsheba's child (2 Sam 12:18). The second was Amnon, murdered by his half-brother Absalom for raping his sister (2 Sam 13:28–29). The third was Absalom himself, who died after attempting to overthrow David (2 Sam 18:14–15). Absalom also fulfilled Nathan's prophesy that David's wives would be given to another, who would sleep with them publicly (2 Sam 16:21–22). The final son to die was Adonijah, who was executed for attempting to subvert King Solomon soon after his coronation (1 Kgs 2:24–25).

BIBLICAL LINKS

"The one who conceals his sins will not prosper, but whoever confesses and renounces them will find mercy." (Proverbs 28:13, HCSB)

"If we say, "We have no sin," we are deceiving ourselves, and the truth is not in us. If we confess our sins, He is faithful and righteous to forgive us our sins and to cleanse us from all unrighteousness." (1 John 1:8–9, HCSB)

"David responded to Nathan, 'I have sinned against the Lord.' Then Nathan replied to David, 'The Lord has taken away your sin; you will not die. However, because you treated the Lord with such contempt in this matter, the son born to you will die.'" (2 Samuel 12:13–14, HCSB)

1 & 2
KINGS

First and Second Kings record the division and destruction of the nation of Israel due to the sins of the kings. Despite prophetic warnings and divine judgments, the northern kingdom embraced idolatry and was destroyed by Assyria. Though several kings attempted reforms, the southern kings also succumbed to idolatry, resulting in the Babylonian Exile.

LOCATION: The events of Kings take place in the kingdoms of Israel (north) and Judah (south). Key locations include Samaria, Mount Carmel, Mount Sinai, and Jerusalem.

ORIGIN: The books of Kings are traditionally attributed to Jeremiah, and were likely written shortly after the Babylonian conquest of Jerusalem (586 B.C.E.) as an explanation of Israel's destruction. Modern critical theories see Kings as the work of a compiler who shared the theological perspective of Deuteronomy.

KEY PASSAGES

1 Kings

Solomon's Reign (1–11)

3:1–28	Solomon Becomes Wise
6:1–9:9	Solomon Builds the Temple

The Division of the Kingdom (12–22)

12:1–19	Rehoboam Divides the Kingdom
12:12–13:34	Jeroboam Establishes Idolatry
17:1–19:21	Elijah Fights Ahab and Jezebel

2 Kings

The Divided Kingdom to the Fall of Samaria (1–17)

2:1–25	Elisha Succeeds Elijah
5:1–27	God Heals an Aramean General
6:8–7:20	Israel Survives the Arameans
9:1–36	Jehu Reigns in Samaria

Judah to the Fall of Jerusalem (18–24)

18:13–20:20	Hezekiah Survives the Assyrians
22:1–30	Josiah Restores the Temple Worship
25:1–21	The Babylonians Destroy

PRINCIPAL FIGURES

God Kings describes God as the Holy One who judges and preserves Israel based on the faithfulness of the kings.

Solomon David's son, who became the wisest king of Israel before falling into foolish idolatry.

Rehoboam Solomon's son, whose kingdom was limited to Judah because he tried to enslave the people of Israel.

Jeroboam The first king of the northern tribes; he built idols to secure power.

Elijah The great prophet who confronted King Ahab of Israel and Baal-worship.

Ahab Ruler of the northern kingdom of Israel, who led the nation into Baal-worship.

Jezebel A Phoenician wife of Ahab, who was eaten by dogs as punishment for murder.

Elisha The successor to Elijah as God's prophet to the northern kingdom of Israel.

Jehu The northern king who ended Ahab's dynasty and eliminated Baal-worship in Israel.

Hezekiah King of Judah, who survived the Assyrian siege of Jerusalem.

Josiah A southern king who restored the Temple and purified Judah from idolatry.

THE WISDOM OF SOLOMON
(1 Kings 3)

After Solomon became king, he went to the city of Gibeon to offer sacrifices to God. In a dream, God invited Solomon to make a request. Solomon recognized that he was young and inexperienced, so he asked God for wisdom to rule well. God was pleased and not only conferred wisdom on Solomon, but wealth and honor as well. He required only that Solomon be obedient to His ways and Law.

Solomon's wisdom was tested when he judged a difficult lawsuit. Two women living in the same house had each given birth to a son. One of the women had rolled onto her son in the night and smothered him. The plaintiff alleged that the other woman was the one whose son had died. She claimed that upon waking and realizing what had happened, the other woman had switched the children before the plaintiff woke up.

The women came to Solomon, each claiming that the living child was her own. Solomon's wisdom was seen in the test he devised to determine who the real mother was. He called for a sword and prepared to cut the child in half. Each woman would get her fair share. One woman found that acceptable, revealing the lack of concern for a child's life that had led to the death of the first son. Simultaneously, the other woman renounced her claim, begging Solomon to let the child live. Her compassion for the child proved that she was his true mother, and Solomon awarded the child to her.

WISDOM IN THE BIBLE

Biblical wisdom is about understanding the way God ordered creation and acting accordingly. As a result, wisdom begins with respecting the Creator of that order (Prov 1:7; Rom 1:21.24). Although Solomon was a wise king, he eventually drifted into disobedience. After a political marriage to Pharaoh's daughter, "just once" (1 Kgs 3:1; Deut 17:17) became 700 wives who eventually seduced him into idolatry (1 Kgs 11).

"All Israel heard about the judgment the king had given, and they stood in awe of the king because they saw that God's wisdom was in him to carry out justice." (1 Kings 3:28, HCSB)

Aleppo
River Orontes
River Euphrates
Tiphsah
Kedesh
Tadmor
(Mediterranean Sea)
Great Sea
Sidon
Damascus
Tyre
Mt. Hermon
Hazor
Mt. Carmel
Megiddo
Mt. Ebal
River Jordan
Gezer
Mizpah
Baalath
Jerusalem
Hebron
Salt Sea (Dead Sea)
Beersheba
Tamar
Ezion Geber
Gulf of Aqaba

Isreal under King Solomon

The United Kingdom of Israel Under David and Solomon

1 & 2 KINGS

After Solomon's death, his son, Rehoboam, tried to hold the kingdom together by force, but the 10 northern tribes rebelled and made Jeroboam their king. As a result, two kingdoms were formed: "Israel" or "Ephraim" in the north, and "Judah" in the south. They would not be reunited for almost 800 years.

Jeroboam's Golden Calves

Jeroboam wanted to secure his throne, and worried that people would return to Rehoboam if they worshipped at Solomon's Temple in Jerusalem.

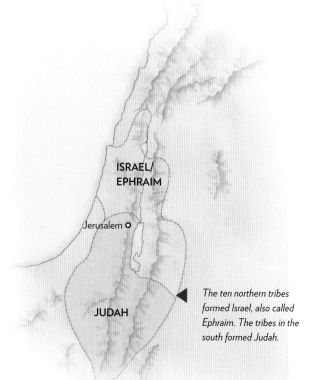

The ten northern tribes formed Israel, also called Ephraim. The tribes in the south formed Judah.

To prevent this, he constructed places of worship within the boundaries of his kingdom. Jeroboam made golden calves and placed one in the south at Bethel, facing north, and the other in the north at Dan, facing south. The symbolic claim was that Ephraim was the dwelling-place of God's glory, like the Ark of the Covenant. Jeroboam opened the priesthood to all Israelite men. Because they remained loyal to Yahweh, the Levites evacuated to Judah, where they could continue to serve in Solomon's Temple.

God Sends a Prophet

Jeroboam's actions showed that he didn't trust God to preserve the kingdom He had given him, and this resulted in swift judgment. God sent a southern prophet to confront Jeroboam at Bethel. God warned the prophet before he left not to accept any hospitality, but to return immediately by a different road.

THE NAMES OF THE NATION

Scholars refer to the period of the 12 tribe's unity under a king as the "United Monarchy." After Solomon, however, the "Divided Kingdom" period saw the one people of God separated into two nations. The northern kingdom was larger geographically and in population. It took the name of its largest tribe, Ephraim. But it was also commonly referred to simply as "Israel." The southern kingdom also took the name of its largest tribe (traditionally the largest of the 12 tribes), Judah.

Upon his arrival, the prophet found Jeroboam offering incense at the altar in Bethel. The prophet pronounced God's judgment against the altar, proclaiming that a future son of David, named Josiah, would defile and destroy it. This was Jeroboam's opportunity to repent. But the king was angered by the prophet's words, and ordered his arrest. As Jeroboam stretched out his hand, it withered and the altar crumbled. Only after he asked the prophet to intercede was the hand restored. Still, Jeroboam retained his idols and restored the altar; the northern kings never abandoned "the sins of Jeroboam."

The Prophet's Disobedience

As the southern prophet returned home, a northern prophet invited him to share a meal. The southern prophet refused, but when the northern prophet claimed divine permission, the southern prophet accepted. At the first bite, God spoke through the northern prophet. The southern prophet would die for his disobedience. And so it happened that a lion attacked the prophet on his road home. Afterward, the lion and the prophet's donkey each stood on opposite sides of the corpse as a sign of God's judgment.

BIBLICAL LINKS

"They have installed kings, but not through Me. They have appointed leaders, but without My approval. They make their silver and gold into idols for themselves for their own destruction. Your calf-idol is rejected, Samaria. My anger burns against them. How long will they be incapable of innocence? For this thing is from Israel—a craftsman made it, and it is not God. The calf of Samaria will be smashed to bits! Indeed, they sow the wind and reap the whirlwind. There is no standing grain; what sprouts fails to yield flour. Even if they did, foreigners would swallow it up." *(Hosea 8:4–7, HCSB)*

"So the king sought advice. Then he made two golden calves, and he said to the people, 'Going to Jerusalem is too difficult for you. Israel, here is your God who brought you out of the land of Egypt.'" (1 Kings 12:28, HCSB)

ELIJAH AT MOUNT CARMEL
(1 Kings 18)

One of the most powerful kings in the history of the northern kingdom was Ahab. He sealed an important alliance between Israel and the Phoenicians by marrying the Phoenician princess, Jezebel. However, Jezebel encouraged Baal and Ashtoreth worship in Israel. As punishment, the prophet Elijah announced to Ahab that he had asked God to cause a drought in Israel. The drought would continue until Elijah prayed for rain. In the interim, God provided for Elijah by sending ravens with food and provisions through a Phoenician widow.

Elijah's Contest

At the end of three years, Elijah invited Ahab and the 850 prophets of Baal and Asherah to the top of Mount Carmel for a contest. Baal's prophets would construct an altar to Baal and slaughter a sacrifice on the wood laid on the altar. But they would not set fire to the wood. They were to ask Baal to do that. Elijah would then do the same and ask Yahweh (God) to set fire to His sacrifice. The Israelites agreed to follow the One that answered.

Baal's prophets spent half the day chanting and even cutting themselves while Elijah mocked them. He suggested that perhaps the prophets of Baal were not calling loudly enough, or that Baal might be asleep or relieving himself. When they were finally exhausted, Baal's servants gave up.

When it was his turn, Elijah set up a traditional altar of 12 uncut stones to God. After placing the sacrifice on the wood he ordered 12 pots of water to be poured over the altar. Finally, he calmly asked God to show the people that He alone was God. Fire fell from heaven and consumed the sacrifice, the wood, the stone altar, and the water.

BAAL AND ASHTORETH WORSHIP

Baal was a storm and fertility god who was worshipped on high hills. Canaanites thought that Baal died and returned through sexual rites worshipping him and his consort, Ashtoreth (later identified as Asherah). This ensured the beginning of the next rainy season, and thus the fertility of crops and flocks.

The Drought Ends

Elijah immediately ordered the people to seize the false prophets. The people took them down to the Kishon brook at the base of the mountain and executed them all. Meanwhile, Elijah kept watch out over the Mediterranean Sea. Soon his servant saw a small cloud growing rapidly. The prophet told Ahab that rain was coming, and left. The drought was over.

"At the time for offering the evening sacrifice, Elijah the prophet approached the altar and said, 'Yahweh, God of Abraham, Isaac, and Israel, today let it be known that You are God in Israel and I am Your servant, and that at Your word I have done all these things.'"

1 Kings 18:36, HCSB)

SYNCRETISM

The Mosaic Covenant was nearly unique among ancient Near Eastern religions for completely forbidding the worship of other gods, even to the point of claiming that those gods did not exist at all. Many pagan cults were willing to accept that deities in different lands who seemed similar to deities in their own land were simply the same gods called by different names. This helps to explain, in part, the attraction of Baal for ancient Israelites. A common Hebrew title for God was Adonai, which meant *Lord*. The Canaanite word for *Lord* was Baal.

BIBLICAL LINKS

"The urgent request of a righteous person is very powerful in its effect. Elijah was a man with a nature like ours; yet he prayed earnestly that it would not rain, and for three years and six months it did not rain on the land. Then he prayed again, and the sky gave rain and the land produced its fruit."
(James 5:16–18, HCSB)

NAAMAN'S LEPROSY HEALED
(2 Kings 5)

Naaman, the commander of the Aramean army, had been very successful against Israel. But he had a skin disease that could not be healed. A slave girl, taken in a raid against Israel, told Naaman's wife of a prophet in Israel who could heal her master. So the King of Aram sent Naaman with a letter to the King of Israel, demanding that he heal Naaman. The Israelite king despaired, thinking that the King of Aram was just trying to pick a fight with him. But, the prophet Elisha (Elijah's successor) sent word that Naaman should come to him.

Naaman Bathes in the River

When Naaman arrived at Elisha's house, the prophet refused to speak to him. Instead, he sent a messenger instructing the general to wash in the Jordan River seven times. Naaman was offended that he was not being treated with the respect he deserved, but his servants persuaded him that he should do this simple thing the prophet asked. When Naaman came out of the water the seventh time, his skin was healed.

An Altar for Damascus

Naaman returned to offer rich gifts to Elisha. This time, Elisha spoke with him but rejected the gifts because he was not the source of the healing. Since the prophet would not accept his gifts, Naaman offered himself as a worshipper of Yahweh. He asked to take a load of dirt back to Damascus so that there would be land there that belonged to God. Naaman promised to build an altar on that land and worship God there.

Elisha's servant, Gehazi, thought that Naaman had been given too easy a deal. He chased after Naaman and claimed that some young men had just arrived who needed clothes and money. Naaman was glad to give more than was asked. But when Gehazi returned, Elisha confronted him over his greed and judged him. Having coveted Naaman's wealth, Gehazi would also receive Naaman's disease.

BIBLICAL LINKS

"He also said, 'I assure you: No prophet is accepted in his hometown. But I say to you, there were certainly many widows in Israel in Elijah's days, when the sky was shut up for three years and six months while a great famine came over all the land. Yet Elijah was not sent to any of them—but to a widow at Zarephath in Sidon. And in the prophet Elisha's time, there were many in Israel who had serious skin diseases, yet not one of them was healed—only Naaman the Syrian.'" *(Luke 4:24–27, HCSB)*

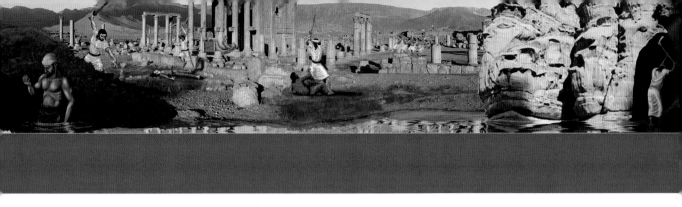

LEPROSY

Naaman's skin disease has traditionally been identified as leprosy. Biblical leprosy, however, does not seem to be the same as modern leprosy (Hansen's disease, Mycobacterium leprae). Nevertheless, the Mosaic designation of skin diseases as signifying divine judgment was taken very seriously. Those with such diseases were put out of their cities and roamed the countryside in bands. Significant Old Testament figures with leprosy included Miriam (Moses' sister), King Uzziah of Judah, and Naaman.

"Naaman responded, 'If not, please let your servant be given as much soil as a pair of mules can carry, for your servant will no longer offer a burnt offering or a sacrifice to any other god but Yahweh.'"

(2 Kings 5:17, HCSB)

TERRITORIAL DEITIES

Many ancient deities were thought to control specific territories. Despite presenting Himself as the Creator of Heaven and Earth, and Liberator from Egypt, even many Israelites thought Yahweh only had power in Israel. Isaiah and Psalms would build on Moses' writing to emphasize God's universal rule in worship and anti-idol rhetoric.

1 & 2 KINGS

THE WAR WITH ARAM
(2 Kings 6–7)

Despite the healing of Naaman, the King of Aram continued to raid Israel. But now it seemed the Israelites always knew where the raids would strike, which caused the king to suspect that Israel had a spy. Although he had been warned that the prophet Elisha knew even his most private conversations, the king ordered a raid to capture Elisha. Without the prophet's divine insights, he believed the Arameans would regain the element of surprise.

Elisha's Mercy

When the Aramean army arrived for Elisha, his servant panicked, but Elisha remained calm. He told his servant that their army far outnumbered the Arameans. The servant looked out and saw an army of fire surrounding the Arameans. Elisha blinded the Arameans and led them into the capital city, Samaria. The king wanted to massacre them, but Elisha rebuked him and ordered the army fed and sent home. This act of mercy stopped the raiding.

The King's Foolishness

Eventually, however, the Arameans invaded Israel again. During the siege of Samaria, the failure of the Israelite king's leadership was illustrated when two women asked him to judge a dispute. In a perverse parody of Solomon's case, the women had agreed to eat one woman's son one day and the other's the next. On the second day, however, the second woman had hidden her child. The first woman demanded that the king compel the second to divide her child between them. The situation not only showed the desperate situation inside the city, it recalled Moses warning about being unfaithful to the Covenant (Deut 28:52-57).

◀ *The city of Samaria was the capital of the northern kingdom of Israel.*

The king's response to the women illustrated his foolishness. Rather than recognize his idolatry as the cause of God's judgment, the king blamed Elisha for all his troubles. He vowed to execute the prophet whose warnings had foiled the Arameans in the past and whose mercy had stopped their raids for so long. But when the king confronted Elisha, the prophet said the famine would end the next day. The Captain of the king's soldiers scoffed that such a thing was not possible. He was told he would see it, but not eat a bite.

The Famine Ends

That night, three lepers outside the city visited the Aramean camp in hope of finding either food or a quick death. The camp was abandoned, but full of supplies. After stuffing themselves, they realized they should tell the city that the Aramean army had gone. The king sent two chariots to investigate and they found that the Arameans had fled to the Jordan River. God had caused them to panic, making them think that they were about to be attacked by the Hittites from the north and the Egyptians from the south. The gates to Samaria were thrown open, and the Captain was trampled to death by the crowd rushing to eat the Aramean supplies.

BIBLICAL LINKS

"The wicked flee when no one is pursuing them, but the righteous are as bold as a lion."
(Proverbs 28:1, HCSB)

"Then they said to each other, 'We're not doing what is right. Today is a day of good news. If we are silent and wait until morning light, our sin will catch up with us. Let's go tell the king's household.'"

(2 Kings 7:9, HCSB)

FOOLISH KINGS

Solomon feared God and became wise (1 Kgs 3), but idolatry made the northern kings fools. When Moses' warnings were fulfilled, they lashed out at the prophets who had served them. They refused to believe that God's punishment was His call for them to return to the blessings of obedience.

JEHU KILLS THE BAAL WORSHIPPERS
(2 Kings 10)

After Ahab's death, his son, Joram, took the throne of the northern kingdom. But God was displeased with Ahab's family for worshipping Baal. He sent the prophet Elisha to anoint Jehu, an army commander, as the next king (2 Kgs 9). God ordered Jehu to eradicate all of Ahab's sons, along with Jezebel, as punishment for their Baal-worship.

Jehu acted swiftly, assassinating Joram, who came out from the town of Jezreel to meet him. Jehu had Joram's body dumped in the vineyard of Naboth, whose property Jezebel had stolen after having Naboth murdered (1 Kgs 21). Jezebel was thrown from an upper window and her body was devoured by dogs. Then, Jehu sent word to the nobles of Samaria ordering them to bring the heads of Ahab's sons to him in Jezreel (2 Kgs 10). When this was done, he went to Samaria to finish his task.

Jehu's Deception

In Samaria, Jehu set out to complete his mission by drawing the worshippers of Baal into an ambush. He announced that though Ahab had served Baal half-heartedly, he would serve Baal fully. He summoned the priests, prophets, and servants of Baal from all over Israel to a ceremonial feast in Baal's honor. Baal's servants were warned that anyone who failed to appear would be killed. Jehu's proclamation ensured that every Baal-worshipper would be present.

When the crowd assembled, Jehu sent them into Baal's Temple. He warned them that this ceremony was only for true followers of Baal, those who had worshipped Baal before Jehu became king. All others were to be expelled. Jehu's men then surrounded the Temple. After offering the sacrifice to Baal, Jehu ordered his men to kill everyone in the Temple of Baal. The Temple was torn down, its pillars burned. The site was then permanently desecrated by being made a public latrine.

God's Blessing for Jehu

Although Jehu ended Baal-worship in Israel, he did not end the worship of Jeroboam's golden calves. Because of Jehu's obedience in destroying the Baal worshippers, God blessed Jehu with a brief dynasty on the throne. But because of his continued use of Jeroboam's calves, Israel continued on the path that resulted in the northern kingdom's destruction by the Assyrians.

JEZREEL

The name Jezreel means "God sows," evoking images of the fertile valley floor on which the town sat. But the name came to be a symbol of thorough-going judgment and destruction. The Omrid dynasty of northern kings ended with Jehu's slaughter of Ahab's family at Jezreel. But because of its continued embrace of idolatry, Jehu's own dynasty would come to an equally bloody end *(Hos 1:4–5)*.

ISRAEL AND ANCIENT SUPERPOWERS

Israel and Judah were small nations occupying strategic roads between the great powers of Mesopotamia (Assyria and Babylon) and Egypt. Both sought security through worship of "powerful" gods and alliances with small neighbors and by becoming clients of great powers. These clever strategies only provoked the wrath of God and the nations.

"Yet Jehu was not careful to follow the instruction of the Lord God of Israel with all his heart. He did not turn from the sins that Jeroboam had caused Israel to commit."
(2 Kings 10:31, HCSB)

BIBLICAL LINKS

"One of the scribes approached. When he heard them debating and saw that Jesus answered them well, he asked Him, 'Which command is the most important of all?' 'This is the most important,' Jesus answered: 'Listen, Israel! The Lord our God, the Lord is One. Love the Lord your God with all your heart, with all your soul, with all your mind, and with all your strength.'" *(Mark 12:28–30, HCSB)*

1 & 2 KINGS

THE ORIGIN OF THE SAMARITANS
(2 Kings 17)

Hoshea was the last ruler of the northern kingdom. He survived an Assyrian attack by agreeing to pay them tribute. But when Hoshea conspired with Egypt, Assyria besieged Samaria. After three years, the city was razed. Assyrian policy toward defeated nations was brutally effective. Everyone was marched away from their homes to new lands. Often, captives were made to walk naked, which resulted in the death of the sick, old, and very young. Those who survived were thoroughly demoralized. Nations the Assyrians deported tended to evaporate into the mists of history.

The Price of Idolatry

The author of 2 Kings insisted that while the rise of new empires and failures of diplomacy were the immediate causes of Israel's destruction, they were not the ultimate reason for its fall. This disaster befell Israel because they had stubbornly sinned against God and been unfaithful to the Mosaic Covenant by worshipping idols. Israel became like the things they worshipped: worthless.

After deporting what remained of the 10 northern tribes, the Assyrians imported new inhabitants from other lands. These people brought the worship of their gods with them but soon discovered that the God of their new land was not pleased with them. After a rash of lion attacks, they asked the Assyrian king to send an Israelite priest to teach them how to worship the

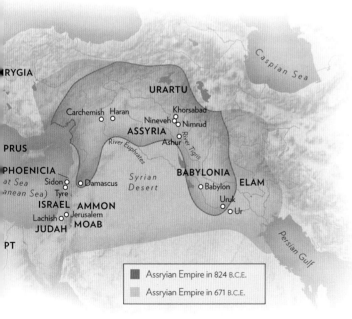

Assyrian Empire in 824 B.C.E.

Assyrian Empire in 671 B.C.E.

EXILE AS PUNISHMENT

Israel's exile seems as harsh as Adam's expulsion from the Garden of Eden (Gen 3). But God had warned the people of Israel about their idolatry repeatedly over some 250 years. The northern kingdom rejected God and His blessings, and so received what their preferred idols could provide: nothing, neither blessing nor protection.

God of the land. The people learned how to serve God according to the Law of Moses. But they observed the Law's ceremonial requirements alongside serving their national gods, including offering human sacrifice.

The Samaritans

These peoples would collectively become known as the "Samaritans." Though they followed many of the Law's requirements, they retained the northern policy of refusing to worship in Jerusalem. Hostility between the Samaritans and the Judeans would surface in the book of Nehemiah and persist into the New Testament era (for example, see John 4).

PAYING TRIBUTE

Conquering powers were sometimes bought off with the promise of annual payments of tribute. Huge sums were demanded, providing vast resources to build the cities of the ruling empire. But these same payments also impoverished the lands paying them and led to rebellion. When successful, the payments ended. When unsuccessful, the rebel nation was destroyed through exile.

"Still, the Lord warned Israel and Judah through every prophet and every seer, saying, 'Turn from your evil ways and keep My commands and statutes according to all the law I commanded your ancestors and sent to you through My servants the prophets.' But they would not listen. Instead they became obstinate like their ancestors who did not believe the Lord their God."

(2 Kings 17:13–14, HCSB)

ASSYRIA'S SIEGE OF JERUSALEM
(2 Kings 18–19)

Within a few years of conquering the northern kingdom, Israel, Assyria turned its attention to Judah, the southern kingdom. But while Israel had been ruled by a faithless king, Judah was ruled by Hezekiah, one of its greatest kings. Hezekiah had removed all idol-worship from Judah and had expanded its borders. But when he tried to assert Judah's independence from Assyria, the Assyrian King Sennacherib sent an army under the Rabshakeh, a senior field commander.

The Assyrians Attack

The Assyrians took the fortified cities of Judah, and Hezekiah stripped the royal treasury and the Temple to pay a huge sum to the Assyrians, in an attempt to buy them off by paying tribute as before. Though he hoped they would withdraw, they continued their advance and laid siege to Jerusalem. When the Assyrians established their lines, the Rabshakeh addressed the city in Hebrew. He warned Judah that words wouldn't save them, and neither would Egypt. He then claimed that Hezekiah had offended God by removing the idols and had authorized Assyria to punish Hezekiah.

The Judean officials asked the Rabshakeh to speak in a language the people would not understand (Aramaic), but he refused. Since the men stationed on the city wall would suffer the effects of the siege, he would speak to them in their own language, Hebrew. The Assyrian warned Hezekiah's soldiers that their king could not be trusted and that God would not rescue Judah. Surrender would allow the people to move to a new, rich land. The Rabshakeh ended by reminding Jerusalem of all the gods the Assyrians had defeated.

Isaiah's Prophecy

Hezekiah called on Jerusalem to ask God for relief, and the prophet Isaiah told the king that the Assyrians would abandon the siege and return home, where Sennacherib would be assassinated (2 Kgs 19). That night, the Angel of the Lord killed 180,000 Assyrian soldiers. The Assyrians abandoned the siege. After returning to his capital at Nineveh, Sennacherib's sons murdered him while he worshipped in the Temple of Nisroch.

BIBLICAL LINKS

"Lord, I seek refuge in You; let me never be disgraced. Save me by Your righteousness. Listen closely to me; rescue me quickly. Be a rock of refuge for me, a mountain fortress to save me." *(Psalm 31:1–2, HCSB)*

ANCIENT WATER SUPPLIES

One necessity for ancient cities was a secure water source. In preparation for the Assyrian attack, Hezekiah improved Jerusalem's defenses by ordering excavation of a 1,750-foot tunnel that channeled the Gihon spring (outside the walls) underneath the city to the pool of Siloam. This project stored water from the spring and made it accessible from within the fortified city. Two teams chiseled through hard rock from opposite directions. The place where the tunnel met was marked by a stone inscription crediting Hezekiah with ordering the project. Discovered in 1838, water still flows through the tunnel today.

"Hezekiah trusted in the Lord God of Israel; not one of the kings of Judah was like him, either before him or after him. He remained faithful to Yahweh and did not turn from following Him but kept the commands the Lord had commanded Moses."

(2 Kings 18:5–6, HCSB)

BABYLON'S SIEGE OF JERUSALEM
(2 Kings 25)

The last king of Judah was Zedekiah. He was an ally of the Babylonians and had been placed on the throne by their king, Nebuchadnezzar. But after 11 years on the throne, Zedekiah rebelled against Babylon, apparently in an attempt to ally himself with Egypt.

The Babylonians Lay Siege

The Babylonians marched against Jerusalem and built a siege wall around the city. No one was able to get in or out. The city lived on what food it had stored, but after two years there was famine in the city. In the end, the Babylonians breached the wall. That night the king attempted to flee but was intercepted and brought back to Jerusalem. The last thing Zedekiah saw before his captors blinded him was the execution of his sons.

The Babylonians razed Jerusalem. The Temple was destroyed and its treasures taken back to Babylon. The houses of the rich were burned and the walls of the city were pulled down. Nothing was left of David or Solomon's city. Nearly everyone who survived was taken into exile in Babylon. Only the poorest were left to tend the vineyards and fields of the land.

The Judeans Flee

Nebuchadnezzar placed a Judean governor, Gedaliah, over what was now the Babylonian province of Judea. He promised that if the inhabitants lived peacefully under Babylonian rule, everything would be fine. The prophet Jeremiah supported the governor. Not everyone was content, however. The king of Ammon encouraged Ishmael, a distant member of Judah's royal house, to assassinate the governor. Fearing the Babylonian response to the murder of their governor, the remaining Judeans and the conspirators fled to Egypt, where they turned from the worship of God to yet more idolatry.

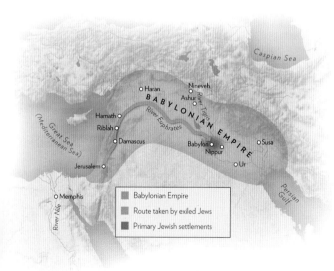

COVENANT CRISIS

The progression from Gen 3:15 through the Noahic, Abrahamic, Mosaic, and Davidic Covenants leads to the crisis of Jerusalem's destruction. God had promised to bless the world through Abraham's seed, but neither a faithful nation (Mosaic Covenant) nor a righteous king (Davidic Covenant) had emerged. Yet the prophets' warnings also offered hope of restoration.

ARCHAEOLOGY AND JERUSALEM'S FALL

In 1970, four arrowheads were discovered at the base of what had been a massive stone defense tower in Jerusalem. The tower had been part of the defenses of the northern wall during the Babylonian siege. The design of the arrowheads was consistent with those known to have been used by Babylonian archers after 600 B.C.E. These artifacts were the first remains of the Babylonian siege to be recovered.

BIBLICAL LINKS

"God, the nations have invaded Your inheritance, desecrated Your holy Temple, and turned Jerusalem into ruins. They gave the corpses of Your servants to the birds of the sky for food, the flesh of Your godly ones to the beasts of the earth. They poured out their blood like water all around Jerusalem, and there was no one to bury them. We have become an object of reproach to our neighbors, a source of mockery and ridicule to those around us."
(Psalm 79:1–4, HCSB)

"Because of the Lord's anger, it came to the point in Jerusalem and Judah that He finally banished them from His presence. Then, Zedekiah rebelled against the king of Babylon."

(2 Kings 24:20, HCSB)

1 & 2
CHRONICLES

Chronicles opens with a genealogy from Adam to the major families of the Israelite tribes. The historical narrative focuses on the history of the Davidic dynasty and the Temple in Jerusalem. Written to Jews in Judea after the Babylonian Exile, Chronicles emphasizes the importance of consistent Covenant loyalty to God.

LOCATION: Most of the events of Chronicles take place in the southern kingdom, Judah. The focus of the book is Jerusalem and the Temple.

ORIGIN: Rabbinic tradition credits Ezra with writing Chronicles, suggesting the book was written after the Babylonian Exile (before 400 B.C.E.). The book describes roughly the same time period as Kings, from the death of Saul (1011 B.C.E.) to the destruction of Jerusalem by the Babylonians (586 B.C.E.).

KEY PASSAGES

1 Chronicles

Genealogies from Adam to Saul (1–10)

(10:1–14) Saul Commits Suicide in Battle

Preparation for the Temple: David (11–29)

13:1–14	David Moves the Ark to Jerusalem
17:1–27	God Makes a Covenant with David
21:1–26:32	David Plans for Temple Worship
28:1–29:31	David Commissions Solomon

2 Chronicles

Construction of the Temple: Solomon (1–9)

3:1–7:22	Solomon Builds the Temple
9:1–12	Queen of Sheba Visits Solomon

History of the Temple: Kings of Judah (10–36)

15:1–19	Asa Renovates the Altar
20:1–30	Jehoshaphat Prays for Protection
26:16–22	Uzziah Defiles the Temple
34:1–35:20	Josiah Repairs the Temple
36:11–23	Babylon Destroys the Temple

PRINCIPAL FIGURES

God Chronicles emphasizes that God is Israel's God and Salvation, rather than idols or the mere presence of the Temple.

David Israel's second and greatest King, who was granted a Covenant with God.

Solomon David's son, who became the wisest king of Israel before falling into foolish idolatry.

Queen of Sheba Ruler of a south Arabian or East African nation, who visited Solomon.

Asa Judean king who suppressed idolatry in Judah, but failed to depend on God consistently.

Jehoshaphat Asa's son, who aided Ahaz and later saw God fight against Edom.

Uzziah Judean king who offered incense in the Temple and contracted leprosy.

Ahaz Judean King who feared Israel and Aram more than God.

Hezekiah King of Judah, who survived the Assyrian siege of Jerusalem.

Josiah The last faithful Judean king who restored the Temple and suppressed idolatry.

THE CAPTURE OF JERUSALEM
(1 Chronicles 11:1–9)

After David was crowned king of all Israel at Hebron, he led his army to Jerusalem. Though the Jebusites who lived there had been defeated in battle during the initial conquest under Joshua, the city itself had not been taken. The Jebusites were confident in their defenses. They boasted that David would never enter the city and that even a blind man could defend it (2 Sam 5:6).

But David sent Joab and a small team of soldiers into the city through the cave used to reach its water source outside the walls. The city fell to David and he made it his capital. Politically, the city was important as an inter-tribal capital, a city not tied to any tribe. But even more importantly, it would become the location for the Temple.

The United Kingdom of Israel
Under David and Solomon

THE TEL DAN INSCRIPTION

In 1993, an inscription dating to the 800s B.C.E. was discovered at Tel Dan in northern Israel. It commemorates an Aramean king's victory over the "King of Israel" and the "King of the House of David" (see 2 Chr 18). It is presently the earliest archaeological evidence for David as a historical figure.

"Then David took up residence in the stronghold; therefore, it was called the city of David."

(1 Chronicles 11:7, HCSB)

DAVID'S CENSUS
(1 Chronicles 21)

In the wake of David's military successes, God became angry with David and permitted Satan to incite the king to take a military census of the nation (2 Sam 24:1–10). Though previous counts had been authorized by God (Num 26:2), David's motivation here seems to have been pride and the sense that his security rested with his army rather than God. David's general, Joab, argued vehemently that David's order would bring God's wrath on the nation. David refused to listen, and the numbering proceeded. Though Joab obeyed the king, he refused to count two tribes: Levi, which was exempt from military service (Num 1:49), and Benjamin, where the Tabernacle had been erected (1 Chr 21:29).

Three Days of Plague

When things began to go badly for David, he realized that he had acted foolishly and sinned and asked God to remove his guilt. God sent a seer named Gad to give David a choice: three years of famine, three months of military disasters, or three days of plague under the Angel of the Lord's sword. David, thinking that God's mercies are greater than man's chose to endure the three days of plague.

When the Angel of the Lord reached Jerusalem, He stood at the threshing floor of a Jebusite resident of the city. David, dressed in ritual mourning clothes, saw the Angel and begged God to spare the people. He acknowledged full responsibility for the census and asked that the judgment fall on himself and his family. Though 70,000 men had already died, God had mercy on Israel and the plague ended.

CORPORATE PERSONALITY

The Bible's concept of "person" is broader than the "individual." A leader's actions and his consequences could be credited to his group (for example, Adam represented humanity), or the group's to its head. This informs Paul's writing about salvation (Rom 5; 1 Cor 15) and the church (1 Cor 12; Col 1).

A Place for the Temple

Gad then instructed David to purchase the threshing floor where the Angel of the Lord had stood. Its owner offered to give it to the king, along with oxen for a sacrifice. But David refused the gift and insisted on paying, not only the cost of the field but the value of its future purpose: the final site of the Tabernacle, and future location of the Temple. God's approval was symbolized by fire from heaven, which consumed the oxen David offered as a sacrifice.

> "David said to God, 'I have sinned greatly because I have done this thing. Now, please take away Your servant's guilt, for I've been very foolish.'"
>
> (1 Chronicles 21:8, HCSB)

MARTIAL NAMES OF GOD

David's sin attributed the nation's strength to its military rather than to God. Several of God's names in the Old Testament speak to His role as the guarantor of the nation's security. *Yahweh Elohim Sabaoth* named Him the Lord God of Hosts. His power was highlighted in the names *El Shaddai* (God Almighty) and *El Gibbor* (Mighty God). God was identified as a source of security and protection with the name *Yaweh Mauzzi* (God Our Fortress).

BIBLICAL LINKS

"Yahweh, if You considered sins, Lord, who could stand? But with You there is forgiveness, so that You may be revered." *(Psalm 130:3–4, HCSB)*

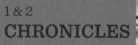

1 & 2 CHRONICLES

After reigning four years, Solomon began construction of a Temple on the site David had purchased. The project included construction of the building itself, along with all its furnishings and instruments for sacrifice. When it was completed, the Ark of the Covenant was deposited in the most holy place: under the cover of two enormous golden cherubim (angels), each with a wingspan of 15 feet. Then the priests sounded trumpets and sang praises to God.

Solomon's Dedication

Solomon stood on a platform before the people and dedicated the Temple with a prayer. He acknowledged God's uniqueness and His promise to David. Solomon confessed that the Creator could not be contained by a building, but asked that God would watch over the Temple and hear Israel's prayers: requests to enforce oaths, pleas for forgiveness, and petitions for aid.

Solomon also asked that God would hear the prayers of foreigners who came because of God's greatness. The king asked that God would grant victory when the people prayed before battle. Solomon even acknowledged that Israel would inevitably fail to keep the Covenant and go into exile (see 2 Kgs 24–25 and 2 Chr 36). But the king also implored God to hear the exiles when they turned toward the Temple and confessed their sin.

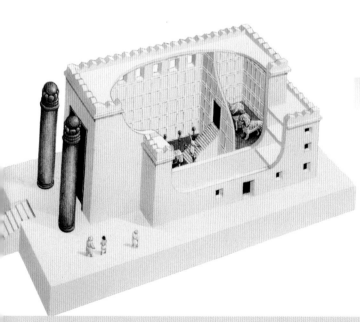

HIGH PLACES AND THE TEMPLE

Israelites could slaughter animals for food anywhere, but Mosaic Covenant sacrifices were to be offered at the Tabernacle/Temple (Lev 17:8–9; Deut 12:5–7). Sacrifice at places sacred to idols (called high places) led to idolatry. Kings who tolerated or built high places were condemned; those who removed them were praised for Covenant faithfulness.

God Accepts the Temple

After Solomon's prayer, fire descended from heaven and consumed the sacrifices he had offered. Then the Temple filled with smoke and the glory of God, so that the priests had to evacuate the building. Herds of cattle and flocks of sheep were sacrificed over the course of seven days to dedicate the Temple and its altar.

The night the celebration ended, God appeared to Solomon in a dream and reaffirmed His Covenant with David. God's message concluded with the warning that though He accepted Solomon's Temple, it would not be a talisman that would ward off the Covenant curses (Deut 28) if Israel was unfaithful to God.

BIBLICAL LINKS

"Heaven is My throne, and Earth My footstool. What sort of house will you build for Me? says the Lord, or what is My resting place? Did not My hand make all these things?" *(Isaiah 66:1–2; Acts 7:49–50, HCSB)*

WORLD'S BIGGEST BARBECUE

The Mother Nature Network reports that the current world records for beef barbecue are held by Paraguay (2008), where 61,600 pounds of meat or 41 cows were cooked, and Australia (2011) for a team marathon barbecue lasting 26.5 hours. In comparison, King Solomon's dedication of the Temple in Jerusalem involved the slaughter of 22,000 cattle and 120,000 sheep and lasted seven days (2 Chr 7:5, 8).

"But will God indeed live on earth with man? Even heaven, the highest heaven, cannot contain You, much less this Temple I have built."
(2 Chronicles 6:18, HCSB)

KING JOSIAH'S RESTORATION
(2 Chronicles 34–35)

Josiah became king of Judah when he was eight years old. At age 16, he began to seek God's favor, and by age 22 he had begun destroying all the idols and high places in Judah and Jerusalem. This purge of idolatry included the execution of the priests of Baal and Asherah. In order to permanently desecrate altars of the idols, Josiah used them to burn the bones of the priests. He even applied these reforms in the territories of the old northern kingdom that had come under his control.

A Book Is Recovered

At age 28, Josiah began a restoration of the Temple complex. It had been more than 300 years since Solomon had constructed it, and after neglect due to the nation's idolatry, the Temple needed a lot of work. People donated money at the Temple and the funds were entrusted to skilled builders.

In the course of the work, "the book of the Law" was found (possibly Deuteronomy). The book was presented to the king, who tore his robes in anguish when it was read to him. It seemed the Mosaic instruction for the kings to make their own copy of the Law to guide their decisions had long been neglected. The king had not recognized the extent of the Israelites unfaithfulness to God's Covenant. But now Josiah saw that the tragedies that had befallen Israel and Judah were the curses promised as judgment on Covenant unfaithfulness (Deut 28).

Josiah Initiates Reforms

Josiah ordered his advisors to seek a word from God, and they returned with a message from Huldah, a prophetess. God affirmed the imminent destruction of Judah. But because of Josiah's penitence over Judah's sin and his humility before God, the king would experience peace during his reign. The judgment would be delayed until after his death.

Josiah completed his reforms by calling the people to reaffirm loyalty to the Mosaic Covenant at a ceremony in Jerusalem. In order to emphasize the basis for the Covenant, the nation then celebrated the Passover in a grand fashion not seen since the days of Samuel. The king and his officials provided sacrificial animals for the assembled people. For the rest of his reign, the people abided by the Law of Moses. Unfortunately, the people's commitment to the Mosaic Covenant ended when Josiah died.

FAILURE OF THE KINGS

At this time in Judah, the primary responsibility of the king was to ensure that his people obeyed the Law of Moses. Josiah's reforms represent the greatest fulfillment of that charge and its human impossibility. Josiah destroyed idols and required obedience to the Law, but he could not change the people's heart (Deut 30:6; Ezek 11:9).

RECOVERY OF THE LAW

Scholarly consensus is that the book recovered was Deuteronomy (or some form of it). Among many features of Josiah's reforms paralleled in Deuteronomy are the centralization of worship, elimination of high places (Deut 12), and the emphasis on Covenant curses (Deut 28). Some have speculated that the document brought to Josiah was a pious fraud, but recent scholarship has argued for the relative antiquity of many features of Deuteronomy. It is not clear how the Law was actually "lost," though it may have been hidden during the Assyrian siege or the apostasies of Kings Manasseh or Amon (2 Chr 32–33).

"So Josiah removed everything that was detestable from all the lands belonging to the Israelites, and he required all who were present in Israel to serve the Lord their God. Throughout his reign they did not turn aside from following Yahweh, the God of their ancestors."

(2 Chronicles 34:33, HCSB)

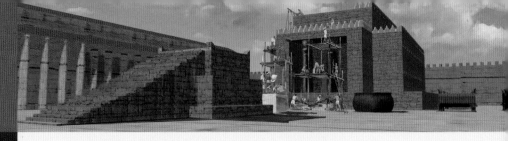

EZRA

Ezra describes the rebuilding of the Temple that began when Zerubbabel brought Jews back to Jerusalem from Babylon. Despite opposition, the Persian king Cyrus' original command was confirmed and aided by Artaxerxes and Darius. The final chapters describe a second return under Ezra and the reestablishment of the Mosaic Covenant.

LOCATION: The events of Ezra are primarily set in Jerusalem. The imperial letters recorded in Ezra would have been written in the Persian city of Susa or Babylon.

ORIGIN: The Hebrew text of Ezra and Nehemiah was received as one book. The later divisions, designated "Ezra" and "Nehemiah," are the memoirs of these men, supplemented by imperial Persian documents and Jewish records. The final version may have been written by Nehemiah or Ezra, about 420 B.C.E.

KEY PASSAGES

Restoration Under Zerubbabel and Jeshua: The Temple (1–6)

1:1–11	Cyrus Orders Construction of the Temple
3:1–13	Jews Start Sacrifices and Construction
4:1–6:22	Opposition Is Overcome and the Temple Completed

Restoration Under Ezra: The Law (7–10)

7:12–28	Artaxerxes Commissions Ezra
9:1–10:17	Ezra Resolves the Problem of Foreign Wives

PRINCIPAL FIGURES

God In the books of Ezra and Nehemiah, God appears as the One who fulfills His promise to restore the Jews to the Promised Land.

Cyrus Persian (Median) king who conquered Babylon and ordered the rebuilding of the Jerusalem Temple.

Zerubbabel Jewish official who led a major migration from Babylon back to Judea.

Sheshbazzar Governor of Judea when Zerubbabel returned from Babylon.

Jeshua The High Priest who supervised the construction of the second Temple.

Rehum Persian official who urged Artaxerxes to suspend work on the Temple.

Shimshai A scribe who joined with Rehum to lobby for work on the Temple to stop.

Artaxerxes Persian (Median) king who suspended work on the Temple until Cyrus' original order to construct it was confirmed.

Darius Persian king who provided support to complete the Temple.

Ezra Scribe who implemented observance of the Law of Moses after the Babylonian Exile.

After years of work, the Temple was still not complete. The foundation had been laid and sacrifices were being offered (Ezra 3), but opposition had delayed the construction (Ezra 4–5). To help fund the work, the Persian king Darius ordered that the imperial treasury be opened to Zerubbabel and Jeshua. Any who opposed the construction of God's House would see the central beam of their own house removed and would then be impaled on it.

With imperial support, and the encouragement of the prophets Haggai and Zechariah, the Temple was finished (516 B.C.E.). The dedication ceremony was much smaller than the one Solomon celebrated when the first Temple was completed (2 Chr 7) but was still a joyous occasion.

Afterward, the people celebrated the Passover for seven days, commemorating God's first liberation of the nation from foreign slavery on the symbolic end of the second liberation from foreign slavery.

THE END OF IDOLATRY IN ISRAEL

The Babylonian Exile ended Israel's national love affair with worshipping idols. The end of formal idol-worship did not mean the end of challenges to Israel's commitment to God, though. Struggles with pagan influences continued; for example, marrying foreign wives (compare Ezra 9–10 with Num 25, Deut 7:3–4, and 1 Kgs 11).

"So the Jewish elders continued successfully with the building under the prophesying of Haggai the prophet and Zechariah son of Iddo. They finished the building according to the command of the God of Israel and the decrees of Cyrus, Darius, and King Artaxerxes of Persia."
(Ezra 6:14, HCSB)

NEHEMIAH

This book describes Nehemiah's efforts to secure the physical and spiritual safety of Jerusalem after the return from exile in Babylon. Despite the support of the Persian king, Nehemiah faced life-threatening challenges from opponents in Samaria. The book records several of Nehemiah's appeals to God for aid and protection.

KEY PASSAGES

Nehemiah Returns to Jerusalem (1–2)

1:1–2:10	The King Commissions Nehemiah to Help Jerusalem
2:11–20	Nehemiah Mobilizes Jerusalem

Rebuilding the Wall In Spite of Opposition (3–7)

4:1–23	Nehemiah Counters Samaritan Opposition
5:1–19	Nehemiah Counters Jewish Oppression
6:1–19	The Wall Is Completed

Reading the Law and Restoring the Covenant (8–10)

7:73–8:12	Ezra Explains the Law of Moses
9:1–31	Judea Confesses the Sins of the Nation
10:28–39	Judea Vows Faithfulness to the Mosaic Covenant

The Reorganization of Jerusalem (11–13)

PRINCIPAL FIGURES

God In the books of Ezra and Nehemiah, God appears as the One who fulfills His promise to restore the Jews to the Promised Land.

Nehemiah The Persian king's cupbearer who was commissioned to rebuild the walls of Jerusalem and became Governor of Judea.

Artaxerxes The Persian (Median) king who suspended work on the Temple until Cyrus' original order to construct it was confirmed.

Sanballat A Samaritan official who conspired to prevent the rebuilding of Jerusalem's walls and to assassinate Nehemiah.

Tobiah A co-conspirator with Sanballat against Nehemiah.

Geshem An Arab who conspired with Sanballat and Tobiah against Nehemiah.

Ezra A scribe who implemented observance of the Law of Moses after the Babylonian Exile.

LOCATION: Nehemiah begins in Susa, but the scene quickly shifts to Jerusalem and the work on the walls. Opposition arose from Samaria, the territory immediately north of Judea.

ORIGIN: The Hebrew text of Ezra and Nehemiah was received as one book. The later divisions, designated "Ezra" and "Nehemiah," are the memoirs of these men, supplemented by imperial Persian documents and Jewish records. The final version may have been written by Nehemiah, or more likely Ezra, about 420 B.C.E.

NEHEMIAH IS SENT TO JERUSALEM
(Nehemiah 2)

Jerusalem was defenseless. That was the report Nehemiah heard when one of his brothers arrived in the Persian capital of Susa from Judah. Nehemiah was heartbroken, and after several days of fasting, he prayed to God. Nehemiah confessed that he and his people had sinned against God, resulting in their current desperate state. He acknowledged that God had warned the nation that sin would lead to exile (Deut 4:25–27), but he also affirmed his faith in God's promise to gather the people back from the ends of the earth if they repented (Deut. 30:1–5).

Nehemiah was the cupbearer to the Persian king. His responsibility to protect the king from poison implied complete trust. It gave Nehemiah an opportunity to speak to the king about Jerusalem. But that opportunity also carried risk. If Nehemiah was seen to be disturbed or nervous, he might be suspected of plotting against the king. So, when the king did in fact question him, Nehemiah was terrified. But he also spoke boldly, telling the king about his concern for Jerusalem.

When the king heard Nehemiah's concern, he asked what Nehemiah wanted. Nehemiah was ready and responded with a detailed request for permission and aid to rebuild the walls of Jerusalem. Nehemiah asked for a leave of absence, material support, a military escort, and letters instructing various imperial officials to help him. The king granted Nehemiah all the supplies and assistance he had requested and sent him to restore the walls of Jerusalem.

THE RETURNS OF THE EXILES

The return of the Jews from captivity in Babylon was not a single event. As the deportation had happened in stages, so did the return. The major phases are represented by Zerubbabel (Ezra 1–2), Ezra (Ezra 7–8), and Nehemiah (Neh 7). These journeys occurred in 538, 458, and 445 B.C.E., respectively.

"The king granted my requests, for I was graciously strengthened by my God."
(Nehemiah 2:8, HCSB)

NEHEMIAH

BUILDING THE WALL OF JERUSALEM
(Nehemiah 3–7)

Nehemiah arrived in Jerusalem and assessed state of the city's walls (Neh 2). He made a nighttime inspection before announcing his intention to rebuild the wall. When he addressed the people, priests, and nobles, they endorsed the project. Officials from the neighboring province of Samaria, however, mocked the people and suggested that the Jews were rebelling against the king of Persia. The restoration of the Temple (Ezra 4) and Jerusalem's walls were a threat to the Samaritans' dominance of the province.

Samaritan Opposition

The families of Jerusalem were each given responsibility for constructing the part of the wall and the gate nearest to their home (Neh 3). But Samaritan leaders conspired to raid the city and attacked Jews coming to help (Neh 4). Nehemiah responded by arming the people and stationing half of them at the low places in the wall. Eventually, the Samaritan leaders attempted to lure Nehemiah into an ambush (Neh 6). When this failed, they accused Nehemiah of treason against Persia.

Further Problems

Samaritan opposition was not the only threat to completing the wall, however. Rather than aid the poor around them, the rich in Jerusalem had made loans for interest, taking control of productive land as collateral (Neh 5). When the poor complained that this left them unable to repay the loans and forced them to sell their children into slavery, Nehemiah became furious. He reminded the nobles of their efforts to buy back Jews who had been sold into slavery to foreigners and commanded them to restore the people's land and the interest they had paid. Resolution of this internal tension allowed Jerusalem's relatively small population to work together effectively, preventing work on the wall from grinding to a halt.

The Wall Is Rebuilt

With the major threats resolved, the work on the wall proceeded quickly. Though there were further attempts to intimidate Nehemiah, the work continued and Jerusalem's defenses were rebuilt. The restoration of Jerusalem provided protection for the residents and encouraged the return of Jewish exiles (Neh 7).

SAMARITAN-JEWISH TENSIONS

Hostility between Samaritans and Jews continued in the inter-Testamental period (400 B.C.E.–30 C.E.). Samaritans built a rival Temple on Mount Gerizim, which a Jewish ruler later destroyed (111 B.C.E.). In 6 C.E., a group of Samaritans desecrated the Temple in Jerusalem by spreading human bones around the outer porches.

CITY DEFENSES

Basic town fortification might include a tower or a small fortress, where people could take refuge during a raid (see Judg 9:46–52). City walls provided better defense and developed into elaborate fortifications involving towers, fortified gates with defended approaches, and double walls designed to absorb the attacks of siege engines. An imperial power's decision to allow a city to rebuild its walls was a significant sign of trust in the city's loyalty to the empire.

"The wall was completed in 52 days, on the twenty-fifth day of the month Elul. When all our enemies heard this, all the surrounding nations were intimidated and lost their confidence, for they realized that this task had been accomplished by our God."

(Nehemiah 6:15–16, HCSB)

NEHEMIAH

After the wall was completed, the people gathered in Jerusalem. Ezra the scribe brought out the Law of Moses and stood on a raised platform among the leading priests, reading the Law from dawn to noon.

The First Sermon

When Ezra unrolled the scrolls, the people stood in respect to hear them read. Unfortunately, the primary language of the people was no longer the classical Hebrew in which the Law had been written. The people spoke Aramaic, which was the common language of the region. Ezra and the other priests translated as they read and also explained what they were reading. Though records of oral proclamation in the Bible began in Genesis, Ezra's preaching was the first explicit example of some already-written part of the Bible being read publicly and explained to the listeners; it was the first sermon.

The people wept as they heard the Law read, realizing how far the nation had fallen from faithfulness to the Covenant and the curses that disobedience had incurred. But they were comforted by Nehemiah and Ezra, who refused to allow their tears. Instead, they sent the people to feast and celebrate the greatness and loving kindness of God. Though understanding the Scripture had initially caused conviction and grief, it ultimately resulted in joy and celebration.

The Feast of Booths

As the Law was read and explained, the people heard the commandment for the "Feast of Booths" (Lev 23:23–43). This festival required the people to live in tents ("booths") for seven days as a memorial to the Exodus journey. The time in the tents reminded them of the purification of the nation as it wandered in the wilderness for 40 years. Leaving the tents for their permanent homes symbolized their arrival in the Promised Land.

The Feast of Booths became a central image through which the people's experience of exile in Babylon and rebuilding of the Temple and Wall of Jerusalem were understood. God had used the exile to purify the nation, just as He had purified the nation through the wilderness wandering. The result in both cases was to be faithfulness to God through the Mosaic Covenant. Celebration of the feast would be a ceremonial reenactment of that purification, which if grounded in actual Covenant faithfulness would help the people to avoid yet another purifying journey through the desert.

BIBLICAL LINKS

"This is why we constantly thank God, because when you received the message about God that you heard from us, you welcomed it not as a human message, but as it truly is, the message of God, which also works effectively in you believers."
(1 Thessalonians 2:13, HCSB)

SECURITY THROUGH COVENANT LOYALTY

Ezra and Nehemiah reflect Israel's post-exile conviction that national security depended on Covenant loyalty. Practically, this led some to emphasize the reading and teaching of the Law to the people and others to focus on the purity of the Temple worship. These emphases are not mutually exclusive and are both visible in the books of Ezra and Nehemiah.

THE PREACHER'S TASK

Ezra's explanation of the Law of Moses to the people brought about conviction and sorrow in people who did not realize the extent of their disobedience to God. Yet Ezra's task was not to destroy, but to comfort those who sincerely turned to Yahweh. This illustrates the job of all preachers in the Bible (the prophets and the apostles) and those who follow in their footsteps: "Afflict the comfortable, and comfort the afflicted, with the Word of God."

"Then all the people began to eat and drink, send portions, and have a great celebration, because they had understood the words that were explained to them."

(Nehemiah 8:12, HCSB)

ESTHER

The book of Esther explains the origin of the Jewish festival of Purim. It traces the rise of Queen Esther and the Amalakite Haman's hatred for Esther's uncle, Mordecai, a conflict that echoes the ancient enmity between Israel and the Amalakites (Exod 15:17; Num 24:7; 1 Sam 15). Esther courageously foils Haman's plot and preserves the Jews.

LOCATION: Esther records parties and plots that occurred in the imperial palace of the Persian king in Susa. Empire-wide events are described near the end.

ORIGIN: The book of Esther is anonymous, but the majority view attributes it to Mordecai. Others have suggested Nehemiah or Ezra. The events occurred during Xerxes' reign, suggesting that the book was written sometime after 486–464 B.C.E., but before the fall of the Persian Empire (332 B.C.E.).

KEY PASSAGES

Esther Becomes Queen (1–2)

1:1–22	The Fall of Queen Vashti
2:1–19	The Rise of Queen Esther
2:21–23	Mordecai Foils a Plot to Kill the King

Esther Foils Haman's Plot (3–7)

3:1–15	Haman Plots to Kill the Jews
4:1–17	Mordecai Exhorts Esther to Intervene
5:1–14	Esther Risks the King's Wrath
6:1–14	Haman Is Forced to Honor Mordecai
7:1–10	Haman Is Executed for Threatening Esther's People

The Feast of Purim Is Established (8–10)

PRINCIPAL FIGURES

God   Though not named directly, God's presence is implied in Esther as the Providential Sovereign over history.

Ahasuerus   The Persian king who was maneuvered into creating and eliminating the threat to the Jews in Persia.

Vashti   Wife of the Persian king, divorced for refusing to appear wearing only her crown for the entertainment of the king's guests at an imperial feast.

Mordecai   A Benjamite and Esther's uncle who prevented the king's assassination and advised Esther on foiling a plot to destroy the Jews.

Esther, also called Hadassah   A beautiful Jewish woman who became Queen and brought down Haman before he could destroy the Jews.

Haman   A descendent of the Amalakites, who conspired to murder Mordecai and all Jews in Persia.

ESTHER FOILS HAMAN'S PLOT
(Esther 3–8)

Haman hated Mordecai. Though the immediate cause was Mordecai's refusal to prostrate himself before Haman, a high official of the Persian king, the rivalry reflected a centuries-old grudge between Israel and the Amalekites. Haman decided to destroy Mordecai and his people. He bribed the king to authorize destruction of the Jews as rebels. He then built his own gallows so that he could personally execute Mordecai.

What neither Haman nor King Ahasuerus realized was that his wife, Queen Esther, was a Jew. The king had conducted a "beauty pageant" to find a new wife, and Esther had kept her nationality secret. Haman also did not know that Mordecai was the queen's uncle. He informed Esther of Haman's plot and suggested to Esther that her coronation might have come precisely so that she could rescue the Jews. His point implied that God's hand had been involved from the beginning. Esther asked Mordecai to pray for her and then approached the king. She invited him and Haman to eat a private feast with her. At the meal, the king asked what she wanted. Instead of answering, she invited him and Haman to another meal.

That night, the king read from the royal histories. They recorded that Mordecai had uncovered a plot to assassinate the king. Haman happened to be nearby, so the king asked how he should reward a great service. Haman thought he was to be honored, so he suggested being dressed in royal robes and paraded on a king's horse, led by a high official. The king then ordered Haman to do just that for Mordecai. Haman was infuriated but obeyed the king's orders. His wife encouraged him with the reminder that the queen was honoring him alongside the king himself with her dinner invitation.

At the second dinner, the king again asked Esther what she wanted. She begged the king to spare her life and that of her people from a murderous plot. The king demanded to know who was behind the plot. Based on Mordecai's report, Esther turned and identified Haman. Haman was hanged on the gallows he had built for Mordecai.

WHERE WAS GOD?

Esther is one of only two Biblical books that make no direct reference to God (Song of Solomon is the other). This explains the books' relatively late acceptance into the Old Testament canon. Yet the book implies God's hand in the providential positioning of Esther as queen and the king reading that a Jew prevented a plot to assassinate him.

JOB

The book of Job is a deep reflection on suffering and the character of God. Job's patience proves that his piety was not a response to God's blessings. But when his friends press their accusations, Job grows impatient and judges God to be unjust. The tension resolves when God humbles and restores Job.

LOCATION: Several of the proper names in Job (Uz, Eliphaz, Temah) are associated with Edom, suggesting the events took place south or southeast of the Dead Sea.

ORIGIN: The book of Job does not claim an author, though one Talmudic source suggests Moses. The events described could have taken place as early as 2000 B.C.E. However, the book likely was written after the 900s B.C.E. and probably predated Ezekiel in the 570s B.C.E. (see Ezek 14:14).

KEY PASSAGES

God Allows Satan to Afflict Job (1–2)

1:6–22	Satan Tests Job
2:1–10	Satan Tests Job Again

The Justice of God's Reign Over Humanity is Debated (3–30)

8:1–7	Bildad Assumes Suffering Indicates Judgment
19:23–29	Job Hopes for Vindication

Elihu Confronts Job and His Friends (31–37)

37:14–24	Elihu Asserts That Men Lack Knowledge to Judge God

God Humbles Job (38–42:9)

God Restores Job (42:10–17)

PRINCIPAL FIGURES

God   In Job, God is the Sovereign Ruler whose power is never in question, but whose justice is questioned in Job's suffering.

Satan   An angelic figure who accuses Job of piety-for-pay and requests permission to afflict Job in order to prove his case.

Job   The main human character whose suffering leads to a confrontation with his friends and eventually with God Himself.

Eliphaz   One of Job's friends who came to comfort, but ended up accusing.

Bildad   A second friend of Job's who afflicted rather than comforted him.

Zophar   Job's third friend who argued with Job instead of sympathizing with him.

Elihu   The young man who alone spoke wisdom to Job and his friends before God spoke.

"Then Job stood up, tore his robe, and shaved his head. He fell to the ground and worshiped, saying: 'Naked I came from my mother's womb, and naked I will leave this life. The Lord gives, and the Lord takes away. Praise the name of Yahweh.' Throughout all this Job did not sin or blame God for anything."

(Job 1:20–22, HCSB)

Job was a very wealthy man, but he was also a good man. He acted with integrity, respected God deeply, and avoided evil. One day, Satan presented himself before God and heard God's praise of Job. Satan was not impressed. He sneered that Job only feared God because God was blessing him. If God took away Job's wealth, Satan insisted, Job would curse God to His face. Though Job had not sinned against God, God allowed Satan to take away Job's wealth.

First, a servant came to report that he was the lone survivor of a raid that had taken all of Job's oxen and donkeys. A second servant told Job that he alone remained after a lightning storm destroyed Job's sheep. Yet a third cried that all the camels had been stolen.

Finally, Job was told that a whirlwind had collapsed the house where his children had gathered, killing them all. Although these messages came one after another, Job acknowledged God's right to rule and did not condemn God.

Satan, however, remained skeptical. When God challenged Satan with Job's faithfulness, Satan replied that Job still had one thing left: his health. Again, Satan insisted that if God removed this last blessing, Job would curse God to His face. God allowed Satan to afflict Job with boils. This time, even Job's wife suggested that it would be better to curse God and die than go on living. Job still refused to judge God's providence, but the countdown clock had begun ticking on Job's patience.

THE PROBLEM OF EVIL

Job's story addresses the question of why an all-powerful, loving God would allow evil. If there is an all-powerful God, He could prevent evil. If that God is good, then He would want to prevent evil. So why is there evil? The answer can involve the value of human free will in spite of evil choices, the value of suffering for refining God's people, or both. Job also emphasizes the importance of trusting God even when answers are not readily apparent.

JOB

Job's friends came to mourn his tragic losses. Following custom, they remained silent until Job spoke, a lament cursing the day of his birth. What followed were a series of arguments debating the justice of God's rule over the world.

Eliphaz, Bildad, and Zophar each assumed that Job's suffering was punishment for hidden sin. Because God gives people what they deserve (Job 11:20) and does so justly (Job 8:3), they concluded that Job must have sinned (Job 4:17). They encouraged Job to act wisely (Job 5:2) and recognize that God had wisdom that men could not fathom (Job 11:6).

His friends' attempt to help Job actually increased his anguish. He was clearly suffering, and he knew that his suffering was permitted by God, but he was not aware of having committed a sin. Since none of the men could see any reason for suffering other than punishment, Job was faced with a dilemma.

Job Questions God's Righteousness

Job had acknowledged the righteousness of God at the beginning (Job 1:21–22). But faced with choosing between God's righteousness and his own, God's wisdom and his own, Job judged God lacking (Job 27:1–6). He agreed that no one could be right before God, but only because they couldn't resist God's power (Job 9:4); even the pure would be impure if God willed it (Job 9:30–31). Job claimed that God destroys the evil and the innocent alike, laughing at their demise (Job 9:22–23). As for wisdom, Job asserted that God could not understand his situation because He has no experience of life as a man (Job 10:4–5). Though the thought terrified him, Job called for a trial in which he could cross-examine God (Job 9:32–35).

Elihu's Counsel

In the end, it was only the young man Elihu, another friend of Job's, who spoke wisdom. Though he agreed with the others that God is always just, he was angry at the three friends for condemning Job without being able to identify his sin (Job 32:3). Yet he was also angry that Job's defense was to judge God to be unjust (Job 32:2). When the choice was between baseless accusations and blaspheming God, Elihu counseled silence until God made matters clear (Job 34:29–30).

BIBLICAL LINKS

"For I am not conscious of anything against myself, but I am not justified by this. The One who evaluates me is the Lord. Therefore don't judge anything prematurely, before the Lord comes, who will both bring to light what is hidden in darkness and reveal the intentions of the hearts." *(1 Corinthians 4:4–5, HCSB)*

DEUTERONOMIC PRINCIPLE

Job and his friends expected God to act justly (see Deut 28). But they also assumed that suffering indicated punishment and blessing vindicated righteousness. Since Job was convinced of his innocence, he decided God was unjust. The book argues that God uses suffering in the lives of the righteous (see Jas 1:2–18).

NAMES FOR GOD: *YAHWEH*

God revealed His proper name to Moses in the desert of Sinai (Exod 3:14). The name means "I AM Who I AM" or "I AM Because I AM," and describes God as the eternal and unchanging God. Many of the names for God in Hebrew are built on God's proper name, Yahweh. These include *Yahweh Yireh* (God Will Provide), *Yahweh M'Kaddesh* (The God Who Sanctifies), *Yahweh Shalom* (God, Our Peace), and *Yahweh Moshiah Goel* (God Your Savior and Redeemer). One name Job would have appreciated was *Yahweh Makkeh* (God Who Strikes).

"God rescues the afflicted by their affliction; He instructs them by their torment."
(Job 36:15, HCSB)

JOB

GOD CONFRONTS JOB
(Job 38–42)

When Job's debate with his friends ended, God addressed Job. Speaking from a whirlwind, God demanded to know who was competent to judge the Creator (Job 38:2). God's first speech (Job 38:4–40:5) amounted to an oral exam in poetic language, exposing Job's ignorance of the natural order. That ignorance left Job unable to assess the justice and wisdom of God's governance (design) of the world. Job admitted that instead of knowing enough to judge the Creator, he knew virtually nothing (Job 40:4–5).

God Reveals Job's Arrogance

God's second speech turned to Job's impotent foolishness (Job 40:6–42:6). God suggested that if Job could defeat human pride and wickedness throughout the world, then God would step aside and let Job become savior and judge (40:7–14). But Job could couldn't even control the great creatures of the natural world. He could neither appreciate nor tame the creature called "Behemoth" (Job 40:15–24). Nor was he able to control "Leviathan" and make him useful (Job 41). Job confessed that God's power and wisdom in ordering the world was far above his ability to understand or judge (Job 42:1–6); he humbled himself before his Creator.

Though Job's friends must have expected the humiliation of Job to be a mere prelude to his destruction by God's wrath, God rounded on them in His final speech (Job 42:7–8). God accused them of not speaking the truth about Him as Job did (see Job 42:2–6). He ordered them to offer a sacrifice but made acceptance depend on Job's intercession for them.

BIBLICAL LINKS

"For you were called to this, because Christ also suffered for you, leaving you an example, so that you should follow in His steps. He did not commit sin, and no deceit was found in His mouth; when He was reviled, He did not revile in return; when He was suffering, He did not threaten but entrusted Himself to the One who judges justly." *(1 Peter 2:21–23, HCSB)*

FORGIVENESS AND INTERCESSION

The Bible often portrays God as angry yet forgiving when a righteous person intercedes. The surprising element in the pattern is that God Himself provokes the righteous person to intercede—for example, Abraham for Abimelech (Gen 20), priests for the people (Joel 2:17), and Amos for Israel (Amos 7:5–6).

A Heart Humbled is Righteous

God had shown grace and forgiveness to Job for arrogantly judging God. Job was allowed to reflect God's character by showing grace and forgiveness to his friends for arrogantly accusing Job of sin without cause. The book ends with God's restoration and expansion of blessing in Job's life, demonstrating that He found a heart He had humbled more righteous than the blameless life Job lived at the beginning.

BEHEMOTH AND LEVIATHAN

When ancients thought of taming the natural world, they might have pointed to the great strength of the ox (Deut 25:4) or the power and speed of the horse (Ps 32:9) as proof of human ability to gain dominion over animals and make them useful in human labor (Gen 1:28). In His dispute with Job, God pointed to other animals that humans had not tamed. "Behemoth" may have been a reference to the hippopotamus, and "Leviathan" a reference to the crocodile. Both were considered dangerous and untamable.

"Get ready to answer Me like a man; When I question you, you will inform Me. Would you really challenge My justice? Would you declare Me guilty to justify yourself?"

(Job 40:7–8, HCSB)

PSALMS

Psalms is a collection of 150 songs that were used both in the public worship of the Temple and in private worship of God. The Psalms are primarily direct addresses to God on the part of their authors. They express deep emotions, including joy, confidence, gratitude, sorrow, and anguish.

LOCATION: Authors are given in the titles of 99 out of the 150 Psalms. David is credited with 73, Asaph with 12, and the sons of Korah with 9. Solomon wrote two, and Moses, Ethan, and Heman each wrote one. Authorship or content indicates that Psalms were written between 1400 and 586 B.C.E.

ORIGIN: Most of the Psalms were written in Jerusalem. Some were written in other locations, such as the Judean wilderness and in Babylon during the Exile.

KEY PASSAGES

Book 1 (1–41)

Psalm 1:	The Song of the Two Ways
Psalm 2:	The Empire of the Son
Psalm 8:	The Creator and His Image
Psalm 16:	Hope of Deliverance
Psalm 22:	The Un-Forsaken Singer
Psalm 23:	The Good Shepherd
Psalm 24:	Who May Worship?

Book 2 (42–72)

Psalm 42:	As the Deer Thirsts
Psalm 49:	True Wealth
Psalm 51:	David's Prayer for Forgiveness
Psalm 71:	An Old Man's Prayer

Book 3 (73–89)

Psalm 74:	A Prayer for Israel
Psalm 89:	Is David Discarded?

Book 4 (90–106)

Psalm 90:	The Song of Moses
Psalm 91:	The Protection of God
Psalm 96–99:	The Royal Songs
Psalm 105:	God's Faithfulness
Psalm 106:	Israel's Unfaithfulness

Book 5 (107–150)

Psalm 107:	God Delivers His People
Psalm 110:	The Coronation of the Son
Psalm 115:	Glory to God Alone
Psalm 119:	The Love of God's Word
Psalm 137:	The Exile's Lament
Psalm 139:	God Is There
Psalm 150:	The Hallelujah Chorus

PRINCIPAL FIGURES

God Appearing by many names, God is consistently the object of worship, praise, and trust in the Psalms.

David Israel's second king, who sang to soothe King Saul and wrote nearly half the Psalms.

Asaph Possibly a Levite who was appointed by David as a musician and performed in the dedication of the Temple.

Sons of Korah Members of a guild of Levitical priests who served in the Temple in Jerusalem.

HEBREW POETRY

One of the primary features of Hebrew poetry is the pairing of lines in a structure known as *parallelism*. Parallelism is found across the Hebrew poetry of the Bible, primarily in Job, Psalms, Proverbs, Ecclesiastes, and Song of Solomon, but also in many other places, such as the prophetic books. There are three major forms of Hebrew parallelism:

Synonymous Parallelism: Two or more lines that communicate the same idea using different words or images.

Antithetical Parallelism: Two or more lines that make a contrast between thoughts or images.

Synthetic (Constructive) Parallelism: Two or more lines that are linked to develop an idea from line to line.

Parallelism is not found in every stanza but being sensitive to these pairings helps make sense of the rhythm and repetition of the Biblical poetry.

Psalm 1 (HCSB)

[1] How happy is the man

Synonymous Parallelism → who does not follow the advice of the wicked

or take the path of sinners

or join a group of mockers!

Synthetic Parallelism → [2] Instead, his delight is in the Lord's instruction,

and he meditates on it day and night.

[3] He is like a tree planted beside streams of water

that bears its fruit in season

and whose leaf does not wither.

Whatever he does prospers.

[4] The wicked are not like this; instead, they are like chaff that the wind blows away.

Synonymous Parallelism → [5] Therefore the wicked will not survive the judgment,

and sinners will not be in the community of the righteous.

Antithetical Parallelism → [6] For the Lord watches over the way of the righteous,

but the way of the wicked leads to ruin.

PSALMS

Psalm 1

The First Psalm contrasts the righteous man (1:1–3) with the wicked man (1:4–5) and summarizes God's response to both (1:6). The imagery highlights the stability of the righteous and the instability of the wicked. This sense of movement is also reflected in the deliberate pace of the first stanza describing the righteous, the hectic tempo of the second stanza describing the wicked, and the blunt brevity of the third stanza suggesting the inevitability of the divine judgment.

The happiness of the righteous is a matter of what he avoids, as well as what he embraces. The psalm sees the righteous man refusing to settle into a pattern of evil (1:1). Instead, he finds joy in God's Law, leading him to let it permeate his thinking at all times (1:2). As a result, the righteous have a source of nourishment that does not fail and which makes them strong and fruitful (1:3).

"The wicked are not like this." Instead of finding stability and strength, there is only a fleeting glimpse of the wicked being blown away in the breeze (1:4). The imagery of the psalm points to the ultimate judgment of God (1:5), which the wicked will not withstand.

The psalm locates the distinction between the ultimate outcome for the righteous and the wicked in the character of God (1:6). The Lord protects the path of the righteous but allows the path of the wicked to reach its ruinous destination. The stark contrast in Psalm 1 is the gateway to the book, casting each psalm as a signpost on the way of the righteous.

WISDOM PSALMS

The literary devices and images in the wisdom psalms are similar to those in Proverbs and Ecclesiastes. They typically contrast the righteous and wicked, and wisdom and folly. These are defined in terms of humility or pride in relation to God and the Mosaic Law. The wisdom psalms include Psalms 1, 19, 37, 73, and 127.

Psalm 73

Psalm 73 tells the story of a singer who almost slipped onto the wrong path. He looked around him and saw that the wicked seemed to grow more and more wealthy. As a result, he began to envy those who were not loyal to God. It seemed that the wicked had an easy life. They had plenty of food and were always in good health. They were proud and powerful, able to do whatever they wanted. They could speak their mind without fear of reprisal. As a result of these things, the wicked became popular. They did not think God noticed their sins.

The psalmist started to wonder if he had been faithful to God for nothing. But when he focused his attention on God, he realized the destiny of the wicked. They stood on shaky ground and would be swept away by sudden disaster.

The singer realized that bitterness had made him foolish, but that God's hand had protected him. God would guide the singer though life and into God's glorious presence after death. Most of all, he realized that God was the most valuable thing in existence. To have God was to have everything.

BIBLICAL LINKS

"Why do you call Me 'Lord, Lord,' and don't do the things I say? I will show you what someone is like who comes to Me, hears My words, and acts on them: He is like a man building a house, who dug deep and laid the foundation on the rock. When the flood came, the river crashed against that house and couldn't shake it, because it was well built. But the one who hears and does not act is like a man who built a house on the ground without a foundation. The river crashed against it, and immediately it collapsed. And the destruction of that house was great!"
(Luke 6:46–49, HCSB)

"For the Lord watches over the way of the righteous, but the way of the wicked leads to ruin."
(Psalm 1:6, HCSB)

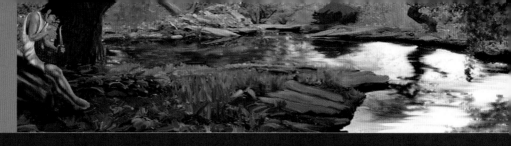

PSALMS

Psalm 2

The Second Psalm completes the introduction to Psalms. Where Psalm 1 speaks of individuals, Psalm 2 addresses the nations. The psalm is set against the background of the Davidic Covenant (2 Sam 7).

God had chosen the son of David to rule His kingdom from Jerusalem. Psalm 2 sees that kingdom encompassing the nations of the earth, which plot rebellion against the rule of God through His Anointed One. God laughs scornfully from His throne in heaven and displays terrifying wrath. God reminds the rulers of the nations that the issue of sovereignty in the kingdom is already settled. The Chosen King rules from Zion, another name for Jerusalem.

David proceeded to proclaim publically what had before been held in secret. David had been anointed king secretly long before (see 1 Sam 16:1–13), and was later publically crowned king (2 Sam 5). So also God had chosen the Son of David (2 Sam 7:12–14), and David sang of the day that this Son of David would be revealed. The nations have been given to the Son. He need only speak to begin to rule. Those who rebel will be destroyed, but those who submit to the Son will be blessed.

Psalm 2 is quoted repeatedly in the New Testament— for example, in Matt 3; Acts 4; Heb 1, 5, 12; and Rev 6, 19.

BIBLICAL LINKS

"Then the kings of the earth, the nobles, the military commanders, the rich, the powerful, and every slave and free person hid in the caves and among the rocks of the mountains. And they said to the mountains and to the rocks, 'Fall on us and hide us from the face of the One seated on the throne and from the wrath of the Lamb, because the great day of Their wrath has come! And who is able to stand?'"
(Revelation 6:15–17, HCSB)

"Pay homage to the Son or He will be angry and you will perish in your rebellion, for His anger may ignite at any moment. All those who take refuge in Him are happy."
(Psalm 2:12, HCSB)

Psalm 110

Psalm 110 identifies itself as a psalm of David. Like Psalm 2, it presumes the Davidic Covenant promises of eternal sovereignty for David's son.

God ("the Lord") speaks to David's heir ("my Lord"), giving the king a seat of honor at God's right hand until the conquest of the nations is complete (110:1). David's son would be enthusiastically supported by God's people and rule in splendor and strength (110:2–3). The king would have a role modeled on that of a pre-Israelite priest-king of Jerusalem, Melchizedek, to whom Abraham had paid homage (Gen 14). The psalm promised that God's power would defeat the nations and envisioned the rule of David's heir extending over the whole world.

Psalm 110 was the most frequently quoted psalm in the New Testament, notably in Jesus' debates with the religious leaders (Matt 22:43–45) and Peter's sermon at Pentecost (Acts 2:34–35).

ROYAL/MESSIANIC PSALMS

The Royal/Messianic psalms (see also Ps 20, 45, 72, and 89) describe the king of Israel in light of the Davidic Covenant. Many modern interpreters see them strictly as hyperbolic songs for coronation ceremonies. The New Testament authors quoted them extensively to argue that Jesus was the promised heir of David.

"This is the declaration of the Lord to my Lord: 'Sit at My right hand until I make Your enemies Your footstool.'"
(Psalm 110:1, HCSB)

PSALMS

Psalm 16

Psalm 16 records David's appeal to God for protection in a time of trouble, quite possibly when David was fleeing from the murderous rage of King Saul (1 Sam 21–27). Despite his suffering, David affirmed his loyalty to God as his greatest good. He identified himself with the joy of the "holy people" in contrast to the sorrows of idolaters (16:3–4), alluding to the comparison of the righteous and wicked in Psalm 1. Using the imagery of the division of the Promised Land (Josh 13–21), David identified God Himself as his inheritance (16:5–6). Because God guided his thought and deeds, David would not be shaken. The grave would not be his final destination, because God's Faithful One would not be abandoned to the grave (16:7–11).

Psalm 16 became a central text in the preaching of both Peter (Acts 2:25–32) and Paul (Acts 13:35).

> *"For You will not abandon me to Sheol; You will not allow Your Faithful One to see decay."*
>
> (Psalm 16:10, HCSB)

BIBLICAL LINKS

"Brothers, I can confidently speak to you about the patriarch David: He is both dead and buried, and his tomb is with us to this day. Since he was a prophet, he knew that God had sworn an oath to him to seat one of his descendants on his throne. Seeing this in advance, he spoke concerning the resurrection of the Messiah: He was not left in Hades, and His flesh did not experience decay. God has resurrected this Jesus. We are all witnesses of this." *(Acts 2:29–32, HCSB)*

Psalm 22

In Psalm 22, David moves from the crisis of feeling abandoned by God in the face of death (22:1–19) to prayer for deliverance (22:20–21) and thanksgiving (22:22–31). David's lament alternated expressions of the reality of his suffering with a determined trust in God. The psalmist bore God's silence (22:2), the sneers of his enemies (22:6–8), and the harm he suffered at their hands (22:12–18). But David's repeated expressions of confidence in God's deliverance reached a climactic crescendo in his final stanza (22:27–31). The psalm exalted that God's act of deliverance would lead families of all nations to worship God as generation after generation heard about God's mighty deed.

Jesus appealed to the powerful lament and hope of Psalm 22 as an expression of His experience of death (Matt 27:46; Mark 15:34). The Gospel writers highlighted the details of the crucifixion and the ways it in which it paralleled the psalm (Matt 27; Mark 25; Luke 23; John 19). Lines 6-8 describe the mocking and ridicule of the psalmist. The onlookers at the crucifixion heaped scorn on Christ, paraphrasing the taunt "He has put His trust in God; Let God rescue Him now" (Matt 27:43). The singer cried out that his hand and feet had been pierced. All four Gospels report that Christ was secured to the cross with nails through hands and feet. The psalmist even reports that his enemies cast lots for his clothing. The Gospels record the fact that the Roman soldiers gambled for Christ's robe (John 19:23–24).

LAMENT PSALMS

The Psalms contain approximately 60 laments (40 percent of their total). Several express national sorrow (for example, Ps 14, 74, 83, and 137), but most are individual (significant examples include Ps 32, 40, 51, 69, and 130). These psalms convey profound hope in God by calling on God despite deep suffering.

"My God, my God, why have You forsaken me? Why are You so far from my deliverance and from my words of groaning?"

(Psalm 22:1, HCSB)

Psalm 8

David recalls Genesis 1–2 in this hymn of praise to God. The psalm is framed by the proclamation of God's glory in the world (8:1, 9). In light of God's magnificence in the heavens (8:1, 3), the psalm asks the question of human significance (8:4). The key lies with 8:2. God could silence sinful pride with the overwhelming display of His glory in nature. But He has chosen to make the greatest display of His glory through the weakness of humanity. For this reason, frail humanity has been given dominion and stewardship in creation (8:4–8, Genesis 1:26-30).

Jesus quoted Psalm 8 in answering the religious leaders of His day (Matt 21:16). The New Testament writers quote Psalm 8 several times to evoke the pattern of divine glory through human weakness (for example, 1 Cor 1:27 and Heb 2:5–8).

> *"Because of Your adversaries, You have established a stronghold from the mouths of children and nursing infants to silence the enemy and the avenger."*
>
> (Psalm 8:2, HCSB)

PRAISE AND CONFIDENCE PSALMS

Psalms of praise are hymns that focus on the majesty and mighty deeds of God, usually with a triumphant tone (for example, Ps 9, 50, 96-99, 116, 124, and 150). Psalms of trust or confidence express affection for God and assurance of His compassion (for example, Ps 11, 62, 116, and 138).

Psalm 23

Psalm 23 uses the imagery of David's experience shepherding his father's sheep (1 Sam 16:11; 17:34–37) to reflect on his relationship to God. In this relationship, however, the former shepherd boy is now the sheep who is dependent on a divine Shepherd (23:1). The tone of the psalm is calm and meditative (23:1–3), turning to direct address (23:4–5) and praise (23:6).

Because God was his shepherd, David was confident that God would provide and protect. The Shepherd would provide good pasture, lead the sheep, and ensure their peace despite the apparent threat of death. The only thing that would chase God's lambs would be His goodness and faithful love. Psalm 23 was the backdrop for Jesus' portrait of the Good Shepherd (John 10:1–18).

THE POPULARITY OF PSALM 23

Psalm 23 is easily the most popular psalm and one of the most familiar passages in the Bible. While it is often spoken as words of comfort at funerals because of its gentle assurance of God's presence in "the darkest valley," it has also had wide impact in music and film. Songs that quote or allude to Psalm 23 include "Jesus Walks" (Kanye West), "Love Rescue Me" (U2), "Sheep" (Pink Floyd) and "Shadow of Deth" (Megadeth). Movies that make use of parts of Psalm 23 include *Pale Rider, Rooster Cogburn, Full Metal Jacket, We Were Soldiers*, and *Titanic*. While some of these songs and movies reflect confidence in the love of God expressed in the psalm, others express the rejection or denial of God's care.

"The Lord is my shepherd; there is nothing I lack. He lets me lie down in green pastures; He leads me beside quiet waters. He renews my life; He leads me along the right paths for His name's sake. Even when I go through the darkest valley, I fear no danger, for You are with me; Your rod and Your staff—they comfort me."

(Psalm 23:1–4, HCSB)

PSALMS

LOVE OF GOD'S WORD
(Psalm 119)

Psalm119

Psalm 119 is the longest and most detailed reflection in the Bible on the nature of God's written Word. It unpacks in extended detail the vision of the righteous man's delight in the Law of God (Ps 1:2).

The poem is written in stanzas, which are poetic lines grouped together like a paragraph in a narrative. The themes of the stanzas reflect the writer's meditation on attributes of God's Word. Each stanza expresses a different quality.

THE LONGEST PSALM

Psalm 119 is the longest chapter in the Bible. But despite its length, it was written to be memorized. The first line of each stanza begins with a Hebrew letter, which progress through the Hebrew alphabet in order, creating an acrostic. English translations often reflect this feature by titling each stanza with its Hebrew letter.

GOD'S WORD...

1–8:	Blesses those who keep it	89–96:	Demonstrates God's eternal faithfulness
9–16:	Preserves from sin	97–104:	Teaches wisdom and understanding
17–24:	Reveals wondrous things to seekers	105–112:	Provides guidance in difficulties
25–32:	Revives and strengthens those who study it	113–120:	Shields and vindicates
33–40:	Teaches reverence and righteousness	121–128:	Yields blessing and judgment
41–48:	Saves and secures	129–136:	Feeds hunger to learn more
49–56:	Builds hope and confidence	137–144:	Highlights the holiness of God
57–64:	Evokes fear and obedience	145–152:	Calls for obedience
65–72:	Trains through discipline	153–160:	Rescues God's people
73–80:	Comforts those shaped by it	161–168:	Prompts praise and brings peace
81–88:	Sustains through affliction	169–176:	Is the delight of those who seek God

BIBLICAL LINKS

"Finally brothers, whatever is true, whatever is honorable, whatever is just, whatever is pure, whatever is lovely, whatever is commendable—if there is any moral excellence and if there is any praise—dwell on these things." *(Philippians 4:8, HCSB)*

"How can a young man keep his way pure? By keeping Your word. I have sought You with all my heart; don't let me wander from Your commands. I have treasured Your word in my heart so that I may not sin against You."

(Psalm 119:9–11, HCSB)

PROVERBS

INTRODUCTION

Proverbs collects the wisdom of Solomon and others. The book presumes that God designed a structure to the world (physically, relationally, and spiritually) and that this structure can be understood. The wise adjusted to how God designed the world and would prosper. Fools who ignored God's wisdom would destroy themselves.

LOCATION: The book of Proverbs primarily draws on the images of city and rural life in ancient Israel, including the marketplace and the city gate.

ORIGIN: The proverbs were primarily written by Solomon, suggesting an origin for most of the book between 970–930 B.C.E. Other material originated with other sources. Solomon's writings were collected by scribes under King Hezekiah, meaning the final form of the book was complete no earlier than 715 B.C.E.

KEY PASSAGES

Solomon's Speeches on Wisdom (1–9)

7:6–24	Fools Fall to Seduction
8:1–38	Wisdom Calls Men to Become Wise

Solomon's Proverbs (10–24)

22:17–24:22	The Thirty Sayings

The Hezekiah Collection (25–29)

25:28–26:28	There Are Many Ways to Be a Fool

The Wisdom of Agur (30)

Wisdom for King Lemuel (31)

31:1–9	Good Kings Rule Wisely
31:10–31	Wise Men Seek an Excellent Wife

PRINCIPAL FIGURES

God   Proverbs sees God as the world's Designer and the source of insight into its structure.

Solomon   David's son who became the wisest king of Israel before falling into foolish idolatry.

Hezekiah   King of Judah, whose scribes collected some of Solomon's wisdom.

Agur   The author of Proverbs 30. Little is known of him.

Lemuel   A young king whose mother taught him the wisdom contained in Proverbs 31.

Chokmah   Wisdom personified as a dignified woman who is a perfect counselor to men, reflecting how God intended Eve to aid Adam (see Genesis 2).

Kesilut   Folly personified as an adulterous woman or prostitute who destroys men, reflecting the effect Satan achieved by successfully tempting Eve (see Genesis 3).

LADY WISDOM
(Proverbs 8)

Though wisdom is not actually a person, Proverbs paints a vivid picture of Lady Wisdom as a dignified woman calling out to men in prominent public places. She offers her blessings to everyone. Even the inexperienced and foolish can become wise if they listen to her. Those who are willing to learn will understand what she says and find her teaching more valuable than precious metals or fine jewels.

The core of Wisdom's teaching in Proverbs is humility before God, the fear of the Lord. In practical terms, this means the wise will hate evil in themselves most of all. Wisdom promises to refine the attitudes, actions, and speech of those who embrace her influence. She is the agent that makes rulers great and anyone wealthy in ways that cannot be measured by money.

Lady Wisdom is the personification of the very structure of the ideas in the mind of God, which He can summon into existence as He summoned the world into existence (see Genesis 1). The implication is that those who understand wisdom will understand how God designed the world to work.

WHAT ARE PROVERBS?

Miguel de Cervantes observed, "Proverbs are short sayings drawn from long experience." They make an observation that evokes appropriate examples. Wisdom consists of both knowing the proverb and knowing when and how the proverb applies.

"And now, my sons, listen to me; those who keep my ways are happy. Listen to instruction and be wise; don't ignore it. Anyone who listens to me is happy, watching at my doors every day, waiting by the posts of my doorway. For the one who finds me finds life and obtains favor from the Lord, but the one who misses me harms himself; all who hate me love death."

(Proverbs 8:32–36, HCSB)

PROVERBS

ADVICE FOR A KING
(Proverbs 31)

Proverbs 31 records the wisdom that King Lemuel's mother taught him (his identity and kingdom are unknown). Her teaching is a compact lesson on leadership and finding the ideal wife, aimed at helping her son become a great man. It exalts the value of wise women in a man's life as a sage mother teaching her son the value of a godly wife.

Motherly Advice

Lemuel's mother begins with advice on the king's leadership. She warns him not to use his power to collect women for himself (31:3). This warning was significant in light of David and Solomon's failures. As a ruler, he must avoid things that would cloud his judgment, which in that time meant wine and strong drink. While people with little to lose might indulge, the leader who does so will end up forgetting God's Law and acting unjustly (31:4–7).

Finally, she challenges him to use his power to defend the defenseless. He must always judge fairly, even when the right decision lies with the poor, who could not give rewards, and against the oppressors, who presumably have the power to exact revenge (31:8–9).

Wifely Virtues

The 22 verses of the king-mother's teaching on a wife (32:10–31) are an acrostic poem. Each verse starts with a letter of the Hebrew alphabet, in order from *alef* to

tav. The poem is also structured as a chiasm, pairing verses from the outside ends of the poem in to the center.

The focal point of this poem is 31:23, in which the king's mother reminds him that the husband of a wise wife will become a great man. The message is consistent with the rest of Proverbs on the significance of a good wife: she is the great glory of her husband (12:4), and the man who finds a good wife is blessed by God (18:22; 19:14).

The expressions of a wise wife's virtues are specific to the ancient culture in which the poem was written. However, the underlying virtues include trustworthiness, industry, entrepreneurial vision, strength, generosity, preparedness, elegance, kindness in counsel, and fear of God (31:11–26). A wise man would seek (31:10) and honor such a wife (31:28–31).

WOMEN IN PROVERBS

Proverbs assumes the dependence of men on key women in order for those men to carry out their responsibilities (see Gen 2). Wisdom is portrayed as a beautiful woman (Prov 8) and men are taught to respect wise mothers and wives. Folly is embodied in the form of a nagging wife or prostitute.

JUSTICE TOWARD THE POOR

The Mosaic Law demanded that judges deliver even-handed justice. This meant giving what was deserved according to the Law and the facts of the case. Judges were not to favor the rich, nor were they to decide in favor of the poor man unjustly (Lev 19:15). Because of the tendency to favor the rich, however, this demand for justice most often took the form of reminders not to accept bribes, favor the rich, or oppress the poor. Rabbinic writings applied this by requiring a rich man to either dress as his poor opponent in court or dress the poor man like himself.

BIBLICAL LINKS

"Your beauty should not consist of outward things like elaborate hairstyles and the wearing of gold ornaments or fine clothes. Instead, it should consist of what is inside the heart with the imperishable quality of a gentle and quiet spirit, which is very valuable in God's eyes." *(1 Peter 3:3–4, HCSB)*

"Charm is deceptive and beauty is fleeting, but a woman who fears the Lord will be praised. Give her the reward of her labor, and let her works praise her at the city gates."

(Proverbs 31:30–31, HCSB)

INTRODUCTION

Ecclesiastes is an older man's meditation on his search for meaning. The book reminds the wise that humility in life's pursuits, tempered enjoyment of its pleasures, and especially reverence of God are essential for seeing life clearly.

LOCATION: Ecclesiastes implies that the experiences the author is reflecting upon took place in Jerusalem, or at least in the nation of Israel.

ORIGIN: The book identifies the author as a "son of David, King in Jerusalem" (Eccl 1:1), who collected and taught proverbs (Eccl 12:9–10). Jewish and Christian tradition identifies Solomon as the author. The experience of wisdom, wealth, and folly argues for an older author, placing the book toward the end of Solomon's reign (971–930 B.C.E.), likely after God confronted Solomon's idolatry (see 1 Kgs 11:1–13).

KEY PASSAGES

Introduction: The Apparent Futility of Life (1:1–11)

The Futility of Prideful Priorities (1:12–6:12)

2:1–11	Pleasure and Possessions Don't Satisfy
2:18–26	Serving Oneself Won't Satisfy
4:4–6:10	Wealth Doesn't Satisfy

The Clarity of Humility (7:1–12:8)

9:1–10	Enjoy a Mortal Life
9:11–18	Respect the Limits of Wisdom
11:1–12:8	Be Content Through Life's Changes

Conclusion: Meaning is Found in Submission to God (12:9–14)

PRINCIPAL FIGURES

God   Ecclesiastes sees God as the Supreme Sovereign, whose ways are beyond human understanding. He is the source of both blessing and judgment.

Qoheleth   The author of the book, a king in Jerusalem who descended from David. The range of personal experience cited suggests wide exposure to wisdom and folly.

"But beyond these, my son, be warned: there is no end to the making of many books, and much study wearies the body. When all has been heard, the conclusion of the matter is: fear God and keep His commands, because this is for all humanity. For God will bring every act to judgment, including every hidden thing, whether good or evil."

(Ecclesiastes 12:12–14, HCSB)

THE TEACHER'S CONCLUSION
(Eccesiastes 12:9–14)

Ecclesiastes is the capstone of Solomon's teaching, reflecting the lessons learned from a long life of wisdom and folly. The Teacher sought wisdom for himself but tried to help others share the blessings of the wisdom he had acquired. This took the form of pondering proverbs, collecting and testing them, and arranging them to be accessible to others. Though the book's refrain, "meaningless/futile," suggests despair, the message is meant to correct the prideful illusions that success can foster.

The Teacher tried to convey hard truths in gracious ways. Those wise sayings were intended to goad the foolish into turning from folly to wisdom. They would serve as deeply embedded nails, firmly holding together lives that threaten to fly apart. The power and insight of true wisdom, he taught, derived from their origin in the One Shepherd of humanity.

Outside of God's wisdom, there would be no end to the novelty that folly would propose. Such study would only weary the one who pursued it. For the Teacher, the knife that cut the fat of folly from the meat of wisdom was the founding principle of all wisdom: the fear of God (Prov 1:7). Submission to God's commands was for all humanity, not only the chosen people of Israel. The message the Teacher wanted to drive home to his students was that the motivation for submission to God was not so much the blessings of this life. Rather, he wanted his students to remember that God would one day judge every act, public or private, good or evil.

FEAR OF THE LORD

The phrase "fear of the Lord" or a variation appears more than 70 times in the Bible. It describes a deep awe and profound respect for God as God, the Almighty Maker of Heaven and Earth, which characterizes true piety in the righteous. It prompts terror of judgment in those the Bible describes as unrighteous.

SONG OF
SOLOMON

The Song of Solomon is a duet that celebrates love. It is also called the Song of Songs, meaning both "Song of Many Songs" and "Solomon's Greatest Song." The Song revels in the fact that despite the Fall (Gen 3), men and women can still share intense joy in marriage. It is also taken to portray God's love for Israel or Christ's love for the Church.

LOCATION: The Song is set in pastoral scenes and Jerusalem. One scene portrays a dream of the Shulamite Woman.

ORIGIN: The Song of Solomon is ascribed to King Solomon as his greatest song (Song 1:1). While Solomon had many marriages to cement alliances, this song appears to have arisen out of a genuine passion between Solomon and the Shulamite Woman. It would have been written between 970 and 930 B.C.E.

KEY PASSAGES

The Origin of The Couple's Love (1–2)

1:7–2:7	The Couple Finds Each Other

The Wedding-Night Songs (3–6:10)

3:1–4:15	The Bride's Anxieties Are Calmed
4:16–5:1	The Couple Consummates Their Marriage
5:2–6:10	The Bride's Fears Are Relieved

The Maturation of the Couple's Love (6:11–8)

7:1–8:4	The Couple Recalls When They First Met

PRINCIPAL FIGURES

God Though not named directly, God's presence is implied in the Song of Solomon as the Author of love and Creator of marriage (see Genesis 2).

The Shulamite Woman The female voice in the Song's duet. She was a rural girl, likely from northern Israel, who came to love and marry King Solomon.

Solomon Israel's third king and author of numerous songs. Solomon is the male voice in the Song's duet.

The Young Women of Jerusalem, The Brothers The Chorus in the Song, functioning both as audience and responders to the voices of the duet.

The perfect love story had come true. The poor country girl, slaving in the fields for her brothers (1:5–6), had been noticed by the glorious king (1:15). Love had blossomed and the marriage had been consummated with joy like the explosion of sweetness in a bite of ripe fruit (4:16–5:1). Surely, it must all have been a dream.

The fear that it couldn't be real plagued the dreams of the Shulamite Woman the night of her wedding (5:2). Having exposed herself fully and irrevocably to her beloved (5:3–5), she feared to find that he was gone. In her dream, she searched for him with a broken heart but was beaten like a prostitute found in the streets at night (5:6–8).

In her dream, the young women who had cheered her pursuit of Solomon now jeered her search, demanding to know what made him so special (5:9). She answered with a recital of his virtues (5:10–16).

At this point, the nightmarish quality of her dream began to resolve into peace. Remembering the goodness of the man she loved calmed her fears and rekindled her joy. The young women were once again encouraging (6:1). Instead of seeking frantically, the Shulamite Woman knew where to find her beloved and was once again confident in the love they shared (6:2–3). The song reaches its crescendo in Solomon's adoring portrait of his new wife (6:4–10).

> *"Eat, friends! Drink, be intoxicated with love!"*
>
> (Song of Solomon 5:1, HCSB)

SEX IN THE BIBLE

While little outside the Song of Solomon is sensual, the Bible has numerous stories involving sex. Examples include the mob in Sodom and Lots' Daughters (Gen 19:4–11, 30–38), the Moabite women (Num 25), and David and Bathsheba (2 Sam 11). Though there are many commands concerning sex (for example, Lev 18), the Bible doesn't denigrate sex. Outside of marriage, the Bible sees sex as highly destructive, but between husband and wife it is celebrated (Song 5:1).

ISAIAH

Isaiah proclaimed judgment on the northern kingdom of Israel as a warning to the southern kingdom of Judah. Yet the prophet's message of judgment was not his final word. God's wrath would be transformed by an ideal king into restoration and fulfillment of the Abrahamic Covenant's blessings on the nation of Israel and the world (see Gen 12).

LOCATION: Isaiah focuses primarily on Jerusalem and Judah, but it also addresses the surrounding nations as well as the regional powers Egypt, Assyria, and Babylon.

KEY PASSAGES

The Message of Judgment (1–39)

5:1–30	God Judges His Vineyard
6:1–13	God Commissions Isaiah
7:1–25	Isaiah Predicts Immanuel
8:1–11–16	David's Heir Will Rule
19:1–20:6	God Refines Egypt and Assyria
36:1–39:8	Out of the Assyrian Pan, into the Babylonian Fire

The Message of Restoration (40–66)

40:1–31	Jerusalem Will Be Comforted
41:1–29	Idols Can't Compare to Yahweh
42:1–25	Isaiah Introduces the Servant
49:1–50:11	The Servant Will Bring Salvation
52:1–12	The Servant Will Triumph Through Suffering
55:1–13	Salvation Is a Feast, Free to All
61:1–11	God's Preacher Will Bring Good News
65:1–25	The Nations Will Enjoy the New Creation

PRINCIPAL FIGURES

God God appears to Isaiah as the True King of the nation of Israel, meaning that He is the Almighty Judge of the nation's sin and also its Savior and Redeemer.

Isaiah The prophet who ministered to four Judean kings during the collapse of the northern kingdom of Israel under the Assyrians. Isaiah may have been a Judean aristocrat.

Ahaz Judean king who rejected Isaiah's offer of a sign validating the prophecy of Jerusalem's deliverance from attack by Israel and Aram.

Shear-Jashub One of Isaiah's sons. His name meant "a remnant shall return," and was itself a prophecy of hope for restoration, though it also implied that judgment would come first.

Immanuel The name of the child Isaiah prophesied would be born of the virgin as the ideal king of God's people. Immanuel means "God with us."

Maher-shalal-hash-baz A second son of Isaiah, who was still an infant at the time Assyria destroyed the northern kingdom of Israel.

Hezekiah King of Judah, who survived the Assyrian siege of Jerusalem.

Cyrus A Persian (Median) king. Isaiah prophesied he would release the Jews from captivity in Babylon to return to the Promised Land.

ORIGIN: The book names Isaiah as its author (1:1), and the New Testament identifies Isaiah as the source of the two main parts of the book, suggesting that the book was written between 750–690 B.C.E. However, many modern scholars argue that the book was written by two different authors: "Proto-Isaiah" (1-39) and "Deutero-Isaiah" (40-66). This view appeals to shifts in the subjects discussed and the words used, and the assumption that prophetic revelation cannot occur (for example, Cyrus lived 200 years after Isaiah; Isa 44:28; 45:1).

THE CALL OF ISAIAH
(Isaiah 6)

King Uzziah was one of the righteous kings of Judah, but when he died, Isaiah had a vision of Judah's true King. The space between the golden cherubim on the Ark of the Covenant had always been thought of as the place where God's glory was enthroned. But now, God had appeared on the throne of Heaven. He was surrounded by angelic beings, each with three pairs of wings. Their voices thundered through the Temple, proclaiming that God was "Holy, holy, holy" and glorious throughout the earth (1:3).

Having seen a clear vision of the glory and holiness of God, Isaiah also saw himself clearly. The effect was devastating. He proclaimed the "woe" of certain judgment on himself, admitting that he was "a man of

unclean lips," an unholy person, a sinner (1:5). But when one of the angelic beings darted towards him it was to make him holy rather than destroy him. The angel took a coal from the altar and touched his lips as a symbol that Isaiah's unrighteousness had been removed.

At that moment, Isaiah heard God's voice. God asked, "Who should I send? Who will go for Us?" Isaiah's response was instantaneous. Echoing the words of Abraham (Gen 22:1) and Moses (Exod 3:4), Isaiah answered, "Here I am." (Isa 6:8)

God gave the prophet a terrible mission. God's people would continue to hear the words of the prophets and watch symbolic messages embedded in their lives. But having rejected those messages for so long, God now condemned them to remain permanently ignorant, blind, and deaf. Like the generation of Israelites who died in the desert, God would cleanse the nation of its unfaithful citizens (Num 14). Their cities would be destroyed and the majority taken into exile (Deut 28:21).

THE MESSAGE OF JUDGMENT

One of the uncomfortable themes of the Bible is that God judges sinners, meaning everyone (Eccl 7:20). Pronouncements of judgment were often intended as calls to repentance, forgiveness, and reconciliation (Isa 55:6). But people could rebel to the point where God condemned them to the consequences of their rebellion (Heb 9:27). Examples include Pharaoh (Exod 4:21), Judah (Isa 6:9–10), and many in Jesus' day (Matt 13:14–15).

ISAIAH

THE PROPHETIC BIRTH
(Isaiah 7)

When God called Isaiah to speak for Him, He warned the new prophet that no one would respond rightly to Isaiah's messages (Isa 6). When God then sent Isaiah to bring a message of comfort to King Ahaz of Judah, the prophet might well have hoped that he had misunderstood God's warning. Unfortunately, Isaiah had not misunderstood; the king refused to believe him.

King Ahaz' Refusal

The Davidic Covenant (2 Sam 7), which promised a son of David would reign on the throne of Israel forever, was threatened by the combined forces of Aram (Syria) and the northern kingdom of Israel (7:1–2). These nations had allied against the rising tide of Assyrian power and demanded that Judah join them. When King Ahaz refused, they conspired to capture Jerusalem, kill Ahaz, and install a puppet on the throne. The king was terrified by the threat.

God sent Isaiah, along with his son Shear-jashub (whose name meant "a remnant shall return"), to speak to Ahaz (7:3). Isaiah reported that there was no reason to fear. God Himself had decided to thwart the plans of Aram and Israel (7:4–8). Isaiah warned that if Ahaz did not stand firm on faith in God, then his line would not be confirmed on the throne (7:9).

A Sign from God

God offered to allow Ahaz to name any sign he wished as confirmation that God would defeat Judah's enemies (7:10–11). Ahaz, however, insisted that he would not ask for a sign, saying "I will not test the Lord" (7:12). Though Ahaz' refusal could have been taken as a pious claim that his faith did not need to be confirmed by a sign, it was actually a rejection of God's message and aid. Isaiah shot back that the house of David (Judah's royal family) was not merely trying his patience, it was testing God's patience (7:13).

BIBLICAL LINKS

"The birth of Jesus Christ came about this way: After His mother Mary had been engaged to Joseph, it was discovered before they came together that she was pregnant by the Holy Spirit.... Now all this took place to fulfill what was spoken by the Lord through the prophet: See, the virgin will become pregnant and give birth to a son, and they will name Him Immanuel, which is translated 'God is with us.'"
(Matthew 1:22–23, HCSB)

Finally, Isaiah informed Ahaz that God would give the house of David a sign. A virgin would give birth and call her son Immanuel, which means "God with us" (7:14). Isaiah then turned to his own son and said that the proof of the prophesied birth was that before Shear-jashub was old enough to be held legally responsible for his actions, Israel and Syria would be defeated by the Assyrians (7:15-16). Judah would survive (7:17). Though Shear-jashub's age at the time of the prophecy is unclear, the reference to him as a "boy" rather than an infant suggests that Aram and Israel would be defeated in the near future.

VIRGIN OR YOUNG WOMAN?

Jewish and Christian scholars have debated whether or not Isaiah's prophecy refers to a virgin or simply a young woman. The Hebrew word *almah* can be translated "virgin" or "young woman" (see Gen 24:43 and Ps 68:25). Jewish scholars point out that the prophet could have used *bethulah*, which can only mean "virgin." Yet, pre-Christian Greek translations (Septuagint) preferred *parthenos* (which means "virgin"). Matthew 1:22-23 quoted the Septuagint's *parthenos*, alluding to Gen 3:15, "seed of the woman." It was not until after 100 C.E. that Jewish translations began to insist on the Greek word *neanis*, which means "young woman."

> "*Therefore, the Lord Himself will give you a sign: The virgin will conceive, have a son, and name him Immanuel.*"
>
> (Isaiah 7:14, HCSB)

ISAIAH

The prophets of the Old Testament often connected judgment and mercy in God's dealings with people. Isaiah 8–11 is an example of this pattern. The birth of Isaiah's son *Maher-shalal-hash-baz,* which means "Speeding to the Plunder, Hurrying to the Spoil" (Isa 8:3), was a sign that Assyria would take Israel captive. They would also overrun most of Judah (8:8), and no alliance, strategy, or prophecy would avert it (8:9–17).

A Pattern of Judgment and Mercy

The purpose of God's judgment of Judah was not the ultimate destruction of His people, but to teach them to fear and trust God. The darkness of judgment would give way to a great light in Galilee (9:1–2). The Assyrians would be destroyed, and a child would be born who would ascend the throne of David and end the cycle of judgment by establishing righteousness in the kingdom (9:6–7).

The judgment-mercy pattern is repeated in 9:8–12:6. In the past, the people of Israel had responded to lesser judgments by boasting they would rebuild better than before. Because they had not returned to the Lord, but continued to oppress the weak, God's anger remained (9:8–10:4). But God's wrath would also fall on Assyria. The Assyrians thought that their gods had made them the destroyers of nations (10:5–14). But the king

of Assyria failed to recognize that he was merely an instrument of God's discipline (10:15–19). God would bring a remnant of His people back and destroy their oppressors (10:20–34).

Isaiah's Prophesy

Once the oppressors of God's people were wiped away, Isaiah prophesied that the seemingly dead stump of the Davidic line would sprout a new branch (11:1). This king would be empowered by the Spirit of God (11:2) and would rule the nation with righteousness (11:4–6). His reign would not only bring peace among men, but harmony to the rest of creation as well (11:6–9). All the nations of the earth would submit to the King as His people returned to the Promised Land (11:10–16).

HANDEL'S MESSIAH

Handel's *Messiah* premiered in Dublin, Ireland, in April 1742. One-third of its songs are quotations from Isaiah, more than any other Biblical book. Legend holds that the tradition of standing for the Hallelujah Chorus began when King George II stood for the song at its London premiere, prompting the crowd to stand with him.

BIBLICAL LINKS

"Now listen: You will conceive and give birth to a son, and you will call His name Jesus. He will be great and will be called the Son of the Most High, and the Lord God will give Him the throne of His father David. He will reign over the house of Jacob forever, and His kingdom will have no end." *(Luke 1:31–33, HCSB)*

"For a child will be born for us, a son will be given to us, and the government will be on His shoulders. He will be named Wonderful Counselor, Mighty God, Eternal Father, Prince of Peace."

(Isaiah 9:6, HCSB)

ISAIAH

Toward the end of Isaiah's ministry in Judah, the Assyrians attacked Jerusalem. During the Assyrian siege, King Hezekiah of Judah, who had succeeded King Ahaz, became desperately ill with a skin infection (Isa 38). Through Isaiah, God warned Hezekiah to prepare for death. The king prayed for healing and Isaiah returned to say that God would deliver Judah from Assyria and Hezekiah from his sickness. As a sign, God caused the sun's shadow to retreat ten steps on the king's staircase (38:7–8).

The Babylonian Threat

Though Hezekiah composed a hymn of humble praise to God (38:10–20), he was also vulnerable to flattery. The king of Babylon had heard of Hezekiah's miraculous recovery (39:1) and may have seen a potential ally. After Hezekiah had foolishly showed the Babylonian ambassadors his wealth, Isaiah delivered a prophecy to the king. He warned that Babylon would become an enemy rather than an ally. Eventually, it would conquer Judah, plundering its wealth and driving its people into captivity (39:5–7).

Unfortunately, Hezekiah's concern for his kingdom did not extend beyond the limits of his own life. When he realized that the Babylonian invasion would not happen in his lifetime, he was content (39:8).

Assurance from God

Despite the dire prophecy, Isaiah also brought comfort to the people of Jerusalem (Isa 40). Captivity would not last forever. There would be a new exodus. The wilderness would become a highway for Israel's return to the Promised Land (40:3–5). Though human lives and plans have no power, God's word would endure (40:6–8). God would exert His strength to bless and restore His flock (40:9–11).

Because God was not dependent upon any counselor or nation, nothing could stop Him from keeping His word (40:12–17). Unlike idols, God was no product of human craftsmanship; He is the Master Craftsman of the universe (40:18–26). Nothing that happened to Judah would escape His notice. His strength would not fail, nor would the strength of those who trusted Him (40:27–31).

DIVINE FAITHFULNESS

God's faithfulness is a major Biblical theme. The pattern of sin, discipline, and restoration in Israel's history portrays God as faithful to His Covenant promises, even when the nation was unfaithful. Their obedience was not the cause of God's favor. Rather, His favor prompted Him to discipline them to faithfulness.

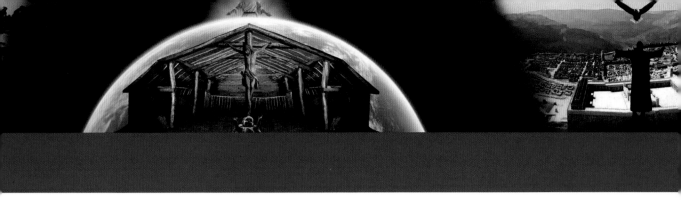

MOCKING IDOLS
(AND THOSE WHO MAKE THEM)

Though God mocks idols in Isaiah 40, the most stinging critique comes in Isaiah 44. The idol-worshipper plants a tree, and when it is grown he cuts it down. He takes some of the wood to warm himself and some to cook his food. The leftovers are shaped into an idol, which he then worships and begs for salvation (44:14–17). God concludes that idolaters are too blinded by folly to see that burning the wood was the more useful act (44:18–20).

"Youths may faint and grow weary, and young men stumble and fall, but those who trust in the Lord will renew their strength; they will soar on wings like eagles; they will run and not grow weary; they will walk and not faint."

(Isaiah 40:30–31, HCSB)

ISAIAH

Isaiah 40–66 shifts focus from Judah in Isaiah's day (around 720 B.C.E.) to the Babylonian captivity (586 B.C.E.) and beyond. A key figure throughout this section is God's Servant. One of the challenges in reading the last third of Isaiah, however, is that the label *Servant* seems to apply to several different figures. The Servant is connected with Jacob or Israel 60 times and the Persian king, Cyrus, is mentioned twice. At other times, the Servant seems to be someone other than Cyrus or the nation of Israel. Determining which figure is in view is a key to reading the "Servant Songs," the four poems that describe the Servant's mission and suffering.

Songs 42, 49, and 50

The first song (42:1–4) describes the Servant as God's chosen one, endowed with God's strength and Spirit. The Servant would be humble and gentle and would persevere to establish universal justice.

The second song (49:1–6) identifies the Servant with Israel, trusting God for vindication in spite of suffering, but then seems to shift from the nation to an individual (see 1 Chr 21). The Servant's mission included bringing Israel back to God (49:5), suggesting an image of the "Prophet like Moses" leading a new Exodus (see Deut 18). Redeeming Israel was too simple a goal, however, so the Servant would also become a light to the nations and salvation for the world (49:6).

In the third song (50:4–9), the Servant claims faithful perseverance in spite of beatings and scorn.

The Final Song

The final song (52:13–53:12) is the most graphic description of the Servant's suffering and victory. The Servant is promised glory despite being disfigured with torture (52:13–15). The Servant would be an unexpected success: a green plant growing from dry ground, a figure without attractiveness or charisma, and disdained by everyone (53:1–3). Yet the Servant would bear the punishment for "our" sins (Israel's and the world's). The Servant would even be executed unjustly because of "My people's" rebellion and buried in a rich man's grave (53:4–9). All this would accomplish God's plan to make the Servant a sacrifice in order to "justify many," bear their sins, and intercede for those in rebellion against God.

IDENTIFYING THE SERVANT

The identity of God's Servant in Isaiah is an old question (see Acts 8:34). Many connect the Servant with Israel (citing, for example, 41:8–9). Others see Cyrus, who ordered the Temple restoration (44:28). The New Testament noted the Servant's redemptive mission (49:5–6) and the details of His death (53:1–9) to identify Jesus as the Servant.

BIBLICAL LINKS

"To this very day, I have obtained help that comes from God, and I stand and testify to both small and great, saying nothing else than what the prophets and Moses said would take place—that the Messiah must suffer, and that as the first to rise from the dead, He would proclaim light to our people and to the Gentiles." *(Acts 26:22–23, HCSB)*

"It is not enough for you to be My Servant raising up the tribes of Jacob and restoring the protected ones of Israel. I will also make you a light for the nations, to be My salvation to the ends of the earth."

(Isaiah 49:6, HCSB)

ISAIAH

Isaiah 55 is a herald's cry in a barren marketplace, offering bread from heaven to all who hunger and thirst (55:1). The imagery is that of a merchant in a bazaar. But the language of economic exchange—something for something—is transformed by the vision of a transaction in which no money or service is given for the meal. What is offered is something for nothing.

The prophet was offering to the people of Israel nothing less than the blessings of God's Covenants with Abraham (Gen 12, 15, 17), Moses (Deut 28), and David (2 Sam 7). These blessings included abundant food, health, and security. Isaiah described these blessings as a banquet to which all were invited freely.

The problem Isaiah envisions is not lack of cash; it is lack of interest. Those in the marketplace are interested in other food and listen to other advertisers (55:2–3). But God made His Covenant with David and his heir. It was firm and would deliver sovereignty over the world to Him (55:4–5).

A Limited-Time Offer

The invitation was free and offered to all, but it was also a limited-time offer. Isaiah urged his listeners to seek God while it was still possible to find Him (55:6). The thoughts and deeds of the people had become wicked and sinful, but those who abandoned their rebellion would find compassion and forgiveness (55:7).

GRACE

One of the great Biblical themes is *grace;* God's favor given without reference to human righteousness and in spite of human sinfulness. Grace is implied in the traditional Hebrew greeting, shalom, meaning "peace"), and is made explicit in the New Testament greeting charis kai eirene ("grace and peace").

Such magnanimity might be difficult to imagine, but God declared that His plans could not be judged by comparison to any human being (55:8–9). The fulfillment of God's promise was as certain as the snow falling from the sky and rain nurturing the crops (55:10–11). God's purpose would be fulfilled: the joy of God's people in His glory (55:12–13).

Open to All

When Isaiah said all were invited, he meant all. God's feast would not be only for Israel, but for everyone who drew near to God (56:1). Those who were ceremonially disqualified from coming to God, such as eunuchs, would find that God offered better than what they had lost (56:2–5). The unchosen nations would find their worship and prayers accepted in God's Temple (56:6–8).

GOD'S GREAT BANQUET

The imagery of Isaiah 55–56 forms the background to Jesus' parable of the banquet (Luke 14:15–23). A great man gave a banquet, but the invited guests were not interested in coming. They made transparent excuses for refusing to come. So the host ordered his servants to bring the poor, maimed, blind and lame. The invited guests who refused to come missed the feast, but those who expected to be passed over enjoyed the host's generosity.

"Seek the Lord while He may be found; call to Him while He is near. Let the wicked one abandon his way and the sinful one his thoughts; let him return to the Lord, so He may have compassion on him, and to our God, for He will freely forgive."

(Isaiah 55:6–7, HCSB)

ISAIAH

The Mosaic Covenant instructed Israel to celebrate a year of Jubilee every forty-ninth year (Lev 25). The celebration was marked by rest for the land, as fields were left unplowed and the people trusted God to provide as He had in the wilderness. Land suitable for growing crops that had been sold was to be returned to the family that had owned it, ensuring that all Israelite families would have the opportunity to provide for themselves. Hebrew slaves were to be released.

It is not clear Israel ever observed this holiday year. Perhaps God's people were not willing to trust God to feed them through a whole year of eating only what they could glean from their unplanted fields. Perhaps they were unwilling to return land or laborers that they had acquired. Whatever their reasons for ignoring the Jubilee, Isaiah prophesied that one day they would experience all of its blessings in full. The first two verses in this passage became the text of Jesus' first sermon (Luke 4:18–19).

A Message of Good News

A divinely anointed preacher would proclaim a message of good news that was particularly for the downcast poor and those in captivity (61:1). The Lord's favor on the oppressed would involve vengeance on the oppressors, but the emphasis here is on the year of blessing rather than the day of vengeance (61:2).

BIBLICAL LINKS

"When John heard in prison what the Messiah was doing, he sent a message by his disciples and asked Him, 'Are You the One who is to come, or should we expect someone else?' Jesus replied to them, 'Go and report to John what you hear and see: the blind see, the lame walk, those with skin diseases are healed, the deaf hear, the dead are raised, and the poor are told the good news. And if anyone is not offended because of Me, he is blessed.'" *(Matthew 11:2–6, HCSB)*

In particular, Isaiah's message was a prophecy of blessing for Jerusalem. The city would be rebuilt and the nations would serve the people of God in the land (61:3–5). Israel, however, would be as priests of God to the nations, whose derision would turn to praise acknowledging God's blessings of His people (61:6–7).

An Eternal Jubilee

God's love of justice and hatred of injustice would motivate His creation of this eternal Jubilee (61:8–9). On that day, the nations would again recognize that God had blessed Israel (6:9), and a hymn of praise would be led by the preacher (6:10). Isaiah's message concluded with the assurance that though the coming of the Jubilee might seem slow and the process hidden like seed planted in the ground, the harvest day of universal righteousness and praise of God would arrive (61:11).

HOPE FOR THE AFFLICTED

The Biblical authors often seemed to "afflict the comfortable, and comfort the afflicted." The prophets vehemently and repeatedly accused the nation and its leaders of unfaithfulness to the Covenant. But they also reassured the faithful remnant suffering divine punishment that God's promises of blessing would be fulfilled in the end.

"The Spirit of the Lord God is on Me, because the Lord has anointed Me to bring good news to the poor. He has sent Me to heal the broken-hearted, to proclaim liberty to the captives and freedom to the prisoners; to proclaim the year of the Lord's favor, and the day of our God's vengeance; to comfort all who mourn."

(Isaiah 61:1–2, HCSB)

ISAIAH

The Book of Isaiah ends with a summary statement about the meaning of Israel's history and future. The Israelites had not become God's people because they had sought Him, but because He had sought them (65:1). God had called Abram and given him an heir (Gen 12, 15, 17); God had called Moses and delivered a people who didn't even know His name from slavery in Egypt (Exod 4). But God repeatedly had to send judges and prophets to recall the nation from rebellion and idolatry (65:2–5), and so the promised curses came (65:6–7, see Deut 28).

The Faithful Remnant

But there was always a faithful remnant. This remnant included Phinehas (Num 25), Ruth and Boaz (Ruth), David (2 Sam 7), Elijah (1 Kgs 18), Hezekiah (2 Kgs 18), and Josiah (2 Chr 35–35). God resolved to preserve the nation for their sake and build a blessed nation (65:8–10). Those who abandoned the Lord, however, would only experience the sword (65:11–12). The servants of God would have joy; the rebels would be destroyed (65:13–16).

NAMES FOR GOD: *ELOHIM*

The Hebrew word *Elohim* could be used to refer to idols ("gods" with a lower-case "g") or to God. Many names for God in the Old Testament are built on Elohim. These names include, *El Olam* (Everlasting God), *El Elyon* (God Most High), *El Roi* (God Who Sees), and *El Shaddai* (God Almighty). Later Persian documents, reproduced in Ezra and Nehemiah, used the name *El Shemayin* God of Heaven) for the God of Israel. Among the names for God found in Isaiah, the prophet used *Elohim Yesha* (God Our Salvation), suggesting that God is not only the source of salvation but is its chief blessing.

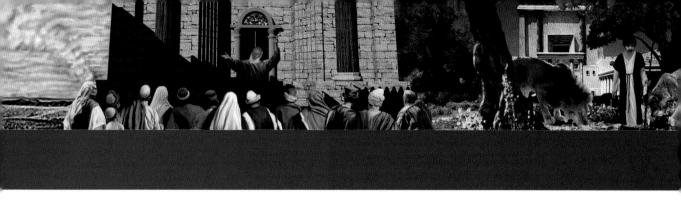

A New Heaven and Earth

The faithful remnant had often suffered alongside the rebels. So God promised that they would experience His blessings in a new heaven and earth, free from the sins of the past (65:17–25). Jerusalem would then be a city of joy where grief would never enter. There would be no infant mortality or early death. People would enjoy the fruit of their labor, and that work would always be blessed. No prayer would be offered as complaint, because God would answer before it was uttered. Even violent nature would enjoy harmony and peace.

Though God did not identify exactly when He would fulfill His promise, He did insist that it was as sure as birth follows the pains of labor (66:9–11). God would come first with fire to execute His wrath and judgment on the wicked (66:14–16). But the righteous would worship God forever (66:18–24).

> *"For I will create a new heaven and a new earth; the past events will not be remembered or come to mind. Then be glad and rejoice forever in what I am creating; for I will create Jerusalem to be a joy and its people to be a delight."*
>
> (Isaiah 65:17–18, HCSB)

FOUND BY THOSE WHO DIDN'T SEEK

Isaiah's reminder that God was the Seeker who found Israel highlights a significant Biblical pattern, applied both to the non-Jewish nations (Rom 9:30; 10:20) and to individuals (1 John 4:10). In part, the pattern offers hope that those who seek God find He was already seeking them.

BIBLICAL LINKS

"Then I saw a new heaven and a new earth, for the first heaven and the first earth had passed away, and the sea no longer existed. I also saw the Holy City, new Jerusalem, coming down out of heaven from God, prepared like a bride adorned for her husband." *(Revelation 21:1–2, HCSB)*

JEREMIAH

Jeremiah describes the career of a prophet who was believed by almost no one and ended up being persecuted by nearly everyone. The book announces Babylon's destruction of Judah and describes the siege of Jerusalem and the aftermath. Yet God's people would be restored and those who cheered their destruction would be judged.

LOCATION: Most of the events occur in and around Jerusalem. The book also describes the experience of Jews who fled to Egypt and Jewish exiles in Babylon.

KEY PASSAGES

The Call of Jeremiah (1)

Prophecies About Judah (2–33)

7:1–34	Jeremiah Condemns the Temple
23:1–40	God Rejects the False Prophets
25:1–29:32	Jeremiah Fights the False Prophets

The Babylonian Conquest of Judah (34–45)

36:1–32	The King Burns the Bible
37:1–39:18	Jerusalem Falls to Babylon

Prophecies About the Nations (46–51)

Reprise of Jerusalem's Fall (52)

ORIGIN: The book identifies Jeremiah as its author and contains the most autobiographical detail of any prophetic book in the Old Testament. Modern scholars have suggested later authors or editors, but little consensus has emerged. The descriptions of Jerusalem's fall suggest that the final form of the book was compeleted not long after 586 B.C.E.

PRINCIPAL FIGURES

God In Jeremiah, God is the implacable Judge of His rebellious people, but also offers hope for the next generation.

Jeremiah Jeremiah was the prophet who both predicted and endured the Babylonian destruction of Jerusalem. He was persecuted by his people and honored by King Nebuchadnezzar of Babylon.

Pashur or Magor-missabib A priest who persecuted Jeremiah. God changed his name from Pashur, meaning "prosperity round about" to Magor-missabib, meaning "fear round about" to reflect the coming judgment.

Zedekiah The last king of Judah, who rebelled against Babylon and was tortured by Nebuchad-nezzar.

Hananiah and Shemaiah Two false prophets who predicted Babylon's defeat and an early release for the Jewish captives.

Jehoiakim The king of Judah, who burned the scroll of Jeremiah's prophecies as it was read to him.

Nebuchadnezzar The king of Babylon, who besieged and destroyed Jerusalem. He honored Jeremiah for his advice to submit to Babylon.

Gedaliah The Jewish governor appointed by Babylon after Jerusalem was destroyed. He was as-sassinated in an abortive rebellion against Babylon.

THE CALL OF JEREMIAH
(Jeremiah 1)

Jeremiah was the son of a priest, living in the territory of Benjamin. When God called him, Jeremiah had the same concerns as Moses (public speaking, Exod 4:10) and Solomon (youth, 1 Kgs 3:7). God, however, had chosen Jeremiah long before that day. Before Jeremiah was even conceived, God had chosen him to be one of His prophets to the nations (1:5). God rejected the idea that Jeremiah's youth was any barrier. In fact, the prophet's long career virtually required that he start early in life.

God demanded that Jeremiah go to whomever God sent him and say whatever God told him to say. God touched Jeremiah's mouth as a symbol of placing His words on Jeremiah's lips. The prophet would stand over nations to proclaim their destruction and offer hope.

Finally, God gave Jeremiah two visions. The first was of the branch of an almond tree *(shaqed),* which gets its Hebrew name from the fact that it awakens *(shaqad)* early in the spring. The vision promised that God would watch *(shoqed)* over His Word and bring it to pass. The second vision was of a boiling pot poured out from the north to the south. This vision promised that disaster would flow over the land of Judah from the north and destroy Jerusalem because of its idolatry. Although the message was horrific, God promised to make Jeremiah an impregnable fortress.

BULLAE AND JEREMIAH

Archaeological excavations in Jerusalem uncovered clay seals, called bullae, dating to about 586 B.C.E., bearing the names of two of King Zedekiah's advisors mentioned in Jeremiah: Gedaliah, son of Pashur, and Jehucal, son of Shelemiah. These advisors tried to stop Jeremiah from advising surrender to the Babylonians (Jer 38:1-13).

"Then the Lord said to me: Do not say, 'I am only a youth,' for you will go to everyone I send you to and speak whatever I tell you. Do not be afraid of anyone, for I will be with you to deliver you. This is the Lord's declaration." (Jeremiah 1:7–8, HCSB)

JEREMIAH

The death of King Josiah (609 B.C.E.) brought further chaos to Jerusalem at an already turbulent time. Babylon had defeated Assyria and would soon best Pharaoh (605 B.C.E.). Egypt occupied most of Judah and had installed Jehoiakim as a puppet king in Jerusalem (608 B.C.E.). Josiah's reforms quickly evaporated into moral and religious chaos despite the restored Temple. In those difficult days, the people of Judah found comfort in the presence of the Temple and its rituals. It was, perhaps, at one of the great feasts (Deut 16:16) that Jeremiah rose to preach what would become his signature sermon.

God warned Jeremiah that any attempt the prophet might make to talk God out of judging His people would be futile (7:16–20). Judah had become stubborn and would not listen and repent (7:21–29). The people mixed the worship of the "Queen of Heaven" with the worship of God (7:18). Without obedience, the sacrifices were meaningless (7:21–23). Judah had even adopted human sacrifice in the valley outside Jerusalem (7:3–33). For all these reasons, Judah's attempt to manipulate God into protecting their sinful society would fall to divine judgment (7:34).

Jeremiah Speaks

Jeremiah condemned the gaping chasm between Judah's moral life and its trust in the Temple. The people chanted "This is the Temple of the Lord" (7:4), drawing comfort from the idea that God would defend His house. But Jeremiah contrasted their hollow words with their concrete deeds of oppression and idolatry (7:5–8).

The Temple had become a "den of robbers" (7:11, see Luke 19:46), a place to retreat for refuge after attacking the vulnerable until emerging to do it again. Jeremiah reminded Jerusalem of the destruction of Shiloh, the original site of the Tabernacle in the Promised Land. Despite its significance, the Philistines destroyed it after capturing the Ark of the Covenant (1 Sam 4).

The Mob Seizes Jeremiah

Near the end of his ministry, Jeremiah delivered this message one last time in the Temple. But this time he prophesied that God was going to cause all nations to curse the city of Jerusalem (26:6).

The priests in the Temple, the false prophets, and the people who had come to worship had enough. They rioted in the Temple courtyard, seized Jeremiah, and were ready to lynch him on the spot. The government officials rushed in, and Jeremiah spoke to the crowd again. He warned them that he had only said what God had instructed him to say (26:12-15).

One official (26:24) reminded the crowd that Jeremiah was saying the same thing that the prophet Micah had said 100 years earlier (26:18, see Mic 3:12).

He reminded the people that King Hezekiah had not executed Micah. Instead the people had repented and the Lord had turned aside from judging the nation (Jer 26:19). He was able to convince the mob to release Jeremiah, but they did not believe Jeremiah's message or repent.

ATTEMPTS TO MANIPULATE GOD

The Bible records numerous attempts to manipulate God through religious ritual. The Tower of Babel (Gen 11), Balaam's sacrifices (Num 23–25), Jephthah's vow (Judg 11), carrying the Ark into battle (1 Sam 4), and Simon the Magician's attempt to purchase the power of the Holy Spirit (Acts 8) are notable examples. They all failed.

"Do you steal, murder, commit adultery, swear falsely, burn incense to Baal, and follow other gods that you have not known? Then do you come and stand before Me in this house called by My name and say, 'We are delivered, so we can continue doing all these detestable acts'? Has this house, which is called by My name, become a den of robbers in your view? Yes, I too have seen it.' This is the Lord's declaration."
(Jeremiah 7:9–11, HCSB)

JEREMIAH

The Babylonian exile of Judah began with the deportation of noble youths as hostages, including Daniel (about 605 B.C.E.). Later, King Jeconiah was taken to Babylon (about 597 B.C.E.). This brought Zedekiah, Judah's last king, to the throne.

Jeremiah's Message

When the neighboring nations sent ambassadors to greet the new king of Judah, God sent Jeremiah to them with a message. Jeremiah wore chains and an ox yoke on his neck, symbolizing captivity and submission (27:1–2). The message was that God had made King Nebuchadnezzar of Babylon His servant. Assyria had been God's instrument to judge the northern kingdom of Israel (2 Kgs 17:7; 1 Chr 5:26). But Assyria had invaded with the intention of destroying God's people forever, so God promised to judge them as well (Isa 10:5–11).

Babylon would be God's new instrument of judgment. Those who resisted King Nebuchadnezzar would be destroyed by the Babylonian army. Those who submitted would remain in their lands. False prophets were predicting victory against Babylon, but the Babylonian empire would last for three generations (27:5–11). Jeremiah repeated this message to King Zedekiah (27:12–15) and the priests and people of Jerusalem (27:16–22). The valuable decorations and instruments remaining in the Temple would be taken to Babylon until God chose to restore them (27:21–22).

A Challenge to the Prophecy

Soon, a false prophet named Hananiah rose to challenge Jeremiah's prophecy. He claimed that God had decided to break the yoke of Babylon and within two years would restore the Temple, King Jeconiah, and the exiled young nobles (28:1–4). Jeremiah responded with a sarcastic, "Amen!" and said he wished it were so. He reminded the people that his prophecy of destruction was consistent with what other prophets had foretold (see Deut 28:47–52, 63–4). The true prophet would be vindicated when his message was fulfilled (see Deut 18:20–22).

PHASED EXILE TO BABYLON

Ancient conquerors did not necessarily begin the process of pacifying the people they conquered with mass deportation. If people were willing to submit, they were often allowed to continue to work their land for the benefit of the imperial power. In addition to levying tribute payments, hostages were often taken from the ruling classes, both as insurance against rebellion and in order to seize the "best and the brightest" for re-education in service of the empire. Installation of puppet kings, destruction of fortified cities, and mass deportation were increasingly severe options for dealing with persistent rebellion. Judah's exile to Babylon essentially followed this process.

The confrontation climaxed with Hananiah taking the yoke from Jeremiah's neck and breaking it to symbolize release from service to Nebuchadnezzar (28:10–11). Later, God sent Jeremiah back to tell Hananiah that the wooden yoke would be replaced with an iron bar (Deut 28:48), and that Hananiah would die within the year for being a false prophet (28:12–17).

BIBLICAL LINKS

"When a prophet speaks in the Lord's name, and the message does not come true or is not fulfilled, that is a message the Lord has not spoken. The prophet has spoken it presumptuously. Do not be afraid of him." *(Deuteronomy 18:22, HCSB)*

"The prophets who preceded you and me from ancient times prophesied war, disaster, and plague against many lands and great kingdoms. As for the prophet who prophesies peace—only when the word of the prophet comes true will the prophet be recognized as one the Lord has truly sent."

(Jeremiah 28:8–9, HCSB)

JEREMIAH

The Babylonian empire threatened the foundation of Israel's existence. God had appointed the House of David (2 Sam 7) to lead the nation to obey the Mosaic Covenant (Exod 20). But relations between Babylon and Judah made it clear that it was only a matter of time before Babylon would decide to destroy Jerusalem and its Temple and end the rule of the House of David. Once that happened, it seemed that God's Covenant with Israel would be finished.

False Hopes from False Prophets

False prophets in Babylon were telling the people there that God would prevent this by allowing Babylon to be defeated by another empire in the near future. But Jeremiah 29 describes a letter Jeremiah sent to the exiles in Babylon, taking God's message where the prophet could not go. As in Jeremiah 27–28, the prophet rejected false hope, but here it was rejected in favor of certain deliverance in the future.

King Zedekiah, Judah's last king, sent ambassadors to King Nebuchadnezzar of Babylon, presumably to convey tribute (29:3). Jeremiah took the opportunity to send his letter with the ambassadors to the exiled leaders and craftsmen of Judah now living in Babylon (29:1–2). The prophet counseled them to accept the common blessings of God, such as shelter, crops, marriage, and children (29:4–6), so that they would flourish in their new home.

God's Plan: Blessing

The blessings mentioned in Jeremiah's message parallel those of Deuteronomy 20:5-10, which lists reasons for exemption from military service. This implied that the exiles were to abandon hopes of a military solution. Most powerfully, Jeremiah counseled them to seek the welfare of the city that had devastated their home and taken them captive (29:7). The exiles of Judah had to let go of resentment and hatred toward Babylon, because humble service would benefit the captives as much as the captors (see Matt 5:43–48, Titus 3:1–2).

LOVE FOR ENEMIES

The Biblical teaching of love for enemies does not refer to affectionate feelings, but to blessing them with service aimed at their genuine good (Jer 29:7; see also Matt 5:43–48). Such actions not only benefit both parties, they are taken to reflect the character of God (Luke 10:25–38; Rom 5:8).

Although it seemed unlikely given their current state, Jeremiah promised that God's plan was not to destroy His people, but to bless them (29:11–14; see Deut 28:1–14). Babylon's power would last for only 70 years, after which God would begin to restore Judah to the Promised Land. At that time, they would call on the Lord and search for Him wholeheartedly. God promised to hear them and gather them back to Jerusalem.

BIBLICAL LINKS

"First of all, then, I urge that petitions, prayers, intercessions, and thanksgivings be made for everyone, for kings and all those who are in authority, so that we may lead a tranquil and quiet life in all godliness and dignity." *(1 Timothy 2:1–2, HCSB)*

"Seek the welfare of the city I have deported you to. Pray to the Lord on its behalf, for when it has prosperity, you will prosper."

(Jeremiah 29:7, HCSB)

JEREMIAH

Israel's repeated inability to remain faithful to the Mosaic Covenant prompted formal renewals of the Covenant under Moses (Exod 34), Joshua (Josh 23–24), Samuel (1 Sam 12), Hezekiah (2 Chr 29–31) and Josiah (2 Chr 34). But each renewal quickly lapsed and ultimately resulted in exile for both Israel and Judah. Another mere renewal would offer no hope of any difference. But Jeremiah prophesied an end to the faithless cycle (Jer 31:31–40).

A New Covenant

In the future, God would make a New Covenant with His people that would fulfill and surpass the Mosaic Covenant (31:31–32). The Old Covenant was marred by spiritual adultery on the part of the nation, but the New Covenant would result in a transformation of the heart (31:33). God's Law would no longer be an external code of duty and demands. Instead, the people's very nature would be faithfulness to God and knowing God would be their heart's desire. In being faithful to God, His people would simply be true to themselves. As a result, God would no longer make previous sins an issue in His relationship with His people (31:34).

God's Promise

God connected the assurance of this New Covenant with His providential rule of creation (31:35–37). Since the faithfulness of God's people would be a result of God's work in their hearts, it would take something that could overpower or outsmart God to cause Him to break it. The promise rests on the implication that no being wiser or more powerful than the Creator exists.

Finally, the New Covenant would one day transform the whole city of Jerusalem into the Holy of Holies, the dwelling place of the glory of God (31:38–40). Under the Mosaic Covenant, only the High Priest could enter the Holy of Holies in the Temple. When the New Covenant was fulfilled, all of God's people would live in God's city, and so dwell in His presence. The New Testament sees this covenant initiated with the crucifixion and resurrection of Christ (Heb 10:19–25) and to be ultimately completed when the heavenly New Jerusalem arrives on earth (Rev 21:9–27).

BIBLICAL LINKS

"It is clear that you are Christ's letter, produced by us, not written with ink but with the Spirit of the living God—not on stone tablets but on tablets that are hearts of flesh." *(2 Corinthians 3:3, HCSB)*

ORIGIN OF THE NAME "NEW TESTAMENT"

Testament is an older English word for covenant or contract. Jesus described His sacrifice as "the New Covenant" (Luke 22:20; see also 1 Cor 11:25; 2 Cor 3:1–14; Heb 8:8–12; 10:16–17). The collection of Bible books that describe Christ's ministry and its implications takes its name from that idea.

ENTERING THE HOLY OF HOLIES

The Holy of Holies (Holiest Place) was the inner chamber in the Temple, where the Ark of the Covenant rested. Only the High Priest could enter this room, and he could only go there once a year to sprinkle the blood of the Day of Atonement sacrifice on the Ark. Entering the Holy of Holies required elaborate ritual preparations designed to cleanse the High Priest of impurity and protect him from being destroyed by God's holy presence (Lev 16). These laws illustrate the significance of Jeremiah's prophecy that all of God's people would dwell in the Holy of Holies forever.

"Instead, this is the covenant I will make with the house of Israel after those days"—the Lord's declaration. "I will put My teaching within them and write it on their hearts. I will be their God, and they will be My people."

(Jeremiah 31:33, HCSB)

LAMENTATIONS

INTRODUCTION

Lamentations is a small collection of funeral dirges over the destruction of Jerusalem. The first four chapters are poems, each of which begins with a Hebrew letter. The first letters of each poem progress through the Hebrew alphabet in order, creating an acrostic. In spite of the mourning over Jerusalem, the book affirms that God intended to refine His people.

KEY PASSAGES

The Lament of Jerusalem (1)

The Judgment of God (2)

Hope for Mercy (3)

The Terrible Siege (4)

Prayer for Restoration (5)

PRINCIPAL FIGURES

God   Lamentations acknowledges God as the just Judge of His people, but appeals to Him as One who looks on His people's suffering with mercy and compassion.

Jerusalem   Jerusalem is personified in Lamentations as a woman confessing her sins and appealing for forgiveness.

Jeremiah   The author of Lamentations speaks as an eyewitness of the destruction of Jerusalem and is brokenhearted for the city (Jer 4:19–22).

LOCATION: Lamentations mourns Jerusalem after its destruction by Babylon, to which the author was an eyewitness. The location of the mourner is not clear.

ORIGIN: The language and anguish of Lamentations is that of an eyewitness to Jerusalem's destruction (586 B.C.E.), but the text does not identify an author. Tradition dating to the Greek translation of the Old Testament (around 200 B.C.E.) attributes the book to Jeremiah. Some modern scholars have suggested other possibilities but have not found consensus.

A PLEA FOR MERCY
(Lamentations 5)

After Jerusalem was destroyed, Babylon took all but the poorest Israelites into exile. Those that remained, like Jeremiah, mourned over the destruction of their city with elaborate poems. The Babylonian siege had stripped away all the pleasant illusions that God would ignore their idolatry as long as they maintained the external forms of the Temple worships. The idols they had served were unable to help them, and their allies had failed them.

Finally, when all had already been lost, they turned to God. They described themselves as orphans and widows, which was surely the simple truth for many of them, remembering God's traditional concern for the poor and defenseless (Ps 146:9; Jer 49:11). The basic necessities of life, once freely available, now had to be purchased from their captors for silver. Food had to be imported to the land that had once flowed with milk and honey.

Their punishment had been long coming, however. The defeated Judeans acknowledged that their fathers had sinned, sowing seeds which they now were reaping. Those who had once been their slaves were now their rulers. The women of Jerusalem had been raped and the elders dishonored by the conquering enemy. Joy had given way to despair, and the cause was the sin of the people.

Much had changed for Judah, but God had not. He was still on His throne and His rule, plan, and kingdom were unscathed. The survivor's plaintive cry struggled with whether God would ever remember them, or would He instead abandon them to the consequences of their sins. They begged God to restore them so that they might return to Him. God's people dared to hope for renewal. Their only fear was that God's righteous anger might result in Him rejecting them as His people forever.

PLEAS FOR MERCY

Pleas for mercy in the Bible acknowledge or imply both the justice of the suffering being experienced and the character of God as the basis for relief. The most important aspect of God's character is *hesed*, which is compassion or loving kindness. Because His love cannot be exhausted, the Bible sees hope for those who turn to God.

"Because of the Lord's faithful love we do not perish, for His mercies never end. They are new every morning; great is Your faithfulness! I say: The Lord is my portion, therefore I will put my hope in Him."

(Lamentations 3:22–24, HCSB)

EZEKIEL

INTRODUCTION

Ezekiel sets the destruction of Jerusalem in the context of highly symbolic visions and public displays. The destruction of Jerusalem threatened the failure of the Abrahamic (Gen 12), Mosaic (Exod 20; Deut 28), and Davidic Covenants (2 Sam 7). Ezekiel explained the reasons for the exile to Babylon and reassured the exiles that God would restore His people and judge their enemies to fulfill His Covenant promises.

KEY PASSAGES

God's Glory in Judgment on Judah (1–24)

3:1–27	God Calls Ezekiel to Be a Watchman
4:1–5:17	Ezekiel Dramatizes the Siege of Jerusalem
10:1–22	God's Glory Leaves the Temple
15:1–17:24	God Uses Parables to Explain His Relationship with Israel
18:1–32	God Rebukes the Exiles' Sense of Victimization
23:1–49	God Compares His People to Two Prostitutes

God's Glory in Judgment on the Nations (25–32)

God's Glory in the Future Kingdom (33–48)

33:1–32	God Calls Ezekiel to Be a Watchman (Again)
37:1–14	God Shows Ezekiel the Valley of Dry Bones

PRINCIPAL FIGURES

God The book of Ezekiel sees God as the Glorious Sovereign who will not tolerate sin, but purifies His people so that they can experience His glory fully.

Ezekiel A leading citizen of Jerusalem and priest who went into exile in Babylon along with King Jehoiachin.

Oholah and Oholibah The northern kingdom of Israel and southern kingdom of Judah are personified as two foolish prostitutes who lusted for Assyrian and Babylonian lovers.

Nebuchadnezzar The king of Babylon. His first attempt to invade Egypt resulted in failure and the rebellion of the smaller nations in Canaan, including Judah. Ezekiel prophesied that God would allow him to conquer Phoenicia and Egypt as a sign of His favor on Babylon.

Pharaoh The title of the ruler of Egypt, known to history as Amasis II or Amhose II, who was defeated in Nebuchadnezzar's second invasion of Egypt.

Gog or Magog A future ruler from the far north who will invade Israel and provoke a final battle with Yahweh.

LOCATION: Ezekiel was written in a village on the banks of the River Chebar in Babylon but describes visions and events taking place in Jerusalem and the regions around Israel.

ORIGIN: The Book of Ezekiel begins with the prophet describing the first of his visions in Babylon (Ezek 1:1) and provides the dates of 11 visions and prophecies (July 593 B.C.E. to April 571 B.C.E.). Internal evidence for a single author includes the literary unity and chronological progression of the book, as well as the consistent use of an eyewitness perspective. Some modern scholars have argued for minor editing by the second generation of exiles in Babylon.

THE CALL OF EZEKIEL
(Ezekiel 3 & 33)

When God called Ezekiel, He gave the prophet a vision in which Ezekiel was presented with a scroll. It was covered with proclamations of woe, mourning, and sadness on both sides (Ezek 2). Then God ordered the prophet to eat the scroll and then speak to the Israelites exiled to Babylon. The vision symbolized God placing His words inside of Ezekiel.

The scroll was sweet like honey, in spite of its bitter words. Yet God warned Ezekiel that the Israelites would not listen to the message. God observed that if He had sent Ezekiel to the Babylonians, they would have accepted the message in spite of the language barrier. God's people, however, would not listen. But God also told Ezekiel that He had made the prophet just as tough as the people to whom he would speak (Ezek 3).

The unpleasant message must have made the prophet wish he could simply remain silent, but God warned Ezekiel that he was being sent as a watchman. A watchman was responsible to sound the alarm when the enemy approached. Ezekiel also would be responsible to preach God's message to His people. If he failed to proclaim God's message through the words God gave or the dramatic actions God directed, then he would be responsible for their suffering. But if he fulfilled his unpleasant task, responsibility for the people's response would lie with them (Ezek 3, 33).

PROPHECY AS DRAMA

Not all prophecies were delivered through sermons. Ezekiel built a model of Jerusalem and lay before it to symbolize its destruction and exile (Ezek 4). Hosea married a prostitute who represented Israel's unfaithfulness (Hos 1–3). Isaiah preached naked for three years to symbolize Judah's march into exile. Jeremiah wore an ox yoke to represent Judah's captivity (Jer 27–28) but also purchased land as an expression of hope for Judah's restoration (Jer 32).

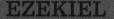 EZEKIEL

THE SIEGE OF JERUSALEM
(Ezekiel 4–5)

Ezekiel began his ministry in the period between the first deportation of Jews to Babylon and the fall of Jerusalem to the Babylonian army in 586 B.C.E. Though other prophets had highly symbolic visions and occasionally dramatized their messages, these elements formed a major part of Ezekiel's ministry. The prophet's greatest dramatic prophecy was performed early in his ministry to the first group of exiles in Babylon.

Act 1

After calling Ezekiel as a prophet, God commanded him to dramatize the coming siege of Jerusalem (4:1–3). Ezekiel took a clay brick, sketched a map of Jerusalem on it, and laid siege. He constructed a wall around the city to trap the inhabitants and prevent resupply. He raised a ramp against the wall for soldiers to reach the defenders, scattered camps around the siege wall, and built siege engines. Finally, he placed an iron plate as a wall and glared at the city from behind it, symbolizing the impenetrability of the Babylonian army and its determination.

Act 2

The second act lasted 430 days—more than a year (4:4–8). God instructed the prophet to lay on his left side for 390 days. He faced north, away from the clay brick, symbolizing the sin of the northern kingdom of Israel. Then for 40 days he lay on his right side, facing south toward the brick, symbolizing the sin of Judah. During this period, God prevented Ezekiel's from moving, so he lay as if bound by ropes. The significance of the 430 days is unclear. Some have suggested that it approximates the 433 years of the monarchy from Saul through Zedekiah. Others note that it fits the 430 years from Ezekiel's deportation (597 B.C.E.) to the Maccabean revolt (167 B.C.E.).

Act 3

The third act of the drama showed the starvation the city would endure (4:9–17). Ezekiel took basic staples and baked bread for food during the 430 days of his siege. He could only eat 8 ounces of bread a day. The catch was that he had to cook it over dried human dung, making it and himself ceremonially unclean. At this

Babylonian Empire
Route taken by exiled Jews
Primary Jewish settlements

point the prophet balked, asking God to spare him that requirement. God relented and allowed him to use dried cow dung instead.

Act 4

The final act took place when God ordered Ezekiel to shave his head and beard with a sharp sword. This act indicated the mourning and shame of the destruction of Jerusalem by the Babylonian army. Ezekiel then showed the fate of the people of Judah by slashing some of his hair with the sword around the model city, scattering some of it to the wind, and burning some of it. But God ordered the prophet to save just a few hairs and fold them in his robe, indicating that God would preserve a small percentage of His people to rebuild the nation (5:1–17).

> *"Take an iron plate and set it up as an iron wall between yourself and the city. Turn your face toward it so that it is under siege, and besiege it. This will be a sign for the house of Israel."*
>
> (Ezekiel 4:3, HCSB)

THE STRATEGIC LOCATION OF JERUSALEM

The Bible sees judgment as God's reason for destroying Jerusalem, but Babylon had other motives. When strong, Judah controlled the coastal and Jordan valley highways from Babylon to Egypt. For Egypt, Judah was a buffer from invasion. For Babylon, it could threaten Egyptian supply lines or support an invasion of Egypt.

RIGHTEOUS WRATH

Human anger is often unjustified and out of control. But the Bible describes God as patient and slow to anger (Num 14:18; Joel 2:13). God's wrath is always a justified response to evil and is proportionate to the spiritual significance of sin.

The Jewish exiles in Babylon had a proverb that sounded like wisdom but was actually foolishness: "The fathers eat sour grapes, and the children's teeth are set on edge" (18:2). They meant that they were being punished because of their fathers' sins, not because of any fault of their own. God swore that He would wipe that saying from their lips (8:3–4). Though the sins of one generation could affect later generations, God insisted that everyone who suffers punishment has earned it by their own actions.

The proverb arose because the people of Judah had misunderstood God's statement at Mount Sinai that He would punish "the children for the fathers' sin, to the third and fourth generations of those who hate Me" (Exod 20:5). They understood this to mean that parents could sin without fear of judgment, knowing that their children would bear the punishment. This view turned God's mercy and patience (Exod 34:6) into permission to sin. The people forgot that God had outlawed punishing innocent children for their parents' sins (Deut 24:16). Instead, what Exod 20:5 meant was that if the children repeated the sins of their fathers, God would not excuse them for simply doing as their parents had taught them. He would punish the wicked even if it took three or four generations to learn the lesson.

Case Studies

God emphasized His point with a series of hypothetical situations that illustrated the principle of individual responsibility. The righteous person would live (18:5–9), but if the son was wicked, the son would die (18:10–13). If the son of a wicked father refused to follow his father's evil example, he would live (18:14–17), but the father would die for his sin (18:18). The principle is that "the one who sins is the one who will die" (18:20; Deut 24:16).

The message then shifts to consider situations in which individuals make radical changes in their lives; repenting of evil or falling from righteousness. The good news was that a wicked person's past sins would

not necessarily determine their destiny. The one who repented in heart and deed would be forgiven and live (18:21–22). God's joy was in restoration, not judgment (18:23). But a person's past righteousness would not give them freedom to sin. Treachery would be met with judgment (18:24).

A Call to Repent

The people objected that God's mercy and justice were not fair, but God observed that those who knew nothing of fairness had no ground to object (18:25–29). He called the exiles to repent of their own sins and get a new heart and spirit (18:30-31; Jer 31:33; Joel 2:28). The alternative was certain judgment, which was not what God wanted for them (18:32).

"*"Throw off all the transgressions you have committed, and get yourselves a new heart and a new spirit. Why should you die, house of Israel? For I take no pleasure in anyone's death.' This is the declaration of the Lord God. 'So repent and live!'"*

(Ezekiel 18:31–32, HCSB)

JUDGING GOD IN THE BIBLE

God's way of doing things often doesn't fit the expectations of people in the Biblical narratives, sometimes drawing fierce criticism (for example, Gen 4:13; Job 32:2; Hab 1-2; Rom 9). Surprisingly, the typical response not only points out the critic's limited, flawed perspective, it displays grace (Ezek 18:25-32; Job 38-42). Rather than destroying the person who displayed blasphemous pride by judging God, the Lord calls them to repent and welcomes the newly humbled critic back into His favor.

BIBLICAL LINKS

"The Lord does not delay His promise, as some understand delay, but is patient with you, not wanting any to perish but all to come to repentance." (2 Peter 3:9, HCSB)

EZEKIEL

THE VALLEY OF DRY BONES
(Ezekiel 37)

In Biblical times, mass deportation into exile was a used as a means to kill cultures. Deported peoples tended to blend into the population and evaporate into the mists of history. It must have seemed that this would be the fate for Israel as well. But God showed Ezekiel a vision of the aftermath of a massacre transformed into hope.

Ezekiel's Vision

The prophet saw a valley floor littered with very old, dry bones (37:1–2). God asked Ezekiel if the bones could live again, and the prophet replied that God alone knew. So God told Ezekiel to preach a message to the bones. God would give them flesh, skin, and breath; they would live and know God (37:4–6).

As Ezekiel preached in his vision, the bones started to move. Skeletons reformed and flesh grew. The preacher summoned the four winds to give life to the bones, and they rose to their feet, a vast army of living men (37:9–10).

When the vision ended, God explained that it was a symbolic picture of the future of the nation of Israel. The bones represented the nation of Israel, which seemed dead and hopeless in exile. But God promised to open the graves (the nations) and bring the people back to life in the Promised Land. God would place His Spirit in them and they would know God (37:11–14).

A Promise to Unite Israel

God promised more than just a return to the situation as it was before the exile. After the vision, God instructed Ezekiel to take two sticks and write the names of the northern and southern kingdoms on them. Then, he was to bind the sticks together into one. When the people asked him to explain, Ezekiel told them that God was going to unite the stick of Israel and the stick of Judah into one branch (37:15–19). The people would return from the lands of their exile and live under the Davidic King ("my servant David"). The nation would be righteous and secure in the land forever, and God would dwell with them (37:20–28).

TOMBS IN THE KIDRON VALLEY

The Kidron Valley lies between the Mount of Olives and the Temple Mount in Jerusalem. The western slope of the Mount of Olives, overlooking the valley, is the location of the oldest Jewish cemetery in the world. It was used as a burial site as early as 1000 B.C.E. Today it contains over 150,000 tombs. Some suggest that this was the location Ezekiel saw in his vision of the valley of dry bones. Jewish tradition also holds that the Kidron Valley will be the place where the final resurrection begins, making those buried there the first to rise to eternal life.

"'You will know that I am Yahweh, My people, when I open your graves and bring you up from them. I will put My Spirit in you, and you will live, and I will settle you in your own land. Then you will know that I am Yahweh. I have spoken, and I will do it.' This is the declaration of the Lord."

(Ezekiel 37:13–14, HCSB)

HOPE OF RESURRECTION IN THE OLD TESTAMENT

Ezekiel 37 is a symbolic vision of return from exile expressed in terms of resurrection. Various passages described miraculous resuscitations, where dead people returned to a normal human life (1 Kgs 17:23; 2 Kgs 4:6, 13:21). But others expected a final resurrection in which the dead would be raised to eternal life, never to die again (Job 19:25–26; Isa 26:19; Dan 12:1–4). Jesus argued that the Torah presumes resurrection (Mark 12:18–27; Exod 3:6).

BIBLICAL LINKS

"And just as the Father raises the dead and gives them life, so the Son also gives life to anyone He wants to." *(John 5:21, HCSB)*

DANIEL

Daniel records the faithfulness of God to four young Jewish noblemen during the Babylonian Exile. The book moves from God's providential control over the lives of individuals to His sovereign rule over empires and history. Conflict runs throughout the historical narratives and visions of this book, between God and His servants, both human and angelic, and among the rulers of this world.

LOCATION: The events and visions in the book of Daniel take place in and around the city of Babylon. Specific locations include the king's palace, the Plain of Dura outside the city, and a vision set in the city of Susa.

KEY PASSAGES

The Life of Daniel (1–6)

1   Daniel Is Faithful to God's Laws

2   Daniel Interprets the King's Dream

3   Daniel's Friends Defy the King (and Survive)

4   Nebuchadnezzar Is Humbled Before God

5   Daniel Reads the Handwriting on the Wall

6   Daniel Survives the Lion's Den

Daniel's Visions (7–12)

9   Daniel Prays for God to Forgive Israel

11   Daniel Predicts the Temple's Desecration

ORIGIN: The book claims Daniel as its primary author (7:1–2), but attributes some material to Nebuchadnezzar (4:1–37). The New Testament affirms Daniel's authorship (see Matt 24:15). The events described took place from 606 B.C.E. through 536 B.C.E. Many modern scholars reject the idea that Daniel could be the author of the book, taking the fact that the book was written in Hebrew and Aramaic to indicate at least two authors. Those who assume that prophetic revelation cannot occur call Daniel 7–12 into question.

PRINCIPAL FIGURES

God   In the book of Daniel, God appears equally concerned with the submission of individuals and nations to His will. He demonstrates faithfulness toward those who are faithful to Him.

Nebuchadnezzar   The king of Babylon whose pride was broken through a series of visions and public humiliations.

Daniel or Belteshazzar   The leader of the four Jewish noblemen. Daniel served three kings and found God faithful as he remained obedient to God.

Hananiah or Shadrach   Along with Mishael or Meshach, and Azariah or Abednego: Daniel's three friends who defied the king and survived the fiery furnace.

The Chaldeans   A group of scholars who studied the stars and interpreted dreams. They functioned as advisors to the Babylonian and Persian kings. Daniel consistently presents them as ineffective and useless.

Belshazzar   The last king of Babylon, defeated by the Persians after "seeing the handwriting on the wall."

Darius   The Persian king whom Daniel served. Though he was manipulated into issuing an edict that sent Daniel to the lion's den, he agonized until Daniel was released.

Son of Man   A heavenly figure who is given eternal dominion over the nations, in apparent fulfillment of the Davidic Covenant.

Gabriel and Michael   Angelic figures sent to explain Daniel's visions.

FAITHFULNESS IN BABYLON
(Daniel 1)

When Judah attempted to renege on its treaty with Babylon, the Babylonians took a selection of sons from noble Jewish families back to Babylon as hostages. Daniel and his friends, Hananiah, Mishael, and Azariah, were among those young men. The primary goal was to ensure the good behavior of the Jewish leaders left behind in Judah. But the policy also served to drain Judah of the most promising members of its next generation and reeducate them for service to the Babylonian king.

The reeducation of the Jewish boys began by giving them new names. The boys' Hebrew names, which honored Yahweh, were replaced with Babylonian names honoring Bel, Nebo, and Aku. Changing their names did not change their allegiance, however. Daniel determined that he would continue to obey God's Law.

Since all the men being trained for the king's service were to eat the king's food, Daniel had to get permission to follow the Jewish dietary laws.

God gave Daniel favor with the Babylonian official, but the man feared what would happen if he disobeyed the king's orders. So Daniel proposed an experiment. For 10 days, he and his friends would eat according to God's Law. At the end of the test period, Daniel and his friends looked better and healthier than those who ate the king's food. God honored Daniel's faithfulness by giving him and his friends wisdom far beyond that of the Chaldeans who advised the king.

DIETARY LAWS IN THE OLD TESTAMENT

The dietary laws in the Mosaic Covenant made it illegal for Israelites to eat some animals, most insects, the blood of animals, and animals found dead (Lev 11, 17; Deut 14). Some scholars suggest these laws prevented disease, others argue the forbidden animals were tied to idolatry, and others think the rules were arbitrary tests of obedience or symbols of distinction from Gentiles.

"God gave these four young men knowledge and understanding in every kind of literature and wisdom. Daniel also understood visions and dreams of every kind." (Daniel 1:17, HCSB)

DANIEL

THE KING'S DREAM
(Daniel 2)

Early in his reign, King Nebuchadnezzar of Babylon had a dream. Since the ancients believed that dreams contained divine messages, the king was anxious to understand it. He also saw an opportunity to test his advisors. Summoning his counselors, he demanded that they not only explain the dream, but also tell him what the dream was.

Nebuchadnezzar Is Distrustful

The advisors objected, saying that to know another man's dreams was beyond their skill; only the gods could do that, and they didn't dwell among men. Nebuchadnezzar decided that his advisors were frauds who had been conspiring to manipulate him with their interpretations, and he ordered their execution.

Though Daniel had not been among the counselors summoned to the king, the execution order covered all of the king's advisors. When the guards came to seize Daniel, he asked for time to hear from God. His friends prayed that God would show him the dream and its meaning. The next morning, Daniel went to the king with the answer. When the king demanded to know if Daniel had figured out the dream, the young prophet deflected credit from himself to God. Daniel told the Nebuchadnezzar that God wanted the king to know what would happen in the future. Nebuchadnezzar likely assumed that God was speaking to him because of his greatness as king of Babylon, but he should have learned from the interpretation of the dream to humble his pride before God.

The King's Dream

Daniel reported that the king had seen in his dream a statue with a head of gold, chest of silver, stomach and thighs of bronze, legs of iron, and feet of iron and clay. A stone broke away on its own and crushed the feet of the statue, which shattered and were blown away in the wind. The stone then became a mountain filling the whole earth.

The meaning was that God had allowed Nebuchadnezzar to build a glorious empire; he was the head of gold. The remaining parts of the statue were empires that would succeed Babylon with decreasing glory but increasing strength, until a strong-but-brittle kingdom concluded the series. It would be destroyed by the rock not shaped by human hands. The rock symbolized a divine, universal kingdom that would never end.

THE ROLE OF MAGI IN BABYLON

Ancients assumed that everything on Earth was connected to something in the heavens. The Greek word *magi*, meaning wise men, refers to those who tried to understand the structure of the universe in order to help people (especially rulers) flourish and succeed. Magi studied astrology, magic, and interpretation of signs and dreams. The New Testament reports that magi saw a star symbolizing the birth of one who would be "King of the Jews." These were the wise men who visited Jesus after His birth in Bethlehem (Matt 2:1–12).

Because Daniel was able to tell him the dream and its meaning, the king spared his advisors, promoted Daniel, and appointed Daniel's friends as governors over the province of Babylon. But the king himself seemed to miss the point of the dream. He failed to acknowledge the supremacy of God's eternal kingdom, which was the goal of human history as revealed by the dream. Instead, he planned a golden statue of himself for the people to worship (Dan 3). Eventually, his pride resulted in a period of temporary insanity (Dan 4).

"No wise man, medium, diviner-priest, or astrologer is able to make known to the king the mystery he asked about. But there is a God in heaven who reveals mysteries, and He has let King Nebuchadnezzar know what will happen in the last days."

(Daniel 2:27–28, HCSB)

BIBLICAL LINKS

"God will bring this about in His own time. He is the blessed and only Sovereign, the King of kings, and the Lord of lords, the only One who has immortality, dwelling in unapproachable light; no one has seen or can see Him, to Him be honor and eternal might. Amen." *(1 Timothy 6:15–16, HCSB)*

DANIEL

King Nebuchadnezzar liked the idea of being the golden head of the statue, the ruler and builder of the most glorious empire, as he had seen in his dream. So he ordered construction of a massive golden statue on the plain of Dura. The officials of the province were assembled before the statue, though Daniel may have remained at court (2:49). In what amounted to a loyalty oath, a herald commanded the assembled nobles to bow to the statue when they heard the instruments play. Almost everyone obeyed.

Daniel's Friends Refuse the King

Although it seems Daniel was not there to encourage them, his friends Shadrach, Meshach, and Abednego refused to bow to the idol. Other advisors saw the opportunity to undermine the Jews who had been promoted ahead of them and denounced them to Nebuchadnezzar. The king's anger smoldered, and he had the men brought to him. He gave them a second chance to worship the statue and warned that no one could rescue them if they refused. The men sealed their fate by contradicting the King; God could rescue them, but whether He chose to do so or not, they would not bow to the statue. Nebuchadnezzar's rage erupted and he ordered the furnace heated to seven times its normal temperature. It was so hot that the soldiers who threw the three Jews into the flames were themselves burned to death.

God Rescues the Faithful

As the king looked on with vengeful satisfaction, he could not believe his eyes. There were four men walking around in the furnace, one of whom looked like a "son of the gods" (3:25). The king inched as close as he dared and called the men to come out. When they did, there was not even a whiff of smoke on them. Nebuchadnezzar decided it was wiser to have that God on his side, so he praised God's power and threatened death to any who disrespected God.

"If the God we serve exists, then He can rescue us from the furnace of blazing fire, and He can rescue us from the power of you, the king. But even if He does not rescue us, we want you as king to know that we will not serve your gods or worship the gold statue you set up."

(Daniel 3:17–18, HCSB)

THE ORIGINS OF RELIGIOUS LIBERTY

Ancient rulers thought angering the gods threatened national security. Rejecting state-mandated religion was treason. Daniel 3 marks the earliest assertion of religious liberty; government is not competent to judge (condemn) sincere religious conviction and cannot coerce religious observance. The most famous Biblical expression of religious liberty was Jesus' statement on paying taxes (Matt 22:21). The command to give Caesar his due while also giving God His due affirms both the legitimacy of government and its limited claim to human allegiance. Believers owe obedience to those in authority over them (Rom 13), except when that obedience requires disobedience to God (Acts 5:29).

BIBLICAL LINKS

"Therefore give back to Caesar the things that are Caesar's, and to God the things that are God's.'"
(Matthew 22:21, HCSB)

DANIEL

Later in his reign, after his building projects had been completed, King Nebuchadnezzar of Babylon had a second disturbing dream (see Dan 2). His wise men were at a loss to interpret it. Finally, Daniel was summoned to hear the king's dream.

The King's Dream

Nebuchadnezzar had seen an enormous tree, visible to the ends of the earth. It provided food and shelter for every creature on earth. But a heavenly figure commanded that the tree be cut down. Only the stump was left, protected by a fence of iron and bronze. Then the vision shifted; the tree became a man living among the animals. The man was insane, and for seven years thought himself to be an animal. The heavenly figure declared that this judgment was to let the world know that God rules the kingdoms of men and gives them to whomever He pleases.

Daniel's Interpretation

Daniel heard the King's dream in stunned silence. When he finally spoke, he lamented that the message applied to Nebuchadnezzar and not to one of his enemies. The king himself was the tree that would be cut down. The king would lose his mind for seven years. Thinking himself an ox, he would live in the fields and eat grass until he acknowledged God's sovereignty over the kingdoms of men. Daniel urged the king to humble himself, but unfortunately, he did not.

Nebuchadnezzar Is Humbled

A year later, the king was walking on the roof of his palace, congratulating himself on the magnificence of his city and empire. A voice from heaven spoke and repeated Daniel's interpretation of the dream. In that moment, Nebuchadnezzar lost his mind. He was taken from the city of Babylon and allowed to wander the fields, likely under guard to keep him safe. His hair grew long and matted. His nails grew long and curved like a bird's claws.

GOD OPPOSES THE PROUD

Blasphemous pride lies at the root of the Bible's view of the human problem (see Gen 3). One of the major patterns in the Bible is the humbling of the proud (Prov 3:34; Jas 4:6). For example, Judah learned that even a pagan girl could be more righteous than he was (Gen 38). Pharaoh found that neither his gods nor his armies could withstand the God of the Hebrew slaves (Exod 7–14). Job learned that he did not know enough to judge God's governance of the universe (Job 38–42). Paul found that he was opposing the Messiah (Acts 9).

After seven years, the king looked toward heaven, his pride finally broken. It was only then that his sanity returned. His advisors and the officials under him recognized that Nebuchadnezzar's sanity had returned. They began to submit themselves to his authority and seek his will once again. The account in Daniel 4 is presented as Nebuchadnezzar's own report, written in praise of the God who had humbled him. The king acknowledged that God is the true and eternal Ruler over angels and men. He can even humble the greatest of kings.

"Now I, Nebuchadnezzar, praise, exalt, and glorify the King of heaven, because all His works are true and His ways are just. He is able to humble those who walk in pride."

(Daniel 4:37, HCSB)

BIBLICAL LINKS

"For though they knew God, they did not glorify Him as God or show gratitude. Instead, their thinking became nonsense, and their senseless minds were darkened." *(Romans 1:21, HCSB)*

DANIEL

Daniel records the breaking of Nebuchadnezzar's pride (Dan 2–4), but it also tells of the breaking of Belshazzar's empire (Dan 5). Darius the Mede had invaded the Babylonian heartland and was near victory. Whether Belshazzar was celebrating a religious festival or simply making a show of bravado in a desperate situation, the king held an opulent feast for 1,000 nobles and got drunk with them. During the feast, Belshazzar ordered the sacred vessels from the Temple in Jerusalem brought out so that he and his guests could drink from them and praise the idols of Babylon.

Daniel Is Summoned

As the cup touched the king's lips, a hand appeared and wrote on the wall. Belshazzar trembled violently and called for the wise men to interpret the sign. He offered to make the one who explained its meaning his the third most important ruler in the kingdom. As was usual in the book of Daniel, the advisors could not understand the sign, so Daniel was summoned.

Daniel spoke of the greatness of Nebuchadnezzar and how he had been humbled before God (Dan 4). But then he accused Belshazzar of failing to learn from his predecessor's example. Instead of humbling himself before the One who held the king's life in His hand, Belshazzar had asserted his superiority over God by using His sacred vessels in drunken worship of idols.

The End of an Empire

The inscription read *"mene, mene, tekel, parsin,"* which is Aramaic for "numbered, numbered, weighed, divided". *Mene* meant that God had numbered the days of the Babylonian empire and that its last day had come. *Tekel* meant that Belshazzar had been weighed in the scales of God's justice and found lacking. *Parsin* meant that the Babylonian empire was being cut apart and given to the Persians.

Daniel refused any reward for giving the interpretation, but the king wrapped him in a royal robe and golden chain, making Daniel the third ruler of Babylon. He held the job for just a few hours. That night Belshazzar was killed by the Persians, paving the way for Darius to rule Babylon.

BIBLICAL LINKS

"Therefore He says: God resists the proud, but gives grace to the humble." *(James 4:6, HCSB)*

FAMILIAR SAYINGS

Daniel 5 is the source for the saying that someone has "seen the handwriting on the wall," meaning a sure sign of doom, usually their own. Other famous sayings from the Bible include, "go the extra mile" (Matt 5:41), "it is better to give than to receive" (Acts 20:31), "no rest for the wicked" (Isa 57:20), and "wolf in sheep's clothing" (Matt 7:15).

"But you his successor, Belshazzar, have not humbled your heart, even though you knew all this. Instead, you have exalted yourself against the Lord of heaven. ... you praised the gods made of silver and gold, bronze, iron, wood, and stone, which do not see or hear or understand. But you have not glorified the God who holds your life-breath in His hand and who controls the whole course of your life."

(Daniel 5:22–23, HCSB)

DANIEL

The Persian Empire was huge; it included everything from modern Turkey to Pakistan and Egypt to modern Afghanistan. In order to rule his vast realm, Darius appointed 120 Satraps, who functioned as regional sovereigns under the Persian king. Daniel distinguished himself above them all, so Darius planned to make him prime minister. But the bureaucrats did everything they could to block Daniel from being set over them. Since there was no flaw in his character or the performance of his duties, their only hope was to catch him between his duty to the king and his duty to God's Law.

A Trap Is Set

The satraps went to the king and, in a show of flattery, praised the king for his divine governance of the empire. They urged him establish the equivalent of a loyalty oath by issuing an edict forbidding everyone from praying to anyone other than Darius for 30 days. Disobedience would mean being cast into a den of ravenous lions. Not realizing their motives or the law's consequences, Darius happily obliged.

When Daniel learned of the law, he simply returned to his house and followed his customary schedule. Three times each day he prayed at the windows facing towards Jerusalem (see 2 Chr 6:36–39). The bureaucrats staked out the house, and when they saw Daniel pray, they denounced him to Darius. The king was determined to rescue Daniel, but the satraps maliciously reminded the king that the decrees of Persian rulers were irrevocable. As Daniel was lowered into the pit, the king called on Daniel's God to save him. The pit was then sealed with the seals of the king and his nobles.

Daniel Is Spared

The next morning, the king rushed to the lions' den and called for Daniel. Daniel answered that God had sent His angel to shut the lions' mouths because he was innocent before God and the king. Daniel was lifted out, and the conspirators and their families were given the opportunity to prove their blamelessness in the same way. So ferocious were the lions, they never reached the floor of the pit. Though cruel, the execution of whole families was typical of Persian policy and was perhaps intended to eliminate the possibility of sons rising to avenge their fathers.

PRAYER IN THE BIBLE

Prayer was a significant act of piety for Hebrews. They often prayed lying prostrate or standing upright with hands uplifted, like a child asking to be picked up. Both postures indicated humility and dependence. The Bible describes God hearing the prayers of women, men, religious people, and even sinners and pagans.

A LION'S DEN

The availability of a den of lions for use as a form of execution was no accident. The Persian kings were known to trap and keep lions as a display of their power. The Persians were also famous for creatively horrific forms of execution, such as inducing insects to eat a living victim covered with milk and honey and sealing a person in a room and then blowing ashes into the room until the person suffocated.

"I issue a decree that in all my royal dominion, people must tremble in fear before the God of Daniel: For He is the living God, and He endures forever; His kingdom will never be destroyed, and His dominion has no end. He rescues and delivers; He performs signs and wonders in the heavens and on the earth, for He has rescued Daniel from the power of the lions."

(Daniel 6:26–27, HCSB)

HOSEA

Hosea is a series of sermons calling the northern kingdom of Israel to return to its covenant of love with God. In the first sermon, Hosea's marriage is introduced as a metaphor for God's relationship to Israel. The verdict of judgment for the purpose of reconciliation becomes the theme developed by the book's remaining sermons.

KEY PASSAGES

Hosea's Marriage to Gomer (1–3)

God's Marriage to Israel (4–14)

4:1–5:15	God Accuses Israel of Sleeping Around
6:1–7:16	God Mourns for Israel
8:1–10:15	God Destroys Israel's False Sense of Security
11:1–13:16	God Decides to Reprise the Exodus
14:1–9	God Promises to Reconcile Penitent Israel

PRINCIPAL FIGURES

God   God is portrayed as the husband whose wife, the nation of Israel, has been unfaithful to Him by chasing after other gods. Rather than divorce Israel, God resolves to reconcile her to Himself.

Hosea   A citizen of the northern kingdom whose marriage and family life serve as a metaphor for Israel's relationship to God.

Gomer   Hosea's unfaithful wife; a symbol for Israel's spiritual prostitution.

Jezreel   Gomer's first son. His name indicated that the dynasty of the current king of Israel would face the same bloody end that the previous dynasty met at the city of Jezreel.

Lo-Ruhama or Ruhama   Gomer's daughter. Her name was a declaration that unfaithful Israel was unloved by God. Her name was later changed to reflect God's enduring love for Israel.

Lo-Ammi or Ammi   Gomer's second son. His name declared that unfaithful Israelites were not God's people. His name was later changed to reflect God's acceptance of Israel.

LOCATION: The sermons in Hosea were delivered in the northern kingdom of Israel, also called Ephraim, probably in the capital, Samaria. A key symbolic location is divorce court.

ORIGIN: Hosea wrote during a period spanning the reign of Jeroboam in the north through Hezekiah in the south (760–710 B.C.E.), indicating that he witnessed the fall of the northern kingdom to Assyria (722 B.C.E.). Much modern scholarship accepts Hosea as the author of the book, though some suggest that later editors compiled the material into its present form.

God called Hosea to be a prophet and instructed him to marry an unfaithful wife (1:1–3). Hosea married Gomer, and together they had only one child, a boy named Jezreel. Hosea gave him this name as a warning that God would wipe out the ruling family of the northern Kingdom of Israel.

Gomer had two more children, a girl and boy, both by other men. God told Hosea to name the girl Lo-Ruhama, meaning "I Don't Love You," as a sign that God would no longer protect Israel from judgment. The boy was named Lo-Ammi, meaning "Not My People," in effect calling him "Bastard," to indicate the breech between God and Israel (1:4–9).

Hosea's marriage and its troubles were quite real, but his marriage was also an analogy for God's relationship with Israel. After the birth of Gomer's children, God had Hosea preach a message that took the form of divorce proceedings (2:2–23). As the aggrieved husband, God accused Israel of having credited her lovers, the idols, with providing her food and clothing. As the Judge, He decreed that Israel would be impoverished and everything she thought the idols had granted her would be lost. But at verdict, God did something unexpected. He sentenced Israel to reconciliation and seduction. He promised to remove her love for Baal and replace it with joy in Himself. Israel would become a faithful wife, pure in her loyalty to God.

The story ended with Hosea finding Gomer and bringing her home. Though she had become a slave, she now belonged to her husband, who restored her to marriage. The children were given new names, meaning "I Love You" and "My People." Paul would later link to this image in his exposition of the grace and love of God (Rom 9:25–26).

REVELATION OF GOD IN SUFFERING

An uncomfortable but significant theme in the Bible is that the character of God is most clearly seen through suffering. Symbolized through divorce court, Israel's unfaithfulness highlighted the unconditional and transforming love of God for His people. God loved His people, and loved them enough not to leave them in their sinful, self-destructive ways.

JOEL

The book of Joel addresses God's people in a time of great distress. Locusts had devoured the crops and fires had swept the countryside. An invasion by a skilled foe was apparently coming soon. God's violent intervention (the Day of the Lord) would come as judgment on the southern kingdom. The people were estranged from God and so were called to repent. But their despair also evoked God's encouragement.

Location   The prophecies of Joel were delivered in the southern kingdom of Judah, most likely in Jerusalem.

KEY PASSAGES

Natural Disasters Devastate Judah (1)

A Call for National Repentance (2:1–17)

God Promises to Bless Judah (2:18–32)

God Promises to Restore the Promised Land (3)

ORIGIN: Nothing is known about Joel, the author of the prophecy that bears his name. Some suggest that the book was written after the Babylonian exile (after 500 B.C.E.), but recent scholarship has argued that the looming foreign invasion suggests a date prior to the fall of Jerusalem (586 B.C.E.), possibly even before the fall of the northern kingdom of Israel (722 B.C.E.).

PRINCIPAL FIGURES

God   Though God judges His people, He is also gracious and compassionate, patient and faithful.

Joel   The focus of Joel's prophecy is on God and God's people. He is not a major figure in the book.

The Priests   Joel calls on the religious leaders of Judah to lead the nation to return to Covenant faithfulness.

The Children of Zion   Joel addresses the people of Judah collectively, promising that their sorrow would be replaced by blessing and joy.

"After this I will pour out My Spirit on all humanity; then your sons and your daughters will prophesy, your old men will have dreams, and your young men will see visions. I will even pour out My Spirit on the male and female slaves in those days."

(Joel 2:28–29, HCSB)

THE PROMISE OF THE SPIRIT
(Joel 2)

The prophet Joel called on the nation of Judah to repent of its faithless violations of the Mosaic Covenant. He reported that if they did so, God would rescue Judah and bless the people. The land itself would turn green and the animals would find easy food. Figs and grapes would grow in abundance as they once had, and the rains would produce overflowing harvests of grain and olives. It would be as if the produce the locusts had destroyed were being given back to the people. All this and more would be evidence of God's presence with His people once again.

The greatest proof of God's grace and favor would be the presence of His Spirit, poured out on all humanity. Both men and women would speak God's truth. Both old and young would be granted divine insight. No one would be left out; even the lowest members of society would receive this richest of gifts from God. Yet the gift of God's Spirit would be a final warning to the world that God's judgment was coming. Only those who called on the name of Yahweh would be saved, and the Lord promised that He would call survivors to Himself. Peter cited this text as the foundation of his sermon to the people of Jerusalem in Acts 2:14-24, explaining the strange events of Pentecost.

THE DAY OF THE LORD

The phrase "Day of the Lord" shows up 18 times in the books written by Old Testament prophets. Variations appear over 45 times in the New Testament. The phrase refers primarily to the final judgment of God on humanity, though it can refer to earlier judgments that foreshadow the final judgment. The Book of Revelation provides the most detailed description of this final judgment.

AMOS

Amos confronted the northern kingdom of Israel at a high point in its military and economic power. He prophesied that the kingdom's social oppression and idolatry would result in swift destruction. Amos demanded the shrines at Bethel and Dan be abandoned, but didn't hope for repentance. Instead, he prophesied that restoration would come only after punishment.

LOCATION: Amos' prophecies were delivered in the northern kingdom of Israel, likely in Samaria, the capital city. At least one oracle, however, was proclaimed at the shrine in Bethel at the southern end of the kingdom.

KEY PASSAGES

The Words of Amos (1–6)

1:1-2:16	God's Judgment Will Target Israel
3:1-16	Israel's Judgment Is Well Deserved
4:1-13	Israel Refuses to Listen to God
5:1-6:14	The Day of the Lord Will Judge Israel

The Visions of Amos (7–9)

7:1-9	God Will No Longer Spare Israel
7:10-17	Amaziah Opposes Amos
8:1-9:10	Israel Will Be Destroyed
9:11-15	Hope for Restoration

ORIGIN: Amos was not a "professional" prophet (1:1). He tended sheep and cared for sycamore figs in the small town of Tekoa, about six miles south of Bethlehem, before God sent him north. The kings mentioned in the book place Amos' preaching sometime between 760 and 750 B.C.E. Modern scholarship provides a wide variety of alternative theories about the origin of the book.

PRINCIPAL FIGURES

God Amos presents God as the Holy Judge who hates the sin and pride of Israel.

Amos A shepherd and farmer from the southern kingdom of Judah, commissioned by God to proclaim judgment against the northern kingdom of Israel.

Amaziah A priest at the royal shrine in Bethel who scoffed at Amos' preaching and was judged to see his family destroyed and to die in exile.

Jeroboam The king of the northern kingdom of Israel, Jeroboam II was a descendent of Jehu (2 Kgs 9–10). He defeated Israel's major enemy, Aram, and was the last strong king in Samaria.

"Seek good and not evil so that you may live, and the Lord, the God of Hosts, will be with you, as you have claimed. Hate evil and love good; establish justice in the gate. Perhaps the Lord, the God of Hosts, will be gracious to the remnant of Joseph."

(Amos 5:14–15, HCSB)

THE DAY OF THE LORD
(Amos 5)

God hated the shrines that the northern kingdom's first ruler, Jeroboam I, had established at Bethel and Dan (2 Kgs 12). In their own way, they were more dangerous than the idols to Baal, precisely because they pretended to be shrines to Yahweh. So when Amos called the Israelites to return to God, they were warned not to seek Him in Bethel. Instead, they were to seek God by abandoning their corruption and oppression of the weak and poor among them.

The people were used to claiming that God was with them. They thought of the northern kingdom as the dwelling place of Yahweh. But God warned them that only by seeking the good would God be with them as

they claimed. Some even longed for the Day of the Lord, in which they thought God would judge all the northern kingdom's enemies. What they failed to realize was that God's judgment would start with them. God hated their feasts and the stench from their sacrifices. Their most beautiful music was mere noise in His ears.

What God wanted from His people was justice to flow like a mountain stream, swift and clear. Righteousness was to course through the land like a river that never failed. He reminded the people that during their wilderness wanderings God had not delighted in sacrifice but had worked to purify the people of their sin and rebellion. So it would be again in their time. God's intent to bring about righteousness among His people rather than continual sacrifices for sin became part of Stephen's sermon before the Sanhedrin in Acts 7 (see 7:42–43).

A PROPHETIC SUCKER PUNCH

The prophets' preaching was not gentle. For example, Amos 1–3 developed a rhythmic pattern of declaring judgment on Israel's enemies, beginning with Damascus. He moved in turn to the Philistines, Phoenicia, Edom, Ammon, Moab, and Judah, eliciting ever-growing acclamation from the Israelites. But the final cheer caught in their throats as the sermon climaxed with a surprise: judgment on their own kingdom of Israel.

OBADIAH

Obadiah records a prophecy against the nation of Edom. Though traditional enemies of the Israelites, Edom had allied with Judah against Babylon (Jer 27:2–7), but then betrayed Judah (Lam 1:2) and cheered the fall of Jerusalem (Obad 12). Obadiah encouraged the Jews by telling them that God would not let Edom's attempt to exterminate His people go unanswered.

LOCATION: The prophecy itself was likely delivered in Judah but spoke about the neighboring nation of Edom in what is now southwestern Jordan.

KEY PASSAGES

God Promises to Destroy Edom (1–9)

Edom Betrays Judah to Destruction (10–14)

The Day of the Lord Will Vindicate God's People (15–21)

ORIGIN: Nothing is known about Obadiah. The similarities between Obadiah and Jeremiah 49 suggest the two prophets were contemporaries. The book may have been written before the final destruction of the city in 586 B.C.E., though more likely it was written soon after Jerusalem fell.

PRINCIPAL FIGURES

God In Obadiah's prophecy, God is the Avenger of His people against those who would see them annihilated as a people.

Obadiah Likely a contemporary of Jeremiah, left in the land after the Babylonian destruction of Jerusalem.

Edom The name of the nation of people descended from Esau, Isaac's son and Jacob's brother.

Teman The name of a major city of Edom, perhaps its capital, personified by Obadiah and substituted for "Edom."

"For the Day of the Lord is near, against all the nations. As you have done, so it will be done to you; what you deserve will return on your own head. ... Saviors will ascend Mount Zion to rule over the hill country of Esau, but the kingdom will be the Lord's."

(Obadiah 15, 21, HCSB)

Sometimes enough is enough. God had had enough of Edom. This nation, located southeast of Judah across the Dead Sea, had been an ancient rival and enemy of God's people. Although Edom and Judah had formed an alliance against Babylon, when the Babylonians invaded Judah, Edom saw the opportunity to be rid of the Jews once and for all. They betrayed Judah, joining the Babylonians and urging the utter destruction of Jerusalem and the inhabitants of Judah.

God was more than a little upset. He mocked the pride of Edom; its mountain fortresses would not withstand God's judgment. Since the Edomites had urged that Jerusalem be stripped, and had broken their treaty with Judah, they would experience the same judgment. The wise leaders of Edom would be thrown down as fools, and the fierce warriors of their capital Teman would cower like little children. The fall of Edom would be a sign to the nations for all who might try to exterminate God's people.

But God would protect His people. They would be a flame to Edom's stubble. The Edomites had taken territory from Judah when the Judeans were exiled to Babylon. So God promised that His people would annex the land of Edom when God took up the throne in Israel.

The prophecy against Edom fit into a larger Old Testament expectation that God would judge the nations and vindicate His people. The result would be that the nations would learn righteousness and respect the God of Israel. The Book of Revelation later took up this theme and saw the rule of God over the nations from Jerusalem fulfilled in the future reign of Christ (Rev 11:15).

JUDGMENT ON THE NATIONS

The Old Testament language of judgment on the nations appears extreme and severe to the modern reader (see especially Ps 137). But these texts were not a vicious celebration of others' pain. Rather, they were part of the greater emphasis on the judgment of God's own people. They highlight the gravity of sin, especially the attempt to exterminate God's people, and the fiercely protective love of God for His people. They must also be understood in light of God's desire to bless the nations through His people (Gen 12:1–3).

JONAH

INTRODUCTION

The book of Jonah condemned Israelite pride by describing Jonah's mission to Nineveh, an Assyrian city. Jonah's unwillingness to preach judgment to Nineveh grew from his certainty that God would use the message to cause repentance. In spite of Jonah's attempt to ensure Nineveh's destruction, the people repented and the city was spared.

LOCATION: The events in Jonah take place in Israel, on a ship at sea, in the city of Nineveh, and just outside Nineveh. Most famously, part of the story takes place inside a large fish or whale.

KEY PASSAGES

Jonah Flees God's Call (1)

Jonah Appeals to God (2)

Nineveh Repents and Is Spared (3)

God Confronts Jonah's Pride (4)

ORIGIN: Though the book itself does not identify Jonah as the author, the Bible seems to ascribe authorship of the story about Jonah to the prophet (see 2 Kgs 14:25) and treats the book as describing historical events (Matt 12:39–41). Jonah ministered during the reign of Jeroboam II (793–742 B.C.E.), the last strong ruler of the northern kingdom of Israel. Modern scholars are deeply divided over the book's genre: many treat it as a parable and question whether the book originated with Jonah prior to the fall of Samaria (722 B.C.E.) or a later writer.

PRINCIPAL FIGURES

God Jonah presents God as the merciful Sovereign over all creation (land and sea) and nations (Israel and Assyria), who will not be refused by those He calls.

Jonah A prophet from northern kingdom of Israel, who wanted to prevent Nineveh from avoiding divine judgment.

The Sailors The sailors manning the ship on which Jonah fled did everything in their power to spare Jonah's life. After tossing Jonah overboard, they became worshippers of Yahweh.

The King of Nineveh The Assyrian ruler who embraced his people's response to Jonah's preaching and ordered formal repentance in Nineveh.

"As my life was fading away, I remembered Yahweh. My prayer came to You, to Your holy Temple. Those who cling to worthless idols forsake faithful love, but as for me, I will sacrifice to You with a voice of thanksgiving. I will fulfill what I have vowed. Salvation is from the Lord!"

(Jonah 2:7–9, HCSB)

JONAH AND THE GREAT FISH
(Jonah 1–2)

Jonah was a native of the northern kingdom of Israel and a prophet. When God ordered him to go to Nineveh and proclaim God's judgment on the pagan city's wickedness, it would have seemed to be a welcome assignment. The Assyrians had been dangerous in the past, but now a period of weakness and internal turmoil in the pagan nation made it the perfect moment for their final destruction.

Despite this, Jonah ran away. He had his reasons, but by running from God, the prophet was only chasing folly. To get away from the Creator of Heaven and Earth, the prophet chose the most dangerous form of travel in the ancient world: sea travel. Ships could be attacked by pirates, just as travelers by land could be robbed. But storms can't sink camels.

Safely away from land, Jonah took a nap below deck. He woke to the sound of a raging storm and the frantic cries of the sailors, demanding to know who had offended the God who was trying to kill them all. Jonah admitted that the storm was his fault and suggested the men throw him overboard as a sacrifice to end the storm. This clever move, suicide-by-sacrifice, would get the prophet out of preaching in Nineveh.

God, however, was not so easily sidestepped. He ordered a great fish to swallow Jonah, and it apparently obeyed more readily than the prophet. God miraculously preserved Jonah's life through three days in the belly of the fish (see Jesus' use of this image in Luke 11:29–32). Finally, Jonah called out to God. Being banished from God's presence was a bad place to be. God caused the fish to vomit Jonah onto the beach, and Jonah took the road to Nineveh. But he didn't like it.

THE GREAT FISH

The book of Jonah does not answer many questions the modern reader might have. What kind of fish or whale swallowed Jonah? How could Jonah survive inside it for three days? The story simply does not say. But the point is in the story as it is told: neither the judgment, nor the call of God, can be avoided.

JONAH

After rescuing Jonah, God again ordered him to preach in Nineveh (3:1–3). This time, Jonah went and proclaimed, "In 40 days Nineveh will be demolished!" Instead of being scorned, the prophet's message was immediately embraced by the citizens (3:4–5). The king expressed Nineveh's consensus by donning mourning clothes (3:6–9). The leaders decreed that every living thing in the city should demonstrate repentance ceremonially and by abandoning evil deeds. Though Jonah's message only declared judgment, Nineveh's repentance indicated hope of mercy. God saw the truth of Nineveh's words in the deeds of her people and lifted the threat of destruction (3:10).

Jonah Resents God's Mercy

After preaching the message of God's judgment through the city of Nineveh, Jonah left in a furious rage. The prophet's angry tantrum clarified the reasons for his initial refusal to preach (4:1). From the beginning he had known that God was merciful and compassionate toward those who repent of their sin (4:2). But Jonah wanted to ensure Nineveh's judgment by not preaching a message that might provoke repentance. Far from speaking with vengeful satisfaction, Jonah had preached in fear that he would be believed. When that happened, he asked God to take his life (4:3). Instead, God simply asked the prophet if his anger was justified (4:4).

God Confronts Jonah

The prophet sat down to the east of Nineveh, watching and hoping that the city might still be destroyed after the threatened 40 days. Though the prophet had made a shelter for himself, God caused a plant to grow overnight to provide shade for Jonah, protecting him from the heat. But the next day, God caused a worm to attack the plant. When Jonah felt the scorching heat of the second day, he complained. God asked if Jonah was being righteous in his anger over the plant. When Jonah insisted that he was, God noted that Jonah cared for something he had no hand in making. Wasn't it appropriate, then, for God to care for the spiritually ignorant creatures of Nineveh? The book ends with the question hanging in the air, leaving its readers to supply an answer.

THE RIGHT TO FORGIVE

Jonah's story highlights several major biblical themes. One is God's desire to extend redemption and blessing to all nations (Gen 12:3). Another is the grace of God toward enemies (Rom 5:10). Most important is the idea that God alone is the arbiter of final judgment and eternal forgiveness (see Matt 7:1–5; 9:2–9; 25:31–46).

> *"Should I not care about the great city of Nineveh, which has more than 120,000 people who cannot distinguish between their right and their left, as well as many animals?"*
>
> (Jonah 4:11, HCSB)

THE PRESERVATION OF NINEVEH

The events in the book of Jonah likely occurred in a period of relative weakness for the nation of Assyria, of which Nineveh was a leading city. Assyrian weakness was a significant factor allowing Jeroboam II (793–742 B.C.E.), ruler of the northern kingdom of Israel, to expand the borders and influence of his kingdom. But with the preservation of Nineveh, the Assyrians began to regain strength. Before long they became God's instrument to judge the northern kingdom of Israel, taking its people into captivity in 722 B.C.E. (1 Kgs 17).

BIBLICAL LINKS

"But I ask, 'Did Israel not understand?' First, Moses said: I will make you jealous of those who are not a nation; I will make you angry by a nation that lacks understanding. And Isaiah says boldly: I was found by those who were not looking for Me; I revealed Myself to those who were not asking for Me. But to Israel he says: All day long I have spread out My hands to a disobedient and defiant people." *(Romans 10:19–21, HCSB)*

MICAH

Micah is a collection of sermons addressed to the southern kingdom of Judah during the reign of Hezekiah. The book alternates condemnation of Judah's sins with promises of hope that would bless all nations. In essence, the book explains how the Abrahamic Covenant would be fulfilled in spite of the sins of Abraham's descendants (Mic 7:19–20).

KEY PASSAGES

Judgment on the Two Kingdoms (1–2)

1:1–16	An Invasion Is Coming
2:1–11	The Wicked Will Be Judged
2:12–13	A Remnant Will Be Restored

Judgment on the Failed Leaders (3–5)

4:1–13	God Will Deliver His People
5:1–15	A Righteous King Will Rule

Judgment on the Covenant People (6–7)

6:1–7:7	God Litigates a Covenant Lawsuit
7:8–20	God's Covenant Will Prevail

PRINCIPAL FIGURES

God   Micah portrays God as the Royal Shepherd and Judge of His people who fulfills His Covenants by making His faithless people faithful.

Micah or Micaiah   A prophet from a small town in Judah, who condemned both Israel and Judah, prophesying restoration under a divine King (2:13).

The Nation of Israel and Judah   Micah addresses the two kingdoms of Israel (north) and Judah (south) separately and collectively as "Jacob" or "the house of Jacob."

The Leaders of Jacob   Micah addresses the leadership of Israel and Judah as specific objects of judgment for their failure to keep the nation faithful to the Mosaic Covenant.

LOCATION: Micah's prophecies were most likely delivered in Jerusalem, capital of the southern kingdom of Judah. They concern events that would take place in the Promised Land of Canaan.

ORIGIN: Micah (1:1) was most likely prophesied between 735–715 B.C.E., roughly concurrent with Isaiah. Modern scholarship has challenged the authorship and dating of Micah 4–7. The primary objections presume that predictive prophecy cannot occur and that a Judean prophet would not have emphasized God's desire to bless the nations (4:1–3; 7:12–17; see Gen 12:1–3).

The prophesied judgment on Jerusalem raised a theological problem for the nation of Israel: what was to become of God's Covenant with David? Jerusalem would fall and the people would go into exile in Babylon (4:10). The goal of the nations was the elimination of God's people, but their intentions were not the same as God's intentions. God would use their aggression to purify His people, who would in turn become a pure instrument of divine judgment on the nations (4:12–13).

The current king in Jerusalem was in trouble, but Micah prophesized that the little town of Bethlehem would give rise to a new ruler over God's people. The king in Micah's day was weak, but the future king would be strong. The king of Judah ruled only two tribes, but the promised king would reunite Israel. Finally, Israel would have the ideal king. This promise prompted at least some strands of later Messianic hopes (see Matt 2:5; John 7:41–42). This king, however, would not merely come from an ancient house; He himself would have his "origin" from eternity (5:2).

The future king would not come immediately. The nation would go through intense pains like a woman in labor, until eventually a specific woman would give birth to the new king. Eventually that new king would gather the scattered people of Israel and become the guarantor of their peace and prosperity.

THE SIGNIFICANCE OF SACRIFICE

Sacrifices were meant to demonstrate the gravity of sin and express dependence on God for a final resolution of sin (Gen 3:15), but they were often used to excuse or enable sin. Micah 6:6–8 represents one of the most concise and forceful statements on the priority of righteousness over sacrifices in the whole Old Testament.

"Bethlehem Ephrathah, you are small among the clans of Judah; One will come from you to be ruler over Israel for Me. His origin is from antiquity, from eternity."
(Micah 5:2, HCSB)

NAHUM

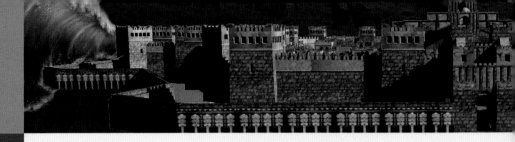

INTRODUCTION

More than 100 years after Jonah, Nahum reassured Judah that God would destroy Nineveh. Though God used Assyria to discipline His people, He would punish them for their attempt to exterminate His people. The prophecy probably encouraged acceptance of King Josiah's reforms, which included eliminating elements of Assyrian religion introduced by King Ahaz (2 Kgs 16:10–16).

LOCATION: The book of Nahum was written in Judah but describes the downfall of the Assyrian city of Nineveh on the Tigris River (across the river from Mosul, Iraq).

ORIGIN: Nahum the Elkashite (1:1) refers to the destruction of the Egyptian city of Thebes in 663 b.c.e. as a recent event (3:8–10) and the destruction of Nineveh as a future event (destroyed by Babylon in 612 B.C.E.). This places Nahum roughly in the period of King Josiah of Judah (639–609 B.C.E.).

KEY PASSAGES

God Is the Defender of His People (1)

God Will Attack Nineveh (2)

God Will Destroy Nineveh (3)

PRINCIPAL FIGURES

God   Nahum presents God as the fierce Defender and Avenger of His people.

Nahum   Nahum, whose name meant "Comforter," does not figure in the book after being introduced as its author.

The City of Nineveh   The book addresses the city of Nineveh as a symbol for the nation of Assyria.

The Assyrian King   Nahum proclaimed the end of the Assyrian kings (1:14; 3:18–19).

The Kingdom of Judah   Nahum briefly addresses Judah, assuring the nation that affliction from the Assyrians is over (1:12– 13) and encouraging them to renew observance of the Mosaic festivals (1:15).

"The Lord is a jealous and avenging God; the Lord takes vengeance and is fierce in wrath. The Lord takes vengeance against His foes; He is furious with His enemies. The Lord is slow to anger but great in power; the Lord will never leave the guilty unpunished."

(Nahum 1:2–3, HCSB)

Nahum begins with the character of God. He is jealous for His people and will avenge them on those who have tried to destroy them. The prophet warns of the fierceness of God's wrath against His enemies. This was not merely personal retribution born out of pain, but the doing of justice proportionate to the crime committed.

God was patient, but once stirred to anger He would not leave justice undone. Nahum implied that those who thought God was weak because He had not acted immediately were in for a nasty shock. Some of the most destructive natural forces known in the Middle East were evidence of His passing. Even the powerful waters, the chaotic sea and the rushing rivers, could not withstand Him. The high mountains provided no refuge against His anger, which flowed down like lava.

Though Nahum's picture of God was as a terror to His enemies, this same God was a fortress to those who sought refuge in His presence. Oddly enough, the safest place to be when God was angry was as close to God as possible.

The city of Nineveh in Assyria, however, had set itself against God. Its leaders had plotted the downfall of the Israelite kingdoms and their God. Nahum encouraged Judah by promising that however strong Assyria seemed, God would crush their power and eliminate their ruler. Though God had used the Assyrians to discipline His people, their role in Israel's history was done. The sign of their defeat would be the execution of their king and his idols. Messengers would bring the joyous news to Judah: the wicked king is dead.

PROPHECY FOR THE OPPRESSED

The rescue of the oppressed is a significant Biblical theme. God rescues His people out of slavery in Egypt (Exodus) and answers their cries when oppressed by the surrounding nations (Judges). He defends the poor, widows, and orphans. This pattern is most prominently displayed in God's rescue of those enslaved and oppressed by sin (John 8:34–36).

HABAKKUK

The book of Habakkuk records the prophet's questions for God and God's answers. Habakkuk raised the problem of God's apparent tolerance of evil in His people and God's justice in using a wicked nation (Babylon) to judge God's people. The book concludes with a hymn of praise to God.

KEY PASSAGES

The First Conversation (1:1–11)

| 1:1-4 | Habakkuk Demands Justice in Judah |
| 1:5-11 | God Reveals His Plan to Use Babylon |

The Second Conversation (1:12–2:20)

| 1:12-2:1 | Habakkuk Objects That Babylon Is Wicked |
| 2:2-20 | God Reveals His Plan to Destroy Babylon |

Habakkuk's Hymn (3)

PRINCIPAL FIGURES

God   Habakkuk describes God as the Holy One who judges His people and the nations.

Habakkuk   A Judean prophet who was amazed at God's strategy for dealing with the sinfulness of nations.

The Chaldeans   Another name for the nation of Babylon, which God used to take the people of Judah into captivity. They were later destroyed by the Persian Empire.

LOCATION: Habakkuk refers to the rise of Babylon (in Mesopotamia, modern Iraq), the Babylonian invasion of Judah, and the subsequent destruction of Babylon.

ORIGIN: Habakkuk (1:1) describes the rise of Babylon as a future event (1:5–6). It is unclear whether the book suggests this will happen in the distant future or more imminently. The first possibility places the prophecy during Josiah's reign (641–627 B.C.E.). The latter places the book during the reign of Jehoiakim (609–598 B.C.E.).

Habakkuk was deeply disturbed by the sin he saw in Judah. The Law of Moses highlighted the ways in which the people were destroying each other, and God had opened the prophets' eyes to see it all around him. But Habakkuk had also become aware that the Law which identified the problem was unable to solve it. The wicked misused the Law to oppress the innocent and pervert justice. So the prophet appealed to God as the only One who could end the violence and oppression (1:1–4).

God's answer shocked the prophet. He would raise up the Babylonians as His agents of judgment on the sin of Judah. The pagan nation would become strong and proud. No fortress would withstand them, and their captives would outnumber the grains of sand on the beach (1:5–11).

As guilty as Judah was, Habakkuk could not understand how God could use the pagan Babylonians to punish His own people. He compared the Babylonians to fisherman who empty the seas of fish and then worship their own nets (1:12–2:1). But God's plan was precisely to use the sinful pride of the Babylonians to humble His people. By teaching them to trust Him, God would make His people righteous and in turn judge the unrepentant pride of their oppressors (2:2–5). The centrality of faith in God for righteousness later became the thesis for Paul's letter to the Romans (Rom 1:17).

Babylon would incur a debt of sin against its neighbors that it could not repay. Their attempts to secure themselves from disaster would sow the seeds of their own demise. The Babylonian conquests would lead to their downfall at the hands of those they had failed to conquer (2:6–17). In the end, the Babylonians' pride would blind them to the fact that their idols were powerless. Though beautifully crafted, they could not speak nor teach wisdom. Trusting in wood and stone overlaid with gold and silver was a fool's path to death (2:18–19). As in the Exodus long ago, God would be vindicated as the only true God against the pagan idols. His word would be fulfilled and the questions and doubts of the world would be silenced in His presence (2:20).

> *"Look, his ego is inflated; he is without integrity. But the righteous one will live by his faith."*
>
> (Habakkuk 2:4, HCSB)

GOD'S USE OF EVIL PEOPLE

The book of Job shows God's use of evil and suffering to refine His people. Habakkuk reaffirms that pattern but also argues that God will deal justly with those who intend sin while unwittingly accomplishing His purposes. Habakkuk insisted that the ability for the righteous to endure depended upon their faith in God's ability to conquer sin in His people and the nations.

ZEPHANIAH

INTRODUCTION

The prophet Zephaniah focuses on the "Day of the Lord," the universal judgment that will begin with God's people and expand to all the nations. The prophet warns Judah to humble itself and repent its rebellion in order to be reconciled to God. He promises that God will purify and rule among them as their King.

KEY PASSAGES

The Great Day of God's Wrath (1:1–2:3)

1:14–2:3   Wrath Should Provoke Repentance

The Judgment of the Nations (2:4–15)

Jerusalem's Doom (3:1–20)

3:1-8   God Will Judge Judah's Leaders

3:9-13   God Will Rule His People

PRINCIPAL FIGURES

God   Zephaniah emphasizes God's role as Sovereign Ruler and judge over His people and the world.

Zephaniah   This prophet may have been a descendent of King Hezekiah of Judah, and so would have been related to King Josiah.

Judah/Jerusalem   The book addresses the Israelites of the southern kingdom of Judah. Their loyalty to Yahweh had been consistently compromised by idolatry.

LOCATION: Zephaniah was likely a resident of Jerusalem and would have delivered his messages there. The locations of the judgments and restoration described focus on Judah and the surrounding nations, but also encompass the whole world.

ORIGIN: Zephaniah delivered his prophecies during the reign of Josiah (639–609 B.C.E.). Scholars debate the timing of the Zephaniah's ministry. Some argue that he wrote early in Josiah's reign to encourage the king's anti-idolatry reforms. Others suggest the book was compiled late in Josiah's reign to condemn the people's insufficient embrace of the reforms.

"Sing for joy, Daughter Zion; shout loudly, Israel! Be glad and rejoice with all your heart, Daughter Jerusalem! The LORD has removed your punishment; He has turned back your enemy. The King of Israel, Yahweh, is among you; you need no longer fear harm."

(Zephaniah 3:14–15, HCSB)

The prophets consistently and thoroughly condemned the sin of God's people. Zephaniah was no exception (Zeph 1:1–3:8). But their failure to be faithful to the Mosaic Covenant did not destroy God's faithfulness to His Covenants with Noah (Gen 9), Abraham (Gen 12, 15, 17), or David (2 Sam 7). Nor did it invalidate God's affirmation of the nation of Israel as His people (Exodus). Instead, God promised that He would purify His people so that they would be completely loyal to Him as their God (Zeph 3:9).

Zephaniah prophesied that God would recall His people who had been dispersed among the nations of the earth. The past rebellion of the nation would no longer shame God's people. Those whose pride had resulted in rebellion against God would be removed. The 40 years of wandering in the wilderness (Num 14) had only temporarily purged the nation of pride, but now God would achieve the permanent humbling of His people (Zeph 3:11–13).

Far from being humiliated, however, God promised that His people would rejoice in reconciliation with God. Their punishment would be removed and their enemy defeated forever. God would both purify the people and rule among them as King (3:14–17). All the hopes of the Davidic Covenant, an eternal King who would forever ensure the blessings of the Mosaic Covenant for God's people and through them for the nations (Abrahamic Covenant), would be fulfilled. Nathaniel would later echo this hope when he met Jesus (John 1:49).

No one of God's people would be left behind when God finally established His rule in Israel. God's joy over them would restore their joy in Him. Those who oppressed God's people would be removed. Instead of being an object of international scorn, God's people would be honored and celebrated among the nations as the conduit of God's blessings to the world (3:18–20).

THE "REMNANT"

God's holiness demanded that the Israelites' sin be judged, but His promises would be broken if the nation were destroyed. Yet in each generation, and especially through the Babylonian Captivity, God preserved at least a small part of the nation in righteousness, ensuring that His people would survive to receive His blessings.

HAGGAI

In the wake of the Babylonian exile, those who returned to Judah had struggled to rebuild their community and had failed to fully restore the worship of God by rebuilding the Temple. When the people committed to rebuilding the Temple, Haggai communicated God's promise to bless the nation with His presence and provision.

LOCATION: The book of Haggai called for the rebuilding of the Temple in Jerusalem and addressed the leaders and people living there.

KEY PASSAGES

Haggai's First Message: Rebuild the Temple (1)

1:1-11	God Calls for the Rebuilding of the Temple
1:12-15	God Affirms the People's Commitment

Haggai's Second Message: The Temple Will Be Glorious (2:1–9)

Haggai's Third Message: The Mosaic Covenant Is Still in Effect (2:10–19)

Haggai's Fourth Message: God Will Restore the Line of David (2:20–23)

ORIGIN: This book identifies Haggai as the source of these prophecies to post-exilic Jerusalem (1:1, 3). The book identifies four distinct oracles and provides dates for each, all occurring within a four-month period in 520 B.C.E. Modern scholarship has been largely content to accept both the authenticity and dating of the book.

PRINCIPAL FIGURES

God   In Haggai, God is portrayed as seeking and deserving the loyalty of His people.

Haggai   A prophet in Jerusalem in the early years after the Babylonian exile whose messages advised and exhorted Judah's political and religious leaders.

Zerubbabel   A leader of the earliest migration of Jews back to Judah after Persia conquered Babylon. He was a descendant of the house of David and became one of the first governors of Judea under the Persians.

Joshua   The High Priest and religious leader of Judah under the Persian Empire.

"For the Lord of Hosts says this: 'Once more, in a little while, I am going to shake the heavens and the earth, the sea and the dry land. I will shake all the nations so that the treasures of all the nations will come, and I will fill this house with glory,' says the Lord of Hosts."

(Haggai 2:6–7, HCSB)

WORK WITH GOD
(Haggai 2:1–9)

In Haggai's first sermon (1:1–15), he had brought up God's pointed observation that the returned exiles were attempting to secure their prosperity apart from a full commitment to the Mosaic Law. Their failure would be reversed, however, if they would seek their prosperity from God. This shift would be marked by prioritizing the rebuilding of the Temple. The leaders had responded and work on the Temple had begun.

In his second sermon (2:1–9), Haggai addressed Zerubbabel the governor and Joshua the High Priest publicly before the people. Though the work had started, the people were discouraged. Haggai addressed their concerns straightforwardly, asking which of them remembered Solomon's Temple. Though it had been nearly 70 years since the Temple was destroyed, there were still some who had memory of its glory. The prophet frankly acknowledged the source of the discouragement; this new Temple seemed like nothing in comparison.

But Haggai's message encouraged the leadership with words reminiscent of David's exhortation when he commissioned Solomon to build the first Temple (1 Chr 28:20). The leaders were to be strong and courageous. God told them that He was with them. He reminded the people that God had promised to be with them when He rescued the nation from slavery in Egypt. Because of His presence, they did not need to be afraid or discouraged.

In particular, God promised that the relative poverty of the people would not impede the building of the Temple. God would shake the earth so that the nations would bring the resources necessary to complete and adorn the Temple. God reminded them that all the silver and gold of the nations was really His wealth. The implication was that since God had decided to ensure the construction of the Temple, He would supply the resources necessary. As a result, the second Temple would become more glorious than the first. Haggai's message of encouragement would be utilized by the author of Hebrews to encourage readers to maintain loyalty to God (Heb 12:25–29).

PUTTING GOD FIRST

Selfishness is distasteful. When it becomes an obsession it is megalomania. But the Bible affirms that God deserves the worship He demands (Ps 29:2; Rev 4:8–11). This does not mean that God needs worship (Acts 17:24–25). Rather, by commanding worship, God calls people to embrace the greatest source of joy and blessing: Himself (Isa 58:13–15).

ZECHARIAH

INTRODUCTION

The prophet Zechariah called the returned exiles to repent for their fathers' sins and return to God. His visions and oracles encouraged the rebuilding of the Temple. He prophesied that this would reestablish the nation as God's Covenant people and point toward the future realization of God's kingdom on earth.

LOCATION: The visions and prophecies of Zechariah were given in Jerusalem. They speak of events in that city in the near future and promise a full implementation of God's rule throughout the world.

KEY PASSAGES

The Night Visions of Zechariah (1:1–6:8)

The Coronation of the High Priest (6:9–15)

The Relationship Between Faithfulness and Ritual (7–8)

The Coming of the King (9–11)

9:9-17   The Davidic King Will Return and Rule

The Restoration of Jerusalem (12–14)

12:9-14   Jerusalem Will Weep Over the One They Pierced

14:1-21   God Will Defend and Bless Jerusalem

ORIGIN: This book is attributed to Zechariah, the son of a priestly family (1:1), and dates chapters 1–7 between October 520 B.C.E. and December 518 B.C.E. Matt 27:9 uses of a quote from Zechariah to introduce an allusion to a longer passage in Jeremiah, which some have taken to suggest that Jeremiah authored Zechariah 9–14.

PRINCIPAL FIGURES

God   As in the other prophets' books, God is presented as the Holy Sovereign of His people, calling them to repentance and promising purification and restoration.

Zechariah   A priest who became a prophet in the days following the return from exile in Babylon, when the Temple was being rebuilt.

Joshua   The High Priest and religious leader of Judea under the Persian Empire, whom God crowned as the spiritual leader of His people.

Zerubbabel   An early Jewish governor of Judah under the Persian Empire.

"Rejoice greatly, Daughter Zion! Shout in triumph, Daughter Jerusalem! Look, your King is coming to you; He is righteous and victorious, humble and riding on a donkey, on a colt, the foal of a donkey."

(Zechariah 9:9, HCSB)

THE RETURN OF THE KING
(Zechariah 9:9–17)

The rebuilding of the Temple and the people to the land did not complete the restoration of God's people. Many still remained in exile, and the Davidic king had not returned to the throne. But Zechariah looked forward to the day when the king would return. He foresaw a day of rejoicing and triumph. The king would come in righteousness and victory, yet humble like King David returning to Jerusalem after Absalom's rebellion had been defeated (2 Sam 15–19). As a result of his return, the nation would no longer need the instruments of war because the king would bring peace with the nations and rule over the whole world. When Jesus later entered Jerusalem on the back of a donkey, it was a deliberate claim to be the king Zechariah prophesied (Matt 21:1–11; John 12:12–15).

God promised the king that because of the blood of the king's covenant sacrifice, God would secure the release of all of the king's people from their captivity. Those who had hope would return to find God had become their Defender. Jesus would later relate this idea to His crucifixion in His last Passover celebration (Matt 26:28; Luke 22:17; 1 Cor 11:25; see also Heb 10:29; 13:20).

The restored nation would be the symbol of God's strength and rule over the nations. God Himself would sound the trumpet and defend His people. The peace promised by the king would be secured by God's victory over the nations, and a jubilant victory feast would celebrate God's preservation of His people. The nation would flourish in the beauty of its people and the bounty of its harvests.

SATAN IN THE BIBLE

The Bible describes Satan as a tempter, accuser, and the instigator of all rebellion against God. The Serpent who tempted Eve was certainly Satan (Gen 3). Zechariah 3 describes Satan accusing the High Priest Joshua before the Angel of the Lord (see Job 1). In the New Testament, he is called the Devil. There, he is the ruler of the angelic beings who rebelled against God (Matt 25:41) and leads the world in rebellion against God (2 Cor 4:4).

MALACHI

The book of Malachi is a large question-and-answer session between God and His people. Together, the questions deny that the people had sinned against God. God's answers justified His wrath and warned the people to repent. He offers forgiveness for those who acknowledge their sin and turn to Him in repentance.

LOCATION: Though no specific location is mentioned in the book, it almost certainly would have been written in Judea, addressing the Israelites living in the Promised Land after the Babylonian Exile.

ORIGIN: Nothing is known about Malachi beyond the ascription of this book to him (1:1). The date of writing can only be tentatively guessed, since no kings or known historical events are mentioned in the book. One common theory dates Malachi as a rough contemporary of Nehemiah (around 444 B.C.E.).

KEY PASSAGES

How Has God Loved Us? (1:1–5)

How Have We Despised God's Name? (1:6–2:9)

Why Do We Profane the Covenant? (2:10–16)

How Have We Wearied God? (2:17–3:6)

How Can We Return to God? (3:7–12)

What Have We Spoken Against God? (3:13–4:6)

PRINCIPAL FIGURES

God   Malachi shows God to be patient and firm, warning His people in order to bring about repentance and restoration.

Malachi   The prophet's name, which means "My Messenger," describes his function in the book as the conduit of God's response to His people's objections.

The Chosen People   The descendants of Jacob, in the form of the nation of Judah, are addressed here as a single person in conversation with God.

The Priests   The religious leadership of Judah are addressed as a single body and chastised for their failure to uphold the Mosaic Covenant.

Elijah   Mentioned at the end of Malachi (4:5–6), God promises that the prophet Elijah (2 Kgs 2) will return to reconcile the people to God before the final judgment.

"They will be Mine," says the Lord of Hosts, "a special possession on the day I am preparing. I will have compassion on them as a man has compassion on his son who serves him. So you will again see the difference between the righteous and the wicked, between one who serves God and one who does not serve Him."

(Malachi 3:17–18, HCSB)

The final element of God's conversation with the people of Judah addressed their slanderous talk about Yahweh (3:13; see Exod 20:7). The people were treating God as a means to an end, seeing obedience to the Covenant simply as an exchange to secure something they saw as more important: material prosperity. This expectation was shattered by the suffering of those who seemed to keep the Covenant faithfully, while the wicked prospered. Instead of trusting God, the people decided that "sin pays." They viewed God as weak at best, an unjust liar at worst (3:14–15).

God, however, insisted that He had not forgotten those who were faithful to Him. God's intentions are symbolized in Malachi by a book written with the names of the faithful, kept in God's presence. This book would be opened on a future day and God would reward those who had been faithful to Him (3:16–17). The book of Revelation describes the opening of this book (Rev 20:11–15). That future day would take full account of the difference between the faithful and the wicked (see Matt 25:31–46). The wicked would be consumed by fire, but the dawn of an eternally righteous world would bring healing to those who had suffered for their faithfulness to God. Their burdens would be lifted and they would overflow with joy (Mal 3:18–4:3).

The prophecy ended with an appeal to "remember" the Law of Moses (4:4). But God would not depend on the people's innate ability to remember and obey. He promised to send Elijah to turn their hearts toward each other (see Lev 19:18). This would prepare God's people for the final judgment by eliminating their selfish arrogance.

Though John was not Elijah himself (John 1:21), Jesus later saw the ministry of John the Baptist as fitting the pattern described here (see Matt 17:10-13).

THE OFFICE OF PRIEST

The Mosaic Covenant set aside the men of the tribe of Levi as priests and servants in the religious life of the nation of Israel. Their task was to seek God's will for important decisions, teach the Law to the people, and operate the sacrificial system in the Tabernacle/ Temple (Deut 33:8–10).

History Between the Old and New Testaments

Under the Persian Empire, the Jews who returned to the Promised Land (538–515 B.C.E.) were organized into the province of Judea, with Jerusalem as its capital. The Persians allowed the Law of Moses to govern the life of the province under the leadership of the High Priest. This made Judea a temple-state within the Persian Empire. Allowing the traditional religion to flourish was designed to keep the peace. Imperial patronage, such as funding the rebuilding of the Temple, ensured support for the Persian Empire. Prayers and sacrifices were offered on behalf of the Persian king. The local governor, such as Nehemiah, was the official responsible for ensuring that imperial interests were maintained and could override the High Priest when necessary.

The Effects of Exile

The cultural impact of the exile was significant. Under the judges and kings, Israel had tended toward adopting pagan cultures through worshipping their idols and intermarrying with gentiles (non-Jews). These practices were decisively rejected under Ezra and Nehemiah's leadership. Covenant faithfulness would be maintained through Temple-worship and personal obedience to the Law of Moses. Another significant change was that Hebrew was no longer the primary language of Judea. Aramaic had replaced it, requiring those who studied the Law to learn Hebrew and to read and explain its meaning to those who did not know Hebrew. It is likely that synagogues, where the Law was read and explained to the people by a teacher *(rabbi),* originated in this period.

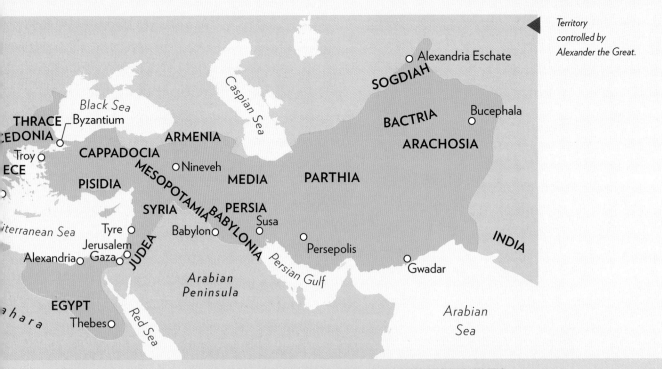

Territory controlled by Alexander the Great.

Judea was part of the Persian Empire from the time of Darius (who conquered Babylon in 539 B.C.E.) until it fell to the Greeks under Alexander the Great (about 332 B.C.E.). The Persians had gained control of Greek cities along the eastern coast of the Aegean Sea around 546 B.C.E. Athenian support for rebellions in these cities led to two major Persian invasions in which their forces were defeated by the Greek city-states at Marathon (490 B.C.E.), Salamis (480 B.C.E.), and Plataea (479 B.C.E.). Abandoning direct military conflict, the Persians developed a policy of causing strife among the Greeks in order to ensure that they didn't unite and that no one city-state became strong enough to challenge Persian interests.

Eventually, however, Philip of Macedon defeated a combined Greek army at Chaeronea (338 B.C.E.) and founded the League of Corinth. He intended to unify the Greeks by focusing them on a campaign against their traditional common foe, the Persians. Philip was assassinated (336 B.C.E.), leaving leadership of the Greeks to his son, Alexander.

The Conquests of Alexander the Great

In 334 B.C.E., Alexander crossed the Hellespont (now known as the Dardanelles, a strait in Turkey that separates Europe and Asia) and began his conquest of the Persian Empire with an army of 30,000 infantry and 5,000 cavalry. He defeated the western Persian Satraps at the Granicus River and quickly moved down the coast, "liberating" Greek cities. In November 333 B.C.E., Alexander defeated a much larger Persian army under Darius III at Issus, the gateway to Syria. Alexander continued south and after razing Tyre, accepted the surrender of Jerusalem (332 B.C.E.), and left Judea as a temple-state under the High Priest. The decisive Greek victory came at Gaugamela (331 B.C.E.), marking the end of the Persian Empire.

Alexander's campaigns continued east to the Indus River, where in the battle of Bucephala (326 B.C.E.) he was wounded by a spear in the chest. He survived that wound, but it and the pressure of his Greek troops to go home forced him to turn back towards Greece. Alexander died at Babylon (323 B.C.E.) without an heir ready to assume his throne. With the succession left unclear, his huge empire broke up into large kingdoms led by his generals.

THE PRESERVATION OF JERUSALEM

During the siege of Tyre, Alexander demanded Judea's support. The High Priest refused, and the Samaritans urged Alexander to destroy their traditional rival. Josephus (Judean Antiquities 11.317–345) claims that Alexander relented when the High Priest surrendered the city and showed him Daniel's prophesy that the Greek king would destroy Persia (Dan 8).

After Alexander the Great died (323 B.C.E.), his generals took control of different areas of the empire. Seleucus gained control of Mesopotamia, while Ptolemy ruled in Egypt. The Battle of Ipsus (303 B.C.E.) secured Ptolemaic control of Judea for a century.

Judea Under the Ptolemies

Under the Ptolemies, Judea continued to be a temple-state led by the High Priest. Though its history is obscure, the New Testament's Sanhedrin may have originated in this period as a High Court or Council of Elders based on the elders who assisted Ezra (Ezra 5:5). The Ptolemies encouraged the adoption of Greek culture, and those who learned Greek had an easier path to success in government and trade. This policy of "Hellenization" appeared to foster an accommodation with pagan culture similar to that which had led to the Babylonian exile. The most vigorous opponents of Hellenism were called Hasidim.

Judea Under the Seleucids

The Ptolemies lost control of Judea after being defeated by the Seleucids at Panium (200 B.C.E.). Seleucid control of Judea would last only 33 years as a result of an aggressive policy of taxation and forced Hellenization. Jewish resistance was mostly passive until the Seleucid king Antiochus IV Epiphanes was ejected from Egypt by Roman diplomatic pressure (167 B.C.E.). Returning through Judea, he found Jerusalem in revolt against Seleucid rule. As punishment, Antiochus Epiphanes determined to eradicate Judaism. He built an altar to Zeus on the main altar in the Temple and sacrificed a pig there. Circumcision and Sabbath observance were outlawed. Possession of a copy of the Law of Moses was punishable by death.

The Seleucids tried to enforce mandatory sacrifices to Zeus in the towns of Judea. Mattathias ben-Hashmon, an elderly priest, was enraged by seeing a Jew sacrifice to Zeus and killed him before escaping into the hills. His son, Judas Maccabeus (whose name meant "the Hammer"), led the Jewish forces that defeated the Seleucids in several key battles (167–166 B.C.E.). Though his initial gains were modest (the Seleucid-chosen High Priest remained and Seleucid troops occupied the citadel in Jerusalem), Judas was able to purify the Temple and rededicate it in what would become the Jewish festival of Hanukkah (165 B.C.E.). Eventually, Judas won a treaty with Rome (161 B.C.E.).

Judas Maccabeus' success was due, in part, to the fact that the main Seleucid forces were engaged in the east. But in 160 B.C.E., they were able to turn their attention to Judea and killed Judas in battle at Beth-horon. Judas' brother Jonathan became the Jewish leader, but was forced to accept the Seleucid-chosen High Priest. But when civil war broke out in the Seleucid Empire (152 B.C.E.), one of the contenders agreed to make Jonathan High Priest and recognize his command of Jewish forces.

An Independent Israel

Jonathan's brother Simeon became leader of Judea when Jonathan was assassinated (143 B.C.E.). The next year, however, Simeon secured an end to paying tribute to the Seleucids. He also renewed the Jewish alliance with Rome. Rome used diplomatic pressure to protect Judea from both the Ptolemies and the Seleucids. Jewish independence from the Seleucids was formally expressed by the popular election of Simeon as ruler and High Priest in 140 B.C.E., meaning that he no longer held these offices as a gift from the Seleucids. For the first time since the Babylonian capture of Jerusalem more than 400 years earlier, Israel was an independent nation.

ROME RISING IN THE WEST

When Alexander the Great died (323 B.C.E.), Rome controlled only the Plain of Latium in central Italy. But by 146 B.C.E., Rome had defeated Carthage, its major rival in the Western Mediterranean, and controlled Italy, Sicily, Sardinia, the Iberian Peninsula, and North Africa. It then turned to the Greek empires.

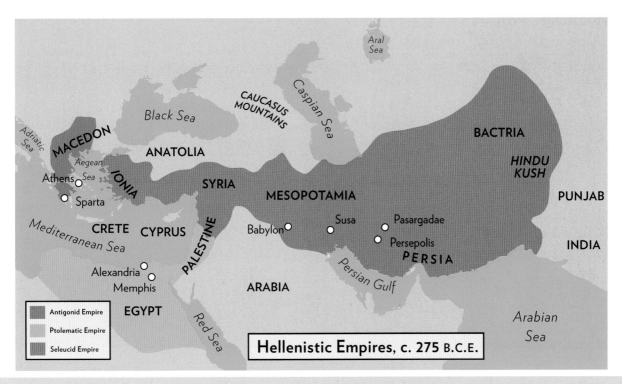

Aral Sea

CAUCASUS MOUNTAINS

Caspian Sea

Black Sea

BACTRIA

Adriatic Sea

MACEDON

ANATOLIA

HINDU KUSH

Aegean Sea

IONIA

SYRIA

Athens

Sparta

MESOPOTAMIA

PUNJAB

CRETE

CYPRUS

PALESTINE

Susa

Pasargadae

Mediterranean Sea

Babylon

Persepolis

INDIA

PERSIA

Alexandria

Memphis

Persian Gulf

ARABIA

Red Sea

Arabian Sea

Antigonid Empire

Ptolematic Empire

Seleucid Empire

EGYPT

Hellenistic Empires, c. 275 B.C.E.

Israel was able to expand its borders under Simeon's descendants, known as the Hasmonean Dynasty. Eventually, the Hasmoneans regained most of the territory David had controlled. Internally, however, tension continued to grow over Hellenization. The Hasmonean kings adopted more and more aspects of Greek culture, including taking Greek names instead of Hebrew names. This trend had religious significance, because these kings also held the High Priesthood and implicated the purity of Judea's Covenant faithfulness.

Priests and scribes who supported the Hasmonean adoption of Greek culture came to be known as Sadducees. The Hasmoneans joined the Sadducees and used them as their primary advisors. The Hasidim, however, resisted the Hellenistic tendencies of the ruling family. They feared that pagan influence would result in divine judgment, as it had in the Babylonian captivity. The priests and scribes who opposed the adoption of Greek culture came to be known as Pharisees.

The End of the Hasmonean Dynasty

The Hasmonean dynasty ended with the struggles between two brothers, Hyrcanus II and Aristobulus II, to secure the throne. Hyrcanus had been appointed High Priest in 76 B.C.E., and Aristobulus had become the military commander. The Sadducees supported Aristobulus and initially succeeded in placing him on the throne. But the Hasmonean governor of Idumea (Edom), Antipater, saw an opportunity to secure power for himself by supporting Hyrcanus.

Both sides appealed to Rome for support and sent representatives to meet with the Roman leader Pompey in Damascus (63 B.C.E.). Pompey ended up assaulting Jerusalem, installing Hyrcanus as High Priest, and deporting Aristobulus to Rome. Antipater was able to develop alliances with key Roman leaders, culminating in his support of Julius Caesar. Caesar rewarded Antipater by making his sons military prefects in Judea.

When Hyrcanus was overthrown in 40 B.C.E., Antipater's son Herod fled to Rome. While he was there, he became friends with both Marc Antony and Octavian (who would become Augustus Caesar in 27 B.C.E.). They got the Roman Senate to declare Herod "King of the Jews," and sent Herod back to conquer his kingdom.

Herod's Reign

Herod continued the policy of Hellenization, introducing Greco-Roman games and buildings to Jerusalem. This policy climaxed with the construction of Caesarea Maritima, his gateway city to the Mediterranean. He even made a large donation to endow the Olympic games in Greece. Herod's greatest achievement, however, was the renovation of the Temple (begun in 19 B.C.E. and finished in 63 C.E.). This was not enough to satisfy the Pharisees, however. When Herod died (4 B.C.E.), a delegation went to Rome to ask for a return to the temple-state form of government in Judea.

After Herod's son proved incompetent, Judea was annexed as the Roman province of Palestine in 6 C.E. The internal affairs of Judea were ruled by the Sanhedrin, supervised by a Roman governor. Other parts of the kingdom were divided among Herod's other sons, who were given the title Tetrarch. The Roman governors struggled to maintain the peace. The first governor, Coponius, tried to impose a direct poll tax. When the Pharisees opposed it, the Romans resorted to force in order to put down the insurrection (17 C.E.). Pontius Pilate, who executed Jesus, became governor around 26 C.E.

HEROD THE GREAT'S RUTHLESSNESS

Herod executed both opponents and family to secure power. Augustus thought it safer to be Herod's pig than Herod's son. From his deathbed, Herod had leading citizens arrested. They were to be killed when he died so that his passing would cause mourning in Jerusalem. This "dying wish" was ignored.

▼ Herod's kingdom of Judea became a Roman territory in 37 B.C.E.

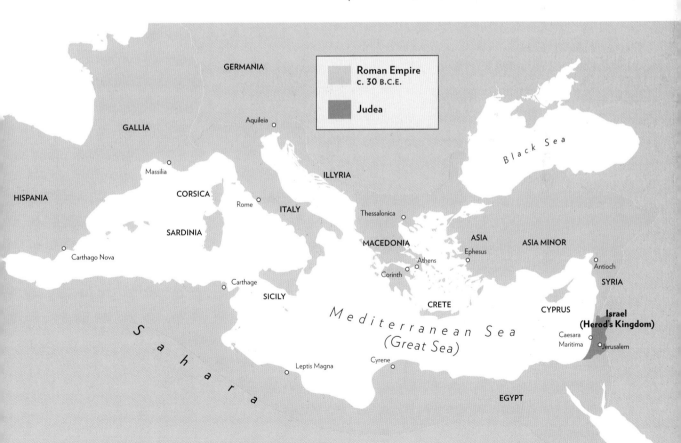

| | Roman Empire c. 30 B.C.E. |
| | Judea |

GERMANIA

GALLIA

Aquileia

ILLYRIA

HISPANIA

Massilia

CORSICA

Rome

ITALY

Black Sea

SARDINIA

Carthago Nova

Carthage

SICILY

Thessalonica

MACEDONIA

ASIA

Athens

Ephesus

Corinth

ASIA MINOR

Antioch

SYRIA

CRETE

CYPRUS

Israel (Herod's Kingdom)

Mediterranean Sea (Great Sea)

Caesara Maritima

Jerusalem

Sahara

Leptis Magna

Cyrene

EGYPT

The New Testament

Scholars classify the New Testament books in different ways, but one of the most common groups them in five categories: the Gospels, History, Pauline Epistles, General Epistles, and Apocalypse.

Gospels

Matthew

Mark

Luke

John

History

Acts

Pauline Epistles

Romans

1 & 2 Corinthians

Galatians

Ephesians

Philippians

Colossians

1 & 2 Thessalonians

1 & 2 Timothy

Titus

Philemon

General Epistles

Hebrews

James

1 & 2 Peter

1-3 John

Jude

Apocalypse

Revelation

MATTHEW

The Gospel of Matthew is the first of four pre-sentations of the good news about Jesus, each of which have slightly different emphases. Matthew was written to present Jesus as the fulfillment of the Old Testament prophecies of Messiah, the anointed Savior of Israel and the world. Matthew quotes the Old Testament directly 61 times. The accounts of the Wise Men (2), the renaming of Simon Peter (16), and several parables are unique to this book.

KEY PASSAGES

Jesus' Preparation for Ministry (1–4:11)

1:18–2:23	The King Is Born
3:1–4:11	Jesus Is Baptized and Tempted

Jesus' Ministry in Galilee (4:12–16:20)

5–7	Jesus Preaches the Sermon on the Mount
13	Jesus Preaches the Parables of the Kingdom
16:13–20	Peter Confesses That Jesus Is Messiah

Jesus' Journey to Jerusalem (16:21–20:34)

17	Three Disciples See Jesus' Glory
19:16–20:16	A Rich Young Ruler Questions Jesus

Jesus' Final Week (21–28)

21–22	The Religious Rulers Prepare to Arrest Jesus
24–25	Jesus Preaches About the End Times
26–28	Jesus Is Crucified and Resurrected

PRINCIPAL FIGURES

God   This book sees God as the Ruler who has sent His Son to rescue His rebellious subjects in fulfillment of His plan for the history of humanity in general and the nation of Israel in particular.

Jesus Christ   Jesus demonstrates divine authority in teaching and miracles, presenting Himself as the Son of God and the Messiah, the Son of David.

Joseph and Mary   Mary is the virgin through whom the Holy Spirit accomplished the miraculous birth of Jesus. Joseph is featured as the protector of his wife Mary and Jesus, his adopted son.

John the Baptist   Jesus' cousin who preached in the Judean wilderness near the Jordan River and heralded the coming of the Messiah. He was later executed by one of Herod's grandsons.

Satan   The chief of the fallen angels, who tempted Jesus in the desert. Matthew records several instances in which Jesus cast out demons (evil spirits under Satan's control).

The Twelve Disciples   Jesus' closest followers and primary students (see Matt 10). Among these, Matthew was a tax collector.

Jesus' Opponents   Primarily the religious leaders who conspired to arrest and have Jesus executed by manipulating the Roman Governor, Pilate.

LOCATION: The events described in Matthew took place primarily in Bethlehem, the area around the Sea of Galilee (northern Israel), and in Jerusalem.

ORIGIN: The book does not name its author, but early manuscripts (from 125 C.E.) attribute the book to Matthew. Most often the author is identified as the Apostle Matthew, though many modern scholars attribute it to a group influenced by the apostle. The book was likely written prior to the Temple's destruction (70 C.E.). Use of the book by early Christian writers indicates it was written before 100 C.E.

WISE MEN SEEK THE KING
(Matthew 2)

After Jesus was born in Bethlehem, a group of foreign sages arrived unexpectedly in Jerusalem. They were Persian magi, wise men who studied dreams, omens, and the stars. During their observations of the night sky, they had seen a sign among the stars. They reported that the star of a new Jewish king had appeared in the sky, and they had come to pay their respects. King Herod, already deeply paranoid about potential rivals to his power, was very concerned. When the king demanded that the scholars of the Law of Moses tell him where the Davidic King promised by the prophets was to be born, they pointed him to Bethlehem.

Herod sent the magi to find God's chosen king and return, claiming that he too wanted to pay his respects. After leaving Jerusalem, the star reappeared and guided the wise men to the house where Joseph, Mary, and the child Jesus were now living in Bethlehem. As Mary held Jesus, the men worshipped Him and presented three valuable gifts: gold, frankincense, and myrrh. Frankincense and myrrh were crystalized tree resin, valued for their medical qualities. These three gifts became the basis for picturing three wise men, though Matthew does not report how many came to visit Jesus.

When the wise men left, God warned them not to return to Herod. God also warned Joseph to take Mary and Jesus to Egypt, identifying Jesus with Israel's experience of taking shelter in Egypt before returning to the Promised Land. When Herod realized that the wise men were not going to lead him to the promised child, he attempted to secure his position by eliminating all the very young boys in Bethlehem, killing every one under the age of two.

THE SYNOPTIC GOSPELS

Matthew, Mark, and Luke are known as the Synoptic Gospels because they share a large body of common material and largely follow the same order of presentation. Many events are described in all three; some appear in two of the three. Scholarly debates over their relationship and sources are commonly called "the Synoptic Problem."

MATTHEW

At the beginning of Jesus' ministry, His cousin John was already preaching in the Judean Wilderness. Fulfilling the role of the wilderness prophet (Isa 40:3), John commanded his listeners to repent their sins. He dipped those who confessed to be sinners in the Jordan River as a sign of their repentance and cleansing (the term for this in Greek is *baptizo*).

John Condemns the Religious Leaders

Religious leaders from Jerusalem came to judge John's preaching, but when John recognized them, he judged them instead. He warned them to repent and not claim their lineage as the basis for their standing with God. He said God didn't need them to fulfill the Abrahamic Covenant (Gen 15) because God had the power make descendants of Abraham out of stones lying on the ground. He warned them that God had judged unfaithful Israelites before. John's threat was particularly sharp because these sects considered themselves the guardians of Covenant faithfulness through the Temple worship (the Sadducees) and teaching the Law of Moses (the Pharisees).

John saw his own preaching as preparation for becoming a greater figure. In contrast to the leaders he condemned, John announced that someone was coming who would not immerse people in water, but would cleanse them with fire and the Holy Spirit. This would be the One who would judge the righteous and the wicked.

John Baptizes Jesus

Eventually Jesus came to John to be baptized. When John balked, Jesus insisted that it was the right thing to do. As John brought Jesus up out of the water, the heavens opened and God's Spirit descended in the form of a dove to land on Jesus. Then a voice from heaven blended the royal pronouncement of Ps 2:7 and the Servant's commission of Isa 42:1, suggesting the imminent fulfillment of the Davidic Covenant (2 Sam 7). Instead of being a confession of sin and repentance, Matthew described the baptism of Jesus as the anointing that began His ministry.

CONFRONTATION: PROPHETS AND PRIESTS

The prophets and priests of ancient Israel did not always get along. John's interaction with the religious leaders is just one example of priests trying to judge prophets and prophets judging priests. This confrontation would be replicated in the attempts of the Pharisees to judge the teaching of Jesus (for example, Matt 9:3, 34; 12:2, 14, 24, 38). Later, when the religious leaders demanded to know by what authority Jesus taught, He would remind them of John the Baptist and their refusal to believe John's warnings (Matt 21:23–27).

"After Jesus was baptized, He went up immediately from the water. The heavens suddenly opened for Him, and He saw the Spirit of God descending like a dove and coming down on Him. And there came a voice from heaven: This is My beloved Son. I take delight in Him!"

(Matthew 3:16–17, HCSB)

THE ORIGINS OF BAPTISM

The Mosaic Law required ritual cleansing as a sign of purification from defilement (Lev 12–15) and sanctification for service (Exod 30:17–21; Lev 8:6). Converts to Judaism also participated in a ritual bath. By applying baptism to penitent Jews, John portrayed them as converts of the heart to their already-professed faith.

MATTHEW

Following Jesus' baptism, the Spirit led Him into the wilderness to be tempted by Satan. After 40 full days of fasting, the Devil challenged Jesus to turn stones into bread. Satan claimed it would satisfy Jesus' hunger and prove that He was God's Son. Satan's suggestion recalled Eve's use of the forbidden fruit to satisfy her hunger (Gen 3:6). Jesus, however, quoted Deuteronomy 8:3 to affirm that God's word (see Gen 3:2–3) should be valued over physical food.

Temptation and the New Adam's Mission

Satan tried again by showing Jesus a vision of Himself standing in a prominent spot in the Temple. The Devil dared Jesus to jump off, reminding Him God had promised to protect His Chosen One (see Ps 91:11–12). This situation seemed designed to cause doubt about God's faithfulness, a similar strategy used against Eve (see Gen 3:4). Again Jesus refused, citing the warning of Deuteronomy 6:16 not to test God.

Finally, the Devil offered Jesus a shortcut to God's goal, Christ's rule over the nations (see Ps 2:8). Instead enduring the pain of crucifixion achieve this goal, He only had to ask (and effectively worship) Satan. This last attempt resembled Satan's offer of the forbidden fruit to Eve as a shortcut to fulfilling God's purpose for humanity (see Gen 3:5). Jesus rejected Satan's offer by affirming Deuteronomy 6:13's prohibition on idolatry.

The Different Temptation Accounts

Mark's temptation account (Mark 1:12–13) simply states that Jesus was tempted by Satan in the wilderness. Matthew's account implicitly contrasted Christ's triumph with Adam and Eve's defeat (Gen 3), suggesting fulfillment of the Genesis 3:15 promise. The subtlety in Satan's approach is that each case offered something legitimate (food, divine protection, and sovereignty) in an illegitimate way (disobedience, doubt, and idolatry). Where Matthew's account highlights the way in which the temptation revealed Jesus as the New Adam, Luke's account (Luke 4:1–13) emphasizes the way the temptation attacked the Father's plan for the Son. Though Satan claimed that doing what he suggested would prove that Jesus was the Son of God, yielding to the temptation would have proved that He was not (see Gen 4).

WILDERNESS PREPARATION

Christ's time in the wilderness was His final preparation for the ministry that began immediately afterward in Galilee (Matt 4:12; Mark 1:12–14; Luke 4:–15; John 1:43; see also Isa 9:2). This pattern in the Bible is shared by Moses (Exod 2–4), David (1 Sam 21–27), and Elijah (1 Kgs 19).

"LEAD US NOT INTO TEMPTATION"

In His model prayer, also called "the Lord's Prayer," Jesus taught His followers to ask the Father not to "bring us into temptation, but deliver us from the evil one" (Matt 6:13). While God does not tempt anyone directly (Jas 1:13), Jesus knew from personal experience that God allows temptation, and that God's grace was sufficient to overcome it (1 Cor 10:13; 2 Pet 2:9).

"But He answered, 'It is written: Man must not live on bread alone but on every word that comes from the mouth of God.'"

(Matthew 4:4, HCSB)

BIBLICAL LINKS

"He humbled you by letting you go hungry; then He gave you manna to eat, which you and your fathers had not known, so that you might learn that man does not live on bread alone but on every word that comes from the mouth of the LORD."
(Deuteronomy 8:3, HCSB)

MATTHEW

THE SERMON ON THE MOUNT
(Matthew 5–7)

Jesus' most famous sermon is known as "The Sermon on the Mount" because Matthew records its delivery on a mountaintop, suggesting a comparison with Moses on Mount Sinai (see Deut 18:15–19). Jesus began by proclaiming God's favor on specific kinds of people who might normally be thought of as disfavored by God (5:3–16); for example, the poor, those who mourn, and those who know themselves to be sinners and yet hunger for righteousness. God would build His kingdom through these people. He then contrasted the "righteousness" of the teachers of the Law ("you have heard it said") with His own teaching ("but I say to you"; 5:17–48). Christ implied that His opponents worked out the details of the Law to enable sin rather than to prevent it. Jesus' standard of righteousness required the moral transformation of the heart.

The Model Prayer

Jesus then turned to the subject of piety (6:1–7:12), warning against using religion as a way of winning praise from men. The centerpiece of the sermon was prayer. Jesus taught a model prayer, which many Christians have memorized to repeat in prayer or to use as a guide for structuring their own prayers to God. Jesus' prayer expressed a desire that God be honored through the submission of the world to His rule and dependence on Him for the daily needs of life. It concludes with a plea for forgiveness of sins and a request for help to avoid future sins.

Jesus taught that praying like this would transform those who prayed with sincere faith into people who honor God as God, trust God's provision, extend humble forgiveness, and value righteousness. Jesus invited His audience to pray for these things in confidence that God would answer graciously, and commanded them to relate to others as they wanted to be treated by God.

The Sermon's Challenge

The sermon concluded (7:13–29) with a series of sharp warnings to avoid the teaching of the religious leaders, which would produce rotten fruit and lead only to judgment. Jesus argued that those who were wise would base their lives on His teaching and be secure against the storms of God's judgment. When He was finished, the people were amazed at the authority Jesus displayed as He spoke.

JESUS' SIGNATURE SERMON

While Matthew's account is the most familiar version of this sermon, Jesus apparently preached different versions in other locations (see Luke 6:17–49). Thirteen of the sayings Matthew records are also repeated in other parts of Luke, for example: "saltiness" (14:34–35), "light of the world" (11:33), and "the model prayer" (11:2–4).

THE SIGNIFICANCE OF THE SERMON

The sermon on the mount is characterized by hope for the downcast, deep connections between faith and the practical life of faith in the real world, and powerful rhetoric and images. But perhaps its greatest attraction is the way in which the life of the preacher, Jesus, matched the message He proclaimed.

"Therefore, whoever breaks one of the least of these commands and teaches people to do so will be called least in the kingdom of heaven. But whoever practices and teaches these commands will be called great in the kingdom of heaven. For I tell you, unless your righteousness surpasses that of the scribes and Pharisees, you will never enter the kingdom of heaven."

(Matthew 5:19–20, HCSB)

MATTHEW

On another occasion, a crowd gathered as Jesus spoke on the shore of the Sea of Galilee. So many people came that He got into a boat and pushed back a bit while the crowd stood on the shore. At this point, Jesus changed His preaching style dramatically. He abandoned the plain language He had used in the Sermon on the Mount (Matt 5–7) and began telling parables, fulfilling Psalm 78:2.

Jesus described a farmer who planted a crop. When he dipped his hand into his bag, he threw the seed everywhere instead of scattering it on the prepared soil. Some fell on the path and was eaten by the birds. Some grew quickly in the rocky soil, but without deep roots was scorched by the sun. Other seed fell among thorns and was choked out. But some seed fell on good soil and produced a miraculously large harvest.

The Purpose of Parables

The disciples asked why Jesus was preaching in parables. He answered by quoting from God's commission of Isaiah (Isa 6:9-10). The parables would confuse those who rejected Christ as Messiah but enlighten and bless those who acknowledged Him. Jesus insisted that the secrets of the kingdom belonged to His followers alone.

The Meaning of the Parable

Jesus concluded by explaining the meaning of the parable to His disciples. The story of the sower used seed as a figure for the Word of God. This made Jesus the sower, proclaiming the gospel to everyone regardless of response. The path represented those who did not understand (accept) Jesus' preaching. The Devil would snatch it away from them. The rocky soil was those who liked the message but would fall away under persecution. The thorny soil was those who would be seduced away from the message by the world's priorities. The good ground represented those in whom the Word bore its intended fruit.

GRACE AND FREE CHOICE

Jesus' parable raises one of the most consistently and vigorously debated aspects of theology: the relationship between God's grace and human free choice. Though theologians have differed widely in their explanations, the most common answers among Orthodox, Protestant, and Roman Catholic theologians have affirmed that people make free choices but need the grace of God in order to freely make good choices (see, for example, John 15:5). Grace is the cause of goodness, not the reward earned by goodness. A common point of division is over whether grace ensures good choices or merely makes them possible.

Jesus told the parable of the sower as an explanation for why people responded to His preaching the way that they did. It does not, however, explain how the different kinds of soil got that way or how they might be transformed from bad to good soil. Instead, it represents an affirmation of those who heard Jesus' message with faith and judgment on those who rejected it in unbelief.

PARABLES IN JESUS' PREACHING

Jesus' parables used a lot of figures (major elements that stand for something else) and often had a meaningful twist (farmers don't throw their seed recklessly, and crops don't usually have such huge yields). The key to the meaning, however, was what the parable affirmed about Jesus and the way God administers His Kingdom.

"For this reason I speak to them in parables, because looking they do not see, and hearing they do not listen or understand. ... But your eyes are blessed because they do see, and your ears because they do hear!"

(Matthew 13:13, 16, HCSB)

THE GREAT CONFESSION
(Matthew 16)

In Caesarea Philippi, Jesus asked the disciples how people saw Him. The disciples answered that the people viewed Jesus positively. There was a sense that He was more than just a Galilean preacher; however, they saw him as the herald of the Messiah rather than the Messiah Himself.

The disciples reported that the religious leaders, the Pharisees and Sadducees, had other views. To them, Jesus was an illegitimate child (John 8:41) or demon-possessed (Matt 12:22–24). They saw Jesus as a blasphemer, someone who claimed the prerogatives of God (Mark 2:6–7), and claimed to be God (Matt 26:63–65; John 10:30–33).

Simon Peter Affirms His Faith

Jesus then asked His disciples who they thought He was. Simon Peter answered "the Messiah, the Son of the living God." Peter's profession of faith in Jesus has come to be known as "the Great Confession," since Jesus' approval made it a model for any other profession of faith in Him. Jesus gave God credit for Simon's faith and reaffirmed his nickname, Peter, which meant *rock*. Jesus announced that He would build His church on "this rock." The phrase *this rock* has been taken to mean Peter, Peter's confession ("You are the Christ..."), or Jesus Himself (see 1 Pet 2:6–8).

Jesus promised to give Peter the keys of the kingdom. Peter would usher people into the kingdom through his proclamation of the gospel (see Acts 2–3, 10). Those who rejected the message would be forbidden entrance to heaven. Those who embraced the gospel would be free to enter. This contrasted Peter's ministry positively with the teachings of the religious leaders, whom Jesus accused of preventing people from entering the kingdom of God (see Matt 23:13; Luke 11:52).

◀ *Jesus did much of His ministry in the region of Galilee.*

Tyre

Caesarea Philippi

GAULANITIS

Korazin

Gennesaret Bethsaida

Capernaum

Cana Magdala Kursi

Tiberias

GALILEE

Sea of Galilee (Sea of Chinnereth)

Nazareth

Nain

DECAPOLIS

River Jordan

Mediterranean Sea (Great Sea)

SAMARIA

Peter Opposes Jesus

Yet when Jesus said that He had to go to Jerusalem to be crucified and resurrected, Peter insisted that he would not let that happen. Jesus rounded on Peter, "Get behind Me, Satan!" Peter's hope for the Messiah did not include His execution. Jesus warned the disciples that the only path to life was for His followers to accept their own crucifixion, but that embracing the cross would allow them to see the kingdom established in Christ.

THE BURIAL OF CHARLEMAGNE

Charlemagne was the greatest European king of the middle ages (742-814 C.E.) and founder of the Holy Roman Empire. When he died, his body was placed in a crypt underneath the cathedral at Aix-la-Chapelle. Tradition holds that when his body was disinterred it was found sitting on a throne surrounded by evidence of wealth and power. His finger pointed to a verse in the Bible on his lap, "What will it benefit a man if he gains the whole world yet loses his life?" Though Charlemagne was personally very pious, the story turns his life into a cautionary tale for those who might be tempted to make earthly position or possessions their highest good.

"But you," He asked them, "who do you say that I am?" Simon Peter answered, "You are the Messiah, the Son of the living God!"

(Matthew 16:15–16, HCSB)

MATTHEW

THE TRANSFIGURATION
(Matthew 17)

Soon after Peter acknowledged Jesus as Messiah in the town of Caesarea Philippi (see Matt 16), Jesus took Peter, James, and John to the top of a tall mountain. While there, He became transfigured before their eyes so that He shone like the sun. His clothing seemed to be like pure light. As the disciples gazed at Him in awe, Moses and Elijah appeared and spoke with Jesus.

God Speaks

Peter was confused but felt like he needed to say something (see Mark 9:6), so he interrupted with the suggestion that he and the other two disciples could set up shrines for the three (Exod 33:7–11; Num 12:5–9). Peter's intention was to honor this special place where heaven and Earth seemed to meet, but his suggestion was both unnecessary and inappropriate. God's intent was to display His glory through His son, not mere buildings, and Jesus was much more than the first among three great prophets.

As Peter was speaking, God's voice interrupted him from a bright cloud. The voice affirmed that Jesus was the Suffering Servant that Isaiah spoke about and also stated that Jesus was the prophet Moses had cautioned the people of Israel to heed (Deut 18:15, 19). The disciples fell on their faces in terror.

Jesus put His hands on the trembling disciples and comforted them. When they looked up, they simply saw Jesus as they had always known Him, standing there alone. Coming down the mountain to the other disciples, Jesus warned them not to tell anyone what they had seen until after He had risen from the dead.

UNDERCOVER MESSIAH

Early in Jesus' ministry, He frequently insisted that no one be told that He was the Messiah (Matt 8:4; 9:30; 12:16; 16:20; 17; Mark 1:44; 5:43; 7:36; 8:26, 30; 9:9; 16:8). Many Jewish people expected a Messiah who would overthrow Roman rule, and Jesus may have wanted to prevent the people from trying to make Him the leader of a popular uprising against Rome (John 11:48–50). He intended to fight His battle on the cross (17:9). It was only later, after the character of His ministry was already established, that Jesus began to make direct claims to be the Messiah.

Untangling the Prophesies

As they walked, the three tried to understand how the prophecies about Elijah coming as a forerunner to the Messiah fit in with all they had seen. Jesus affirmed the prophecy that an Elijah-like figure would come and call for repentance in Israel (Mal 4:5–6). He then asserted that in this sense Elijah had come, but that the nation had not listened to him. Instead, he was persecuted and killed. Jesus reminded them that He would suffer in the same way. Then they realized that Jesus was talking about John the Baptist, who had been executed by King Herod Antipas. He was the one who had fulfilled the prophecy about Elijah.

"While he was still speaking, suddenly a bright cloud covered them, and a voice from the cloud said: This is My beloved Son. I take delight in Him. Listen to Him!"

(Matthew 17:5, HCSB)

MATTHEW

When Jesus approached Jerusalem for the last time before the crucifixion, He sent two disciples ahead to take a donkey and its colt from the next village so that He could ride the colt into the city. If confronted, they were to simply say, "the Lord needs them," and they would be permitted to go. Matthew reports that Jesus was intentionally fulfilling Zechariah 9:9, which described the Davidic King coming to Jerusalem on a donkey's colt. This entrance also recalled Solomon's ride to his coronation on David's mule, suggesting that Jesus was the Son that Solomon was unable to be (2 Kgs 1:33). Mark stated that the colt had not been ridden before (Mark 11:2). The presence of the colt's mother would have helped to keep the young animal calm as it was being ridden for the first time, explaining why Matthew reports that both were taken.

Jesus' Arrival in Jerusalem

The disciples did as instructed, and when they brought the colt they placed their robes on its back as a saddle for Jesus. A very large crowd gathered along the road, hailing His arrival. Many spread their robes along the road as a royal carpet (see 2 Kgs 9:13). Others spread freshly cut branches. As He passed, the crowds acclaimed Jesus as the Davidic King. The cry, "Hosanna to the Son of David!" was equivalent to "God save the King!" The crowd described Him as "the blessed One" (Ps 118:25–26). Jesus accepted their acclamation, but

Luke (19:39–40) and John (12:19) report that the religious leaders were frustrated with the crowds and tried to get Jesus to calm them.

FICKLE CROWDS?

The people of Jerusalem acclaimed Jesus as He entered the city before Passover. But just a few days later, a crowd before the Roman Governor yelled "Crucify Him!" When the Governor offered to release Jesus, they demanded the release of the criminal Barabbas instead. Then, as Jesus was led to His crucifixion, women lined the road weeping. While it may appear the people of Jerusalem couldn't make up their minds, it is more likely that the group which called for Jesus execution was composed of the religious leaders and their close supporters, not the general population of the city.

BIBLICAL LINKS

"Rejoice greatly, Daughter Zion! Shout in triumph, Daughter Jerusalem! Look, your King is coming to you; He is righteous and victorious, humble and riding on a donkey, on a colt, the foal of a donkey." *(Zechariah 9:9, HCSB)*

The Effect of Jesus' Arrival

The city, which was packed with Jews from all over Israel and the international Jewish community for the Passover festival, was rocked by the commotion. The whole city was buzzing to know who had arrived to such excitement. Matthew reports that the crowds added to their declaration that Jesus was the Son of David by describing Him as a prophet from Nazareth.

"Then the crowds who went ahead of Him and those who followed kept shouting: Hosanna to the Son of David! He who comes in the name of the Lord is the blessed One! Hosanna in the highest heaven!"

(Matthew 21:9, HCSB)

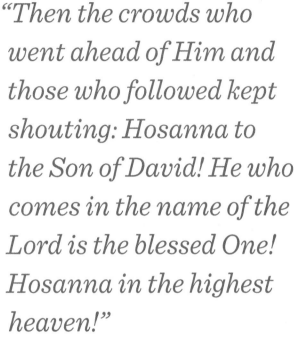

TENSIONS IN JERUSALEM AT PASSOVER

Israel was required to celebrate Passover at the Temple, expanding Jerusalem's population by as much as three times during the festival. Passover celebrated the Jews' release from slavery in Egypt, the Jewish equivalent of Independence Day. For the Roman occupiers, it was a situation in which they feared that revolt could erupt at any moment.

MATTHEW

JESUS DEBATES THE RELIGIOUS LEADERS
(Matthew 22)

When Jesus entered the Temple during the Passover week, the religious leaders attempted to trap Him with His own words. The Pharisees, religious leaders who rejected Gentile culture, came first and asked Jesus about whether the Mosaic Law permitted paying taxes to Caesar. Questions over paying Roman taxes had sparked riots in the past, but Jesus recognized the trap and asked for the kind of coin used to pay Roman taxes. Since it had an image of Caesar, it would have been offensive to Jews as a graven image (graven, or carved, images were forbidden by the Law of Moses due to their use in idolatry; Exod 20:4). But bearing Caesar's image, it could also be considered to belong to him. In response to the question, Jesus said to give Caesar what belonged to him, but to be sure to give God all that He is due.

Jesus Answers the Sadducees

The Sadducees, the religious leaders who only accepted the books of Moses (Genesis through Deuteronomy), then asked their best brain-stumper. They asked about a hypothetical situation in which a woman was widowed by a series of husbands. The question was which one would be her husband in the resurrection. Since the Sadducees thought that the books of Moses didn't teach resurrection, the question was designed to show the absurdity of resurrection. Jesus denied that people would enter eternal life married and then turned the

tables on the Sadducees. He noted that God had told Moses, "I am the God of Abraham..." (Exod 3:6). Since Abraham had been dead over 400 years, and yet God was still his God ("I am" not "I was"), Jesus concluded that Abraham was alive in the presence of God.

JESUS AND THE TEACHERS

Jesus' confrontations with the religious leaders often highlighted their competing interpretations of the Old Testament and the authority to teach it. In this context, Jesus' assertions that they did not understand or had not read the Old Testament correctly would have been particularly galling (Matt 21:16, 42; 22:29, 31; Mark 2:25).

BIBLICAL LINKS

"This is the declaration of the LORD to my Lord: 'Sit at My right hand until I make Your enemies Your footstool.'" *(Psalm 110:1, HCSB)*

Jesus Questions His Questioners

In the end, Jesus asked the Pharisees about the identity of the Messiah. They affirmed that Messiah would be David's son. Jesus then quoted Psalm 110:1, recalling that David was inspired by the Spirit. Since fathers outranked their descendants, Jesus asked how David could call his descendent "Lord." No one could answer, so that put an end to the questions.

"Jesus answered them, 'You are deceived, because you don't know the Scriptures or the power of God.'"

(Matthew 22:29, HCSB)

TAXES: A SENSITIVE SUBJECT

Few people like to pay taxes, and the Jewish people of the first century C.E. were no exception. For them, however, more was at stake than "lower taxes" or "paying your fair share." Roman coins were engraved with images of the Emperor or pagan gods. Even to carry them could be considered participation in idolatry for devout Jews. Some Jews even incited tax revolts against the Romans. One such revolt was led by Judas the Galilean in 6 C.E. The result was the slaughter of thousands of Jews and the deportation of even more. It was hard enough for Jews to pay taxes to pagan overlords; they certainly did not want to hear another Jew preach that it was right for them to do so.

MATTHEW

Matthew, along with the other four Gospels, describes the crucifixion and resurrection of Jesus (Matt 27:1–28:1). But even the resurrection was not the end of Jesus' work. Jesus appeared to the disciples in Jerusalem and told them to return to Galilee for a final period of instruction. The closing story in Matthew's Gospel refers to "the 11 disciples" gathered on a mountain in Galilee to meet with the risen Jesus. Peter, who had denied knowing Jesus three times, was present (John 21:15–19). It was Judas who was missing, having committed suicide in despair over his betrayal of Jesus (Matt 27:3–10).

Jesus Calls the Disciples

When Jesus came, the disciples worshipped Him. But the confidence and faith of their worship was mixed with ongoing struggles to understand and accept everything that had happened. Jesus, however, did not scold them for their doubts, nor did He attempt to answer all their questions in that moment. Instead, He comforted them and gave them a job to do.

In light of His resurrection, Jesus stated that He had entered into His reign as sovereign over creation (see 2 Sam 7:13). All authority over both heaven and Earth belonged to Christ. On that basis, He commanded them to go and make new disciples. Their goal was not merely to call Israel or the Jews dispersed through the nations to follow Jesus. Instead, they were responsible for making disciples of people from every tribe, culture, language, race, and nation.

THE MISSIONARY MOVEMENT: ACTS AND BEYOND

The book of Acts begins the story of Jesus' followers obeying His command to carry the gospel to all nations (see also Mark 16:15, Acts 1:8). Tradition says the original disciples reached Spain in the west, south to Ethiopia, north to Ukraine, and east to India. In 2013 there were 2.35 billion self-described Christians, and an estimated 1.65 million international missionaries and full-time Christian workers. Unfortunately, Jesus' followers have often faced the hostility He predicted. The book of Acts also describes persecution of missionaries such as Paul and Silas (Acts 16). By some estimates, over 100,000 Christians are killed each year for their faith.

The Making of New Disciples

Jesus emphasized two essential aspects of making disciples. The first was the "initiation rite" that identified new disciples with Christ, baptism. Baptism was to be administered in the name (in the authority of) the Father, Son, and Holy Spirit. The second element was teaching those new disciples to observe all of what Christ had commanded.

It was a daunting task. Not only was the world larger than they knew, but Jesus had warned them that they would face the same hostility He had faced (Matt 24:29). Yet Matthew reported that the One who had conquered death also promised that He would be with and would empower His disciples until the end of the age.

"Go, therefore, and make disciples of all nations, baptizing them in the name of the Father and of the Son and of the Holy Spirit, teaching them to observe everything I have commanded you. And remember, I am with you always, to the end of the age."

(Matthew 28:19–20, HCSB)

MARK

The Gospel of Mark is the second of four presentations of the good news about Jesus, each of which have slightly different emphases. Mark explains how Jesus could be the Jewish Messiah and Lord of the Gentiles even though He was crucified by the Romans. The major themes in Mark are the significance of following Christ (8:34), the kingdom of God, and the place of the crucifixion in Jesus' mission.

KEY PASSAGES

Galilee: Proclaiming the Kingdom (1:1–8:21)

2:1–12	Forgiveness and Healing for a Lame Man
5:1–20	Relief for a Demon-Possessed Man
5:21–43	Healing of a Bleeding Woman
7:1–23	Condemnation of the Religious Leaders

Road to Jerusalem: Teaching About Discipleship (8:22–10:52)

9:1–13	Jesus' Glory Is Revealed
10:32–45	Jesus Teaches About Suffering and Service

Jerusalem: Revelation of the Messiah's Mission (11–16)

11:15–12:44	Jesus Confronts the Religious Leaders
14–15	The Betrayal and Crucifixion of Jesus
16	The Messiah's Mission Succeeds: The Resurrection

PRINCIPAL FIGURES

God This book envisions God as the Creator and Ruler of Creation who is also the Father of Jesus Christ.

Jesus Christ The Son of God who concealed His identity as Messiah so that the crowds who applauded His miracles would not misunderstand His mission.

John the Baptist The wilderness preacher who baptized Jesus at the beginning of His ministry and was later executed by Herod Antipas.

The Sick and Demon-Possessed One of the major types of people toward whom Jesus directed His ministry, resulting in miraculous healings and removal of demons.

The Sinners Though used to describe all humanity in other parts of the New Testament (Rom 3:23), in the Gospels this term refers especially to Jews who were not faithful to the Mosaic Covenant, particularly as the Pharisees understood it.

The Twelve Disciples Named in Mark 3:13–19, these were Jesus' closest followers and most intimate students. Jesus explained His full identify to them, while insisting that they keep it a secret until after His crucifixion.

The Religious Leaders The established Temple priests and teachers of the Law, who conspired to arrest Jesus and have Him executed.

LOCATION: Mark describes the ministry of Jesus in Galilee (northern Israel) and Jerusalem. Key locations include the town of Capernaum on the north shore of the Sea of Galilee, Nazareth, and the road to Jerusalem.

ORIGIN: The book of Mark does not name its author, but tradition associates it with John Mark, the cousin of Barnabas and companion of Paul. Papias (120–130 C.E.), an early Christian writer, associated Mark with Peter (see 1 Pet 5:13). This places the writing of the book in Rome in the 60s C.E.

FORGIVENESS OF THE LAME MAN
(Mark 2:1–12)

Jesus established his base of operations in the town of Capernaum, on the north shore of the Sea of Galilee. One day, people gathered in the house where Jesus was teaching. Since Jesus had already gained a reputation for miracles, some of the people brought a paralyzed man to be healed. They couldn't get in through the door, so they carried the man onto the flat roof of the house. After peeling away a section of the roof, they lowered him down on to a mat. Jesus saw the faith of these men through their actions, and so He looked at the paralyzed man and forgave him of his sins.

The religious leaders thought that Jesus was committing blasphemy, since only God can forgive sins against God. Jesus, however, knew exactly what they were thinking. Instead of claiming that they had misunderstood Him or suggesting that people can forgive sins against God, Jesus confronted them. He asked, "Which is easier: to say 'Your sins are forgiven,' or 'Get up and walk?'" On the one hand, no one could verify if the man's sins were forgiven, but everyone would be able to see if he could walk or not. On the other hand, if Jesus had blasphemed by forgiving the man's sins, then God certainly would not allow Jesus to heal him.

Jesus then proved His authority to forgive sins by looking down at the man and telling him to get up, take his mat, and go home. Immediately, the man leaped up and pushed through the astonished crowd. Once the man left, the people exploded with praises to God. They had never seen anything like it before.

THE MESSIANIC LOGIC OF JESUS' MIRACLES

Jesus claimed that His miracles validated His teaching, in particular His claim to be Messiah and exercise divine authority (John 10:37–38). The other three Gospels display this logic and tie it to Jesus' fulfillment of Isaiah's prophecy about a divinely appointed preacher of good news to the poor (Matt 11:1–6; Luke 7:18–23; see Isa 61:1–2).

"Who can forgive sins but God alone?"

(Mark 2:7, HCSB)

MARK

As Jesus ministered in Galilee, He gained a reputation for healing the sick. Jairus, the leader of a synagogue, had heard of his skill. When his daughter became ill, Jairus asked Jesus to heal this young girl. Jesus agreed to help and went with him.

The Woman in the Crowd

As they were pressing through the crowd, a woman who had suffered a hemorrhage for 12 years approached. She had gone to many doctors, but they had only added to her suffering. The Mosaic Law taught that someone with an uncontrolled emission of bodily fluids was unclean and made anyone they touched unclean (Lev 15). But the woman pressed through the crowd to get to Jesus. When she got close, she reached out and touched the hem of his robe. In that instant the flow of blood ceased. Instead of Jesus being made unclean, the woman was made clean. This surprising result demonstrated that Jesus' purity could not be tarnished by sin. Instead, contact with Jesus purified sinners (see Lev 6:25–27).

Jesus immediately stopped and asked, "Who touched my robe?" The disciples were stunned at the question. They pointed out how large and thick the crowd was, with people pressing in around Jesus. But Jesus wasn't asking them; He was calling on the woman to tell the crowd what had happened to her. When she approached Jesus, she trembled and told her story. Jesus affirmed her faith and confirmed her healing.

PURITY LAWS

Mosaic Law contained ritual purity laws, distinguishing clean from unclean. Usually, when unclean things touched clean things, the clean became unclean and had to be purified. Occasionally, however, the "unclean thing became clean—purified and dedicated to God." Among other things, the purity laws symbolized the divisive effect of sin on human relationships with God and others.

UNABLE TO WORK THERE

Jesus' healing miracles in the towns around the Sea of Galilee contrast with His "inability" to do the same in His home town of Nazareth (Mark 6:5). Mark's point was not that the absence of faith left Jesus powerless, because Jesus did heal a few sick people there. Instead, the point was that Jesus refused to perform like a magician in order to impress skeptics.

The Dying Girl

As she left, people came from the synagogue leader's house to report that his daughter had died. Jesus overhead them, and told him not to worry. When they entered the house, Jesus told the ritual mourners to be quiet or they would wake the sleeping girl. They laughed at Him, but He kicked them out and went to the child's bed. Then, He simply took her hand and told her to get up. Immediately she got up. The family was amazed, but Jesus warned them to keep silent about what He had done, perhaps to avoid the inevitable delay that the crowds would create after finding that the girl was alive.

"While He was still speaking, people came from the synagogue leader's house and said, 'Your daughter is dead. Why bother the Teacher anymore?' But when Jesus overheard what was said, He told the synagogue leader, 'Don't be afraid. Only believe.'"

(Mark 5:35–36, HCSB)

MARK

As Jesus and His disciples made their final journey to Jerusalem, Jesus briefed them on what would happen when they arrived. He told them that He would be handed over to the religious leaders, who would condemn Him to death. They would hand Jesus over to the Romans, who would torture and execute Him. But Jesus also told them that He would rise from the grave after three days.

An Inappropriate Request

At that sensitive moment, James and John thought it would be a great idea to ask Jesus for a favor. Jesus wisely asked what they wanted from Him. It was a great chance to rethink, but they plunged ahead and asked to be given the top spots when Jesus became King. Jesus gently told them that they didn't know what they were asking for and implied that they could not bear the suffering He was facing. Again missing a perfect opportunity to be quiet, they insisted they could take whatever Jesus could. Jesus told them that they would share His suffering but said that the spots of honor at His left and right hands had already been reserved, though He did not say for whom.

A SERVICE-ORIENTED SOCIETY

Jesus' teaching that greatness came through service gradually transformed Western expectations of those with political and economic power. Instead of seeing public offices or business merely as an avenue to accumulate personal power and prestige, those in such positions have an obligation to serve the best interests of their constituents and clients. Government serves by securing the natural rights of the governed. Officials who serve well receive greater honor. Business serves through the products and services it creates. Those that serve best earn more clients and trade. Though corruption and fraud do persist, reelection and profit can also be signs of genuine service.

BIBLICAL LINKS

"You call Me Teacher and Lord. This is well said, for I am. So if I, your Lord and Teacher, have washed your feet, you also ought to wash one another's feet." *(John 13:13–14, HCSB)*

The Path to Greatness

When the rest heard what James and John had asked, they were angry (probably because they hadn't thought of it first). So Jesus called them all together. He reminded them of the blindingly obvious fact that pagan rulers used their power to serve themselves. He then told them that this is not how it works in God's administration. In fact, greatness would be achieved through serving others. The principle was that the greatest would be the One who served the most, the best, at the deepest point of need. Jesus told them this was exactly why He had come: to give His life as a ransom so everyone else could live.

> *"...whoever wants to become great among you must be your servant, and whoever wants to be first among you must be a slave to all. For even the Son of Man did not come to be served, but to serve, and to give His life—a ransom for many."*
>
> (Mark 10:43–45, HCSB)

WASHING THE DISCIPLES' FEET

Jesus' last symbolic act of service before His crucifixion came when He washed the feet of His disciples at the beginning of the Last Supper (John 13:12–15). Jewish culture considered this task so humiliating that it was reserved for slaves, preferably Gentile slaves. When the disciples "Teacher" and "Master," performed this task, however, it forcefully illustrated that Jesus understood His role to be that of a servant (see Isa 42, 49–40, 53). This symbolic act also set the example Jesus expected all of His people to follow.

JESUS CLEANSES THE TEMPLE
(Mark 11)

After His triumphal entry of Jerusalem, Jesus entered the Temple complex and attacked the tables of the money-changers and sacrifice sellers. Merchants were not particularly popular among the ancients (see Jas 4:13–17). They were often accused of fraud, including using false weights to cheat customers.

The Role of Temple Merchants

Although they were unpopular, the merchants had a place in Israel's sacrificial system. The Law of Moses permitted those travelling long distances to sell the animal they intended to sacrifice and carry the money to the Temple so that they could purchase an animal once they arrived and make a sacrifice there (Deut 14:24–26). Also, since the silver coins minted in various places around the Roman Empire were of differing sizes and purity, the Temple only accepted shekels minted in the city of Tyre, which were among the most pure and consistent in size. Unfortunately, these services designed to aid worshipers came to be a means of defrauding them.

Jesus Condemns Pride and Extortion

Jesus explained His action by citing Isaiah 56:7 and Jeremiah 7:11. The Temple was to be a place of prayer for everyone. Instead, it had become, in the minds of the people, a defense for sin. Jesus' statement clearly indicts the fraud running rampant among the merchants. But His quote of Isaiah 56:7 implicated the pride and nationalism of His day. As in Jeremiah's time, Israel had come to see the Temple as the talisman that ensured their special relationship with God no matter what they did. Both the pride and extortion of Jesus' day contradicted Solomon's vision for the Temple as a place of penitent and humble prayer for everyone (1 Kgs 8:41–43).

JESUS WASN'T ALWAYS GENTLE

Jesus was often gentle but also displayed righteous indignation. He became angry when the religious leaders refused to affirm helping a crippled man on the Sabbath (Mark 3:5), when He judged unbelief (Matt 11:21, also Matt 23), and when He saw the destructive force of sin and death (John 11:33).

Jesus' actions increased His standing with the crowds who had been defrauded by the merchants (see also Matt 21:14-16). But the religious leaders, who likely benefited from the system, were enraged. For them, it was one more reason to destroy Jesus.

BIBLICAL LINKS

"I will bring them to My holy mountain and let them rejoice in My house of prayer. Their burnt offerings and sacrifices will be acceptable on My altar, for My house will be called a house of prayer for all nations." *(Isaiah 56:7, HCSB)*

"Then He began to teach them: 'Is it not written, My house will be called a house of prayer for all nations? But you have made it a den of thieves!'"
(Mark 11:17, HCSB)

AN INVITATION TO WORSHIP GOD

Although only Israelites were permitted to enter the courtyard of the Temple and offer sacrifices there, the Temple itself was intended to be a house of prayer for all nations (1 Kgs 8:41–43). Solomon's hope was that when Gentiles saw God's glory displayed in His answers to their prayers, they would become worshippers of God. This suggests that the distinction between Jew and Gentile was not intended to be a permanent rejection of non-Jews. The distinction not only illustrated the separation between God and the Gentiles, it also provided a way to express God's desire that the separation be overcome. The Gentile who became a worshipper of God was no longer simply a Gentile, he or she became one of God's people.

LUKE

The Gospel of Luke is the third of four presentations of the good news about Jesus, each of which have slightly different emphases. Luke dedicated his Gospel to Theophilus with the explanation that he intended to provide a well-researched, orderly account of the life and ministry of Jesus Christ. His goal was to assure his readers of the truth of what they had been taught about Jesus as the Savior.

LOCATION: The events in Luke's Gospel take place in Bethlehem, around the Sea of Galilee (northern Israel), and in Jerusalem. The Temple was the scene of much of Jesus' public ministry in Jerusalem.

KEY PASSAGES

Preparation for Jesus' Ministry (1:1–4:15)

1:5–80	The Birth of John the Baptist
2:1–40	The Birth of Jesus Christ

Jesus' Ministry in Galilee (4:16–9:50)

4:16–30	Jesus Is Rejected in Nazareth
7:36–50	Jesus Eats with a Pharisee

Jesus' Journey to Jerusalem (9:51–19:27)

10:25–37	The Parable of the Good Samaritan
15:1–31	The Parable of the Lost Son
19:1–10	Jesus Visits Zacchaeus

Jesus' Ministry in Jerusalem (19:28–21:38)

Jesus' Arrest and Crucifixion (22:1–23:56)

22:7–38	The Last Supper

The Resurrection of Jesus (24:1–53)

ORIGIN: Though the Gospel does not name its author, most ancient works dedicated to someone were not anonymous. Literary features connecting this Gospel to Acts suggest they were written by the same author. Internal details in Acts and early church tradition suggest the author was Luke, the beloved physician and companion of Paul. The book was likely written between 65–85 C.E.

PRINCIPAL FIGURES

God   Luke emphasizes God's sovereign rule over history and grace towards sinful humanity as the Father who sent His Son to be the Savior of the world.

Jesus Christ   Jesus speaks and acts with divine authority, demonstrating that He is Messiah and Lord (a true deity; Luke 2:11).

Holy Spirit   The Holy Spirit is referred to throughout Luke as the One who empowers people, including Jesus, for specific tasks.

Theophilus   The name Theophilus means "One Who Loves God," and this has led scholars to argue over whether the name refers to an individual friend of Luke's or is a general dedication to anyone who loves God.

Gabriel   An angelic being who announces the two miraculous births in Luke (John the Baptist and Jesus).

Zechariah and Elizabeth   A priest and his barren wife who are promised a son who will prepare the way for the Messiah.

Mary   A virgin who is promised that she will bear the Messiah though a miraculous conception by the Holy Spirit.

The Disciples   Luke focuses on the twelve main disciples but also refers to a larger group of Christ's followers, "the Seventy."

The Outcasts   A group composed of tax collectors, sinners, prostitutes, the sick, and the poor that were the primary focus of Jesus' ministry.

The Opponents   Primarily the religious leaders who attempted to embarrass and later to kill Jesus. This group also included civil officials such as Herod Antipas and Pilate, the Roman Governor.

Zechariah was a priest working in the Temple. Although both he and his wife Elizabeth were righteous people, she had been unable to bear a child. Both were now too old to have children, but as with Abraham and Sarah, God had other plans.

God sent the angel Gabriel to speak with Zechariah while he was burning incense inside the Temple. Gabriel told Zechariah that Elizabeth would bear a son who would be set apart to God. He would turn people's hearts toward God in preparation for the coming of the Messiah. Zechariah doubted the message, so Gabriel told the priest that he would be unable to speak until the promise was fulfilled.

When it became clear that Elizabeth was pregnant, she went into seclusion for five months. When she finally gave birth, her neighbors and family came to celebrate. They wanted to name the baby boy after his father, Zechariah. But the silent priest signaled for a tablet and wrote the name the angel had given, "His name is John!" With that expression of faith acknowledging that God's promise had been fulfilled, Zechariah's speech was restored. He prophesied that God was bringing the Messiah to save His people from their enemies, and that John would be the one to prepare the way for the Promised King.

THE ROLE OF THE FORERUNNER

Zechariah's prophecy pulled together the expectations of a prophet who would precede the Messiah (Isa 40:3–4, Mal 3:1, 4:5). John the Baptist's role was to redirect the expectations of his contemporaries away from a political or military deliverer to one that would save them from their greatest enemy, their sin.

"And child, you will be called a prophet of the Most High, for you will go before the Lord to prepare His ways, to give His people knowledge of salvation through the forgiveness of their sins."
(Luke 1:76–77, HCSB)

LUKE

Caesar Augustus wanted a census taken of the whole Roman Empire. In Herod's territory, the head of each household was required to return to his ancestral home, along with his family, to be counted in the census. This meant Joseph had to leave Nazareth in Galilee and travel south to Bethlehem, because he was a descendent of David's family. Apparently he had already taken up the responsibility to care for Mary, though they were not yet married, because she traveled with him. While in Bethlehem, Mary gave birth and laid her son in a feeding trough because there was no other place for them to stay.

An Angel Appears

Nearby, there were shepherds caring for flocks in the fields. An angel appeared to them in the night. The shepherds trembled in the bright light, but the angel told them not to be afraid. He reported that there was great news for everyone, a Savior who was Messiah the Lord had been born in David's town. They were to look for a baby wrapped in cloth, lying in a feeding trough. Then an army of angels appeared, praising God with the words "Glory to God in the highest heaven, and peace on earth to people He favors!" After the angels disappeared, the shepherds went to see the child and repeated the message the angel had given.

Jesus Is Named Son of God

After eight days, the child was circumcised as the Law of Moses commanded (Lev 12:3) and named Jesus. Then He was brought to the Temple to be dedicated as a firstborn son to God (Exod 13:12). While there, Simeon and Anna, a righteous man and a prophetess, sought them out. Though both declared that God's promise of a Messiah was being fulfilled in Jesus, it appears that they only spoke of this to Joseph and Mary. Herod's reputation for executing rivals was well-known in Jerusalem and may have prompted them to be discreet.

DATING THE CENSUS

Luke ties the date of Jesus' birth to a Roman census ordered by Caesar Augustus. Luke also reports that the Roman official Quirinius was in charge of the census in the Roman province of Syria. The problem is that Jesus is known to have been born before Herod's death in 4 B.C.E., but Roman records list Quirinius as the Governor (legatus) of Syria in 6–7 C.E., 10 years after Herod died. Some scholars have suggested that the text could mean that the census happened before Quirinius was Governor. Others suggest that he was Governor twice.

WHAT'S THE DATE?

The calendar in use throughout the Western world is the Gregorian Calendar, developed by Pope Gregory XIII in 1582 C.E. Though this book uses the international practice of describing dates as "C.E." (Common Era) and "B.C.E." (Before the Common Era), many readers will be familiar with the traditional "B.C." (Before Christ) and "A.D." (Anno Domini, Latin for "the Year of the Lord"). The index year, marking the difference between B.C.E./B.C. and C.E./A.D. is the year of Jesus' birth, as calculated in the sixth century C.E. by the monk Dionysius Exiguus. An error in the calculation, however, leads to the odd effect of dating Jesus' birth between 7–4 B.C.E. or "Before Christ."

"Now, Master, You can dismiss Your slave in peace, as You promised. For my eyes have seen Your salvation. You have prepared it in the presence of all peoples—a light for revelation to the Gentiles and glory to Your people Israel."

(Luke 2:29–32, HCSB)

LUKE

After returning from the wilderness and Galilee (4:1–15), Jesus came to Nazareth where He had been raised. On the Sabbath, He entered the synagogue and read from the scroll of Isaiah. Jesus read from Isaiah 61:1–2 but ended the reading in the middle of verse 2, saying that He was proclaiming God's favor. Jesus sat down to begin His sermon and declared that they were hearing the promised preacher speak. The rest of Isaiah 61:2 spoke of the day of God's judgment. Jesus' decision to stop with the proclamation of favor was consistent with the primary purpose of His ministry (see John 3:17). But on other occasions, Jesus taught that He would "finish the sentence" by returning later to execute the Day of Judgment (see Matt 21:31–46).

The Skeptics of Nazareth

The people were amazed at the power of Jesus' preaching about God's grace. Yet, they also rejected Jesus' assertion that He was the promised preacher. They refused to accept that the One they knew as Joseph's son was the Messiah. Jesus anticipated their next line, "Doctor, heal yourself." If Jesus could do all these wonderful things, why were He and His family so poor? The people cynically demanded that Jesus produce miracles as they had heard He did in Capernaum.

Jesus answered the people's proverb with one of His own, "No prophet is accepted in his hometown." Israel's pattern had always been to reject the prophets God sent. Those who would have been expected to believe the prophets did not (Israel). But those who would not have been expected to receive them, did (Gentiles like the widow in the Phoenician town of Zerephath, whose small amount of flour and oil lasted through a three-year famine [1 Kgs 17:8–24], and Naaman, the Syrian general who was healed of leprosy by Elisha [2 Kgs 5:1–17].) This answer enraged the people in the synagogue, and so they drove Jesus out to throw Him off a cliff. But before they could push Jesus over the edge, He simply walked away through the crowd.

THE SCRIPTURE IS FULFILLED

The Gospel writers assert or quote Jesus as claiming that a particular event "fulfilled" the Scripture over 20 times. Many of these Old Testament quotations were direct prophecies about the Messiah, such as the place of His birth, the purpose of His life, and details about the way He died. Other "fulfillments" were incidents that followed an important precedent or pattern, such as Jesus' family taking refuge in Egypt (Matt 2:15) and the people refusing to believe Jesus' teaching (Matt 13:14).

A Pattern of Rejection

This account of the rejection of Jesus in His hometown of Nazareth also sets up a pattern for Luke's whole account of Jesus' life and ministry. As with the other Gospel writers, Luke would describe the miraculous feedings, healings, and exorcisms that Jesus did. He would also consistently point out that Jesus was rejected, just as many of the prophets had been (6:23; 11:47, 49–50; 13:33–34; 20:9–19).

A PREACHER TO THE POOR

Jesus' concern for the poor reflected God's character (Ps 68:5–10), seen in the Exodus (Exod 2:23–24) and Mosaic Law (Exod 23:11; Lev 25). This concern was expected of the Davidic King (Ps 72:1–4; Isa 11:4). The apostles also prioritized care for the poor (Acts 6:1–7; 2 Cor 8-9; Jas 1:27).

"He began by saying to them, 'Today as you listen, this Scripture has been fulfilled.' They were all speaking well of Him and were amazed by the gracious words that came from His mouth, yet they said, 'Isn't this Joseph's son?'"

(Luke 4:21–22, HCSB)

LUKE

At one point in Jesus' ministry, a scholar of the Mosaic Law found an opportunity to test Jesus, perhaps thinking that he could be the judge of Jesus' teaching. The scholar asked Jesus what he had to do in order to receive eternal life. Jesus answered with a question, asking what the Law taught. The scholar gave the commonly accepted summary of the Law's teaching: love God wholeheartedly (Deut 6:5) and love your neighbor as yourself (Lev 19:18).

Jesus affirmed the man's answer but knew that this scholar misunderstood the purpose of the Law. Instead of seeing it as God's instrument to reveal human sinfulness and to point to the Righteous One, the Messiah, the scholar thought he could make himself righteous through his obedience.

The scholar then asked a second question, "Who is my neighbor?" His question challenged Jesus to define the boundaries between who qualified as "my neighbor" and who did not. Jesus refused to instruct the scholar in how he could make himself righteous. Instead, He deliberately answered a different question. He did this by telling a story about a man traveling down from Jerusalem to Jericho.

Compassion from an Unexpected Source

As the man traveled this steep road, he was attacked by robbers and left half dead. Though a priest and a temple worker passed by, they did nothing to help. But then the last person a Jew could expect help from, a Samaritan, stopped to help. The Samaritan tended the man's wounds and took him to an inn, where he paid for lodging and promised as much money as needed to cover the expenses while the man recovered.

Who Proved to Be a Neighbor?

Jesus then turned to the scholar and asked His question: who proved to be a neighbor to the wounded man? The question refocused the discussion away from the boundaries of duty, where obedience became disobedience, to a person's character. The scholar grudgingly

BIBLICAL LINKS

"For while we were still helpless, at the appointed moment, Christ died for the ungodly. For rarely will someone die for a just person—though for a good person perhaps someone might even dare to die. But God proves His own love for us in that while we were still sinners, Christ died for us!" *(Romans 5:6–8, HCSB)*

answered, "the one who showed mercy" (refusing to acknowledge he was a Samaritan). Where the scholar of the Law had challenged Jesus to set boundaries to obedience, Jesus challenged the scholar to look beyond the parable recognize those who showed mercy to the helpless enemy, and become like Him.

When Jesus made a Samaritan (hated by Jews) the hero of His story, He was criticizing the hatred implied in the scholar's attempt to designate some classes of people as outside his responsibility to love. But an even greater critique was suggested by Jesus' refusal to affirm the scholar's desire to make himself righteous. Jesus simply dismissed his question out of hand.

AUGUSTINE'S INTERPRETATION

Augustine (354–430 C.E.), the great Christian writer and bishop in North Africa, identified several levels of meaning in the parable of the Good Samaritan. In one book, he noted that the parable meant that people should care for everyone they meet. But Augustine also identified Jesus as the ultimate example of a loving neighbor. In another book, Augustine explained how Biblical history was summarized in the parable. Satan had attacked and left humanity half-dead in sin. The Law of Moses didn't change that sad fact. But when Christ came, He rescued and provided for those destroyed by sin.

"But a Samaritan on his journey came up to him, and when he saw the man, he had compassion."
(Luke 10:33, HCSB)

LUKE

The Pharisees taught Covenant faithfulness. They rejected those who collaborated with the pagan Romans (tax collectors) and those who didn't follow the Law of Moses (sinners). When they saw that Jesus extended fellowship to these people, even though He didn't affirm or enable their sin, they were upset.

Jesus' Use of Parables

Jesus told a series of parables to explain His actions. The first described a shepherd who rejoices more over finding 1 lost sheep than the 99 that were safe in the fold. The second told of a woman celebrating over finding one lost coin. In each of these stories, Jesus was comparing himself to the seeking shepherd and woman. Just as these characters valued what was lost and rejoiced when what was lost was found, so Jesus' fellowship demonstrated how He valued those He had come to seek and to save (Luke 19:10). These parables also illustrated God's joy over those who repented and returned to Him.

The Prodigal Son

The climax was the story of the lost son, traditionally called the "prodigal son." The younger of two sons went to his father and asked for his share of the inheritance. It was a horrible request, essentially saying the son preferred the money to his father's life. Surprisingly, the father granted the request and the son left. He wasted his money, and when famine struck, he found himself feeding unclean animals to make ends meet. Even the slops started to look tasty.

When the he came to his senses, he realized that he had committed what would be considered an unforgivable sin against his father. Despairing of ever being forgiven, he decided to ask to be an indentured slave in his father's household (see Lev 25:39–55). His father saw him coming and instead of turning him away, the father ran to embrace his son. The younger son confessed his sin and said that he was not worthy to be called a son. But the father wouldn't hear it. Instead, he ordered a party to celebrate the younger son's return.

The dutiful older son refused to celebrate. He had never received the party he thought he had earned. The son that deserved death was getting the party. The father urged him to celebrate, but the story left the older son's decision hanging in the air for the Pharisees to answer.

OPEN-ENDED PARABLES

Jesus often told parables that asked questions, such as the Two Foundations (6:26–49) or the Two Debtors (7:41–43). Others left a story unresolved, such as the Barren Tree (13:6-9) or the Rich Man and Lazarus (16:19–31). Each invited listeners to decide or resolve the story wisely in light of Jesus' teaching.

A Challenge to Celebrate God's Grace

The problem that this last parable posed for the Pharisees lay in the symbolic significance of its key characters. The parable clearly made God the gracious Father and the sinners of Jesus' day the younger son. This left the Pharisees to identify with the dutiful older brother who was unhappy that the Father did not reward his sons according to their merits but instead was gracious to the once wicked but now penitent younger son. Jesus was challenging them to give up their pride and instead celebrate the fact that God is gracious towards sinners. Jesus' decision to leave the story unfinished put its resolution in the hands of His listeners. They would either join the celebration of God's grace or turn their backs on God.

"I tell you, in the same way, there is joy in the presence of God's angels over one sinner who repents."

(Luke 15:10, HCSB)

LUKE

The people of Jericho heard that Jesus and His disciples were passing through. They gathered along the road to see Him, perhaps in hopes of seeing a miracle. They saw one, if not necessarily the kind they expected.

Zacchaeus the Tax Collector

One of the people who went to see Jesus was a man named Zacchaeus, whose name meant "righteous." When people called his name, it must have been with a sneer, because Zacchaeus was a traitorous crook; he was a tax-collector. He paid the Romans a set fee but was free to collect as much as he could and keep the profit for himself. It was essentially government-approved extortion, and Zacchaeus had become very wealthy doing it.

Jesus Speaks to Zacchaeus

Zacchaeus was also a short man. He couldn't see over the crowd, and they had no interest in letting him through. So he climbed a tree to catch a glimpse of Jesus. When Jesus got there, He looked right up at the tax collector and addressed him as "Righteous" (Zacchaeus). But when Jesus said it, something changed.

Jesus ordered Zacchaeus to climb down from the tree. Then He told the tax collector that He was going to stay at his house that day. Far from being an imposition, it was a sign of honor to be asked for hospitality.

Zacchaeus scrambled down and welcomed Jesus with joy. Jesus had taken the most despised man in town and gave him the greatest honor.

The crowds complained that Jesus was honoring such a sinful man, but Zacchaeus demonstrated the change Jesus' words had caused by repenting of his greed. He publically vowed to give half of his wealth to help the poor. He also committed to make restitution for his extortion by repaying his victims fourfold (see Exod 22:1).

Jesus affirmed that Zacchaeus had experienced the salvation He had come to bring to Israel.

THE SON OF MAN

Jesus called Himself "Son of Man" 83 times in the Gospels. The phrase was used over 90 times of the prophet Ezekiel and emphasized his humanity in contrast to God's divine nature. But Jesus' use of the term appears to have more in common with Daniel's description of "one like a son of man" (Dan 7:13–14). Daniel described this figure as being established before God with glory and dominion over the nations in an eternal kingdom. There, the "Son of Man" appears to be a divine figure who fulfills the promise of the Davidic Covenant.

Salvation for the Faithful

When Jesus said that salvation had come to Zacchaeus "for he too is a son of Abraham," Jesus was not claiming that being a physical descendent of Abraham made Zacchaeus a candidate for salvation. Instead, the point was that in demonstrating a penitent, life-transforming faith, Zacchaeus had shown that he had the faith of Abraham. Jesus concluded by affirming that He had come to bring salvation to anyone who had this kind of faith, no matter how sinful they were.

ROMAN TAX COLLECTORS

Romans imposed direct taxes (tribute) on land and persons. Indirect taxes were levied against local governments (excise and inheritance taxes, or tolls). The Romans' "tax farming" system allowed speculators to bid on tax contracts that were paid upfront. The system encouraged high bids (and so high tax revenue), extortion, and tax revolts. Jews who become tax collectors for the Romans were seen as greedy traitors, leveraging the power of the occupiers' swords to exploit and victimize their own people.

"For the Son of Man has come to seek and to save the lost."

(Luke 19:10, HCSB)

THE LAST SUPPER
(Luke 22)

The religious leaders had come to see Jesus as a threat due to His popularity as a miracle worker, but Jesus' triumphal entry into Jerusalem made them afraid that arresting Him in a public place would spark a riot. Their fear allowed Jesus to reach the first day of the Passover Feast and celebrate it with His disciples.

A Place for Passover

That morning, Jesus sent Peter and John into Jerusalem to prepare for the ceremonial meal of lamb, bitter herbs, unleavened bread, and wine (see Exod 12). Finding available space large enough to accommodate the meal seemed impossible so close to Passover, since the city was crowded with so many pilgrims who had also come to celebrate the feast. But Jesus told them to look for a man carrying a jug of water, which would have been an unusual sight because at that time women were the ones who carried water. They were to follow him to his house and tell the owner that Jesus wanted to use his guest room to celebrate the Passover. Following Jesus' instructions, they found a place big enough for them all to celebrate the feast.

A Warning of Betrayal

When the time for the meal came, Jesus told His disciples that He had been anticipating this Passover meal before His suffering began. It would be His last before becoming the sacrificial lamb that the feast prefigured and that God intended Him to become in the crucifixion. At some point in the meal Jesus also issued a warning. The one who would betray Jesus to His death was sitting with Him. Though Jesus was going to the cross in submission to God's will, the betrayer was acting for his own sinful reasons and would be judged. The disciples immediately began to try to figure out who it would be. But when Judas left, the rest failed to realize that he was the one Jesus was speaking about.

A New Covenant

The supper followed the normal course of a Passover meal, with two major changes. When Jesus took the bread and broke it, He gave it to the disciples and described it as His body. Jesus also took the final cup and told them that this was the new covenant of His blood. Each was given for them. He commanded them to celebrate the meal in remembrance of Him.

Jesus' final Passover supper linked His death with the celebration of the Mosaic festival of Passover. The original Passover commemorated the miraculous liberation of Israel from bondage in Egypt. The Passover lamb recalled the sacrificial blood that protected the firstborn of the Hebrews from death when spread on the door posts and lintels. The connection Jesus made implied that His death would accomplish a greater liberation by securing salvation from sin for all people in Himself. Jesus also linked His death to the inauguration of Jeremiah's "New Covenant" (Jer 31:31).

PASSOVER AND THE LAST SUPPER

The way in which the Gospels describe the timing of the Last Supper has led to some confusion among readers. Matthew, Mark, and Luke describe Jesus as celebrating the Passover meal, while John indicates that Passover was eaten after sundown on Friday. This has led some to conclude that that the Gospel writers were confused about the events leading up to the crucifixion. However, each Gospel has the crucifixion on Friday and the Last Supper on the night before (Thursday). It seems that Jesus celebrated the Passover meal a day early, on the first day of the Feast of Unleavened Bread (Thursday), and then was crucified at about the traditional time of the sacrifice of the Passover lamb on Friday.

"And He took bread, gave thanks, broke it, gave it to them, and said, 'This is My body, which is given for you. Do this in remembrance of Me.' In the same way He also took the cup after supper and said, 'This cup is the new covenant established by My blood; it is shed for you.'"

(Luke 22:19–20, HCSB)

JOHN

INTRODUCTION

The Gospel of John is the last of four presentations of the good news about Jesus, each of which have slightly different emphases. John wrote his Gospel to convince his readers that Jesus is the Messiah and God's Son, so that they might have life through faith in Him (20:31). The author argues that Jesus' miracles validated His teaching (10:38; 20:30). The most significant of these miracles is His resurrection.

LOCATION: The events in John are set in Galilee (northern Israel) and Jerusalem. Key locations include Jacob's well in Samaria, the town of Bethany near Jerusalem, and the Temple.

KEY PASSAGES

Introducing the Eternal Word Made Flesh (1:1–18)

The Revelation of Jesus in Word and Deed (1:19–10:42)

3:1–21	Nicodemus Questions Jesus About Salvation
4:1–42	Jesus Saves Samaritans
6:1–71	Jesus Provides the Bread of Life
10:1–21	Jesus Is the Good Shepherd

The Revelation of the Messiah's Mission (11:1–12:50)

11:1–44	Jesus Raises Lazarus from the Dead

The Revelation of Jesus in Suffering and Victory (13:1–20:31)

17:1–26	Jesus Prays in the Garden of Gethsemane
18:1–19:42	Jesus Is Betrayed and Crucified
20:1–31	Jesus Is Raised and Appears to His Disciples

The Way Forward for Jesus' Followers (21:1–25)

ORIGIN: This book is anonymous, but tradition associates it with the Apostle John, the "beloved disciple." Early Christian sources (100–125 C.E.) quote from the book, which suggests it was written prior to 100 C.E. Some scholars argue for a date prior to 70 C.E.

PRINCIPAL FIGURES

God　God exists as the Eternal Father of the Divine Son in fellowship with the Holy Spirit, and loves the world enough to provide salvation in His Son.

Jesus Christ　The eternal Word who is both Creator and Savior of the world. Because He is fully divine, He reveals the invisible God (Father) and is the location of God's glory (the true Temple).

Holy Spirit　Also God, who empowered the ministry of the Son and who would be sent by the Son from the Father to draw people to faith in Jesus and empower the life of believers.

Nicodemus　A Pharisee and member of the ruling council in Jerusalem (the Sanhedrin) who questioned Jesus in a nighttime meeting and eventually became a believer.

The Twelve Disciples　John focuses on Thomas, who doubted the resurrection, and Peter, who denied Jesus three times but was restored when Jesus provoked three affirmations of love.

Mary and Martha　Sisters who trusted Jesus to raise their brother Lazarus from the dead because they believed Jesus was Resurrection and Life itself.

Mary Magdalene　A wealthy woman who anointed Jesus' feet and was one of the first to see Him after the resurrection.

The Jews　This title does not refer to all Jewish people. The religious leaders, especially the Pharisees, considered themselves "the real Jews" because of their detailed Torah observance.

NICODEMUS VISITS JESUS
(John 3)

One night, a man lost in his own spiritual darkness came to question the new Teacher that had risen among the people. The visitor was not just any questioner; he was one of the noted Pharisees of his day, Nicodemus. He assured Jesus that the religious leaders knew He came from God, implying that Jesus should clearly identify Himself as a teacher or prophet. The implication was that Jesus needed to submit Himself and His teaching for the approval of the religious leaders.

But Jesus didn't let Nicodemus set the terms of the conversation. Instead, He immediately asserted that unless someone (presumably Nicodemus) was born again by God's power, that person would never enter God's kingdom. When Nicodemus challenged Jesus' metaphor of rebirth, he was also rejecting the idea that

his obedience to the Law of Moses didn't qualify him for heaven. But Jesus' point was that only God could make rebellious people faithful (see Ezek 36:25–27). Since like gives birth to like, sinful people could only produce sin. Only the righteous God could confer righteousness.

Nicodemus still refused to understand, so Jesus rebuked him. If Nicodemus refused to enter the kingdom on Jesus' terms, then he would understand nothing further. Jesus insisted that the Nicodemus look to Him for salvation. Jesus told Nicodemus that He would be lifted up, referring to His coming crucifixion, and that He would draw all men to Himself.

Just as God had graciously provided healing for His people during the Exodus, so God's love for the world would provide salvation in His Son for all who believe in Him. Jesus' mission was not to destroy the world, but to secure salvation in Himself. Those who believe in Him would avoid judgment. Those who did not believe were already condemned. The decisive question for humanity was whether or not they would embrace Christ's light. Jesus stated that what people do with Him demonstrates whether they depend on themselves or on God for salvation.

BORN AGAIN

Christians use the phrase "born again" to describe the divine gift of new life. Catholics tie this to their understanding of baptism, while Protestants connect it to conversion through faith. Some of the more famous figures to claim the label include former U.S. President Jimmy Carter and Watergate figure Chuck Colson.

JOHN

THE WOMAN AT THE WELL
(John 4)

Jesus was travelling from Judea to Galilee. The route He took went through Samaria, which was an unusual choice for a Jew. Due to the animosity between the Jews and the Samaritans, most Jews at the time would have avoided Samaria.

When Jesus needed to rest, He stopped and sat by a famous well. While He was there, a Samaritan woman came to draw water. Jesus stunned the woman by asking her for a drink. Since Jews and Samaritans didn't associate, she asked why he was speaking to her.

Jesus Offers Water of Life

Jesus said that if she realized who He was, she would ask Him for water. He wouldn't give brackish well water, but living (fresh, running) water (Isa 55; Jer 2:13). She scoffed that He didn't even have a bucket. Surely He was not greater than Jacob, who had dug the well. But Jesus insisted that He was and pointed to the kind of water each provided as proof. Water from Jacob's well gave life, but one needed to keep coming back. But one drink of Jesus' water would satisfy forever, giving eternal life.

The woman liked the idea of forgoing trips to the well, but Jesus told her that this was not the problem His water would solve. Jesus called attention to the moral chaos of her marriages to highlight the value of His water (Isa 1:16). Water from the well would wash her clothes, but the water Jesus offered (salvation) would cleanse her from her sins.

The woman was stunned that He knew the intimate details of her life and called Jesus a prophet. She then asked Him to settle the ancient dispute between Samaritans and Jews about where God was to be worshipped. While Jews affirmed that covenant sacrifices had to be offered at the Temple in Jerusalem, Samaritans argued that they were to be offered at Mount Gerazim. But the issue was not "where," it was "who." Again, Jesus returned to the woman's sinfulness. He said that God was looking for those who would worship in spirit and in truth (14:6; 15:26).

JESUS AND WOMEN

Jesus affirmation of women contrasted starkly with His culture (Luke 13:16). He condemned thoughtless attitudes of men towards women (Matt 5:28–29; 19:8). Women travelled among His disciples (Matt 27:55) and sat under His teaching (Luke 10:39). Most significantly, women were the first to witness the resurrection (John 20:1–19).

Jesus and the Samaritans

Jesus' gracious offer of salvation in spite of His clear knowledge of her sinful life led the woman to recognize Jesus as the Messiah. She rushed into the town to tell the people of her discovery. When the Samaritans came to Jesus, they asked Him to stay with them, which He did for two days. By accepting their hospitality, Jesus showed that the breach of fellowship between the people of Judea and Samaria was healed in Him (see 1 Kgs 13:7–10). During his visit, many there came to believe that He was the Messiah.

GRACE AND TOUGH LOVE

When the woman at the well met Jesus, she did not realize that He already knew her life story. It was not a pretty picture. Five divorces suggested that the men in her life saw her as a worthless wife. The fact that she was coming by herself to the well instead of with the other women from the town suggests that those who knew her story shunned her. But Jesus neither rejected her nor minimized her sin. Instead, His knowledge of her life demonstrated that He was not offering grace blindly. He knew who she was and loved her anyway, offering salvation that would transform her life.

"But an hour is coming, and is now here, when the true worshipers will worship the Father in spirit and truth. Yes, the Father wants such people to worship Him. God is spirit, and those who worship Him must worship in spirit and truth."
(John 4:23–24, HCSB)

JOHN

Around Passover time, a large crowd came to Jesus on a mountain near the Sea of Galilee. Jesus decided to feed them, but there was not enough food available for so many. One of Jesus' disciples found a boy with five loaves of bread and two fish. Jesus broke these into pieces for the disciples to distribute. Miraculously, the bread and fish multiplied in His hands. After everyone had eaten their fill, they collected 12 baskets of left-overs. Amazed by the meal that fed so many with so little, the people declared Jesus the Prophet that Moses had promised (Deut 18:15) and wanted to crown Him king.

The Crowd Begs for Food

The next day, the crowd followed Jesus to Capernaum. Jesus accused them of following Him for the food, not because they believed He was the Messiah. He claimed to have food that would confer eternal life and urged them to seek that instead. When the people asked what God wanted them to do, Jesus told them to believe in Him as the Bread of Life.

The people asked Jesus to feed them repeatedly, as they envisioned Moses doing in the wilderness. But Jesus corrected them; Moses had not fed the Israelites, God had fed the people in the desert. God was now giving them Christ, the Bread from Heaven. Jesus promised that everyone who believed in Him would have eternal life and be resurrected.

Jesus Offers Himself

Jesus' claim to be the Bread from Heaven was too much for the authorities. They insisted on seeing Jesus as Joseph's son, rather than as God's Son. Jesus implied that their disbelief was divine judgment and insisted that He was the Bread of Life. He then pressed the issue of their unbelief by intensifying the image of life-giving bread. Just as bread does no good to those who will not eat, Jesus told them that only those who ate His flesh and drank His blood would live forever.

CHRISTIAN CANNIBALISM?

Early Christians affirmed their faith in Jesus as the Bread of Life by obeying Christ's command to take communion "in remembrance of Me" ("this is my body," and "this is my blood," Luke 22:14–21). As Jesus had done, they used bread and wine as the elements to be consumed in this meal. But the language of eating the body and drinking the blood of Jesus sometimes resulted in Christians being accused of cannibalism. Defenders of Christianity dismissed this accusation by appealing to the exemplary moral character of Christians, especially their well-known emphasis on the value of all human life.

The people recoiled from the claim, rejecting both a crassly literal understanding of Jesus' metaphor (one must commit cannibalism in order to be saved) and the metaphor's link between eating and believing in Jesus. Jesus warned the disciples that the Spirit was the only One who could overcome disbelief. When some of the disciples left, Jesus asked the remaining 12 if they were leaving also. Peter, however, affirmed that Jesus alone could confer eternal life through His teaching.

BIBLICAL LINKS

"Now this is His command: that we believe in the name of His Son Jesus Christ, and love one another as He commanded us." *(1 John 3:23, HCSB)*

"What can we do to perform the works of God?" they asked. Jesus replied, "This is the work of God—that you believe in the One He has sent."

(John 6:28–29, HCSB)

JOHN

Around the time of the Feast of Dedication (Hanukkah), Jesus rose to condemn Israel's religious leadership as poor shepherds of God's flock, the people of Israel. His speech echoed the accusations of the prophets (especially those in Ezekiel 34 and Jeremiah 23) and Psalm 23. Where God had promised to take up the role of Shepherd of the nation, Jesus implied this spoke of Him.

The Role of the Shepherd

Jesus described Himself as the only legitimate entrance into the fold and as the Shepherd who cares for the sheep. Others sneak in only to steal and kill the sheep. But Jesus would defend the sheep by laying down His life for them. Those who belonged to Him would hear His voice and follow, both Jews and Gentiles. Some of the religious leaders thought Jesus was possessed by a demon, but others considered that demon possession could not explain His words and deeds.

Later, the leaders demanded a simple statement on whether or not Jesus was the Messiah. Christ responded that He had shown them through His works, but that they didn't believe Him. The religious leaders had seen Jesus healing and performing other miracles but consistently tried to find fault with Him. This pattern had climaxed when they expelled a man Jesus had healed from the synagogue because the man insisted that Jesus was from God (9:1–41). Not only did the religious leaders refuse to believe that Jesus' miracles proved

that He was the Messiah, they were trying to prevent everyone else from following Him. Even so, they would not be able to prevent anyone from following Jesus because the Father had given them into Christ's hand.

The Charge of Blasphemy

Jesus argued that since no one could defeat the Father, no one would be able to defeat Jesus, either. His summary, "I and the Father are One," served to distinguish Jesus from the Father ("I and the Father"), but also included Himself in the statement of God's unique divinity ("are One"). Jesus' statement was a rephrasing of a famous statement called the Shema (Deut 6:4). Shema is the Hebrew word for *hear,* and was used as the name for the most concise statement in the Mosaic Covenant of the assertion that there is only one God: "Hear O Israel, the Lord our God, the Lord is One."

BIBLICAL LINKS

"My anger burns against the shepherds, so I will punish the leaders. For the LORD of Hosts has tended His flock, the house of Judah; He will make them like His majestic steed in battle." *(Zechariah 10:3, HCSB)*

The leaders immediately moved to stone Jesus, so He asked them for which of His miracles was He being executed. They answered that they were not going to execute Him for the miracles He had done but for His interpretation of their meaning. In their eyes, Jesus was merely a man and so had blasphemed by claiming to be God. Jesus reminded them that the Scriptures described created beings with divine language (Ps 82:6). Angelic messengers could be called "gods" and "sons of God." Therefore, there could be no problem with the supreme messenger from God, the Messiah, calling Himself the "Son of God." Again, Jesus insisted that His works validated His connection to the Father.

SHEPHERD IMAGERY IN THE BIBLE

Many prominent figures in the Bible were shepherds. Abel, Jacob, Moses, and David all tended sheep. Abraham also had large flocks. The primary job of a shepherd was to guide the sheep to good pasture and water and to protect them from predators. Leaders in Israel came to be described as shepherds (Zech 10:3). God even applied the image to Himself (Ps 23, Ezek 34). In the New Testament, the title *pastor* is the Greek word for *shepherd*.

"If I am not doing My Father's works, don't believe Me. But if I am doing them and you don't believe Me, believe the works. This way you will know and understand that the Father is in Me and I in the Father."
(John 10:37–38, HCSB)

JOHN

THE RESURRECTION OF LAZARUS
(John 11)

When one of Jesus' close friends, Lazarus, fell desperately sick, his sisters, Mary and Martha, sent for Jesus to heal him. When Jesus got the message, He said that Lazarus' illness would not end in death but in the glory of God. Jesus loved Lazarus and his sisters, but in order to maximize the display of God's glory in the situation He waited two days before starting toward their home in Bethany. The disciples feared that by going so close to Jerusalem, the religious leaders would kill Jesus, but they were determined to go with Him.

Lazarus Dies

While they were travelling, Lazarus died. Jesus knew it had happened and told His disciples that Lazarus had fallen asleep, but that He would wake him up. The disciples thought Lazarus was recovering, so Jesus explained clearly that Lazarus was dead.

When Jesus arrived, Lazarus had been in the tomb for four days. Some religious leaders had come to comfort the family, but as soon as Martha heard Jesus was coming she abandoned them and went to meet Him. Her grief poured out with the confession that if Jesus had been there, Lazarus would not have died. Yet she affirmed that God would still do whatever Jesus asked. Jesus told her that her brother would rise from the dead, and she acknowledged her belief in the eventual resurrection of the righteous. But Jesus told her that He was life itself and that those who trusted Him would survive death and live forever. Martha believed Him.

Lazarus Is Restored

Jesus went to the tomb with the sisters, angered by the grief death had caused them. He wept with them, and the observers took this to indicate the depth of His love for Lazarus. They were wrong. His love was even stronger than mere tears.

When Jesus ordered the tomb opened, Martha's faith faltered. She warned Jesus that Lazarus had been dead four days and his body would reek with the stench of decay. Jesus reassured her that if she would trust Him, then she would see God's glory. When the tomb was opened, Jesus thanked the Father for always hearing Him and stated that His goal was to convince the bystanders that God had indeed sent Him. Finally, Jesus called for Lazarus to come out. He did, restored to full health. Jesus' love for Lazarus had triumphed even over death, and the result was that many of those who had seen believed in Jesus (11:45).

BIBLICAL LINKS

"And just as the Father raises the dead and gives them life, so the Son also gives life to anyone He wants to."
(John 5:21, HCSB)

RESURRECTIONS IN THE BIBLE

Some scholars distinguish between *resurrection* and *resuscitation* in the Bible. When that distinction is made, the term *resurrection* is used to describe physically rising to eternal life after death. The term *resuscitation* is not intended to suggest that the person was comatose or had not died. Instead, it means that the person merely returned to mortal life. The Bible reports six miraculous resuscitations: two in the Old Testament (1 Kgs 17:8–24; 2 Kgs 4:18–37), two in Jesus' ministry (Mark 5:35–43; John 11:17–44), and two in Acts (Acts 9:36–42; Acts 20:9–12). Each person presumably died again. The only permanent resurrection was Jesus.

FAITH: CAUSE AND EFFECT

Jesus often affirmed that people were blessed through their faith in Him (for example, Luke 7:50, 8:25, 17:19, and 18:42). But John's account of the resurrection of Lazarus puts the emphasis on Jesus' love as the motivation for His decision to raise Lazarus. The resurrection was the event that caused people to put their faith in Him. In that sense, faith was the result of the miraculous resurrection, not its cause.

"Jesus said to her, 'I am the resurrection and the life. The one who believes in Me, even if he dies, will live. Everyone who lives and believes in Me will never die— ever. Do you believe this?'"

(John 11:25–26, HCSB)

ALL GOSPELS

THE TRIALS OF JESUS
(Matthew 26:47–27:26; Mark 14:43–15:15; Luke 22:47–23:25; John 18:2–19:16)

Each of the four Gospels provides an account of the final days of Jesus, noting different details. Some of these differences have been the basis for claims that the authors disagree. This unified summary suggests that the accounts can be understood as complementary rather than contradictory.

Jesus Is Arrested

After celebrating the Passover meal, Jesus and His disciples went to the Garden of Gethsemane on the Mount of Olives, where Jesus agonized in prayer over His impending death. Just after midnight, Judas brought a large crowd to arrest Jesus. Judas met Jesus with a traditional greeting kiss, the signal identifying Jesus for the guards, who took Him into custody.

Jewish Trials of Jesus

Jesus was taken first to Annas, a former High Priest, to be interrogated. As the religious leaders gathered at High Priest Caiaphas' house, Jesus was hauled in to hear contradicting testimony from several false witnesses. Finally, the High Priest demanded to know if Jesus was the Messiah. Jesus calmly affirmed that He was the divine Son of Man. The High Priest reared back, tore his robes, and cried that Jesus had blasphemed.

During the trial, Peter snuck into the High Priest's courtyard. But when the servants questioned him, he denied knowing Jesus three times, as Jesus had predicted. The rooster crowed, and Jesus looked at Peter, who fled weeping. Judas responded to the verdict by throwing the money he had been paid on the floor, denouncing his own betrayal of an innocent man. Later he hanged himself.

Roman Trials of Jesus

Though the religious leaders wanted Jesus executed, they feared inciting a riot. So they brought Jesus to Pilate, the Roman governor, where they accused Him of committing treason by setting Himself up as a king. This strategy unintentionally implied that treason against Caesar was a higher crime then blaspheming the God of Israel. Pilate was amazed by Jesus' calm authority, but when Jesus said that He was not an earthly king, Pilate decided He was no threat.

Still, the religious leaders demanded that Jesus be executed. Realizing that Jesus was a Galilean, Pilate passed Jesus off to Herod Antipas, the ruler of Galilee. Herod had heard of Jesus and wanted to see some miracles. Jesus maintained His dignified silence, refusing to perform for the king. So Herod's soldiers mocked Him, beat Him, and sent Him back to Pilate.

Growing more concerned, Pilate proposed to have Jesus flogged and released, but the religious leaders pressed for execution. Pilate spoke to the gathered people and offered to release Jesus as part of a Passover tradition which freed a condemned criminal. But the religious leaders provoked the crowd to demand the release of the robber Barabbas instead. Meanwhile, Pilate's wife frantically warned him that a dream had shown her that Jesus was a righteous man who should not be harmed. Though Romans considered dreams divine messages, Pilate brushed her off.

Instead, Pilate ordered a severe flogging for Jesus, but it wasn't enough. Pilate told the religious leaders to execute Jesus themselves. When they spat back that Jesus was guilty of blasphemy, Pilate realized that they were determined that Jesus be executed, and just as determined to see the Romans do it. The religious leaders implied that Pilate would be denounced as a traitor to Caesar if he did not execute Jesus.

Frustrated, Pilate asked if they wanted him to execute their king. The ironic response was, "We have no king but Caesar," contradicting the traditional Jewish claim that God is the true King of Israel (Judg 8:23; 1 Sam 8:7). When Pilate finally granted the execution order, he washed his hands before the crowd, symbolizing refusal to take responsibility for Jesus' death.

AUTHORITY TO EXECUTE

Most interpreters take the statement, "it is not legal for us to put anyone to death" (John 18:31) to mean that the Jews did not have authority to execute anyone at all. Yet the Sanhedrin executed other Jews in this period (notably, Stephen in Acts 7:54–60; see also John 8:1–11). Also, a Temple inscription from this period threatening execution for any Gentile that entered was found in 1871 (see also Josephus, War 5:2). Since the charge before Pilate was treason, however, this statement may have been a more narrow assertion that treason against Caesar was under Roman jurisdiction, not the Law of Moses.

By mid-Friday morning, Pilate sentenced Jesus to be crucified. Before He was led away, the Roman soldiers again mocked His claim to be the Messiah, the King of the Jews. They dressed Him in a red robe and put a crown of thorns on His head. Though Jesus had been cruelly flogged, He was now forced to carry His cross. At some point along the way, Jesus grew too weak to carry it farther and stumbled under its weight. The Roman soldiers picked Simon of Cyrene out of the crowd to carry the cross to the execution site. Women in the crowd mourned for Jesus, but He mourned for them and told them that judgment was coming on Jerusalem.

Jesus on the Cross

The crucifixion site outside the city walls was called *Golgotha,* meaning "Place of the Skull." It is not clear how the location got its name. The soldiers gave Jesus wine mixed with gall and myrrh as a mild sedative, likely to make attaching Him to the cross easier. This was done with three nails; two through the wrist or hands and one through the heels or feet.

Jesus' enemies suggested that He prove that He was the Son of God by coming down from the cross. Instead, Jesus prayed that God the Father would forgive them. Others were there to mourn. Jesus' mother Mary was present, along with one of the disciples (likely John). Jesus asked that disciple to care for His mother.

Two robbers were crucified along with Jesus. They also mocked Him, but one repented. He observed that they deserved their punishment, but Jesus was an innocent man. He expressed his faith in Jesus by asking that he be remembered when Jesus began to rule in God's kingdom. Jesus promised that the man would join Him in paradise that day.

After erecting the crosses, the soldiers attached a plaque naming the crime of the accused. In Jesus' case, Pilate wrote "This is Jesus of Nazareth, the King of the Jews." The religious leaders demanded that the plaque say only that Jesus claimed that title. Pilate dismissed them out of hand. While this went on, the soldiers gathered at the foot of the cross to gamble for Jesus' clothes.

"Why Have You Forsaken Me?"

Jesus hung on the cross for about six hours. Around noon the sun went dark, signifying the sin, sorrow, and judgment of the day. As the afternoon wore on, Jesus cried out "My God, My God, why have You forsaken Me?" Though some have suggested that Jesus had expected God to rescue Him and was in despair, Jesus' repeated statements about His intention to die in Jerusalem make this unlikely.

Instead, His cry indicates the deep spiritual suffering that came with the physical pain. The Aramaic phrase began with the word *Eli,* meaning "my God." But some thought He was calling on Elijah (Eliyahu). Jesus rasped that He was thirsty, so a sponge with sour wine

was lifted to His lips. Then Jesus spoke His final words, saying, "It is finished" and committing His spirit to God the Father. The earth trembled and the Roman centurion overseeing the crucifixion declared Jesus innocent, observing, "Truly, this was the Son of God." Others left beating their chests as a sign of mourning and repentance.

Aftermath

Not realizing that Jesus had died, the religious leaders asked Pilate to order the criminal's legs broken. This would ensure a quick death and allow burial before the day ended. Leaving the condemned men on their crosses would have defiled the land for the Passover feast.

Pilate allowed it, but when the soldiers found Jesus already dead they chose to pierce His side with a spear in order to confirm His death.

Joseph of Arimathea, a member of the Sanhedrin who was a secret disciple of Jesus, asked Pilate for Jesus' body. Mary Magdalene and several other women hastily prepared the body for burial by wrapping it in linens packing with spices intended to speed decomposition of the body. They placed the body in a chamber carved into rock and covered it with a stone. When the body had decomposed, the bones would be placed in a "bone box" so that the tomb could be used again.

DEATH BY CRUCIFIXION

Crucifixion was a gruesome form of torture. Hanging by outstretched arms put pressure on the breathing muscle, making breathing difficult. Victims pushed up from the feet to ease the pressure but could not stay up long. Eventually victims died from blood loss or suffocation. Christian interpreters often note that the physical torture Jesus suffered could not compare with the mental and spiritual anguish of bearing the sins of the world.

THE RESURRECTION OF JESUS
(Matthew 27:62–28:15; Mark 16:1–8; Luke 24:1–49; John 20:1–21:23)

After Jesus' body was sealed in the tomb, no one believed that He would rise from the dead after three days as He had prophesied. However, the religious leaders did think Jesus' disciples might steal His body and claim He had risen. They asked Pilate to place a guard on Jesus' tomb for a few days. Pilate gave them a detachment of Roman soldiers to ensure the tomb remained undisturbed.

The Tomb Is Opened

Saturday passed uneventfully. But just before dawn on Sunday, the earth quaked as an angel rolled back the stone from the mouth of the tomb. The stunned soldiers fell to the ground and fled. Later they accepted bribes to say that the disciples had stolen the body while the soldiers slept. The religious leaders assured them that they would protect the soldiers if Pilate disciplined them for sleeping on duty.

As dawn broke, Mary Magdalene and several other women went to the tomb to complete the burial rituals. When they saw the stone rolled away, Mary Magdalene rushed to tell Peter and John that Jesus' body had been stolen. The other women went on into the tomb and saw two angels, one of whom said that Jesus had risen. The women were to tell the disciples that Jesus would meet them in Galilee. As they fled in speechless joy and fear, Jesus appeared to them. He repeated the angel's message as they worshipped Him and touched His feet.

After hearing the report from the women, Peter and John raced to the tomb. The two found the grave cloths folded, but no body. They apparently believed the report that the body had been stolen, not the report that Jesus had risen, and went back to their homes.

Meanwhile, Mary Magdalene returned to the tomb in tears. There she encountered the two angels, who asked her why she wept. She told them her Lord's body had been stolen and she didn't know where it was. As she turned away, she saw a man who she took to be the gardener and asked if He knew where the body had been taken. He simply spoke her name and His voice cut through her grief. Jesus told her to let Him go and tell the disciples that He would ascend to the Father.

Jesus Appears to the Disciples

Later that day, two disciples were travelling on the road to Emmaus, a town seven miles northwest of Jerusalem. A man they did not recognize joined them, and they were amazed when He didn't seem to know what had happened. They told Him they had followed a great prophet who they hoped would be the Messiah. He had been crucified, and they didn't believe the resurrection reports. Jesus told them they were foolish for not believing the prophets and explained what the Scriptures said about the Messiah's life, death, and resurrection. When He broke bread and gave thanks that afternoon, they finally recognized Him. They raced back to Jerusalem to report what they had seen to the other disciples.

That night, 10 of the remaining 11 disciples gathered in the room where they had eaten the Passover meal with Jesus. As they discussed the day's events, Jesus appeared to them. They thought they were seeing a ghost, but Jesus let them examine the scars from the nails in His hands and feet, and the spear wound in His side. Finally, He ate some fish to prove that He was not a ghost.

Jesus told the disciples that He was sending them to preach His gospel to the world (*apostle* means "sent one"), breathed on them to symbolize the Holy Spirit who would come, and left. Finally, the disciples (now apostles) believed. Only Thomas, who was not there, continued to doubt. One week later Jesus appeared to them again, with Thomas present. When Thomas saw Jesus, he declared the Risen Savior to be "My Lord and my God!" Jesus met with the disciples several more times in Galilee over the next 40 days before ascending to the Father, as He promised.

HARMONY OF THE RESURRECTION ACCOUNTS

The four Gospels have differences in how they report the resurrection. Some think these accounts are contradictory; others argue they reflect only different literary emphases. Some questions about the order of events cannot be conclusively answered from the Gospel accounts. The summary presented here represents one possible harmonization of the Gospel narratives and does not include Mark 16:9–20, which does not appear in the earliest and best manuscripts of that Gospel.

"'Why are you looking for the living among the dead?' asked the men. 'He is not here, but He has been resurrected!'"
(Luke 24:5–6, HCSB)

ACTS

INTRODUCTION

The book of Acts tells of Jesus' followers as they carry out His command to spread the gospel of salvation by faith in Christ throughout the world. It emphasizes the power of the gospel to overcome the divisions among peoples, especially Jews and Gentiles (non-Jews), as well as God's intention to save and use unexpected people.

LOCATION: Acts describes events in Jerusalem, Judea, Samaria (north-central Israel), and Paul's missionary journeys through the eastern half of the Roman Empire.

KEY PASSAGES

The Spirit Empowers Gospel Proclamation (1:1–2:47)

Christians Bear Witness in Jerusalem (3:1–5:42)

5:1–11   Ananias and Sapphira Lie to the Holy Spirit

Witnesses in Judea and Samaria (6:1–8:40)

6:8–8:4   Stephen Becomes the First Martyr

The Conversion of Saul/Paul (9:1–31)

Peter Preaches to the Gentiles (9:32–12:24)

10:1-48   Cornelius Becomes the First Gentile Convert

12:1-19   Peter Is Rescued from Prison

Headed to the Ends of the Earth (12:25–28:28)

13:1–14:28   Paul's First Missionary Journey

15:1–35   The Jerusalem Council Welcomes Gentiles

16:1–21:16   Paul's Second and Third Missionary Journeys

21:17–28:28 Paul's Arrest and Journey to Rome

ORIGIN: Acts was written by the same author as the Gospel of Luke (Acts 1:1-2, Luke 1:1–3). Though the author is not named, internal evidence allows the reasonable inference that the author was Luke, a companion of the Apostle Paul. Written after the Gospel of Luke, Acts was probably produced between 65–90 C.E.

PRINCIPAL FIGURES

God   God stands behind the narrative of Acts as the Sovereign Lord of history, accomplishing His plans to bless all nations through the seed of Abraham.

Jesus Christ   The promised Messiah of the nation of Israel, who commissioned His people to carry the gospel to the world.

Holy Spirit   The divine Spirit sent by Christ to unify His people and empower their proclamation of the gospel.

Stephen   A Greek-speaking Jewish Christian who became the first Christian martyr (someone executed for being a Christian).

Peter   The spokesman of the apostles, who preached the first Christian sermon in Jerusalem and brought the gospel to the Gentiles (non-Jews) by preaching to the Roman centurion Cornelius.

James   The leader of the church in Jerusalem, who oversaw the Jerusalem Council.

Saul/Paul   A Pharisee who led the persecution of Christians, but was converted when Christ appeared to him and commissioned him as an apostle to the Gentiles.

THE ACENSION AND PENTECOST
(Acts 1–2)

Jesus' last conversation with His disciples occurred on the Mount of Olives. He instructed them to remain in Jerusalem until the Holy Spirit empowered them to testify about Jesus throughout the world. As He spoke, Jesus rose into heaven and angels appeared, saying that Jesus would eventually return in the same way.

The disciples continued to meet together until Pentecost, the spring harvest celebration. On that day, a sound like a hurricane filled the house where they met and tongues of fire, symbolizing the Spirit, rested on each of them. The disciples emerged and began to speak to the gathering crowd about Jesus. The crowd was amazed to hear the disciples speaking the native languages of all Jerusalem's visitors. Some, however, thought the disciples were drunk.

Peter reminded the crowd that it was only nine in the morning; no one was drunk yet. This was what the prophet Joel had predicted. God had poured out His Spirit on His people, signifying that those who called on the Lord would be saved (Joel 2:21).

Jesus is that Lord. They had seen Jesus do miracles, and Peter told them that even the crucifixion had been according to God's plan, confirmed by the resurrection. David had said that God would not "leave me in Hades, or allow Your Holy One to see decay" (Ps 16:10). But anyone could visit David's grave, so he could not have been speaking of himself. Instead, he spoke of the Messiah, who God said would sit at His right hand until all His enemies were defeated (Ps 110:1).

The people were convicted by Peter's message and begged to know what they should do. Peter called them to repent and be baptized as followers of Jesus. Then they too would receive the Holy Spirit as a sign that God's promise was being fulfilled in them.

THE ROLE OF LANGUAGES IN THE BIBLE

God's judgment of humanity at Babel resulted in different languages and thus prevents humanity from cooperating in sin as easily as it could if there were only one language. In light of Isaiah 33:17–19, the crossing of the language barrier at Pentecost suggests that the judgment of Babel is being withdrawn in Christ.

ACTS

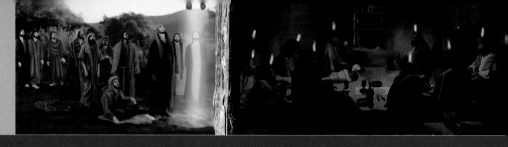

Saul was a Pharisee, zealous for Israel's Covenant faithfulness. He saw the Christian movement as a threat to that purity and tried to eliminate it. After Stephen was stoned for being a Christian (Acts 7:54–60), Saul led a sweeping inquisition. He even secured letters from the High Priest allowing him to arrest Christians in the synagogues of Damascus for trial in Jerusalem.

As Saul and his companions neared Damascus, they were ambushed. Saul was blinded by the light of a heavenly figure and heard His voice. The figure asked Saul, "Why are you persecuting Me?" Saul begged to know who was speaking, and the figure identified Himself as Jesus. He ordered Saul to go into Damascus and wait for instructions.

In Damascus, Jesus appeared to a disciple named Ananias and commanded him to go to Saul and restore his sight. Ananias objected that this was a suicide mission, since Saul had come to arrest Christians. But Jesus insisted, because He planned to use Saul to carry the gospel to the nations and their leaders. Ananias obeyed, and Saul's sight was restored. As his obedience to Jesus' commission took him across the Roman Empire, Saul would use the Roman name by which he became famous: Paul.

PAUL'S UNDERSTANDING OF HIS CALLING

Paul was a Pharisee, but that "righteousness" counted against him (Phil 3:4–7). Despite all he knew, he still willfully disbelieved and blasphemed Christ (1 Tim 1:12–13). But Paul wrote that this was why Christ called him. If He could save Paul, Paul thought Jesus could save anybody (1 Tim 1:14–17).

"He commanded us to preach to the people and to solemnly testify that He is the One appointed by God to be the Judge of the living and the dead. All the prophets testify about Him that through His name everyone who believes in Him will receive forgiveness of sins."

(Acts 10:42–43, HCSB)

Cornelius was a God-fearer. He prayed and cared for the poor. But he was also a Roman centurion—a Gentile (non-Jew). He could not share the Mosaic Covenant without being circumcised, an operation few adult men chose to undergo. But God loved Cornelius anyway, so an angel told him to send some of his servants to ask the Apostle Peter to visit him.

As Peter prayed, he too saw a vision. A sheet came down from heaven with every animal on Earth in it. A voice told Peter to kill and eat. But Peter objected to eating the unclean animals. The voice responded that Peter must not reject what God had made acceptable. When the messengers arrived, God's Spirit commanded Peter to go with them. At Cornelius' house, Peter explained that though faithful Jews could not have fellowship with Gentiles, God had shown him that the gospel was for all nations. Peter acknowledged that God didn't show favoritism but accepts anyone who turns to Christ.

While Peter preached the gospel, the Spirit poured Himself out on the Gentiles who were listening. What followed was a repeat performance of Pentecost (Acts 2). In light of this evidence, Peter baptized the Gentile believers, signifying that they were part of Christ's church (no surgery required).

DIETARY LAWS AND THE GOSPEL

The Mosaic Covenant's dietary laws (for example, Lev 20:24–26) effectively prevented Jews from eating in the homes of Gentiles. These laws clearly distinguished God's people from the pagan nations, but they became a barrier to demonstrating the equality of humanity under the gospel and the fellowship shared by everyone who is a follower of Jesus. Peter's vision recalls an earlier aspect of Jesus' teaching and ministry. Jesus had taught that it was not the food one ate that defiled a person, rather it was what came out of their heart in their speech and actions that made one unclean (Mark 7:14–23). This statement immediately preceded His ministry to a Gentile woman (Mark 7:24–30), demonstrating that His gospel is for everyone.

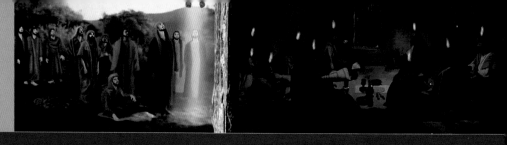

ACTS

In the wake of Cornelius' conversion (Acts 10) and the spread of the gospel outside of Israel (Acts 11–14), some began to argue that Gentiles (non-Jews) had to submit to the Mosaic Covenant in order to be accepted as God's people (15:1, 5). Paul and Barnabas argued against these teachers in Antioch, but it became clear that a consensus needed to be reached in Jerusalem.

Who Are God's People?

When Paul and others went to Jerusalem, the apostles and elders gathered to discuss the issue. After much debate, Peter clarified the question by reminding the group of his experience with Cornelius. God had already decided the issue by sending Peter to preach the gospel to the Gentiles and then affirming their faith by granting them the Holy Spirit (15:7–9). Since God had decided that the Gentiles would be admitted without converting to Judaism, to decide otherwise would be to test God. In fact, Peter reminded them, Israel's historic inability to keep the Law demonstrated that Jews were saved by God's grace rather than by Law-keeping, just as Gentiles were.

After Barnabas and Paul described what they had seen God do on their missionary journey, Jesus' brother James summarized the matter. He stated that the reports of Peter and the rest were clear fulfillment of God's plan, prophesied in Amos 9:11–12 and Isaiah 45:12. Unless the council was to insist on testing God by rejecting what He was already doing, the only

question before the group was a practical question: how could Gentile converts and observant Jewish Christians demonstrate that they were the one people of God together?

A Plan for Fellowship

The primary point of fellowship for Jewish culture was hospitality and shared meals. To eat with someone was to show acceptance and approval of them. James reminded the council that a basis for Jew-Gentile fellowship already existed in the Law's requirements for foreigners living in Israel (Lev 17–18). These foreigners did not have to convert to Judaism but were asked to abstain from behavior that would defile the Jews they lived with.

JEWISH CHRISTIANS

Today, Judaism is a religion quite distinct from Christianity, but the earliest Christians did not see themselves as followers of a new religion that was distinct from that of the nation of Israel. They saw themselves as embracing the fulfillment of what the Law and the Prophets taught. As a result, the relevant question when Cornelius became a believer in Jesus was not "Are we still Jewish?," but "Must Cornelius and other Gentiles become Jewish in order to become Christians?"

On that basis, James suggested that Gentile Christians abstain from eating the meat of the animals that had been sacrificed to idols, consuming blood (directly or in meat), and sexually impure behavior. This basis for fellowship was already familiar to the God-fearers and clearly indicated respect for Jewish Christians who continued to observe the Law, but not conversion to Judaism as such.

THE ROLE OF THE LAW OF MOSES

Paul saw the Law as a tutor pointing to Christ by highlighting human sinfulness and Christ's righteousness, but he rejected attempts to use the Law to earn salvation (Gal 2:16). While accepting Paul's teaching, Christians today differ on how the Law relates to following Jesus. Many see the Law of Moses as revealing the character of God but not as a set of rituals to be followed. Some argue that it can be a direct basis for public policy, while most see its contemporary relevance in indicating broader values and principles that should be found in any just society.

"He made no distinction between us and them, cleansing their hearts by faith. Now then, why are you testing God by putting a yoke on the disciples' necks that neither our ancestors nor we have been able to bear? On the contrary, we believe we are saved through the grace of the Lord Jesus in the same way they are."
(Acts 15:9–11, HCSB)

ACTS

On his second missionary journey, Paul took Silas and Timothy as assistants. They traveled through western Turkey and intended to continue along the Black Sea. However, Paul had a vision in which a man from Macedonia, on the other side of the Aegean Sea, asked Paul to come there.

Philippi

After crossing to Europe, Paul and Silas went to Philippi, a city of Roman citizens, that was the local capital. Since there was no synagogue there, they went to the unofficial Jewish meeting place. A merchant named Lydia believed their message of the Messiah and sheltered them. While there, they encountered a slave who had been possessed by demons. Paul healed the slave, angering her owners. Though the real source of their anger was the loss of income from their slave's fortune-telling, they accused Paul of treason (teaching that Jesus was king, not Caesar).

The magistrates had Paul and Silas beaten and imprisoned. That night there was an earthquake, which damaged the jail cells, making it possible for the prisoners to escape. The jailor, assuming that the prisoners had escaped and fearing severe punishment, was ready to attempt suicide. But Paul intervened, telling him that miraculously all the prisoners were still there. The man believed the gospel and tended Paul's wounds.

Thessalonica and Berea

In the city of Thessalonica, Paul preached in the synagogue for three weeks. Some Jews and a number of Gentiles (non-Jews) believed. But others rejected and rioted. They brought Paul and Silas to the magistrates, accusing them of replacing Caesar with Jesus. Here, however, the magistrates released the missionaries. When Paul and Silas went on to Berea, the Jews there examined the Scriptures to confirm their teaching.

Paul travelled from city to city, spreading the gospel.

Athens

Paul went on to Athens and was troubled by the idols he saw. He spoke in the marketplace and was invited to speak on the Areopagus, a gathering place to hear visiting speakers. Paul talked about the altar "To An Unknown God" and announced that he would introduce his listeners to that God. He described the majesty of God and even quoted some Greek poets, but when he got to the resurrection of Christ many refused to listen further. Some, however, believed his message.

Corinth

The last stop in Europe was the city of Corinth. Again, Paul went first to the synagogue. Eventually, however, he gave up on the Jews there because they repeatedly and violently rejected his teaching and focused on the Gentiles. God encouraged Paul with a vision, and he stayed in Corinth for 18 months. When the synagogue leaders finally complained to the magistrate, they charged Paul with Jewish heresy. However, the magistrate wasn't interested in Jewish theological disputes and dismissed the case.

Paul's missionary travels in Europe continued (Acts 20:1–5) and the churches he founded in these cities endured. Five of his letters were written to the churches in Corinth (1 & 2 Corinthians), Thessalonica (1 & 2 Thessalonians), and Philippi (Philippians). Each became part of the New Testament.

PAUL'S MISSIONARY STRATEGY

Paul usually went first to city synagogues. His preference paralleled Biblical history (Rom 1:16; Gen 12:3). Also, the people in synagogues were familiar with the Old Testament, so they had the best background for understanding and receiving his message. Additionally, cities were strategic points where Paul could efficiently communicate ideas that could then be disseminated to surrounding areas (Acts 19:9–10).

"The people here [Berea] were more open-minded than those in Thessalonica, since they welcomed the message with eagerness and examined the Scriptures daily to see if these things were so."
(Acts 17:11, HCSB)

ACTS

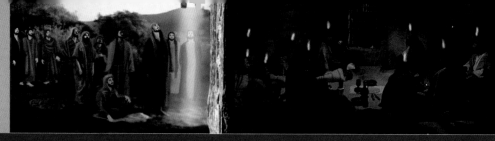

PAUL'S JOURNEY TO ROME
(Acts 21–28)

God had told Ananias that He would use Paul to take the gospel to "Gentiles, kings, and Israelites" (Acts 9:15). Paul did eventually preach before kings and Caesar, but in an unexpected way. Paul was traveling to Jerusalem when a prophet named Agabus met him. Agabus told Paul that he would be arrested and given into the power of the Romans.

Paul's Arrest

When Paul reached Jerusalem, he entered the Temple (Acts 21). A riot broke out over rumors that Paul had defiled the Temple by bringing a Gentile into the area reserved for Jews. The Roman soldiers had to step in. The soldiers intervened again at Paul's public defense and once more during the examination by the Sanhedrin, the ruling council of Jewish religious leaders. As a result, the Roman commander decided to transport Paul to Caesarea where the Roman Governor Felix had his residence and could deal with the matter (Acts 22–23).

The High Priests' representative acted as Paul's accuser in the trial before the Governor. He accused Paul of being a religious agitator who had defiled the Temple. He claimed that Paul was being dealt with according to the Law, but that the Roman commander had prevented it. Paul answered that he had not caused any disturbance, but that he was a Christian and had been bringing an offering to the Temple when others had sparked a riot. His summation was that he was really

on trial for believing in the resurrection of the dead, meaning the resurrection of Jesus in particular. The Governor was familiar with Christianity but held Paul for two years hoping that Paul's friends would give Paul money to bribe the governor for release. Ultimately, Felix left Paul in prison as a political favor to the religious leaders (Acts 24). Paul's patience had outlasted the Governor's tenure in office.

Paul Appeals for a Trial

The new Governor, Festus, soon called for Paul. Festus asked Paul to accept trial in Jerusalem. The religious leaders had requested this in hopes of ambushing Paul along the way and killing him. Paul refused to be handed over to them and appealed to Caesar Nero for trial. Festus had to grant the request, but before Paul left for the trial, he and King Agrippa allowed Paul to entertain them with his story (Acts 25–26).

Paul traveled to Rome by ship, though it was not an easy journey. Despite Paul's warning of a coming storm while in port on Crete, the captain sailed anyway. The ship eventually wrecked on Malta, though miraculously, no lives were lost. Ultimately, Paul reached Rome for his trial in front of Caesar.

Though the sequence of events is not related in Acts, tradition holds that Paul was eventually released for a time. Some believe that he reached Spain before returning to Rome where he was rearrested and beheaded by Nero's order sometime before 68 C.E.

THE RIGHT OF APPEAL TO CAESAR

Caesar Augustus secured imperial power by collecting Roman offices. One was Tribune, an office that allowed him to veto any magistrate's decision. But Tribunes also heard appeals by Roman citizens who claimed unfair trial. Though Caligula abolished the right, Seneca convinced Nero to reinstate it about the same time Paul was arrested (58 C.E.).

"But Paul said: 'I am standing at Caesar's tribunal, where I ought to be tried. I have done no wrong to the Jews, as even you can see very well. If then I am doing wrong, or have done anything deserving of death, I do not refuse to die, but if there is nothing to what these men accuse me of, no one can give me up to them. I appeal to Caesar!'"

(Acts 25:10–11, HCSB)

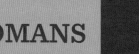

ROMANS

INTRODUCTION

The book of Romans is a letter written by the Apostle Paul to Christians in the city of Rome. It is a deep reflection on the gospel of salvation from sin through faith in Jesus Christ. Paul develops the argument that the gospel is God's plan for salvation for all people and addresses the implications of that claim for understanding the history of the nation of Israel and living the Christian life.

KEY PASSAGES

The Gospel of God's Righteousness (1:1–17)

God's Righteous Wrath Against Sinners (1:18–3:20)

1:18–2:11	God Has Been Patient with Sinners
3:1–20	God's Wrath Is Justified

God's Righteousness in Salvation (3:21–8:29)

3:21–31	God Saves Those Who Trust Christ
4:1–24	Abraham Is the Example of Salvation Through Faith
6:1–23	Salvation Releases People from Slavery to Sin
8:1–39	There Is No Condemnation for Those in Christ

God's Righteousness to Jews and Gentiles (9:1–11:36)

10:1–17	Righteousness Comes Through Faith in Christ

Living Out God's Righteousness (12:1–16:27)

12:9–13:10	Love Drives the Righteous Christian Life

PRINCIPAL FIGURES

God   Romans presents God as a holy and just God who judges sinners and as the justifier who shows mercy to all who trust Christ.

Jesus Christ   The son of David and Son of God who pours out God's love and rescues those who trust Him from sin's power and consequences.

Paul   Author of Romans, who hated the presence of sin in his own life and wanted Jews and Gentiles to share the salvation he experienced.

The Romans   The recipients of Paul's letter were Christians living in the city of Rome, not all Roman citizens, nor even all the people living in the city of Rome.

Abraham   Father of the nation of Israel, used by Paul as an example of salvation through faith prior to the **Law of Moses**.

Adam   The first human and cause of sinfulness in humanity. In Romans, Adam's fall and its effects are compared with Christ's sacrifice and its effects.

LOCATION: The city of Rome in central Italy was the capital of the Roman Empire and residence of the Roman Emperor. Gaining favor of the church there was the key point in winning government toleration of Christianity.

ORIGIN: Paul wrote Romans in order to introduce himself and his teaching to the church in the city of Rome. Paul had not visited the city before and planned to make the city his base for preaching in Spain. The letter was likely written from the Greek city of Corinth in late 55–56 C.E.

UNRIGHTEOUS, DECLARED RIGHTEOUS
(Romans 3:9–31)

Paul spends the first few chapters of his letter arguing that all humanity is sinful and stands under God's judgment. Sin affects every individual; everyone is unrighteous (3:10–18). This is the obvious conclusion when people are held up against the moral standard of the Law of Moses. No one will vindicate their life in God's eyes by appealing to the Law; that is not its purpose (3:19–20).

Paul's argument is neither arrogant nor vicious. He describes himself as a sinner (5:8, see also 1 Tim 1:15), and emphasizes the problem of sin in order to make sense of God's solution. While the Law can't save, it and the Old Testament prophets point to the righteousness God would provide through faith in Christ (3:21–22). Everyone is a sinner and under the judgment of God, but salvation is available to every sinner through faith in Christ (3:23–34). Through Christ, God remains holy and just in His judgment on sinners, and yet also declares righteous every person who has faith in Christ (3:25–26).

Adam and Eve refused to trust God and instead embraced blasphemous pride (Gen 3). God calls people to admit their sinfulness (humility) and depend through faith on Christ's work on their behalf (trust). This eliminates prideful boasting about human righteousness, whether by Jews or Gentiles (3:27–30). Rather than reject the Law, Paul wrote that this upholds the central teaching and purpose of the Law (3:31).

THE SYMBOLIC SIGNIFICANCE OF THE CROSS

The cross of Christ is the center of Christian theology, as witnessed by its near-universal presence in Christian art and architecture. It points to the historical event of Christ's crucifixion. It also demonstrates the severity of sin and judgment while at the same time displaying Christ as the substitute who bears that punishment for sinners. The cross expresses the depth of God's love by setting it in the context of God's holy wrath.

1 & 2
CORINTHIANS

Paul's letters to the Corinthian Christians address a church he founded and led for several years. After his departure, however, the church suffered internal strife and the influence of false teachers. The Corinthian letters defended Paul's authority as an apostle and addressed the major problems facing the church.

LOCATION: Corinth was a major Greek city and center of commerce on the isthmus connecting central Greece to the Peloponnese (southern Greece).

ORIGIN: Paul most likely wrote his Corinthian correspondence between 54 C.E. and early 55 C.E. while in the city of Ephesus. Some scholars have argued that the two letters were originally three separate letters. All existing copies of the Corinthian correspondence, however, demonstrate the two-letter arrangement reflected in modern Bibles.

KEY PASSAGES

1 Corinthians

Church Factions (1–4)

1:18–2:5	God's Methods Seem Foolish
3:1–17	God Gets the Credit for His Servant's Work

Sex, Lawsuits, and Marriage (5–7)

Worship Wars (8–14)

12:12–31	The Church Is a Body Whose Parts Serve Each Other
13:1–13	Love Transforms Selfishness into Service
14:1–40	Use Gifts to Serve Others

The Resurrection (15)

Collection for the Poor in Jerusalem (16)

2 Corinthians

The Integrity of Paul's Ministry (1–7)

1:3–7	Suffering Serves Others
3:7–4:18	The Gospel Ministry Is Superior to Moses' Ministry

Collection for the Poor in Jerusalem (8–9)

Response to the Super-Apostles (10–13)

12:1–10	God's Strength Is Seen in Weakness

PRINCIPAL FIGURES

God Paul emphasizes God's grace in working through weak agents to glorify Himself and comfort His people.

Jesus Christ Jesus is identified in Corinthians as the Suffering Servant and Risen Lord of the Church.

Holy Spirit Also called the Spirit of Christ, God's Spirit is the divine Agent who unifies and empowers the church through the loving use of His gifts in service to others.

Paul Despite Paul's vigorous defense of His authority as an apostle, he presents himself as a slave of the church, whose role depends on God's grace shining through His weaknesses.

Apollos An evangelist in the early church era. Factions within the church at Corinth claimed him, the Apostle Peter, the Apostle Paul, and Jesus as source of their ideas.

The Super-Apostles False teachers who, in 2 Corinthians, claimed to have the authority to judge Paul's teaching and correct his presentation of the gospel.

THE RESURRECTION IS KEY
(1 Corinthians 15)

Paul insisted that the resurrection of Christ from the dead was essential to the truth of the gospel he proclaimed. Christ had died for our sins, as the Scriptures had prophesied, and had risen from the grave three days later. Paul affirmed that over 500 people had seen the risen Jesus, implying that his readers could seek them out to confirm what Paul was saying (15:1–11). By making this claim, the apostle treated the resurrection as an historical event, not a mythological fable.

The resurrection was critical to Paul's preaching because without it, the Good News was simply a lie. Christ's death would be just another Roman execution, not an atoning sacrifice acceptable to God. If faith in Christ did not resolve the eternal consequences of sin, then Christians, who so often suffered for Christ, were

pitiful fools (15:12–19). But if Christ has really risen from the dead, then sin has been conquered (see Gen 3:15). The resurrection proves that Adam's failure has been superseded by Christ's victory for those who trust Him. Christ's victory ensured fulfillment of God's rule over history (15:20–28).

After dealing with some of the Corinthians' foolish thinking about the resurrection (15:29–49), Paul concluded by celebrating God's promise of resurrection for believers. He pointed out that corrupted things could not enter the eternal age and explained how the resurrection makes it possible for mortals to enter God's kingdom. Those who are in Christ will be transformed when He returns. What was once mortal will become immortal. Death and the grave will be stripped of their power over Christians (15:50–58).

UNITY IN NEW TESTAMENT CHURCHES

The most common problem in churches in the New Testament era was lack of unity. False teachers, ethnic nationalism, and outright sin in congregations caused many problems. Since the goal was the unity of genuinely different people (1 Cor 12), differences not caused by sin had to be embraced. The apostle's answer focused on the common ground shared in the gospel (Eph 4) and submission to the Lordship of Christ, expressed in love (1 Cor 13–14).

In Paul's letter to the Galatians, he aggressively defends of the gospel of salvation by grace through faith in Christ. Paul argues that Gentiles do not need to submit to the Mosaic Covenant for salvation. He also argues that the Holy Spirit's work on a Christian's character achieves true righteousness, while human efforts to keep moral rules always fail.

LOCATION: Galatia was a Roman province in what is now west-central Turkey.

ORIGIN: Scholars debate whether Paul wrote Galatians early (49–50 C.E.) or later (53–58 C.E.). The earlier date would make this one of Paul's first letters and place it before the Jerusalem Council (Acts 15).

KEY PASSAGES

There Is Only One Gospel (1:1–2:21)

2:11–14	Paul Rebukes Peter
2:15–21	Union with Christ Through Faith Applies Salvation

God Justifies by Faith, Not the Mosaic Law (3:1–4:31)

3:1–5	Salvation Comes by Hearing with Faith
3:6–9	Abraham Was Saved by Faith
3:10–25	The Law Leads to the Cross, Which Fulfills the Abrahamic Covenant
3:26–4:11, 21–31	The Gospel Makes Sons; Misuse of the Law Makes Slaves

God Sanctifies by the Spirit of Christ, Not the Mosaic Law (5:1–6:18)

5:19–21	People Can't Become Righteous by Keeping Rules
5:22–26	The Spirit Makes People Righteous

PRINCIPAL FIGURES

God God is the Father who sent Christ to redeem those under the Law and adopt them as His children.

Jesus Christ Christ is the fulfillment of the Abrahamic Covenant who sets Christians free from the condemnation of the Mosaic Law.

Holy Spirit The Spirit of Christ dwells in Christians as the promise of their full experience of salvation and the One who empowers the transformation of their character.

Paul In Galatians, Paul is the fierce protector and servant of the Galatian Christians through his defense of the gospel.

Peter The leader of the apostles who is rebuked by Paul for undercutting the gospel of grace by his hypocrisy in Antioch.

Abraham Paul's primary example establishing the fact that God did not intend the Law of Moses to save people **from sin.**

The Judaizers The false teachers who taught that Gentiles must embrace the Mosaic Covenant to be saved and that Christians need to obey the Law of Moses to live a righteous life.

"For through the law I have died to the law, so that I might live for God. I have been crucified with Christ and I no longer live, but Christ lives in me. The life I now live in the body, I live by faith in the Son of God, who loved me and gave Himself for me."

(Galatians 2:19–20, HCSB)

Paul reminded the Galatians that they had not received God's Spirit by keeping the Law of Moses but by hearing with faith (Gal 3:1–5). His primary example that salvation comes through faith was Abraham, who was declared righteous because he believed God. This would be God's pattern for Abraham's descendants and for the nations blessed through Abraham (Gal 3:6–9).

Paul pointed out that the righteousness of the law depended upon perfect obedience. Those who failed that test were cursed. The glory of the gospel was that Christ had borne the curse for everyone. The pattern of divine blessing through faith in Christ rather than through works fulfilled God's promise to Abraham about his seed (Gen 12:7; 17:8). That promise could not be set aside by a later contract, the Mosaic Covenant (Gal 3:10–18).

The priority of God's promise to Abraham and pattern of blessing faith led to the question of why God instituted the Mosaic Covenant. Paul insisted that the Law was not a bad thing, though he condemned its misuse to foster self-righteous pride. Rather, the Law humbled people's pride by highlighting their sinfulness and their inability to conquer their own sin. The Law functioned as a tutor, teaching people to look for the Promised One (Gen 3:15) and to recognize Him when He came (3:19–26).

SARAH AND HAGAR

Paul saw an analogy of salvation in the way God's promise of a son for Abraham was fulfilled (Gal 4:21–31). Abraham tried to seize the promise by sleeping with the slave Hagar, who gave birth to a slave (Ishmael). Only when Abraham and Sarah trusted God was the promised son born (Isaac). Similarly, those who insist on earning righteousness (misusing the Law) find only slavery, while those who trust God receive His promise.

EPHESIANS

INTRODUCTION

Paul's letter to the Ephesians hails the accomplishment of God's eternal purposes in Christ. It refers to the inclusion of the Gentiles (non-Jews) in the Abrahamic Covenant and the reconciliation of Jews and Gentiles in Christ. The letter also describes the impact of the gospel on family life and introduces the image of the "Armor of God" for resisting Satan's temptations.

LOCATION: Ephesus was a Greek city and served as the capital of the Roman province of Asia Minor, in what is now western Turkey.

KEY PASSAGES

God's Eternal Purpose in Christ (1:1–3:21)

2:1–10	Jesus Rescues People from Death to New Life
2:11–22	Jesus Creates a Unified Humanity

Living Out God's Purpose in Christ (4:1–6:24)

4:1–16	Christ Has Blessed His People to Walk Together
5:15–6:4	Christ Has Redeemed Marriage and Family
6:10–20	Christ Has Provided Armor for Resisting Satan's Attacks

ORIGIN: Though the book identifies Paul as the author (1:1) and the earliest Christian writers affirmed that claim, some modern scholars suggest it was written by a later disciple of Paul. The absence of the address "to the Ephesians" in several early manuscripts has led some to conclude that Ephesians was letter that Paul intended to be sent to several different cities. The letter was likely written while Paul was imprisoned in Rome, between 61–62 C.E.

PRINCIPAL FIGURES

God   Ephesians presents God as the Providential Lord of History whose gracious plan is fulfilled in Christ.

Jesus Christ   Jesus is the Unifier who overcomes the barriers between humanity and God, among different races, and within families.

Paul   The author of Ephesians, writing from prison to encourage the church he pastored for several years (Acts 19).

Tychicus   The messenger who took Paul's letter to the Ephesians and informed them of the details of his situation in prison.

"For you are saved by grace through faith, and this is not from yourselves; it is God's gift—not from works, so that no one can boast. For we are His creation, created in Christ Jesus for good works, which God prepared ahead of time so that we should walk in them."

(Ephesians 2:8–10, HCSB)

LIFE IN CHRIST
(Ephesians 2)

Though Paul celebrated the accomplishment of God's plan of salvation in the believers at Ephesus (1:3–14), he made sure to remind them of their spiritual history. Like all of fallen humanity, they were once spiritually dead in sin (2:1), implying that they were as unresponsive to spiritual prodding as a dead body is to being kicked. As dead people, they did what all spiritually dead people do. They rebelled against God, chasing sinful desires or even good desires in sinful ways. They stood under the wrath of God (2:2–3).

But God intervened in human history. Acting out of a wealth of mercy and deep love for humanity, God made believers alive in Christ. This was not due to the attractiveness of spiritually dead, decaying sinners. It was simply a gift of God's grace. But God didn't stop there. He has taken believers and seated them with Christ in heaven, guaranteeing that the glory of His grace would be displayed in them for eternity (2:4–7).

Paul reminded the Ephesians that they were saved by God's unmerited favor (grace), which they received through faith in Christ. Even this faith was not a human creation that earned God's favor; it too was a gift from God. In short, God's way of saving people ensured that they could not boast in their own insight or effort. Instead, they would acknowledge that God had remade them in Christ. Their good deeds were to be seen as the result of God's grace, not its cause (2:8–10).

AUTHORSHIP IN THE NEW TESTAMENT

Some scholars claim that certain New Testament letters are pseudonymous, or written under a false name. They argue that this practice was an understood and accepted way of honoring a teacher, perhaps used when students collected and published the teacher's ideas. On the other hand, some modern scholars have argued that pseudonymous authorship was always malicious. Early Christian pastors used false claims to apostolic authorship (pseudonomy) as grounds for rejecting books as part of the New Testament.

PHILIPPIANS

In his letter to the Philippians, Paul expresses gratitude for the Christians in Philippi. He praises the Christians' growth in righteousness and encourages their continued humility and unity. The apostle also warns them against false teachers who attempt to undercut the effect of the gospel. Finally, Paul thanks the Philippians for supporting him during his imprisonment.

KEY PASSAGES

The Priority of Advancing the Gospel (1:1–20)

1:3–11	The Philippians Helped to Advance the Gospel
1:12–20	Paul's Highest Desire Was That Christ Be Honored

Preservation of the Philippians' Witness (1:21–4:9)

1:21–29	Christians Must Be Excellent Citizens
2:1–18	Christ Is the Model for Humble Service
3:1–21	Only Christ Can Make People Righteous

Paul's Gratitude for the Philippians' Support (4:10–23)

PRINCIPAL FIGURES

God Philippians views God as the ultimate Judge who grants significance to His people's suffering, their deliverance, and the resources to accomplish His goals.

Jesus Christ Jesus is presented as the source of significance and righteousness, whose humility became the model for Christian service to others.

Paul The apostle in chains, Paul expresses gratitude for the Philippians and a desire to preserve their place in the defense of the gospel.

Epaphroditus A Christian from Philippi whose sacrificial service epitomized the Philippians' love for Paul.

False Teachers Philippians identifies several kinds of false teachers. Some preached the gospel in hopes of causing Paul trouble in prison, others promoted legalism, and some claimed that Christians could sin without restraint.

Saints in Caesar's Household Mentioned at the end of the letter, these Christians were evidence that the gospel was making inroads into the Emperor's family and closest servants.

LOCATION: Philippi, in modern Greece, was the ancient capital of Macedon (Alexander the Great's kingdom), later resettled by Romany army veterans as a Roman colony. It was the first place the gospel was preached in Europe (Acts 16:6–40).

ORIGIN: The letter claims Paul as the author (1:1) and supplies personal detail throughout. Modern scholarship is almost unanimous in accepting Paul as the author. Tradition holds that the letter was written while Paul was imprisoned in Rome (61–62 C.E.) awaiting his appeal to Caesar (see Acts 25).

"... work out your own salvation with fear and trembling. For it is God who is working in you, enabling you both to desire and to work out His good purpose."
(Philippians 2:12–13, HCSB)

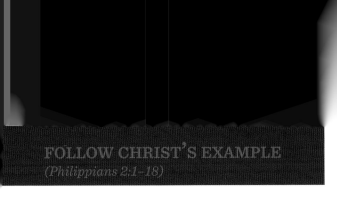

Paul saw Jesus as both the Divine Savior and the perfect example of what a human being should be. As a result, he called on the Philippians to work together to become more and more like Christ. Since Christians share the common ground of knowing Christ and His love and being united to Him by the Spirit of God, the apostle urged his readers to act accordingly. He challenged them to operate with one mind and not be divided by petty rivalry or conceit. The virtue that was most important for maintaining unity would be humility, considering others more important than one's self (2:1–4).

The supreme example of humility is Jesus. He was fully divine from eternity but did not regard His equality with the Father as a reason to reject the Father's will and avoid the role of Savior. Instead, He poured out His life for everyone by taking on human nature and form. From this position, He humbled himself completely by obeying the Father's will that He bear the penalty for sin in humanity's place, even though that meant suffering death on a cross. This greatest and deepest of all service resulted in the highest of all honors. The Father has exalted the name of Jesus so that one day everyone will bow to Christ's authority and confess that He is the Sovereign Lord, to the glory of God the Father (3:5–11).

Paul expected that this pattern of humble obedience would be reproduced in the lives of the Philippian Christians. As Christ had submitted to the Father, they were to obey God with the reverence He is due. But Paul also encouraged them that they would be joining God in the work He was already doing in them. In practical terms, this meant obeying God joyfully rather than grudgingly. Reflecting Christ's character in this way would cause them to stand out against the backdrop of their culture like bright stars in the night sky and would validate Paul's ministry of the gospel (3:12–18).

DEFENDING THE GOSPEL

The confession that "Jesus is Lord" sounded like treason to Rome, for whom "Caesar is Lord." But Jesus taught that the transformed lives of His followers would cause people to join them in glorifying God (Matt 5:16). Peter added that Christ-like lives would put to shame those who slandered believers (1 Pet 2:12). Paul expected the conduct of Christians to adorn the gospel (Titus 2:9–14; Phil 1:27).

COLOSSIANS

In Colossians, Paul addresses Christians in a church he had never visited. His letter exalts Christ as the Lord of creation and the church, and then uses that idea to combat various false teachings threatening the church. Focusing on Christ would enable Christians to reject sin and embrace righteousness in their church, in families, and with non-Christians.

KEY PASSAGES

Thanksgiving and Prayer for the Colossians (1:1–14)

The Supremacy of Christ (1:15–2:23)

1:15–23	Christ Is Lord over Creation and the Church
2:8–23	Christ Is Superior to the False Teachers

Life Under the Lordship of Christ (3:1–4:6)

3:1–4	Focus on Christ as Lord
3:5–11	Submit to Christ by Rejecting Unrighteousness
3:12–17	Submit to Christ by Embracing Righteousness

Greetings from Paul's Companions (4:7–18)

PRINCIPAL FIGURES

God   Colossians describes God as the Father who loves His Son and sent Him as the Messiah.

Jesus Christ   Colossians focuses on the supreme excellence of Christ as the eternal Son of God, Creator and Ruler of the World, Savior and Lord of the church.

Paul   Paul describes himself as the servant of the gospel and so the servant of all Christians through his suffering for Christ.

Epaphras   The founder of the church in Colossae (1:7), who sought Paul's help with the problems there.

False Teachers   The false teaching in Colossae may have been a version of legalistic Judaism originating in the Greek-speaking Jewish community outside of Judea. Whatever its origin, it seems to have aimed at undercutting the supremacy of Christ.

LOCATION: Colossae was a small city in Asia Minor, now southwestern Turkey, near the major road from Ephesus to Mesopotamia.

ORIGIN: Paul wrote to the Colossian Christians in response to a visit from their founding pastor, Epaphrus. The letter was likely written from Rome during Paul's imprisonment (61–62 C.E.) awaiting his appeal to Caesar (Acts 25). Some modern scholars have rejected Paul's authorship of Colossians, suggesting that a later disciple of Paul's wrote the letter.

"Therefore, as you have received Christ Jesus the Lord, walk in Him, rooted and built up in Him and established in the faith, just as you were taught, overflowing with gratitude."

(Colossians 2:6–7, HCSB)

Paul often opened his letters with prayer for his readers, introducing a significant theme for the message he was communicating. In Colossians, he prayed that his readers would know God's will in a practical way so that their behavior would reflect well on their Lord and please Him, resulting in good works and a growing relationship with God. He also asked that they be fortified with God's power to continue living for Christ, joyfully giving thanks to God who had empowered them to become part of His kingdom of God's Son in the first place. The Colossians hadn't always been citizens of Christ's kingdom. They had once been under the tyranny of darkness. But in Christ they had been rescued and forgiven (1:9–14).

Thinking of what Christ had done for the Colossians led Paul to reflect on who this Savior is. The apostle wrote that Christ perfectly reveals the invisible God and is the Ruler of all creation. His place at the head of creation is not because He is the greatest creature, but because He is the Creator of all things and the One in whom creation holds together and makes sense (1:15–17). Christ is also the head of the Church, which is His body. Having risen from the dead as the first who will never die again, He will be acknowledged as first in all things. God the Father has revealed the full measure of the divine glory in the Son by reconciling His creation to Himself through Christ's blood shed on the cross (1:18–20).

Paul urged his readers to see that it was this Glorious Lord who had taken alienated, hostile rebels and reconciled them to God. Not only had He overcome their rebellion, He was also removing sin from their lives. As the Colossians continued to live for Christ, His death would continue to transform them into righteous citizens of God's kingdom. This, Paul insisted, was the Savior he served and the gospel he proclaimed (1:21–23).

HOUSEHOLD CODES

Ancient philosophers wanted households to function in a way that would strengthen society, and they often wrote household codes, or lists of duties. The apostles adapted this tradition, but they describe reciprocal relationships, not just the duties owed to the head of the family. They also give the greater honor to wives, children, and slaves by addressing them first and directly, often comparing them favorably to Christ. The apostles believed the gospel would transform families, and in turn transform society.

1 & 2 THESSALONIANS

In his letters to the Thessalonians, Paul reminded them of his integrity and concern for them, in spite of the fact that his ministry there was brief (Acts 17:1–9). His letters focus on correcting various misconceptions about the return of Christ (Day of the Lord) and encouraging the Thessalonians to help each other to live righteous lives in expectation of that day.

KEY PASSAGES

1 Thessalonians

Paul's Ministry to the Thessalonians (1–3)

1:2–10   The Thessalonians Were Exemplary Christians

Paul's Call to Sanctification (4–5)

4:1–12   God Will Sanctify Christians

4:13–18   Christians Won't Miss Christ's Return

5:1–11   Christians Should Be Ready for Christ's Return

2 Thessalonians

God Will Judge the Unrighteous (1)

The Coming of the Day of the Lord (2)

2:1–4   The Final Judgment Had Not Yet Started

2:5–12   The Man of Lawlessness Will Come First

Living in Light of Christ's Return (3)

PRINCIPAL FIGURES

God   The Righteous Judge of humanity, who has delivered believers from wrath through Christ.

Jesus Christ   The One who will come to rescue believers and destroy the enemies of God.

Paul   The apostle who brought the gospel to Thessalonica and nurtured the new Christians there.

The Man of Lawlessness   Paul's name for "The Beast" of Revelation. This figure will oppose God and blasphemously claim worship as God.

That Which/He Who Restrains   Possibly the Holy Spirit, working through the church and human government, who prevents the rise of the Man of Lawlessness until the proper time.

> *"For God did not appoint us to wrath, but to obtain salvation through our Lord Jesus Christ, who died for us.... Therefore encourage one another...."*
>
> (1 Thessalonians 5:9–11, HCSB)

LOCATION: Thessalonica, modern Salonika (Thessaloniki), was the capital of the Roman province of Macedonia in northeastern Greece on the coast of the Aegean Sea.

ORIGIN: Paul's letters to the Thessalonians were likely some of the earliest New Testament writings (50–51 C.E.) and were probably written from Corinth. Some scholars argue that 2 Thessalonians was written first, and that the order of the two books in the New Testament was determined by length rather than date of writing (1 Thessalonians is longer).

The Christians in Thessalonica were concerned about some of their number who had died. Paul encouraged them by pointing out that since Jesus had risen from the dead, God would also raise Christians from the dead. Both living and dead Christians would hear the shout of the archangel and the trumpet of God when Christ returned. The dead would rise first and the living would join them to meet Christ in the clouds (1 Thess 4:13–18).

As for the day of Christ's coming, Paul did not know when that would be. He reminded them that it would come as an unpleasant surprise for the world. Not expecting Christ to judge them, sinful humanity would think itself secure only to be destroyed. Paul encouraged Christians, however, to live with the future in mind. Instead of acting like creatures of the night, Christians are to be serious and prepared for battle against sin, wearing the armor of faith, love, and hope. They could stand firm in the assurance of God's promise that they would not experience His wrath but would live with Jesus who had died for them (1 Thess 5:1–11).

Unfortunately, the Thessalonians got the idea that they had missed Christ's return. Paul reassured them that they had not. He told them that God's judgment would not begin until there was a climactic rebellion against God, led by the "Man of Lawlessness." This figure would promote himself as the supreme object of worship, standing in God's Temple and claiming to be God (see Dan 9:27). Paul reminded his readers that something held him back for the proper time. The principle of rebellion was already present, but there was Someone who prevented the Lawless Man from being revealed. Once he came, however, he would use Satan's power to deceive the willfully blind world, just as Pharaoh had hardened his heart and in turn been hardened by God. In the end, the Lawless one would be destroyed by the glory of Christ's coming (2 Thess 2:1–12).

THE DAY OF THE LORD

The New Testament develops the Old Testament teaching on the Day of the Lord. It associates the final judgment with the Messiah's role as King. He will come to defend His people and eliminate evil by destroying those who oppress the helpless and by establishing justice. So the New Testament describes Jesus as both gentle to the weak and fierce toward the wicked who refuse to repent.

The books of Timothy consist of two letters Paul wrote to Timothy, the young pastor of the church in Ephesus. The first letter challenges him to rebuke false teachers and help the Christians under his care to honor the leaders in government, church, and family that He had placed over them. The second letter prepares Timothy to lead the church in Ephesus after Paul's impending execution.

KEY PASSAGES

1 Timothy

Correcting Problems in Ephesus (1:1–4:5)

1:3–17	Paul's Life Answers the False Teachers
2:1–7	Christians Should Pray for Their Rulers
3:1–13	Churches Must Have Godly Leaders

Exhortations to Pastor Timothy (4:6–6:21)

4:11–5:2	Pastors Must Lead With Integrity
6:3–1	Greed and False Teaching Go Together

2 Timothy

Paul's Greeting (1:1–5)

Encouragement to Stand Firm in the Gospel (1:6–2:13)

1:8–12	Don't Be Ashamed of the Gospel

Exhortation to Endure Despite Challenges (2:14–4:8)

3:1–9	Difficult Days Will Come
3:10–17	Scripture Gives Wisdom for Salvation

Paul's Appeal for Aid (4:9–22)

PRINCIPAL FIGURES

God   In these letters, God is seen as the Divine Sovereign who has created the world and desires the salvation of all people.

Jesus Christ   Paul identifies Jesus as the Divine Savior who suffered under Pontius Pilate and will return to judge the living and the dead.

Paul   Paul presents himself as an unlikely convert, whose life and ministry demonstrates the grace and power of God. He writes to Timothy as a father to a son.

Timothy   The son of an Israelite mother and Greek father who became a travelling companion of Paul and, as a relatively young man, the pastor of the church in Ephesus.

False Teachers   The letters to Timothy mention several false teachers by name. They seem to have been teachers of a legalistic understanding of the Mosaic Covenant who were motivated by greed.

LOCATION: Ephesus was a Greek city and served as the capital of the Roman province of Asia Minor, in what is now western Turkey.

ORIGIN: Both letters present themselves as personal correspondence from the Apostle Paul to his younger disciple, Timothy. 1 Timothy would have been written in a period of freedom (61–63 C.E.), and 2 Timothy just prior to his execution (64–67 C.E.). Many modern scholars, however, have claimed that the letters were pious forgeries, composed by unknown Christian authors for supposedly noble purposes.

Paul had been trained as a rabbi in the tradition of the Pharisees, so he was very concerned about the use and misuse of the Mosaic Covenant. Paul accused false teachers of totally misunderstanding the Law. The problem was not the Law itself. When used properly, to highlight the need for salvation and to identify the Righteous Savior, it was a great good. But it was not meant for those who were already right with God; rather, it addressed sinners of all kinds to show them their sinfulness. The Law condemned every form of human pride and self-righteousness, all of which runs counter to the gospel of grace through humble faith in Jesus that God had entrusted to Paul (1:3–11).

Paul thanked Christ for calling him, strengthening him, and declaring him faithful. When Jesus had confronted him on the Damascus Road (Acts 9), Paul had not been strong or faithful. At that point, he had been a blasphemer, a persecutor, and a willfully arrogant sinner. Each of these was a greater sin than any he had mentioned earlier, such as murder or sexual immorality (see 1:9–10). However, acting in ignorance and unbelief did not excuse a scholar of the Law (see Rom 1:18).

Paul's point was that his great guilt was the perfect opportunity for God to show the depth of the mercy, love, and grace in Christ. The great lesson Paul had learned, his "trustworthy saying," was that Christ had come precisely to save sinners. By acknowledging himself to be the greatest of sinners, Paul became exactly the kind of person Jesus had come to rescue. So Paul saw his own story as an encouraging example for everyone else. If Jesus could save him, then Jesus could save anybody. That made Jesus worth worshipping (1:12–17).

"This saying is trustworthy and deserving of full acceptance: 'Christ Jesus came into the world to save sinners'—and I am the worst of them."
(1 Timothy 1:15, HCSB)

TITUS

The letter to Titus provides Paul's instructions for organizing healthy churches to his young disciple on the island of Crete. It focuses on Godly leadership, the intergenerational mentoring of younger Christians, and the relationship of the churches to non-Christians. False teachers are a less immediate threat than in the letters to Timothy.

LOCATION: Titus was working with new churches on the island of Crete at the southern end of the Aegean Sea.

ORIGIN: The letter identifies Paul as its author (1:1) and was likely written about the same time as 1 Timothy (about 61–63 C.E.). The two letters share some common themes and similar content. As with the letters to Timothy, many modern scholars have argued that the letter to Titus was a forgery.

KEY PASSAGES

Instructions for Godly Church Leaders (1)

1:5–9	Pastors Must Live and Speak the Truth
1:10–16	Godly Leaders Contrasted with False Teachers

Instructions for Developing Godly Christians (2)

2:1–10	Mature Christians Mentor New Christians
2:11–15	Godly Behavior Validates the Gospel

Instructions for Living Among Non-Christians (3)

3:1–11	Christians Should Serve Their Neighbors

PRINCIPAL FIGURES

God   This letter describes God as the Gracious Savior who loves humanity and is merciful.

Jesus Christ   Jesus is presented as the Great God and Savior, sent by God the Father, who justifies and pours out God's Spirit on those who believe the gospel.

Holy Spirit   The Spirit of God who cleanses and gives new life as He is poured out on believers.

Paul   The apostle describes himself as a slave of God whose mission is to build the faith and godliness of believers.

Titus   A young Greek disciple of the Apostle Paul, sent to the island of Crete to organize the churches there.

"But when the kindness of God our Savior and His love for mankind appeared, He saved us—not by works of righteousness that we had done, but according to His mercy, through the washing of regeneration and renewal by the Holy Spirit."

(Titus 3:4–5, HCSB)

One of the great challenges for Christians in the New Testament era was living in a genuinely pagan culture. Working out the practical details of loving enemies (Matt 5:44) and neighbors (Luke 10:29) while remaining faithful to Christ required a lot of wisdom. Paul encouraged Titus to remind the Christians on Crete to honor the authorities God had placed over them, to avoid slander and quarreling, and to be gentle and kind to everyone (3:1–2).

Instead of being proud and elitist, Christians were to have compassion for those around them by remembering their own sinful past and how they had been changed by God's grace. Paul reminded Titus that no one starts out righteous. Every Christian was once foolish and rebellious toward God, deceived and enslaved by their passions. The kindest, most loving believer once harbored envy and hatred in their heart (3:3).

Remembering their past would also prompt Christians to remember how it all changed. In mercy and love, God had taken the initiative to send His Son. Christ saved people, not because of their righteousness but purely by applying mercy and purifying new life in God's Spirit. God declared people righteous as a gift of grace. This was what gave them a confident hope for eternal life (3:4–7).

Paul counseled Titus to insist on the grace of God in the gospel. Remembering God's grace would lead Christians to imitate Christ's love by serving the good of their unbelieving neighbors. Forgetting God's grace would lead them into self-righteous pride. Those who refused to humble themselves before God's grace could not be part of the community of believers (3:8–11).

REGENERATION

Regeneration refers to being created anew, "re-generated." The concept can refer to the renewal of the whole creation (Matt 19:28) or to individuals becoming a new creation in Christ (Titus 3:5). Jesus was using this idea when He said, "Unless someone is born again, he cannot see the kingdom of God" (John 1:3).

PHILEMON

The book of Philemon is a personal letter from Paul asking Philemon to forgive and welcome back a runaway slave, Onesimus. The letter does not explicitly order Philemon to treat Onesimus' conversion as liberating him from slavery. However, Paul's argument clearly was designed to motivate Philemon to treat Onesimus as a free brother in Christ.

LOCATION: The letter implies that Onesimus journeyed from Colossae (southwestern Turkey) to Rome as a runaway slave, met Paul in Rome, and returned to Colossae bearing this letter.

KEY PASSAGES

Greeting and Prayer for Philemon (1–7)

Paul's Appeal for Onesimus (8–22)

8–9	Though Paul Could Command, He Asked out of Love
10a	Onesimus Had Become a Christian
10b–11	Onesimus Had New Value
12–16	Onesimus Was No Longer a Slave, But a Brother
17–22	Paul Put Onesimus on a Level with Himself

Paul's Final Greetings and Blessing (23–24)

ORIGIN: Philemon identifies Paul as its author (1:1). The letter was likely written from Rome during Paul's imprisonment (61–62 C.E.) awaiting his appeal to Caesar (Acts 25). Despite the intensely personal nature of the letter, a number of modern scholars have argued that the letter was a pious fraud by a later disciple of Paul.

PRINCIPAL FIGURES

God   The letter calls God "Father," suggesting both His eternal relationship to Jesus and His authority as the Creator of humanity.

Jesus Christ   Jesus is described in this letter as Paul's owner and Lord, suggesting that He is the only legitimate owner of Christians.

Paul   The apostle describes himself as an old man and prisoner of Christ, who was instrumental in the conversions of both Philemon and Onesimus.

Philemon   A Christian slave owner to whom Paul appealed to receive Onesimus as a brother. Possibly a resident of the city of Colossae.

Onesimus   A runaway slave who converted to Christianity under Paul's teaching, while the apostle was in prison.

> "For perhaps this is why he was separated from you for a brief time, so that you might get him back permanently, no longer as a slave, but more than a slave—as a dearly loved brother."
>
> (Philemon 15–16, HCSB)

NO LONGER A SLAVE
(Philemon 8–22)

While Paul was in Rome, awaiting his appeal to Caesar (Acts 25), a young man named Onesimus came to be of valuable help to the imprisoned apostle. The only problem was that Onesimus was a runaway slave. A runaway slave in the Roman Empire could be forcibly returned to his master or even put to death. On the other hand, the Mosaic Law made it illegal to return a runaway slave (Deut 23:15). So Paul did what he could; he gave Onesimus the gospel. Having experienced reconciliation with God, Onesimus came to desire reconciliation with his master, Philemon. At that point, Paul saw a unique opportunity to demonstrate the transformative power of the gospel and seized it by giving the runaway slave a letter to carry to his master.

Paul had helped Philemon become a Christian and knew the love that Christ had placed in Philemon's heart (6–7). So instead of simply giving Philemon an order, the apostle made an appeal for Onesimus on the basis of love (8–9). While Onesimus had helped Paul in his physical prison, Paul had helped Onesimus out of his spiritual prison. Onesimus had become a Christian, and that changed everything. Once he had been useless, but now he was useful to both Paul and Philemon (10–11).

The apostle told Philemon that he was sending Onesimus back in spite of how helpful he had been, seeing to Paul's needs while he was imprisoned. Paul was sure that Philemon would have wanted Onesimus to continue helping Paul if he knew of the situation. But since he did not know, Paul did not want to take what Philemon would willingly give. So Paul was sending Onesimus back with Paul's letter of explanation (12–14).

The emotional peak of the letter came when Paul suggested that perhaps the temporary separation caused by Onesimus' flight had been God's way of giving him back forever, if not in the way a slave owner might expect. Paul insisted that the man he was sending back was no longer a slave. Onesimus was now far more valuable than any slave; he was a beloved brother in Christ (15-16). If Paul and Philemon were coworkers in Christ's service, then so was Onesimus. Paul urged Philemon to treat Onesimus as he would Paul (17).

HEBREWS

INTRODUCTION

The book of Hebrews argues that Christ's New Covenant is superior to the Mosaic Covenant by demonstrating Christ's superiority to the Levitical priesthood and the Temple's sacrificial system. It warns Jewish Christians not to abandon their loyalty to the Messiah by returning to Torah observance as a way to achieve self-righteousness.

LOCATION: The book of Hebrews makes reference to the sacrificial system of the Temple in Jerusalem but does not indicate the location of either its author or its recipients..

KEY PASSAGES

Jesus Is the Supreme Revelation of God (1–2)

1:1–14	God Reveals Himself Through Jesus
2:5–18	Jesus Identified with Humanity

Jesus Is the Supreme High Priest (3–10)

4:14–5:10	Jesus Is Our High Priest
7:1–28	Jesus Is Superior to the Levitical Priests
8:1–13	Jesus Brought the New Covenant
9:1–10:18	Jesus Is the Supreme Sacrifice

Jesus Is the Supreme Example and Object of Faith (11–12:13)

11:1–30	God Has Always Blessed Faith in Him
12:1–14	Faith in Christ Calls for Endurance

Christian Life Under Jesus' Supreme Lordship (12:14–13:21)

ORIGIN: Hebrews does not name its author, though he was associated with the Apostle Paul (13:23). Tradition attributes Hebrews to Paul. Medieval and modern suggestions include Luke, Barnabas, and Apollos. The letter was likely written during or just after the persecution that happened under Nero (beginning in 64 C.E.) and before the destruction of the Temple (70 C.E.).

PRINCIPAL FIGURES

God In Hebrews God is the Father of Jesus Christ and the God of the Covenant who disciplines those He loves.

Jesus Christ Jesus is described as the Superior Revelation of God and the source of the New Covenant, which is the only hope for salvation from sin and judgment.

Melchizedek The priest-king of Jerusalem who received a tithe from Abraham (Gen 14). In Hebrews he is used as evidence of a priesthood that is both distinct from and superior to Aaron and the Levites under the Mosaic Covenant.

Aaron and the Levitical Priests The first High Priest and the tribe of priests under the Mosaic Covenant who foreshadowed Christ and were superseded by Him.

Abraham The major example of faith among the heroes of the Old Testament.

HIGH PRIEST OF THE NEW COVENANT
(Hebrews 7)

The author of Hebrews argued that Jesus was superior to the priests of the Mosaic Covenant (5–6). The author based his case on a comparison of Jesus and Melchizedek, the priest-king of Jerusalem in Abraham's time (Gen 14; Heb 7:1–3). Abraham had acknowledged Melchizedek as a legitimate priest of God by offering him a tithe. The author of Hebrews applied the ancient idea that a man's descendants were subordinate to him. In this case, that meant that the Levites were subordinate to Abraham, who had submitted to Melchizedek. Since Jesus had become a priest like Melchizedek (5:6), He was superior to the Levitical High Priest (7:4–10).

With a new High Priest came a New Covenant which, in contrast to the Mosaic Covenant, would succeed in making people righteous (7:11–19; see Jer 31:31–34). The New Covenant, with its new High Priest, fulfilled God's oath that the Son of David would be a priest forever (7:20–22; Ps 110:4). In the natural course of life, every priest from the tribe of Levi died and had to be replaced by another priest (7:23). Though Jesus also had died, His resurrection ensured that He could be a priest forever and always mediate between God and His people (7:24–25).

Jesus' resurrection demonstrated His superiority as a priest by showing the superiority of the sacrifice He offered. Priests under the Mosaic Covenant had to offer sacrifices on a yearly basis to atone for their own sins. Only then could they offer a sacrifice for the sins of the nation, which also had to be repeated every year. Jesus, however, was a holy and innocent sacrifice, which only needed to be offered once (7:26–28).

THE WARNING PASSAGES

Hebrews contains warnings about drifting from God's final word (2:1–4), stubborn hearts (3:7–4:13), lack of spiritual growth (5:11–6:12), disloyalty to Christ (10:19–39), and refusing God's Word (12:14–29). Modern scholars debate whether these verses indicate that salvation can be lost or describe the fate of those whose commitment to Christ was insincere. The primary function of the warnings, however, was to exhort believers to persist in their faith in Christ.

JAMES

The book of James was written to Jewish Christians outside of Israel and consists of a series of short sermons focusing on the application of faith in the lives of individuals and Christian communities. The book's major themes include faith, trials, the rich and poor, and humility.

LOCATION: The book addresses Jewish Christians outside of Israel, most of whom would have been living in the eastern half of the Roman Empire (mainly modern Italy, Greece, Turkey, Syria, Egypt, and Libya).

ORIGIN: The book identifies James as its author (1:1). Tradition holds that this is Jesus' half-brother, who was the leader of the church in Jerusalem (Acts 15). Some suggest the writing is a pious fraud. Granting James of Jerusalem as the author suggests that the book was written between 40–62 C.E.

KEY PASSAGES

Tests of Christian Faith (1)

1:2–18   Enduring Trials and Temptations

1:19–25   Being Doers of the Word

The Application of Faith (2)

2:1–13   Favoritism Denies the Gospel

2:14–26   Claims of Faith Are Vindicated by Deeds

Pure Speech and Wisdom (3)

3:1–12   The Most Deadly Pound of Meat

Pride and Humility (4)

4:1–12   Repent of Selfish Pride

Judgment and Prayer (5)

PRINCIPAL FIGURES

God   The Only God who gives good gifts and works through the poor, and who also judges the proud.

Jesus Christ   The glorious Lord who is the "owner" of Christians and chose to identify with the poor rather than the rich.

The Rich   The rich in James include both wealthy Christians and those who use their wealth to oppress others and exalt themselves.

The Poor   The poor in James are primarily Christians who lack basic material necessities.

Abraham   Abraham is James' primary example of genuine faith.

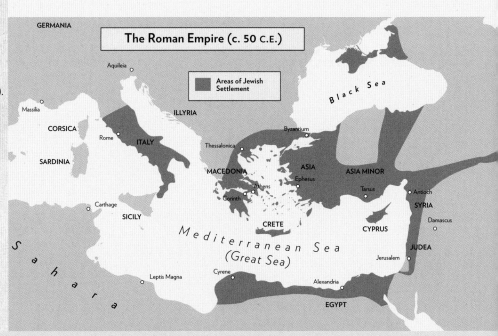

The Roman Empire (c. 50 C.E.)

Areas of Jewish Settlement

GERMANIA · Aquileia · Massilia · CORSICA · SARDINIA · Rome · ITALY · ILLYRIA · Carthage · SICILY · Thessalonica · MACEDONIA · Athens · Corinth · CRETE · Byzantium · ASIA · Ephesus · ASIA MINOR · Tarsus · Antioch · SYRIA · CYPRUS · Damascus · JUDEA · Jerusalem · Leptis Magna · Cyrene · Alexandria · EGYPT · Black Sea · Mediterranean Sea (Great Sea) · Sahara

DOERS OF THE WORD
(James 1:19–27)

James was concerned with reminding his readers that they should pay attention to God's Word. Though conviction often provokes an angry response, Christians are to prefer hearing what God has to say through the Scripture to protecting their pride. The angry rejection of God's message due to wounded pride will prevent the accomplishment of God's righteousness. James insisted that those who embrace the gospel's promise of release from sin would receive the Word of God, enabling them to abandon sinful practices (1:19–21).

> *"Therefore, ridding yourselves of all moral filth and evil, humbly receive the implanted word, which is able to save you. But be doers of the word and not hearers only, deceiving yourselves."*
>
> (James 1:21–22, HCSB)

But James was also concerned that his readers could deceive themselves. A positive emotional response to the Word was meaningless if it did not result in actual obedience to its message. Passive listening made little sense to James. The man who doesn't correct the flaws he sees when he looks in a mirror is a fool. But the wise student of God's Word would embrace its teaching as the law that sets him free from sin's control. The one who persists in obedience would experience God's blessings in his life (1:22–25).

The test of a person's response to God's Word would come in three major areas: control of the tongue, care for the helpless, and dealing with sin in one's own life. James wrote that controlling the tongue was among the most difficult things for a person to do (3:1–12). Religious observance that did not accomplish this was worthless; it only cloaked the unrighteous heart within. The result of genuine submission to God's word was not ritual; it was care for the defenseless. It resulted in taking care of those who seem worthless in the eyes of society and refusing to tolerate sin in one's own life (1:26–27).

SERMONS IN THE NEW TESTAMENT

The New Testament records many public speeches and sermons by Jesus, the apostles, and other Christians in the four Gospels and the book of Acts. More easily overlooked, however, is the fact that letters were a significant way in which someone could "speak" to others when the author could not be physically present. The letters of the New Testament would have been read out loud in their entirety by the recipients, making them a kind of sermon.

1 & 2
PETER

INTRODUCTION

Peter's letters encourage Christians to stand firm in following Christ in spite of persecution. In particular, he emphasizes that Christians should not suffer for actual crimes, but that their character should validate the life-transforming claims of the gospel. He warns against false teachers and against becoming discouraged that Christ has not yet returned to judge the world.

KEY PASSAGES

1 Peter

Salvation for Those in Exile (1:1–2:10)

1:3–12   Christians Are Called to Hope

1:13–2:10   Christians Are Called to Holiness

Living as Citizens of Heaven in a Hostile World (2:11–4:11)

2:11–17   Virtue Validates the Gospel

Living through Suffering (4:12–5:14)

4:12–19   Christians Should Suffer for the Right Reasons

2 Peter

Grace for a Transformed Life (1)

1:16–21   The Prophet's Message Was Fulfilled in Christ

Judgment on False Teachers (2)

Assurance of the Day of the Lord (3)

PRINCIPAL FIGURES

God   Peter describes God as the merciful and holy God who protects and purifies His people and will judge the world.

Jesus Christ   The Savior who experienced unjust suffering at the hands of sinners in order to fulfill the Father's will, and who will return to execute God's judgment.

Holy Spirit   The glorious Spirit of Christ who guided the authors of Scripture and empowers Christians to know and obey God.

Peter   The apostle who, when imprisoned in Rome and facing execution, wrote to encourage suffering Christians and pastors/elders.

False Teachers   Teachers who effectively denied the authority and mission of Christ by encouraging Christians to sin without restraint and denying that there would be a final judgment.

LOCATION: Peter wrote from "Babylon" (1 Pet 5:13), which likely symbolized Rome. His audience was Christians in what is now northern and western Turkey.

ORIGIN: Both letters identify the apostle Simon Peter as their author (1 Pet 1:1; 2 Pet 1:1). His execution under Nero places both letters prior to 68 C.E. 2 Peter was likely written just before Peter's death (2 Pet 1:13–15). Some modern scholars have argued that the letters are a pious fraud, written as late as 110 C.E.

"You are being protected by God's power through faith for a salvation that is ready to be revealed in the last time."

(1 Peter 1:5, HCSB)

THE DAY OF THE LORD
(2 Peter 3)

In the last chapter of 2 Peter, the apostle returns to an important subject from his first letter, the Day of the Lord (1 Pet 4:7–19). Peter is referring to the time of God's final judgment on the rebellious and sinful world in which His people live. This subject was important to the Old Testament prophets (see Isa 2; Joel 1:15–2:11; Amos 5:18-27; Zeph 1), and the apostles followed their example in calling God's people to righteousness in light of the coming judgment of the wicked (for example, 1 Cor 1:8; 1 Thess 5:1–11; 1 John 4:17–18).

Scoffers would sarcastically demand to know when God's promised judgment would come, confident that it never would. Peter reminded his readers that the scoffers' objections ignored the fact that God had created the world in the first place (Gen 1). They also forgot that when God released the waters in Noah's day, every living thing on Earth was destroyed. This time, the world would be destroyed by fire.

Peter reassured his readers that God was not delaying the judgment because He was unready. People might get impatient with the passage of time, but time does not wear God down. He can endure a thousand years as easily as a day. Instead, God was being patient, waiting for everyone who would to repent of their sins and turn to Christ.

The gospel call for unbelievers to repent was urgent because there would be no warning to prepare people for the day of judgment. It would spring on them like an unexpected explosion and end with the complete destruction of this world. For believers, the knowledge that this day would come should provoke them to invest their lives in God's eternal kingdom, rather than in the very things that would be destroyed by judgment. What matters is the new heavens and new Earth, were everything will be put right.

SUFFERING IN THE NEW TESTAMENT

Though the New Testament expects that Christians will avoid the final judgment, it clearly affirms that they will suffer in this life (for example, John 16:33; Phil 1:29–30). Sometimes this is the result of persecution (John 15:20), and at other times it is a way of refining the faith of God's people (Jas 1:2–12).

1, 2, & 3
JOHN

The three letters of John (1–3 John) addressed churches facing false teaching and needing assurance that those who believed in Christ had eternal life. They address those who had set themselves against Christ by denying that He had come in the flesh. John encouraged love among Christians as the major sign of salvation.

LOCATION: No specific places are named or alluded to in 1–3 John, but early Christian writers held that John ministered in Ephesus towards the end of his life.

KEY PASSAGES

1 John

God Is Light: Embracing the Truth (1:1–3:10)

1:5–2:2	Walking in the Light
2:15–28	Don't Love the Things of the World

God Is Love: Living Together (3:11–5:21)

3:11–4:21	Love Like Christ
5:13–21	Confidence in Christ

2 John

Walking in Truth and Love (1–6)

Rejecting Deceptive Teachers (7–13)

3 John

Faithfulness to Word and Deed (1–8)

Contrasting Figures (9–13)

ORIGIN: None of the letters names its author, though 2 and 3 John identify their author as "the Elder." Tradition has identified the Apostle John as the author. Literary connections between the letters and the Gospel of John are often taken to support this identification. If correct, the letters were likely written toward the end of the apostle's life, probably between 85–100 C.E.

PRINCIPAL FIGURES

God These letters describe God as "light" and "love." He is identified often as the Father of Jesus Christ.

Jesus Christ Jesus is presented as the eternal Son who embraced human nature, becoming a sinless man while remaining fully divine. John emphasizes Jesus' mission to express God's love and destroy the works of the Devil.

Holy Spirit Treated as distinct from the Father and Son, yet equal to them. The Spirit is called Love (because He possesses the divine attribute of love completely) and is God's gift to believers, enabling them to know the truth, overcome the world, and reject false teaching.

The Elder The author's self-description in 2 and 3 John, likely identifying both advanced age and leadership within the churches to whom he wrote.

The Elect Lady Possibly an individual woman hosting a church in her home, or a literary reference to the whole church in all its specific locations.

False Teachers Identified as "antichrist," meaning "against Christ," in 1 John for denying that Christ embraced human nature. Specific sinful leaders are named in 3 John.

LIFE-GIVING LOVE
(1 John 4)

John calls his beloved readers to love each other. The kind of love John calls for can come only from God, and showing this love proves that a person has been reborn and knows God. Those who do not love this way show that they simply do not know God, because He is love itself.

To explain divine love, John points his readers to the cross of Christ (see John 19). God sent His Son to give life to sinful people—not because they wanted it, but because loving those who do not deserve it is just who God is. Though humanity stood under the wrath of God (Rom 2:5), God sent Christ to be our peace. John reminds his readers that experiencing God's love transforms people so that they love others in the same way.

Confidence in God's love comes through the assurance God's Spirit gives that the eyewitness accounts about the Savior are true (see 1:1–4). Confidence in the truth of the gospel leads to open confession that Jesus is God's Son and the Savior of the world (see John 4:42), and it is this faith that brings people into a right relationship with God. When the love God gives reaches full maturity in people, causing them to love like God loves, it eliminates all fear of the final judgment. Fully experiencing and understanding God's love gives complete confidence that the believer has peace with God through Jesus.

LOVE IN THE NEW TESTAMENT

The assertion that "God is love" (1 John 4:8) and the warning that sinful humans are objects of God's wrath (Eph 2:3) seems contradictory to many readers. Yet they are expressed together in the crucifixion of Christ. God's wrath is poured out on a person, but that person is the willing substitute for guilty humanity. The wrath of God highlights the love of God.

"This is how we have come to know love: He laid down His life for us. We should also lay down our lives for our brothers."

(1 John 3:16, HCSB)

INTRODUCTION

Jude is a short book that declares divine judgment on false teachers and exhorts Christians to help each other remain faithful to God. The book uses examples of judgment from Old Testament history and Jewish tradition to demonstrate the inevitability of God's judgment on those who corrupt the truth of the gospel.

LOCATION: Nothing in the letter indicates where its author or recipients were located.

ORIGIN: The letter identifies its author as Jude, a brother of James, seeming to expect that the recipients knew both. This was most likely Jesus' half-brother (Mark 6:3) and brother of James the leader of the Jerusalem church (Acts 15). The letter was likely written before 68 C.E.

KEY PASSAGES

Exhortation to Contend for the Faith (1–4)

The Old Testament History of Judgment (5–13)

The Prophecy of Enoch (14–16)

The Prophecy of the Apostles (17–19)

Appeal and Hymn of Praise (20–25)

PRINCIPAL FIGURES

God   Jude describes God as loving His people. He is the Savior and object of worship and glory forever.

Jesus Christ   Jesus is the Messiah, Master, and Lord who protects His people and who will return to judge the wicked.

Holy Spirit   Jude mentions the Holy Spirit as the One who empowers the prayers of God's people.

Jude   The letter's author, who intended to write about the salvation Christians share, but who had to challenge his readers to deal with false teachers among them.

Michael   The archangel (ruling angel) who, according to Jewish legend, argued with the Devil over Moses' body.

Enoch   A descendent of Adam, who walked with God and was taken into God's presence without dying (Gen 5:18–23). Jude quotes from a book written after 300 B.C.E., which claimed to be authored by Enoch.

"Now to Him who is able to protect you from stumbling and to make you stand in the presence of His glory, blameless and with great joy, to the only God our Savior, through Jesus Christ our Lord, be glory, majesty, power, and authority before all time, now and forever. Amen."

(Jude 24–25, HCSB)

RESISTING FALSE TEACHERS
(Jude 17–25)

Jude reminded his readers that the existence of false teachers who would trouble God's people should come as no surprise. Peter had predicted that scoffers would come into the church and make a display of following their own desires rather than submit to Christ. They would create divisions because they would have no part in what unifies God's people, the presence of the Holy Spirit.

Jude urged Christians to remain firmly in the love of God as God had loved them. He taught them to do this in three ways. First, Christians stay in God's love by strengthening their commitment to the faith, which had been delivered to them by the apostles. Second, prayer that is empowered by God's spirit will foster the love of God in the one who prays (see Rom 8:15–16). Third, a hope that is fixed on Jesus' mercy, which will give eternal life, evokes a deep love for God.

The believers' confident expectation of mercy in Christ would in turn motivate them to show mercy toward those who experienced doubts because of the influence of the false teachers. Though the false teachers themselves are condemned, their followers should be gently and patiently won back to the truth. Even those who had embraced the sinful lifestyles the false teachers encouraged were to be rescued, though believers were to take care not to fall prey to their sins.

Jude closed his letter with a prayer of praise to God. All praise, glory, majesty, and power belong to God from eternity, today, and forevermore. That glorious God is both able and willing to protect His people so that they will stand in His presence, fully blameless and full of joy. The faithfulness of God's people would not be ensured by the strength of their will. Instead, the grace of God would ensure the strength of their faith in Him.

HERESY IN THE NEW TESTAMENT

The Greek word *hairesis* often means nothing more than "choice" or "sect." But it also came to refer to groups that caused division due to sinful pride (1 Cor 11:19) or to prideful teaching that undermined faith in Christ (2 Pet 2:1). Heresy, then, was not merely incorrect teaching. It was teaching that turned people away from Christ's gospel of grace.

REVELATION

The book of Revelation was written to encourage Christians to endure persecution by remaining faithful to Christ. John assured his readers that Christ is the glorious Lord who will execute God's judgment on rebellious humanity and its demonic leaders. God's purpose for creation and humanity will be fulfilled as God dwells with redeemed humanity.

LOCATION: The book of Revelation indicates that it was written on the island of Patmos in the Aegean Sea. It describes a worldwide apocalypse.

KEY PASSAGES

What You Have Seen: John's Vision of Jesus (1)

What Is: Letters to Seven Churches (2–3)

What Will Take Place After This: The Apocalypse (4–22)

4:1–5:14	The Throne Room of Heaven
6:1–9:21	The Great Tribulation
15:1-16:21	The Great Tribulation, Continued
19:11–21	Armageddon: The Last Battle
20:1–15	Judgment of Satan and Sinful Humanity
21:1–22:5	The New Heaven and New Earth

ORIGIN: The book identifies "John" as its author. Though this could be an otherwise unidentified author, it is most likely the apostle John. Some modern scholars have argued the work was a pious fraud. The earliest Christian authors stated that the book was written under the Roman Emperor Domitian, 81–96 C.E., who persecuted Christians toward the end of his reign.

PRINCIPAL FIGURES

God   God is the Almighty Sovereign over creation and history, who accomplishes the purpose for which He created the world.

Jesus Christ   Christ is referred to as a glorious lamb, killed as the sacrifice for sin, who now executed judgment on the Devil and those who persisted in rebelling against God.

John   The author of the Book of Revelation, who saw the visions described in the book.

The Angel   John's guide throughout the vision of heaven and the end times.

The Woman   A symbolic figure for the nation of Israel, the church, or perhaps for Mary, the Mother of Jesus.

The Beast   The leader of the human rebellion against God in the last days.

The Prostitute   A symbolic figure standing in contrast to the Woman.

THE REVELATION OF JESUS CHRIST
(Revelation 1:1–19)

John was in a very ordinary place when he saw an extraordinary vision. He was in exile on the island of Patmos because of his preaching about Jesus. On a Sunday, which Christians called the Lord's Day to honor Christ's resurrection on the first Easter Sunday, the Holy Spirit opened John's eyes to see Jesus (compare to Isa 6).

A voice like a trumpet commanded John to write what he saw and send it to seven churches. What he saw was One like the Son of Man in Daniel's visions, standing among seven golden lampstands (see Dan 7:13; 10:5–6). The lampstands were a heavenly version of the Temple's menorah (Exod 25:31–40), which symbolized the light of God's glorious presence (see also Zech 4:1–14).

The focus of the vision, however, was on the Son of Man. The setting suggested the work of a priest, trimming the wicks to ensure the light symbolizing God's glory burned bright. His clothing suggested both royal and priestly status, and His symbolic physical appearance indicated wisdom, purity, life, and power. A sword came from His mouth, an image that identified Him as the One who would execute the final judgment (Isa 11:4; 49:2; 2 Thess 2:8).

John fell prostrate before the glorified Lord, but Jesus touched him and said that he did not need to be afraid. Jesus declared that He was the resurrected Lord who could liberate people from death or condemn them to it. Jesus then ordered John to write what he saw according to a simple outline: "what you have seen, what is, and what will take place after this" (1:19). Readers often move quickly to the graphic descriptions of the final judgment, but John's opening vision is essential; Jesus is not only the Savior, He is also the final Judge of sinful humanity.

INTERPRETING THE BOOK OF REVELATION

The major approaches to Revelation differ in how they relate the book to history. The Preterist (past) view sees the book fulfilled, fully or partially, in the Temple's destruction (70 C.E.). Idealists see a symbolic clash between God and Satan. Historicist views attempt to map the prophecies of Revelation onto world history. Futurist interpretations understand Revelation 4–22 as prophesying actual events in the future in general or more specific detail.

REVELATION

The Bible began with the first human couple in a sinless world, having fellowship with God in the Garden of Eden (Gen 1–2). But the introduction of sin into the story presented a divine dilemma (Gen 3). If God judged sin, as His holiness required, then there would be no fellowship between God and the people He had made in His image. Satan would have succeeded in ruining God's very good creation. On the other hand, showing mercy out of love while ignoring sin would leave sinful humanity cut off from God and each other forever. Again, God's purpose for creation would fail.

A Heavenly City

John's final vision was that God's purpose for creation would be fulfilled. Where a sinless couple fell in the Garden, there would one day be a heavenly city on Earth where a redeemed humanity would never sin again. God would dwell with a sinless humanity and there would be no mourning or death (21:3–4). Those who had acknowledged their thirst (Isa 55, Matt 5:6) and found satisfaction in Christ (John 4:14) would inherit God's kingdom. Those who persisted in their rebellion would share the eternal judgment reserved for Satan (21:8, 20:7–15).

John described the New Jerusalem in fantastic terms, a beautiful city almost beyond description. One of its most notable features, however, is what is missing. John saw neither Temple, nor sun or moon. These would not be necessary, because the glorious presence of the Father and Son would fill the city (21:22–23). Every race, tribe, and language would be represented there (21:24–27).

God and Humanity Reunited

The story of the Bible answers the question: how can God be just and yet justify fallen people and rescue creation while remaining righteous? The first hint of the answer came in God's promise to Adam and Eve of the seed of the woman who would defeat the snake and lift the curse (Gen 3:15). John's vision promised a future with the curse lifted (22:1–5).

PEARLY GATES

The image of Peter standing at the Pearly Gates to welcome people to heaven is partially correct. The Book of Revelation describes the heavenly city as having gates of pearl which never close and 12 foundations made of precious stones. The streets are paved with gold, suggesting that the most coveted commodities on Earth will be no more valuable than packed dirt or cobblestones would have been in an ancient town. But it is Jesus who will order the Lamb's Book of Life opened to admit those whose names are written there—those who embraced the gospel of repentance from sin and faith in Jesus as Savior and Lord.

John's vision concluded with the warning that those who persisted in rebellion would be judged and that those who were cleansed by Christ would regain the Tree of Life (Gen 2:9). But this warning became an invitation from the Spirit of God and His people (described metaphorically as "the bride of Christ," the object of His supreme love) to come and drink of the living water given as a gift, and so enter God's kingdom (21:17).

"Both the Spirit and the bride say, 'Come!' Anyone who hears should say, 'Come!' And the one who is thirsty should come. Whoever desires should take the living water as a gift."

(Revelation 22:17, HCSB)

THE TRIUMPH OF GOD

Though Revelation is challenging to read, its point is simple and clear: God wins. Satan's rebellion and humanity's sin will be defeated. So the Nicene Creed affirms, Jesus "shall come again, with glory, to judge the quick and the dead; [His] kingdom shall have no end. ... [there shall be a] resurrection of the dead, and the life of the world to come."

The Apocrypha

APOCRYPHA

This book has focused on introducing readers to the Bible as it has been unanimously received by both Jews and Christians. Eastern Orthodox, Protestant, and Roman Catholic traditions accept the same list of New Testament books. Similarly, the 22 books of the Hebrew Bible (listed as 39 books in English translations) are also unanimously accepted by Jews, as well as all Christian traditions.

There is, however, a list of disputed books associated with the Old Testament. The history of this second list is complicated, though the conclusions are clear enough. The Orthodox and Roman Catholic Churches accept some of these texts as Scripture; Jews and Protestants accept none of them as Scripture.

Defining and Naming the Disputed Texts

The list itself is difficult to define, with some versions naming as many as 18 texts. These texts include histories, fictional narratives, wisdom literature, songs, prophetic literature, philosophy, and apocalyptic text. Most were written in Greek. These texts were written between 300 B.C.E. and 100 C.E.

Even the name for this collection of texts is disputed. Protestants commonly refer to these books as the Old Testament Apocrypha, or simply the Apocrypha. This Greek word means "hidden" or "set aside" and was first used to describe this body of material by Origen (184-253 C.E.). Roman Catholics prefer the term deuterocanonical, which means "second list." As used by modern Roman Catholics, the term is intended to convey "second" in sequence, not "secondary" in authority.

Debates over Canonical Status

The New American Bible, a Roman Catholic English-language translation, lists seven books that do not appear in the Hebrew Bible. Two other Old Testament books are expanded with texts from this "second list" (Esther and Daniel). Roman Catholic scholars argue that the New Testament alludes to or quotes texts from this list (compare Heb 11:35 with 2 Macc 7:12). The fact that the New Testament most often uses the Septuagint (a Greek translation of the Old Testament) to quote the Old Testament is also taken to affirm the second list, which was often included in the Septuagint. Though notable early Christian bishops did not accept the second list, others did, and that trend grew until the Reformation era and the formal endorsement of the second list by the Council of Trent (1545-1563 C.E.).

Protestant scholars note that Jews considered divine prophecy (the basis for the Old Testament writings) to have ceased by 400 B.C.E., a view that they see reflected in the second list itself (see 1 Macc 4:45-46; 9:27; 14:41). These scholars conclude that the second list does not claim for itself a level of authority equal to the Hebrew Bible, nor did the Jewish people see these texts as Scripture. Protestant scholars also argue that the New Testament does not actually quote texts on the second list and that familiarity with traditions they describe does not constitute endorsement of them as Scripture.

They insist that Jesus' acceptance of "the Law and the Prophets" (Matt 7:12) refers to the Hebrew Bible, not the second list.

Protestants point out that the earliest Christian lists of the Old Testament (for example, Melito of Sardis's list, 170 C.E.) did not include books from the second list and that significant Christian leaders explicitly rejected these books as Scripture (for example, Athanasius). Cardinal Cajetan, who led the Roman Catholic investigation of the reformer Martin Luther, published a *Commentary on All the Authentic Historical Books of the Old Testament* (1532 C.E.) that did not include any books from the second list. Protestants conclude that there is no historical consensus supporting acceptance of the second list as Scripture.

An Important Source for Jewish History and Thought

Christian debates about the canonical status and doctrinal value of the second list should not, however, obscure their generally acknowledged importance in providing insight to Jewish history and thought in the period between the Old and New Testament eras.. Historians and students of the Greek language of the era continue to find these texts valuable.

WHERE TO FIND THE SECOND LIST

The 18 texts comprising the Septuagint's additions to the Hebrew Bible can be found grouped together after the books of the Hebrew Bible in the New Revised Standard Version. The texts that the Roman Catholic Church accepts as deuterocanonical can be found in the New American Bible, where they are listed as part of the Old Testament.

THE SECOND LIST

Texts accepted by the Roman Catholic Church as deutero-canonical

Tobit (Tobias)
Judith
Additions to the Book of Esther
1 Maccabees
2 Maccabees
Wisdom of Solomon
Sirach (Ecclesiasticus, Wisdom of Ben Sira)
Baruch (including the Letter of Jeremiah)
Additions to the Book of Daniel
    Prayer of Azariah
    The Song of the Three Jews
    Susanna
    Bel and the Dragon
1 Esdras (3 Ezra or 2 Esdras)
2 Esdras (3 Esdras or 4–6 Ezra)
Prayer of Manasseh
Psalm 151
3 Maccabees
4 Maccabees

APOCRYPHA

The Hebrew Bible contains seven books that, when translated in modern Bibles, are listed together as 12 "historical" books. The books of Joshua, Judges, 1 & 2 Samuel, 1 & 2 Kings, 1 & 2 Chronicles, Ezra, Nehemiah, and Esther comprise this list. The description of these books as "historical" does not suggest that all other Old Testament books are fictional. Instead, they indicate a focus on historical narratives about the nation of Israel from the conquest of Canaan through the return from exile in Babylon. The "second list" adds four books to these, along with a short addition to the Hebrew text of Esther.

Tobit (or Tobias)

Tobit was written around 200 B.C.E. and tells the story of Tobit, an exile from the northern kingdom of Israel, and his wife, Sarah. The book also describes the journey of Tobit's son Tobias, who travels to the city of Media to collect a debt. On the way he is opposed by an evil spirit, Asmodaeus (a demonic figure in Persian mythology), and aided by the angel Raphael. The book describes God as the Holy Ruler of Heaven, who shows love and mercy to His people no matter where they live.

Judith

Judith was likely written after the Maccabean revolt (167 B.C.E.) and tells the story of Judith, a Jewish widow who assassinates a Babylonian general in order to protect the people of her city. She is presented as an example of piety and righteousness under the Mosaic Law. Her death at age 105 evoked great mourning among her people.

Additions to the Book of Esther

The Greek translation of Esther was written around 100 B.C.E. by Lysimachus, a Greek-speaking Jew of Jerusalem. The 107 verses added to the Hebrew text did not originally constitute a separate document, but were added in the process of translation, creating an interpretive paraphrase of the Hebrew original. These verses insert clear references to God, which the Hebrew text lacks, and stress the power, knowledge, and holiness of God.

1 Maccabees

Written around 100 B.C.E., 1 Maccabees describes the revolt of the Maccabees against the Seleucid king Antiochus IV Epiphanes, who had defiled the Temple and attempted to destroy Judaism. The book also describes the expansion of the independent Jewish state through the reign of John Hyrcanus. 1 Maccabees emphasizes the importance of the efforts of godly leaders under the sovereignty of God.

2 Maccabees

2 Maccabees was written around the time of 1 Maccabees and is a shorter and more theological interpretation of the events described in 1 Maccabees. It emphasizes faithfulness to the Mosaic Covenant through Temple observance and ritual purity. The book celebrates Jewish resistance to the pagan influences of Greek culture.

HANUKKAH

When Antiochus IV Epiphanes attempted to destroy Judaism, one of his most important acts was to desecrate the Temple in Jerusalem. He did this by sacrificing a pig on the main sacrificial altar in front of the Temple, because Mosaic Law regarded pigs as unclean. After the Maccabean victory, however, the Temple was cleansed and observance of the Mosaic Covenant was reinstated. Though the account of the rededication of the Temple in 1 Maccabees is brief, it is the setting for the Jewish holiday of Hanukkah.

Tradition holds that a very small container of holy oil kept the *menorah* (the seven-lamp stand of the Mosaic Covenant) burning in the Temple for eight days while more holy oil was prepared. Commemorated in Hanukkah (or Chanukah), the Festival of Lights, an eight-lamp stand is used to signify each of the eight days the original lamp was kept burning. The festival is celebrated in late November or early to mid-December and involves giving gifts and traditional games and songs.

APOCRYPHA

The Hebrew Bible has five books of poetry and six prophetic books. In modern Bibles these are listed as the 5 poetic books and 17 prophetic books. The "second list" adds two books (Wisdom and Sirach) to the list of poetic books and one (Baruch) to the prophetic books, along with several distinct texts attached to the Hebrew/Aramaic text of Daniel.

Wisdom of Solomon

The first of the two poetic books in the second list is the Wisdom of Solomon, written after 200 B.C.E. Though the book uses the parallelism of Hebrew poetry, it is written in elegant Greek. The Wisdom of Solomon presents God as Wisdom itself, demonstrating this aspect of His character most clearly in the history of the nation of Israel.

Sirach (Ecclesiasticus, Wisdom of Ben Sira)

Sirach was written in Hebrew around 180 B.C.E. by the teacher Sira and translated into Greek approximately 50 years later by his grandson, Sirach. This book is the longest of those on the second list, and much of its content is structured in the form of pairs of parallel lines like the book of Proverbs. Sirach teaches about a wide variety of topics, but its most famous passage is "In Praise of Famous Men" (Sir 44–50).

Baruch (Including the Letter of Jeremiah)

Baruch was written between 166 B.C.E. and 1 B.C.E. and presents itself as the work of the prophet Jeremiah's scribe, Baruch ben Neriah (see Jer 36). The book includes a confession of the sins of God's people and a prayer for divine restoration. Baruch then shifts to poetry, praising wisdom and encouraging the people of Israel. The sixth chapter of Baruch is a distinct text describing itself as a letter from Jeremiah to the Jewish exiles in Babylon (compare with Jer 29:1–23). The letter is a sermon to the exiles warning them of the impotence of idols and the folly of worshipping them.

Additions to the Book of Daniel

The additions to the Greek text of Daniel are distinct units rather than scattered comments and explanations. They are found at the end of Daniel 3 and form chapters 13 and 14, added to the original 12 chapters in the Hebrew text.

Prayer of Azariah   The Prayer of Azariah is placed between what is Daniel 3:23 and 3:24 in the original Hebrew/Aramaic text and was probably written between 200–100 B.C.E. It, along with the Song of the Three Jews, is offered as a description of what happened while Shadrach (Hananiah), Meshach (Mishael), and Abednego (Azariah) were in the fiery furnace. The prayer confesses the sins of the nation of Israel, prompting God to send an angel to protect the three Jews from the flames.

The Song of the Three Jews The Song of the Three Jews is a hymn of praise to God. The song opens by describing God as "blessed" throughout creation. It then calls on the various works of God in creation to praise God, repeating the formula, "Bless the Lord, you …; sing praise to Him and highly exalt Him forever." The song progressively narrows its focus to the three Jewish men in the furnace, calling on them to praise God for rescuing them from the power of the flames.

Susanna The story of Susanna forms Chapter 13 of the Greek version of Daniel. In this story, Daniel investigates the accusations of two lustful elders against Susanna, a beautiful woman who had refused their attempts to seduce her. Their combined testimony threatened to lead to her execution, but God stirred a young Daniel to intervene. He separated the two elders and found the flaws that exposed their testimony as lies, thus establishing his reputation for wisdom among the Jewish exiles.

Bel and the Dragon Chapter 14 of the Greek version of Daniel tells the story of the exposure of the Babylonian god Bel as a mere idol and Bel's priests as frauds. Bel's priests invited the king to place food in the Temple of Bel and seal the doors. But Daniel pointed to the footprints of the priests and their families on the floor, evidence that they had entered and eaten the food. Afterward, the king showed Daniel a dragon and insisted that it was a god. But when Daniel killed the dragon, the king threw him into the lion's den for six days. While there, God sent the prophet Habakkuk to feed Daniel.

SUSANNA IN ART AND MUSIC

The story of Susanna has inspired numerous paintings and pieces of music. Artists who painted scenes from the story included Rubens, Rembrandt, and Picasso. Handel wrote an oratorio based on the story in 1749, eight years after his *Messiah*. Shakespeare also refers to the story in *The Merchant of Venice*.

GLOSSARY

Abrahamic Covenant   God's promise to give Abraham the land of Canaan (see "promised land"), make him into a great nation, and give him a son through whom God would bless all nations.

apostle   A title meaning "sent one," it refers to those Jesus commissioned directly to preach the gospel after His resurrection.

ark (Noah's Ark)   A very large ship that God ordered Noah to build in order to rescue his family, the birds, and the land animals from God's judgment in a worldwide flood.

Ark of the Covenant   A wooden chest overlaid with gold and decorated with two angels that carried the Ten Commandments.

Christ   (see Messiah)

covenant   A contract between two parties, sealed by an oath.

crucifixion   A form of execution used by the Roman Empire on rebels and other criminals.

Davidic Covenant   God's promise to give King David a descendent who would sit on the throne of Israel forever.

disciple   A student or follower of a teacher, especially the 12 primary followers of Jesus.

divided kingdom   The period of time in which the nation of Israel was divided into northern and southern kingdoms, called Israel and Judah, respectively.

Gentiles   Non-Jewish people, synonymous with the phrase "the nations."

gospel   Literally "good news," it refers to the New Testament message of salvation from sin by faith in Jesus' gracious death and resurrection.

Hellenism/Hellenists   The embrace of Greek culture by non-Greek peoples. In the New Testament, Hellenists were Jews who adopted Greek language and culture.

high place   A hilltop or high platform used for offering sacrifices, especially to idols.

idols/idolatry   Worship of fictional gods or actual demons, usually through carved images.

Immanuel   A name or title meaning "God with us." Used for the Messiah, it indicates both God's presence and His favor on His people.

Israel   Name meaning "prince of God" given to Jacob. Israel later becomes the name of the nation comprised of the 12 tribes rescued from slavery in Egypt. Also used to refer to the northern kingdom during the "Divided Kingdom" period.

Jews, the   A term based on the name "Judah," it can refer to all Israelites after the Babylonian Exile. In the New Testament, it most often refers to a more narrow group: Israelites who considered themselves pure followers of the Law of Moses.

Judah   Named after one of Jacob's sons, this tribe became the ruling tribe and an independent nation during the "Divided Kingdom" period.

Levites   An Israelite tribe descended from Jacob's son, Levi. Chosen by God to provide the priests of the Mosaic Covenant.

Messiah   Hebrew term meaning "anointed one." Used especially to refer to the anticipated figure that would fulfill the covenant promises of God to Israel and the nations.

Mosaic Covenant   The treaty establishing a formal relationship between God and the nation of Israel at Mount Sinai, delivered through Moses.

New Covenant   God's promise to rescue us from sin and its consequences, fulfilled in the death and resurrection of Jesus.

Noahic Covenant   God's promise that He would not judge humanity with a universal flood again.

Palestine   Roman province roughly equivalent to ancient Israel or the modern state of Israel and the Palestinian territories.

Passover   A feast commanded by the Mosaic Covenant to celebrate God's liberation of the Israelites from slavery in Egypt.

Pentecost   The spring harvest feast in Israel; also refers to the conferral of the Holy Spirit on the first Christians as the beginning of their mission to preach the gospel to the nations.

Pharisees   A Jewish religious sect that emphasized ritual purity; Jesus' primary opponents.

priest/High Priest   Religious officials tasked particularly with operating the Mosaic Covenant's sacrificial system. The leading official was called the High Priest.

promised land   The land of Canaan which God promised to give to Abraham, Isaac, Jacob, and their descendants.

prophet   One who speaks for God, often through prediction of future events.

Sadducees   A Jewish religious sect that emphasized the Temple sacrificial system.

Samaritans   Traditional enemy of the Jewish people who claimed to observe the Mosaic Law, but refused to offer sacrifices at the Temple in Jerusalem.

Sinners   A term in the New Testament which can refer to Jews who failed to keep the Law of Moses or to any human being, Jew or Gentile, who has violated God's moral law.

syncretism   The blending of different religions, a common and accepted practice in the ancient world, but considered a concession to idolatry by Judaism and Christianity.

Tabernacle   The tent which served as the temporary, mobile place of sacrifice for the Israelites under the Mosaic Covenant.

Temple   Refers primarily to the permanent location of Mosaic Covenant sacrifices in Jerusalem. The first Temple was built by King Solomon and destroyed by the Babylonians. A second Temple was built after the Babylonian exile and renovated by King Herod. The second Temple was destroyed by the Romans in 70 C.E.

Torah   Meaning "law," the name for the first five books of the Old Testament; also called the Books of Moses.

United Kingdom   The period of time in which the 12 tribes of Israelites were unified under one king. Three kings ruled over a united Israel Saul: David, and Solomon.

Zealots   Religious-political Jews dedicated to the overthrow of Roman rule in Palestine.

RESOURCES

Old Testament References

Hill, Andrew, and John Walton. *A Survey of the Old Testament.* Grand Rapids: Zondervan, 2009.

Longman III, Tremper. *Introducing the Old Testament: A Short Guide to Its History and Message.* Grand Rapids: Zondervan, 2008.

Merrill, Eugene. *Kingdom of Priests: A History of Old Testament Israel.* Grand Rapids: Baker, 2008.

Walton, John H. *Chronological and Background Charts of the Old Testament.* Grand Rapids: Zondervan, 1994.

New Testament References

Alexander, T. D. *Discovering Jesus: Why Four Gospels to Portray One Person?* Wheaton: Crossway, 2010.

House, H. Wayne. *Chronological and Background Charts of the New Testament.* Grand Rapids: Zondervan, 2009.

Köstenberger, Andreas, and Justin Taylor. *The Final Days of Jesus: The Most Important Week of the Most Important Person Who Ever Lived.* Wheaton: Crossway, 2014.

Lea, Thomas, and David Allen Black. *The New Testament: Its Background and Message.* Nashville: B & H Academic, 2003.

Witherington III, Ben. *New Testament History: A Narrative Account.* Grand Rapids: Baker, 2003.

General Bible References

Bartholomew, Craig, and Michael Goheen. *The Drama of Scripture: Finding Our Place in the Biblical Story.* Grand Rapids: Baker Academic, 2004.

Brisco, Thomas. *Holman Bible Atlas: A Complete Guide to the Expansive Geography of Biblical History.* Nashville: Holman Reference, 1999.

Hamilton, James. *What is Biblical Theology?: A Guide to the Bible's Story, Symbolism, and Patterns.* Wheaton: Crossway, 2014.

Hays, J. Daniel, and J. Scott Duval, eds. *The Baker Illustrated Bible Handbook.* Grand Rapids: Baker, 2011.

Roberts, Vaughn. *God's Big Picture: Tracing the Storyline of the Bible.* Downers Grove: InterVarsity Press, 2009.

Reading the Bible

Ryken, Leland. *How To Read the Bible as Literature.* Grand Rapids: Zondervan, 1984.

Hays, J. Daniel, and J. Scott Duval. *Grasping God's Word: A Hands-On Approach to Reading, Interpreting, and Applying the Bible.* Grand Rapids: Zonvervan, 2012.

Fee, Gordon, and Douglas Stuart. *How to Read the Bible for All Its Worth.* Grand Rapids: Zondervan, 2003.

Plummer, Robert. *40 Questions About Interpreting the Bible.* Grand Rapids: Kregel Academic & Professional, 2010.

Recommended Free Online Resources

- Bible.org (bible.org)
- Bible Gateway (biblegateway.com)
- Biblia.com (biblia.com)
- Blue Letter Bible (blueletterbible.org)

Free Bible Apps
(for iOS, Android, and Kindle Fire)

- Bible.is
- Faithlife Study Bible
- GloBible

conflicts between science and faith, 11, 17
constructive parallelism, 125
contextual clues, 12
Corinth, 293
Corinthians, 298–299
Cornelius, 289
coronation of the Son psalms, 128–129
creation, 17
cross of Christ, 297
crucifixion of Jesus, 282–283
cult prostitution, 36
curses, 50
Cyrus, 108, 144

D

Daniel, 180
    Belshazzar's drunken worship of idols, 188
    book, 180, 336–337
    faithfulness tested in Babylon, 181
    golden statue, 184
    humbling of King Nebuchadnezzar, 186–187
    King Nebuchadnezzar's dream, 182–183
    lions' den, 190
    religious liberty origins, 185
Darius, 108, 190
David, 72
    capture of Jerusalem, 101
    census, 102–103
    Chronicles, 100
    Davidic Covenant, 78–79, 205
    versus Goliath, 76–77
    judgment, 81
    meets Bathsheba, 80
    psalms, 124
        coronation of the Son, 128–129
        God and humanity, 132
        good shepherd, 133
        suffering to praise, 130–131
    Son of David expectations, 79
Day of the Lord
    1&2 Peter, 321
    New Testament, 309
    Old Testament, 195
Deborah, 62–63
Delilah, 62, 67
demon-possessed people, 248
Deuteronomy, 54–57
dietary laws, 181, 289
disputed books, 332–337
divine love and faithfulness, 150, 323
doom, 189
dreams, 35

E

Ecclesiastes, 140–141
Edom, 198–199
Ehud, 62
Eleazar, 48
Eli, 72
Elihu, 118–120
Elijah, 86–87, 216
Elimelech, 68
Eliphaz, 118
Elisha, 88–92
Elizabeth, 256
Elohim, 158
Enoch, 324
Epaphras, 306
Epaphroditus, 304–305
Ephesians, 302–303
Er, 36
Esther, 116–117, 334
ESV (English Standard Version), 8
Eve, 18–21
even-handed justice, 139
evil, 119
exile to Babylon, 164
Exodus, 38
    Ark of the Covenant, 45
    golden calf idolatry, 44
    Israelite exodus from Egypt, 40–41
    Mosaic Covenant, 42–43
    overview, 38
    parting the Red Sea, 41
    rise of Moses, 39
explanatory notes, 9
Ezekiel, 172–177
Ezra, 108–115

F

fall of humanity, 18
familial marriage, 31
famine, 69
fear of the Lord, 141
Feast of Booths, 114
firstborn son priority, 33
flood, 22–23
forgiveness, 122, 202
formal and functional equivalence, 8
frankincense, 229
fulfilling the Scripture, 260

G

Gabriel
    birth of John the Baptist, 257
    Daniel's vision, 180
    Luke, 256

Galatians, 300
Gedaliah, 160
genealogies, 25
General Epistles. See 1–3 John; 1&2 Peter; Hebrews; James; Jude
Genesis, 16
    Abrahamic Covenant, 26–27
    Adam and Eve sin, 18
    binding of Isaac, 28–29
    Cain, 20–21
    creation, 17
    flood, 22–23
    genealogies, 25
    God's judgment, 19
    Jacob steals Esau's blessing, 32–33
    Joseph, 34–35
    Judah's transformation, 36–37
    overview, 16
    Rebekah's faith, 30–31
    Seth, 21
    Tower of Babel, 24–25
genres, 12
Geshem, 110
Gideon, 64–65
God
    grace and human free choice, 236
    judging, 177
    judgment, 19
    love, 13, 323
    manipulation attempts, 163
    martial names, 103
    names, 121
    reunited with humanity, 328–329
    revelation in suffering, 193
    triumph in Revelation, 329
    word, 134
    wrath, 175
Gog, 172
golden calves idolatry, 44, 84–85
Golgotha, 282
Goliath and David, 76–77
Gomer, 192
Good Samaritan parable, 262–263
Good Shepherd, 276–277
Good Shepherd psalm, 133
Gospels. See specific names of gospels
the Great Confession, 238–239
Greeks, 4–5, 222
Gregorian Calendar, 259

H

Habakkuk, 208–209
Hadassah, 116
Hagar, 301
Haggai, 212–213

Nahum, 206–207

Naomi, 68

NASE (New American Standard Bible), 8, 332

Nathan, 72

Nazareth rejection of Jesus, 260

Nebuchadnezzar, 160, 164
    Daniel, 180
    dream, 182–183
    Ezekiel, 172
    golden statue, 184
    humbling, 186–187

Nehemiah, 110–115

New Covenant, 317

new disciples, 246–247

new heaven and earth, 328–329

New Testament, 7
    See also specific names of books
    crucifixion of Jesus, 282–283
    Day of the Lord, 309
    heresy, 325
    letters as sermons, 319
    love, 323
    pseudonymous authorship, 303
    resurrection of Jesus, 284–285
    suffering, 321
    trials of Jesus, 280–281
    unity, 299
    Word of the Lord, 10

Nicodemus, 270–271

Nineveh, 202, 206

NIV (New International Version), 8

NLT (New Living Translation), 8

Noah, 16, 22–23

Numbers, 48–53

O

Obadiah, 198–199

Oholah, 172

Oholibah, 172

Old Testament, 6
    See also specific names of books
    categories, 15
    Day of the Lord, 195
    pagan cultures, 53
    Psalms, 124
    slavery, 41

oldest Jewish cemetery, 178

Onesimus, 314–315

open-ended parables, 265

Orpah, 68

Othniel, 62

outcasts, 256

P

pagan cults
    syncretism, 87
    Old Testament, 53

papyrus, 4

parables. *See* Jesus Christ, parables

Paradise Lost, 18

parallelism, 125

paralyzed man miracle, 249

Pashur, 160

Passover, 243, 268–269

Paul
    conversion, 288
    Jewish Christians acceptance, 290–291
    letters
        1&2 Thessalonians, 308–309
        1&2 Timothy, 310–311
        Colossians, 306–307
        Corinthians, 298–299
        Ephesians, 302–303
        Galatians, 300
        Philemon, 314–315
        Philippians, 304–305
        Romans, 296–297
        as sermons, 319
        Titus, 312–313
    missions, 292–294

Pauline Epistles. *See* Paul, letters

Pearly Gates, 328

Pentecost, 287

personal responsibility for sin, 176–177

Peter
    Acts, 286
    ascension and Pentecost, 287
    Galatians, 300
    Great Confession, 238–239
    inclusion of the Gentiles, 289
    Jesus
        denying, 280
        resurrection, 284–285
        transfiguration, 240–241
    Law of Moses, 291
    letters, 320–321

Pharaoh, 40, 172

Philemon, 314–315

Philippi, 292

Philippians, 304–305

Philistines, 67, 76–77

Phinehas
    Joshua, 58
    Numbers, 48
    zeal, 52–53

pleas for mercy, 171

poetic disputed books, 336–337

Poetry books. *See specific names of books*

Pontius Pilate, 280–282

power, 10

praise psalms, 130–131, 134

prayers
    Azariah, 336
    "the Lord's Prayer," 233
    postures, 190
    Sermon on the Mount, 234–235

pride, 186

primogeniture, 33

prodigal son parable, 264–265

prophecies not delivered through sermons, 173

prophetic disputed books, 336–337

prophets. *See specific names of prophets*

Protestant scholars disputed books, 332–333

Proverbs, 136–138

Psalms, 124
    coronation of the Son of David, 128–129
    God and humanity, 132
    good shepherd, 133
    Hebrew poetry, 125
    laments, 131
    love of God's word, 134
    praise and confidence, 134
    suffering to praise, 130–131
    wisdom and folly, 126–127

pseudonymous authorship, 303

Ptolemies, 222

purity laws, 250

Q–R

Qoheleth, 140

Queen of Sheba, 100

Rahab, 58–59

Raiders of the Lost Ark, 73

reading the Bible, 9, 12–13

Rebekah, 16, 30–37

refinement through suffering, 49

regeneration, 313

Rehoboam, 82

Rehum, 108

religious liberty, 185

rescuing the oppressed, 207

resurrection
    hope in Old Testament, 179
    Jesus Christ, 284–285
    Lazarus, 278
    versus resuscitation, 279

resuscitation, 279

Revelation, 326–329

Roman Catholic disputed books, 332